Paolo Sorrentino's
Cinema and Television

Paolo Sorrentino's Cinema and Television

EDITED BY

Annachiara Mariani

intellect

Bristol, UK / Chicago, USA

First published in the UK in 2021 by
Intellect, The Mill, Parnall Road, Fishponds, Bristol, BS16 3JG, UK

First published in the USA in 2021 by
Intellect, The University of Chicago Press, 1427 E. 60th Street,
Chicago, IL 60637, USA

A catalogue record for this book is available from
the British Library.

Copy editor: MPS Limited
Cover designer: Alex Szumlas
Cover image: Photo by ©Gianni Fiorito.
Frontispiece image: Photo by ©Gianni Fiorito.
Production manager: Jessica Lovett
Typesetter: MPS Limited

Hardback ISBN 978-1-78938-396-6
Paperback ISBN 978-1-78938-375-1
ePDF ISBN 978-1-78938-376-8
ePUB ISBN 978-1-78938-377-5

Printed and bound by CPI Antony Rowe, UK

To find out about all our publications, please visit our website.
There you can subscribe to our e-newsletter, browse or download our current
catalogue and buy any titles that are in print.

www.intellectbooks.com

This is a peer-reviewed publication.

Contents

Figures

Acknowledgements

First and foremost, I would like to express my sincere gratitude to Dr Flavia Laviosa, the creator and chief editor of the new book series *Trajectories of Italian Cinema and Media,* and the founder and editor of the *Journal of Italian Cinema & Media Studies (JICMS).* This edited collection is the second publication from the *Trajectories* book series; Dr Laviosa invited me to assemble the book after we completed the work on a special issue of the *JICMS* on Italian filmmaker Paolo Sorrentino. I am honoured that she entrusted me with this important task, and I will forever be grateful for her assistance, patience, professionality and expertise. Without her invaluable help, this book would not have been possible. I must also thank my colleague and mentor Flavia Brizio-Skov for her unfailing willingness to advise me in several aspects of this project.

A special note of thanks is due to Sorrentino's customer designer, Carlo Poggioli, for granting me an interview at Cinecittá on a very hot August day. It was an honour to talk to him and learn about his work and draw from his wisdom on cinema. Similar thanks are in order to Sorrentino's official photographer, Gianni Fiorito, who granted me permission to use his stunning photos for this publication and to Martina Prosperi and Paolo Pedullà from Wildside for their legal authorization.

I also give sincere thanks to the renowned Italian film scholars who agreed to blind-review the individual chapters included in this book and the entire manuscript; their comments were fair and most helpful. I am also greatly honoured that Dr Giancarlo Lombardi provided the Foreword to this book. His expertise and intellectual acumen were an important addition to this collection.

My most heartfelt thanks go to Dr Adrian Del Caro, Department Head of the Modern Foreign Languages and Literatures department at the University of Tennessee (UT), Dr Amy Elias, Director of the UT Humanities Center, and the UT Office of Research and Engagement for their generous publication-funding grants.

My sincere thanks also go to Pasquale Verdicchio and Loredana Di Martino who granted me permission to reprint Monica Facchini's article, which previously appeared in their *Encounters with the Real in Contemporary Italian Literature and Cinema* (Cambridge: Cambridge Scholars Publishing, 2017).

Finally, I am especially grateful to the scholars who authored the chapters of this volume, not only for their impressive contributions to an important and timely dialogue on Sorrentino's *oeuvre*, but also for their extraordinary patience during the lengthy publication process. Last but not least, I would like to thank my family, my husband Brendan McConville and my daughter Reesie for their endless encouragement.

Foreword

Giancarlo Lombardi

College of Staten Island, Graduate Center, CUNY

Of Visibility, Celebrity and Power: Sorrentino's Society of Spectacle

The opportunity of reflecting on the oeuvre of Paolo Sorrentino in a brief preface to a series of essays that ponder on disparate aspects of the director's rich production allows me to consider the recurring tropes linked to questions of power, visibility and celebrity in his recent works. In *The Young Pope* (2016), Lenny Belardo, ascended to papacy under the new name of Pius XIII, defines himself since the very beginning of his pontificate by his refusal to appear in public. To the faithful, his image is virtually shielded by that cloud of smoke that emanates from his perennially lit cigarette, that same smoke that, in the credit sequence, ensues from the fall of a meteorite that brings a doppelganger of the omnipresent and hypervisible John Paul II to the ground. Since his very inaugural address, proffered in complete darkness, Lenny stages his own rebellion against a system he now dominates by calling for renewed ascetic reflection. In his speech, the young Pope Pius XIII surprises his followers, that he accuses of a lapse in faith, by refusing to show them his face and body, whose traits will only be revealed through their eventual renewal of faith: his pontificate stands in stark contrast with that of John Paul II, who breached the auratic distance of his predecessors by overexposing himself in images and actions.

Of all pontiffs, John Paul II is most certainly the one we can consider to have achieved unparalleled celebrity status – his desire to be *among the people* took him across the world multiple times, drawing an uncommon following from those age groups most often disassociated from religious matters. While Woytila inspired the very creation of the figures of the so-called *Papa Boys*, viewers learn that Lenny predicates detachment as a mean to exorcize his solitude as a child. And this call for detachment speaks to an allure of mysticism that eventually colours his actions with an aura of sainthood. The journey of the young Pope, who surprised the world with his unexpected conservatism, shockingly terminates right as he finally opens himself to the adoring crowd of Venice: his inability to be *among the people* is fatal to him, as the series ends on his possible death on the steps of St. Marks.

Once considered within the larger corpus of Sorrentino's work, *The Young Pope* transcends its religious context in order to appear as yet another meditation on power from the *auteur* who already experimented with long-form narrative in the Oscar-winning *La grande bellezza* (2013) and most recently with *Loro* (2018) and who expounded on this very same topic not only in these two works, but also in *Il divo* (2008), and albeit indirectly, in many of his other works, often touching upon questions that connected celebrity status with power and (in)visibility, on the power granted by both visibility and invisibility, and on the multiple (in)visibilities of power.

Let's begin with the end: the two-part cinematic re-visitation of the final years of the Berlusconi era engages most directly with questions of visibility and invisibility. Much of *Loro 1* unspools its narrative in the very absence of its protagonist: after all, as the title itself connotes, this is not a movie about Silvio Berlusconi (lui), but about those who witnessed, facilitated or suffered through his ascent to power (loro). The very first image of Berlusconi is that of his face tattooed in a prostitute's lower back about to be engaged in a sexual act. And long before he enters the screen, which he eventually dominates in *Loro 2*, his presence is felt through his phone calls, announced by a large LUI appearing on cell phone screens. The viewers are plunged into a cold and hypnotizing narrative in medias res that immediately likens them to the goat that we see at the very beginning of the film. Mesmerized by a television screen and frozen to death because of an AC unit that mysteriously mimics a countdown on its thermostat, the audience of *Loro* is immediately asked to participate in a guess game that will facilitate a correct decodification of the film. Already invoked by the titular preference of pronouns to first and last names, Sorrentino's strategy is to stimulate the viewer cognizant of the many scandals of the Berlusconi era to identify characters who appear on screen without ever being named. Is Riccardo Scamarcio portraying Gianpaolo Tarantini, the entrepreneur from Puglia who recruited escorts for Berlusconi's parties? And is his partner the infamous Patrizia D'Addario? The game starts immediately, and it continues throughout the two films, culminating with a long sequence far into *Loro 2*, when at the very end of a long conversation between Berlusconi and one of his long-time partners, the former finally calls him by name, Fedele, thus facilitating the identification with Fedele Confalonieri while making the most of the symbolic connotations of that very name, evoking the faithfulness, or lack thereof, of Berlusconi's entourage, and the role such entourage played in his downfall. *Loro* is particularly rewarding for viewers familiar with Berlusconi's biography exactly because it brings to the screen all those men and women who derived their celebrity status through their involvement in Berlusconi's affairs, be they personal or political. And what is made visible sheds indirect light on what is left out, on the characters and events that Sorrentino has chosen, or has possibly been forced to leave out. Berlusconi's children are never portrayed, nor, unsurprisingly, is Ruby Rubacuori, who most directly provoked his downfall.

In *Loro,* cinematographer Luca Bigazzi's sought to reflect, in formal terms, the luxuriant decay that connoted the Berlusconi era. 'Je suis l'empire à la fin de la décadence' recited one of the most quoted poems by Paul Verlaine, *Langueur* (1884), long associated with the very conceptualization of literary Decadence, but also inspired by the figure of Nero, who watched Rome burning before him. That same Decadence inspired Sorrentino in his re-visitation of political, social and moral corruption in *Il divo* and *La grande bellezza*. The former recounts the final arc of the long career of Giulio Andreotti, as shortly before being considered a possible candidate for the Presidency of the Republic, he was accused of mafia collusion, and his entire political legacy tainted by a trial that eventually returned a guilty sentence. The latter paints a much larger tableau of Roman society at the onset of the new century, moving freely across several different environments, all equally betraying a profound sense of incipient decay.

Long suspected of holding on to power with illicit means, Giulio Andreotti is portrayed by Sorrentino as a man haunted by the ghosts of his past. Visible only to him, the ghost of Aldo Moro in sweats, reflected in his bathroom mirror, acts as a reminder of an impending doom. In a society that moves, or better, dances frantically around him, Andreotti has long remained still, holding on for dear life to a power that, as he famously once said, 'logorates those who don't have it'. Ever present, ever visible, yet probably responsible for all sorts of ignominious actions committed in total invisibility, Andreotti is portrayed by Sorrentino in his last public moments, shortly before disappearing from the public scene forever.

Jep Gambardella, the protagonist of *La grande bellezza*, holds different claims to visibility and omnipresence, on a social scene that he intended to dominate since his arrival in Rome decades earlier. As a social arbiter, his stated goal was not only to be present at every party, but to be able to cause their undoing. An updated version of Fellini's Marcello, failed novelist, failed journalist turned publicist, Jep lives in an opulent Roman apartment overlooking the Coliseum, long considered a symbol of that very decadence evoked by Verlaine in his famous poem. And the many parties staged on its terrace, always ending with dancing trains that are famous and beautiful because 'they don't go anywhere', seem to stage that very decadence that is further evidenced by the mysterious presence of someone who's even more powerful and privileged than Jep and his socialite friends. Let's not forget that even in *Loro*, Berlusconi is surpassed by the mysterious God, who is eventually revealed to live in his Sardinian villa. I'm thinking of the man who lives upstairs from Jep, and whose smaller balcony overlooks his apartment. The contrasting symbol of invisibility to Jep's utter visibility, this mysterious man is not only the protagonist of a public sexual encounter that is found to be disturbing even by Jep: he is also revealed, at the very end, to be a long time fugitive of the law, and a self-described engine of the rotten Italian economy. It becomes evident, therefore, that the society of spectacle, and of those who have found ways to manage it, exploiting it to their own convenience and effectively manipulating its victims, has long been a constant preoccupation of Sorrentino's oeuvre, in its timely and multifaceted meditation on power and its relation to questions of visibility.

The essays that comprise this important volume, which is the first edited collection in English on Sorrentino, significantly expand on some of the issues I have raised. The polyphonic contributions from a diverse group of international scholars concentrate mostly on the recent works of the Neapolitan *auteur*, adopting a wide spectrum of theoretical frameworks, ranging from psychoanalysis to ecocriticism, which will allow readers and experts in the field to capture the eclectic quality of Sorrentino's rich production.

Introduction:
The Creative and Artistic Trajectory of
Paolo Sorrentino

Annachiara Mariani

The University of Tennessee

*In all the stories I tell, the struggles of my characters are the struggles
I have within me.*

(Paolo Sorrentino in Hogan [2020])

In his article on Paolo Sorrentino, Mark Olsen asserted that 'Italian filmmaker Paolo Sorrentino creates movies of overwhelming imagery that is indulgently decadent and starkly beautiful, conveying emotions that are terrifying and touching' (2019). Although there is a rich variety and a profound depth in Sorrentino's ethos, the diverse perspectives in this collection of essays coalesce to a thematic unity across his films. Olsen's assessment is in line with the recurring Sorrentinian topos that unites these essays: the human struggle against the loss of relevance. Sorrentino's films and television series showcase a wide variety of unique characters, including musicians, politicians, athletes, gangsters, popes, film directors, actors and rock stars. Yet, they all share the same existential dilemmas, inner moral struggles and deep introspections. In an interview with Paiella (2019), Sorrentino confirms this tendency:

'I do like to talk about these characters who are caught at the moment of their decline and they tend to develop a melancholic outlook. They are afraid of death and they inevitably make the wrong decisions and it's something that does happen when in aging they have one last burst of vitality and this can become pathetic and ridiculous. These kinds of moods and feelings are very much in tune with how I feel, and I like talking about them. It is true that I've focused on male characters and older male characters'. His characters' existential dilemmas and conflicts reflect his own, as confirmed by the epigraph at the beginning of this introduction, and I therefore refer to his *oeuvre* as 'self-introspective and contemplative art'.

The fourteen articles featured here examine the human postmodern condition of Sorrentino's eclectic harmony, and pave the way for new ideological and theoretical approaches to his cinematography. Sorrentino's indisputable status as a renowned auteur has been established and advanced by numerous film studies scholars.[1] As Claudio Bisoni stated, '[e]ven before *La grande bellezza* (2013) triumphed with the Academy Award for Best Foreign Language Film in 2014, Sorrentino's films had been long considered works of "industrial" auteur cinema: they were able to compete successfully in international festivals thanks to a negotiation of an individual visual style and characters that are firmly rooted within Italian society' (Bisoni 2016: 251). In a similar vein, Alex Marlow-Mann asserted with confidence that, 'given his degree of control (over settings, characters, gestures, editing strategies, music) together with the considerable thematic parallels between his films, the coherent stylistic aesthetics since his debut film, Sorrentino's films are prime candidates for auteurist analysis' (Marlow-Mann 2010: 162). Likewise, Alan O'Leary – in 'What is Italian Cinema?' – made the following observation: 'As its most internationally visible products, Sorrentino's films assert the "authentic" Italian cinema to be that which directly recalls the auteur cinema of the so-called golden age' (O'Leary 2017: 19).

Other scholarship has pointed out that Sorrentino's work offers a compelling example of what has been termed 'postmodern impegno/postmodern engagement' (Antonello and Mussgnug 2009: 4,11). In view of this, Millicent Marcus has remarked the following:

> Sorrentino's post-realism aesthetics, irony and ethics of political engagement can coexist with his vogue for postmodern stylistic virtuosity – including the use of pastiche, abundant citation, semiotic playfulness, imagistic saturation, decorative exuberance, flamboyant camera work, performative excess, over-the-top musical score, obtrusive editing, theatrical lighting, dazzling set design.
>
> (Marcus 2010:248)

Although some scholars have pointed out the sexist and misogynist nature of Sorrentino's views (Hipkins 2008; Mariani 2017; O'Rawe 2018), recent studies have upheld that his use of comic irony and 'double irony' undermines the apparent sexism in his films. According to Simor and Sorfa, the director hyperbolizes the object of desire for parodic purposes through his excessive film style; the 'sexist' presentation of female beauty thus becomes a humorous subversion. This ironically expressed ambiguity is the main characteristic of Sorrentino's humour (Simor and Sorfa 2017: 212).

Besides the articles mentioned above, one of the most extensive critical examinations of Sorrentino's work can be found in Russell Kilbourn's *Paolo Sorrentino's Cinema: Commitment to Style* (2020). Through accurate close readings of the director's works, the author addresses crucial leitmotifs of Sorrentino's production style, and underscores the director's ability to imbue his cinema with a sense of social consciousness and responsibility.

Sorrentino's global breadth, his unique visionary style and distinctive aesthetics, his weighty poetics and his stunning compositions (thanks also to Luca Bigazzi's photography) *tout court* make him a contemporary director worthy of scrutiny. The purpose of this book is to rediscover and deconstruct Sorrentino's current exegesis, highlighting his auteurist traits in order to present a more extensive picture of his cinematic *opus*. Paolo Sorrentino's cinematic career started in the late 1990s, when – as a screenwriter – he wrote and directed his first short films, *Un paradiso (A Paradise)* (1994), *L'amore non ha confini (Love Has No Boundaries)* (1998) and *La notte lunga (The Long Night)* (2001), the latter launching his lifelong collaboration with Indigo Film. His first feature film, *L'uomo in più (One Man Up)* (2001), received praise and prizes at the 58th Venice Film Festival, and marked the start of a long-term working relationship with Neapolitan actor Tony Servillo. It was, however, with his second feature film, *Le conseguenze dell'amore (The Consequences of Love)* (2004), that he truly stepped into the limelight, winning five 'David di Donatello' and three 'Nastri d'argento' awards. In 2006, he directed the dystopian *L'amico di famiglia (A Family Friend)*, and in 2008 his much-acclaimed biopic on Giulio Andreotti, *Il Divo*. The latter was awarded the Jury Prize at the Cannes International Film Festival, thereby placing Sorrentino at the centre of a nationwide cinematic and political debate. *Il Divo* also impressed festival juror Sean Penn, leading to their collaboration in *This Must Be the Place* (2011), Sorrentino's first English-language film. In 2014, *La grande bellezza (The Great Beauty)* won an Oscar and a Golden Globe for Best Foreign Language Film, as well as a BAFTA Award and five EFA Awards. In 2016, *La Giovinezza (Youth)* gained an Oscar nomination for Best Original Song and two Golden Globe nominations for Best Supporting Actress and Best Original Song. The film won three European Film Awards. Additionally, in 2016, Sorrentino wrote and directed *The Young Pope*, his first English-language, Italian drama television series for HBO, Canal + and Sky Atlantic, whose stellar cast included Jude Law, Diane Keaton and James Cromwell.

His 2018 biopic, *Loro*, which centres on the four-time Italian Prime Minister Silvio Berlusconi, offers a timely analysis of the overindulgence of power-hungry individuals. In this film, Sorrentino scrutinizes the multifaceted personality of the tycoon (played once again by Toni Servillo) during a turbulent period in his life, as his marriage to Veronica Lario (interpreted by Elena Sofia Ricci) ends and his political power is threatened. Sorrentino skilfully threads together the stories of a wide variety of characters with different social backgrounds, as they attempt to either flatter him or dissociate themselves from him. In 2020, SKY Atlantic and HBO aired the sequel to *The Young Pope*, called *The New Pope*, which again featured a star-studded cast. *The New Pope* saw the return of Jude Law and Silvio Orlando, complementing a new cast that included John Malkovich, Marilyn Mason and Sharon Stone. Film critics didn't hesitate to praise the sequel: one of these characterized it as 'gorgeous, audacious, confusing, and shockingly sexy' (Mancuso 2020). Sorrentino is presently working on another biopic starring Jennifer Lawrence, based on the life of the New York mafia wife-turned-police-informant, Arlyne Brickman. The film is an adaptation of the non-fiction crime story by the Pulitzer Prize–winning reporter, Teresa Carpenter, called *Mob Girl: A Woman's Life in the Underworld (1992)*. To add to this list of achievements, Sorrentino also published a novel, *Hanno tutti ragione* (*Everybody's Right*) (2010), and two collections of short stories, *Tony Pagoda e i suoi amici* (*Tony Pagoda and His Friends*) (2012) and *Gli aspetti irrilevanti* (*The Irrelevant Aspects*) (2016). In 2017, finally, he authored *Il peso di Dio. Il Vangelo di Lenny Belardo* (*God's Weight. Lenny Belardo's Gospel*), which is a collection of dialogues from the series *The Young Pope*.

The fourteen essays contained in this book, which is the second publication in the new series *Trajectories of Italian Cinema and Media,* are the result of a rigorous and challenging selection process. They shed an innovative light on hermeneutical traits that have not been sufficiently addressed in existing studies. The overall focus of this book is on the second phase of Sorrentino's production, starting from *This Must Be the Place* (2011), which inaugurates his more recent, transnational works. Although some of the essays make references to his earliest films, specifically to *One Man Up* and *Il Divo*, this collection underscores the trajectory of Sorrentino's production on an international scale. From this perspective, *This Must Be the Place* constitutes a point of departure into the director's transnational phase, and a movement away from his primarily Italian audience.

The contributors to this book masterfully examine Sorrentino's authorial trademarks, his 'excessive visuals, scathing humour and a yearning for spirituality' (Simor and Sorfa 2017: 212), as well as the grand themes of memory, nostalgia, aging, love, the thirst for fulfilment, the search for the self, identity crisis, human estrangement, marginality, irony and power. In so doing, they offer new theoretical angles, hermeneutical perspectives and cues for discussion while enriching existing literature. Although they refer to previous scholarship, the contributions here go further, advancing unique perspectives that, at times, deconstruct the established assumptions and paradigms of Sorrentino's hermeneutics.

Part One of this book, entitled 'Examining and Deconstructing Sorrentino's Ethos', opens with Ellen Nerenberg's comparative analysis of the theme of nostalgia in *Youth* and *The Young Pope*. In her chapter 'Private Pain/Public Places: Sights, Sightings and Sounds of Nostalgia in *Youth* and *The Young Pope*', Nerenberg claims that 'nostalgia in Sorrentino's *oeuvre* provides a *modus faciendi pelliculas*'.

Nostalgia is an elaborate concept that acts as a catalyst for the plot, one that is 'visualized, somatized and gendered', embracing and involving masculinity, reformation, deformation and remorse. The author furthers that this concept is present at every semiotic level in Sorrentino's audio-visual texts, and may manifest different and even contrasting epistemologies. Nerenberg maintains that 'nostalgia itself is not a monolithic category', and she uses Svetlana Boym's well-established discussion on 'restorative' and 'reflective' nostalgia to analyse the film and the television series. Through her elaborate comparison of the two screen texts, Nerenberg explains how nostalgia reveals an alternating and dual nature, which looks backwards into memory and history, and forward into the future.

The examination of the director's ethos continues with Mimmo Cangiano's analysis of a Romantic and Modernist Sorrentino. In 'Against Postmodernism: Paolo Sorrentino and the Search for Authenticity', Cangiano deconstructs the most common assertion about Sorrentino's postmodern penchant, stating that his cinematic oeuvre challenges postmodernist theories of identity by focusing on romantic and modernist leitmotifs, such as the search for identity and authenticity in life. Cangiano backs his argument up by highlighting Sorrentino's characters' proclivity to follow their sensory impulses, and their incessant urge to travel. In his view, these traits demonstrate that the characters' flawed perspectives are rooted in an unreal world. He maintains that Sorrentino's archetypal figure is a man who, in seeking himself, attempts to construct meaning from the conflict between his stable and ephemeral identities. Cangiano states that Sorrentino's cinema simultaneously supports and suppresses postmodern readings of his work; reflecting this interpretation, the *mise en abyme* of his entire poetics coincides with the characters' journey from nihilism to meaning, and therefore with the creation of art in life.

The third chapter in this first section features Monica Facchini's examination of the spectacular realism and unamendability of reality in *The Great Beauty*.[2] According to Facchini, Sorrentino's film exposes contemporary society in all its contradictions. The film highlights, on the one hand, the reality of a society based on spectacle and, on the other hand, the turmoil of human existence, with its disquiet and frailties. The author's argument combines Guy Debord's theory of the 'Society of the Spectacle', Maurizio Ferraris' ideas on the 'unamendability of reality' and Pier Paolo Pasolini's concept of death as the moment that, like a fictional story or montage, gives our existence a stable and unchangeable meaning. Facchini argues that in Sorrentino's award-winning film the double reality of the spectacle coexists: one shiny and visible, the other uncomfortable and hidden. Eventually, the film tears away the mask of the spectacle, recognizes its inauthenticity and reveals the 'trick' behind the illusory pursuit of pleasure. The main character, Jep, epitomizes the weakness of a mundane Roman life, and exorcizes the fear of death by unmasking society's artificiality and excesses. However, Facchini notes that the director finds authentic beauty precisely in the intrinsic vulnerability caused by aging and the fear of death. Moreover, she argues that 'death in *The Great Beauty* serves as that unamendable element of reality, which prompts the protagonist to look at life with different eyes and with a renovated awareness of its meaningfulness'. Through an analysis of Sorrentino's cinematic style, Facchini proposes a reading of the film as an 'inverted' journey, one that does not go 'from life to death', as Céline would have it, but, from death to life.

The last chapter in this opening section is written by Lydia Tuan. She argues that Sorrentino employs a distinctive cinematic style that is linked to theories of cinematic excess, particularly those advanced by Kristin Thompson in four representative films: *One Man Up*, *Il Divo*, *The Great Beauty* and *The Young Pope*. Tuan shows how Sorrentino's formal excess becomes temporally and spatially evident through the analytic attention to its aesthetic. Employing Elizabeth Freeman's notion of chronobiopolitics, she argues that the director frequently slows down or speeds up time so as to portray his protagonists' thoughts, memories and flashbacks in a way that reflects their suspended states. Distancing herself from Kristin Thompson's view of excess as a formal element, she gives the term a more literal meaning. Tuan thus views excess as extra, overflow, surplus, 'more than' an anticipated quantity. In doing so, she argues that Sorrentino employs a style that relies on techniques being used to an unusual degree, formulating the notion of 'excess as style'. She manages to effectively demonstrate that Sorrentino's aesthetics is inextricably linked to his manipulations of time and space. She skilfully states that:

> through extended establishing shots and presentations of non-linear cinematic timelines, Sorrentino's temporal excess and spatial excess produce each other, allowing viewers to formally engage with the idea of decay and slow destruction, which mirrors the slowness of personal decay felt by Sorrentino's protagonists through their estrangements from their professional lives.

The second part of this collection is dedicated to 'Sorrentino's Real and Symbolic Spaces', and showcases four chapters that trace the literal and metaphorical spatial trajectory of the director's audio-visual texts. Matteo Gilebbi's chapter, entitled 'Posthuman Sorrentino: *Youth* and *The Great Beauty* as Ecocinema', opens the discussion by suggesting that the standard interpretation of Sorrentino's cinematic world as dominated by a human-privileged – or anthropocentric – perspective of the environment is incorrect. According to Gilebbi, 'in *The Great Beauty* and *Youth* a posthuman condition informs the interaction between the characters and their undivided natural and cultural environments'. Struggling to find meaning in the frailty of their human condition, Sorrentino's characters seek kinship with nature and the biosphere, exemplifying a posthuman condition in a world devoid of hierarchies and human privileges. This endorsement grants ecocinematic qualities to Sorrentino's latest films, where a crossover with ecology reveals the presence of a biosphere that exists alongside and beyond human understanding and control. Moreover, the author maintains that Sorrentino's narrative helps us to reconsider our ethical and political role in the Anthropocene, where we are decisive agents of global ecological transformation.

Neatly following on from Gilebbi's argument, Alex Gammon's chapter on 'Rome's Vocalization Through Architecture in *The Great Beauty*' suggests that Sorrentino's films attribute anthropomorphic qualities to architecture and natural elements. Unlike Federico Fellini's *La dolce vita* (1960), where the relationship between the characters and architecture is antithetical and unresponsive, Gammon cogently demonstrates that *The Great Beauty* creates a stage where people can establish a fruitful dialogue with monuments, churches and ruins, thus inspiring a rebirth from their materiality. Gammon advances the hypothesis of a dialectic between Roman architecture and film, viewed as vocalizing entities through which the protagonist Jep re-establishes his identity and rediscovers his inspiration. Hence, architecture gains a vocal quality through film that allows Rome to interact with the film's protagonists. Gammon convincingly argues that 'the architecture becomes a conduit for truth in the protagonist's identity by vocalizing existential freedom to him'.

The discussion of Sorrentino's metaphorical spaces continues with Michela Barisonzi's chapter '*The Great Beauty*: A Journey Through Art and Relations in Search for Beauty'. Countering the widespread criticism that Sorrentino's films all feature a dichotomy between form and substance in relation to beauty, Barisonzi argues that *The Great Beauty* is a meditation on this duality, which points to the place where true meaning and 'beauty' reside: human relations. The chapter creates a dialogical discourse on the social nature of aesthetics, and offers a nuanced investigation into the elements of beauty used throughout the film, by promptly tearing them down, thus revealing their emptiness. By referring to Alain Badiou, Gilles Deleuze, and John Urry's theories, Barisonzi argues that the award-winning film offers a new definition of beauty by bringing together the two components of the binary opposition. The author argues that 'true beauty emerges from relationships'. However, she clarifies that relationships must first be deconstructed in order to leave space for the rediscovery of beauty. This idea is epitomized by Jep, when he says the following words: 'we are all on the verge of desperation, all we can do is look each other in the eyes, keep each other company, and make fun of each other'. Only by acknowledging this existential truth can one overcome appearance (form) and rediscover true beauty (substance). Barisonzi thus maintains that, in *The Great Beauty*, Sorrentino does not prefer form to substance but, rather, re-examines the concept of aesthetic beauty. He does so by transferring true beauty to a substance found in unconventional, physical and symbolic places, such as love, a true friend, school children's games or a father's tribute to his son. The author's stance is cleverly summarized by this remark: '[B]eauty is not in objects, but in life conceived as the precarious and everchanging sum of human fragilities and relationships'.

Carla Molinari's 'The Urban Dimension as Film Character: Rome in *The Great Beauty*' concludes this second part. It focuses on the intersection between cinema and architectural studies, and on the former's influence on the latter. Considering Francois Penz and Walter Benjamin's theories, the author claims that *The Great Beauty* can be used to understand and analyse architectural spaces and their cinematic relations. She proposes a methodology for examining cinematic texts from an architectural perspective. Molinari emphasizes Rome's relevance and its fictional representation in *The Great Beauty*, underlining the power of cinema in the narration and transformation of the urban context, and anticipating the spaces of the future. In particular, she examines Sorrentino's choice of locations and use of montage, music and dialogue to create two different urban dimensions, based on two different kinds of Rome: one dark, contemporary and brutal, the other sublime and beautiful, though trapped in the past. Thus, the author argues that through its use of Rome, *The Great Beauty* can be considered an example of the 'city-genre' as defined by Andrew Webber (2008).

The third part of this collection is entitled 'A Journey into Sorrentino's Psyche'. It opens with Russell Kilbourn's chapter 'The "Primal Scene": Memory, Redemption and "Woman" in the Films of Paolo Sorrentino', which examines gender and female marginalization in *The Great Beauty* and *Youth*. It offers an interesting new perspective on Sorrentino's aesthetics and on his highly gendered cinematic world. Rather than deconstructing the way in which Sorrentino objectifies the female form, Kilbourn delves into his motivation. Having established his theoretical perspective, and what he calls 'the Sorrentinian subject', Kilbourn furthers some interesting claims about the function of the image as an aesthetic spectacle, which is unquestionably central to Sorrentino's cinema. Invoking the role of the 'gaze' and the 'stare' as elaborated in disability studies, the author examines Sorrentino's fascination with non-normative identities, which function as radical othering, shedding a more ironic light on the masculine subject. He thus links the objectification of the female form to the director's proclivity for images of deformed and/or grotesque bodies. Kilbourn traces an increasingly complex trajectory in the portrayal of gender in Sorrentino's films, which is problematized by the connection of the memory of the primal scene with secular or postsecular redemption.

The emergence of Sorrentino's subconscious in his films is the focus of Sandra Waters' chapter 'Anxiety (of Influence) and (Absent) Fathers in Sorrentino's

English-Language Narratives'. Waters analyses the mirror effect between Sorrentino's fatherless characters and himself, in an attempt to break the fourth wall between the diegetic and the extra-diegetic narrative. Through a psychoanalytical reading of *Youth*, *This Must Be the Place* and *The Young Pope*, she upholds that Sorrentino is not a mere twenty-first-century reiteration of Fellini; rather, his frequent citations of Fellini's films serve as a catalyst to delve deeper into the director's psyche, and not merely to 'mimic' his predecessor in a Bloomian fashion. As his characters' fictional lives are spent searching for either their ancestors or a Hitchcockian McGuffin, Waters boldly suggests that the director uses the camera to address his troubling past in his art, to seek his own missing *objet petit a*, to exorcize his loss and demonstrate his superiority over his predecessors (i.e. Fellini and Pasolini). Waters concludes that 'any deficiencies, failures or crises depicted by the fathers, sons, and father figures on screen is counteracted by the success of Sorrentino himself off screen [...] who becomes a "strong" poet-director, perhaps even overshadowing his own poetic forerunners'.

The part dedicated to the journey into Sorrentino's psyche ends with a chapter by Nicoletta Marini-Maio, entitled "'È solo l'alito di un vecchio". Obscenity, Exchange Regimes, and the Catastrophe of Aging in *Loro*'. Drawing on Francesco Ceraolo, Ida Dominijanni, Michel Foucault and Massimo Recalcati's political and psychoanalytical theories, Marini-Maio claims that the diptych *Loro* is a public display of the obscenity of neoliberal power, and a parody of Silvio Berlusconi's physical and political deterioration. Moreover, she suggests that the hedonistic, Berlusconian regime exhibits 'the erotization of power relationships' and 'the commodification of the self' that typify neoliberalism. The author maintains that *Loro* visualizes the economic and power exchange so typical of neoliberal societies, where 'the Law literally coincides with enjoyment and desire'. These power dynamics are mainly represented by 'the aesthetic of the orgy' and 'the libidinal tension between the aged male body and the young women', which become a constant thematic narrative in *Loro*. Consequently, the young women that are featured in the film are political bodies that 'shine a light on the fundamental condition of Berlusconism'. Marini-Maio defines Sorrentino's cinema as a postmodern political allegory, because it presents facts as they manifest themselves without examining their causes. This process produces 'signifiers that acquire emblematic value on their own from their existence as simulacra'. She explains how the film's non-linear and fluid narratives build around the deictic ambiguity of the title *Loro*, creating 'a disorienting fluctuation of points of view and mechanisms of identification'. Skilfully, the disorientation of the form mirrors the political turmoil so typical of neoliberalism.

The fourth and final part of this collection features essays on 'Sorrentino's Post-secular Pope'. It opens with a second chapter by Russell Kilbourn, '*The Young*

Pope's Credit Sequence: A Postsecular Allegory in Ten Paintings'. Here Kilbourn argues that the ironic transmediation of the ten paintings reproduced in *The Young Pope*'s opening credit sequence allegorizes the series' engagement with the contradictions of the current postsecular era. The author approaches the ten artworks in terms of their analogical – that is, their diegetic, characterological or thematic – connections to *The Young Pope*, and to Sorrentino's *oeuvre* in general. Kilbourn's reading of this television series deepens the sociocultural and aesthetic analysis of digital media as expressed through Sorrentino's complex and enigmatic use of the image. His chapter responds to the discussion on the reception of this series, which criticizes the current state of the Catholic Church and examines the nature and value of religious faith in the twenty-first century. Kilbourn also addresses the crucial underlying issue of how to analyse, evaluate and understand Sorrentino's conceptual, stylistic and/or affective 'contradictions'. The author's focus on the thesis of postsecular allegory offers an alternative assessment of Sorrentino's position as an auteur, and in doing so makes references to some key texts on allegory. The essay thus draws on a number of authoritative thinkers on this subject: Angus Fletcher on allegory, Northrop Frye on irony, Roland Barthes on connotation and denotation, Gilles Deleuze on the time image and on the poverty of cinema, Fran Kermode on rhetoric. Finally, Kilbourn stresses the pivotal role of digitally enhanced production in *The Young Pope*, endorsing 'its status as digital and allegorical event'.

Pertinently following on from Kilbourn's argument, Monica Jansen and Maria Bonaria Urban's chapter on 'The "Fabrication" of Religion in *The Young Pope*: the Double Irony of Post-Secular "Icono*clash*"' addresses the post-secular question through the theoretical lenses of Bruno Latour's 'icono*clash*' and Birgit Meyer's 'sensational form' of religion. By presenting several examples of 'iconoclash' within the series, the authors show how the director accomplishes this through his 'double irony' narrative strategy, which is indicative of Sorrentino's interpretation of the post-secular. The chapter explores *The Young Pope*'s insoluble contradiction between 'the mystery of a transcendental "beyond" and the "world-making" practices of art and religion', which is embodied by Pius XIII, thus between humanism and transcendence. The authors make a persuasive case for reconciling this dichotomy within Sorrentino's 'excessive cinematic style', between 'post-metaphysical conscience' and the desacralization of the sacred that is inherent in the 'fabrication of religion'. The authors maintain that, through the rhetorical device of 'double irony', the series disavows the power of the Church and reveals its transcendence.

The last part of this book contains a chapter by Anna Manzato and Antonella Mascio, on *The Young Pope* as a form of 'celevision'. They examine how celebrities impacted on the writing and the reception of the series, as well as their role in making *The Young Pope* a transnational phenomenon. The concept of celevision mainly entails celebrities' participation in television shows, which has been facilitated by the collapsing boundaries between, and the cultural legitimization of, cinema and television. Manzato and Mascio consider a range of texts linked to medial, para-textual discourse and to Facebook pages, which have accompanied the broadcasting of each episode. Supported by several theoretical models borrowed from the field of celebrities studies, the two authors cunningly analyse how celebrity is constructed within and outside the text. They reveal that the discourse on these celebrities – which they call an extra-diegetic type of celevision – overshadows any reflection on the filmic text itself. Conversely, an intra-diegetic narrative trajectory involves the increasing celebrity status of the main character, Pope Pius XIII; the authors argue that part of the show's popularity rests on this dual celebrity-building strategy.

Regarding celebrity status outside the text, Manzato and Mascio cite several newspapers, from reports that cover *The Young Pope*'s premiere at the 2016 Venice Film Festival to positive reviews published months later, written by journalists and film critics alike. They reproduce enthusiastic comments in the Italian and American press that use Sorrentino's character to portray the series as a Copernican revolution, filled with Sorrentinian leitmotifs – his 'magical realism' trait *in primis*. This astonishing coverage is intended to influence the audience's interpretation, and the press' focus on directors and actors allows celebrity events to be constructed. Thus, a celebrity status is attributed to the individual participants in the series, 'but also more generally to the product itself, which takes on a peculiar resonance thanks to the superposition of cinema and television'. The authors maintain that *The Young Pope* is a typical example of 'complex television', because it constructs celebrity culture through various stages: transmedia storytelling, orienting paratexts, new authorialities and social networking. Finally, the celevision status of *The Young Pope* impacts on the social realm through the symbolic power exercised by the media.

Finally, my interview with Carlo Poggioli, Sorrentino's costume designer, concludes this collection of essays. The captivating stories about his career and his collaboration with the director add another dimension to our understanding of Sorrentino's work and his eclectic harmony.

To conclude, this book clearly opens the field for a novel and unique exegesis of Sorrentino's *opus*, without disregarding previous hermeneutical approaches. It also aims to correct certain misconceptions about Sorrentino's work. For many years now, various film critics have considered him a pretentious filmmaker, denigratingly referring to Sorrentino as the new Fellini,[3] thus implying that he mimics Fellini's cinematic style and motifs. Yet, many Italian and international directors (such as Woody Allen in *Stardust Memories* [1980]) have included Fellinesque elements in their films, which fell short of plagiarism with-out, however, being stigmatized in the same way. In my opinion, Sorrentino's style reflects the ancient Latin concept of *imitatio*. In his entry on 'Imitation' (*mimesis, imitatio*) in *The Encyclopedia of Ancient History*, Michael Fronda defines imitation as 'an author's conscious use of features and characteristics of earlier works to acknowledge indebtedness to past writers' (Bagnall et al. 2012: 3416). Imitation recurs in nearly every work by Greek and Roman authors. To clarify this, Fronda explains that 'ancient theoretical discussions of imita-tion agree that good imitation required more than simple copying. An imitator was expected to emulate many models, join imitated material seamlessly to his own, reshape and vary it for its new context, and improve upon it' (Bagnall et al. 2012: 3416). Closer scrutiny of Sorrentino's films reveals that the director indeed operates within the terms of ancient *imitatio*. His emulation of some of Fellini's films, including *La dolce vita* (1960), *8½* (1963), *Giulietta degli spiriti* (*Juliet of the Spirits*) (1965) and *Roma* (1972), does not simply replicate these films, but rather reshapes them into a more contemporary and transnational mould, informed by his singular aesthetic of a (post)modernized Italy and, in particular, Rome.

In keeping with the aims of the *Trajectories of Italian Cinema and Media* series, this volume is intended to provide a forum for diverse approaches to, and transnational perspectives on, Paolo Sorrentino, a new auteur of Italian cinema, whose 'self-introspective and contemplative art' and unique aesthetic touch have had – and continue to have – a profound impact on national and transnational film studies.

NOTES

1. For an up-to-date list of publications on Sorrentino, see the bibliography at the end of this volume.
2. Facchini's article first appeared in Loredana Di Martino and Pasquale Verdicchio (eds.), *Encounters with the Real in Contemporary Italian Literature and Cinema*, Cambridge: Cambridge Scholars Publishing, 2017.
3. See the online article written by James Killough, 'Why Paolo Sorrentino is and isn't the new Fellini': http://www.purefilmcreative.com/killough-chronicles/why-paolo-sorrentino-is-and-isnt-the-new-fellini.html. Accessed 10 February 2018.

REFERENCES

Antonello, P. and Mussgnug, F. (eds) (2009), *'Postmodern Impegno': Ethics and Commitment in Contemporary Italian Culture*, Bern: Peter Lang.

Bagnall, R., Brodersen, K., Champion, C., Erskine, A. and Huebner, S. (eds.) (2012), *Encyclopaedia of Ancient History*, Malden, MA: Wiley-Blackwell.

Bisoni, C. (2016), 'Paolo Sorrentino: Between engagement and *savoir faire*', in G. Lombardi and C. Uva, *Public Life, Imaginary, and Identity in Contemporary Italian Film*, Oxford: Peter Lang, pp. 250–62.

Hipkins, D. (2008), 'Why Italian film studies needs a second take on gender', *Italian Studies*, 63:2, pp. 213-34.

Hogan, M. (2020), 'Interview to Paolo Sorrentino', *The Guardian*, 5 January, https://www.theguardian.com/film/2020/jan/05/paolo-sorrentino-my-characters-struggles-are-the-struggles-i-have. Accessed 9 January 2020.

Kilbourn, R. (2020), *The Cinema of Paolo Sorrentino: Commitment to Style*, New York: Columbia University Press.

Killough, J. (2013), 'Why Paolo Sorrentino is and isn't the new Fellini', *Pfc Everything as a Story*, 10 December, http://www.purefilmcreative.com/killough-chronicles/why-paolo- sorrentino-is-and-isnt-the-new-fellini.html. Accessed 10 February 2018.

Mancuso, V. (2020), '*The New Pope* review: John Malkovich leads a sermon on faith, corruption, and club bangers', *Collider*, 1 July, https://collider.com/new-pope-review-hbo/. Accessed 1 September 2020.

Marcus, M. (2010), 'The ironist and the auteur: Post-realism in Paolo Sorrentino's *Il Divo*', *The Italianist*, 30, pp. 245-57.

Mariani, A. (2017), 'The empty heterotopic (non-)space of Sorrentino's female characters in *The Great Beauty* and *The Consequences of Love*', in S. Byer and F. Cecchini (eds), *Female Identity and Its Representations in the Arts and Humanities*, Newcastle upon Tyne: Cambridge Scholars Publishing, pp. 168-84.

Marlow-Mann, A. (2010), 'Characters engagement and alienation in the cinema of Paolo Sorrentino', in W. Pope (ed.), *Italian Films Directors in The New Millennium*, Newcastle upon Tyne: Cambridge Scholars Publishing, pp. 161-73.

O'Leary, A. (2017), 'What is Italian cinema?', *California Italian Studies*, 7:1. DOI: https://escholarship.org/uc/item/7z9275bz.

Olsen, M. (2019), 'Paolo Sorrentino on Loro, Silvio Berlusconi and the art of the sensual party', *Los Angeles Times*, 1 October, https://www.latimes.com/entertainment-arts/movies/story/2019-10-01/paolo-sorrentino-toni-servillo-loro-silvio-berlusconi. Accessed 10 January 2020.

O'Rawe, C. (2018), 'Editorial: Contemporary Italian film culture in the light of #MeToo', *The Italianist*, 38:2, pp. 151-52.

Paiella, G. (2019), 'Paolo Sorrentino on Berlusconi's "Bunga" parties and Jude Law's papal speedo', *Condé Nast*, 20 September, https://www.gq.com/story/paolo-sorrentino-loro-new-pope-interview. Accessed 10 January 2020.

Simor, E. and Sorfa, D. (2017), 'Irony, sexism and magic in Paolo Sorrentino's films', *Studies in European Cinema*. DOI: 10.1080/17411548.2017.1386368.

Sorrentino, P. (1994), *Un paradiso (A Paradise)*, Italy: Polymedia.

Sorrentino, P. (1998), *L'amore non ha confine (Love Has No Boundaries)*, Italy: Indigo Film.

Sorrentino, P.(2001a), *La notte lunga (The Long Night)*, Italy: Indigo Film.

Sorrentino, P. (2001b), *L'uomo in più (One Man Up)*, Italy: Indigo Film.

Sorrentino, P. (2004), *Le conseguenze dell'amore (The Consequences of Love)*, Italy: Indigo Film.

Sorrentino, P. (2006), *L'amico di famiglia (A Family Friend)*, Italy: Indigo Film.

Sorrentino, P. (2008), *Il Divo*, Italy: Indigo Film.

Sorrentino, P. (2011), *This Must Be the Place*, Italy, France and Ireland: Indigo Film and Medusa Film.

Sorrentino, P. (2012), *Tony Pagoda e i suoi amici (Tony Pagoda and his Friends)*, Milan: Feltrinelli.

Sorrentino, P. (2013a), *Hanno tutti ragione (Everybody's Right)*, Milan: Feltrinelli.

Sorrentino, P. (2013b), *La grande bellezza (The Great Beauty)*, Italy and France: Indigo Film.

Sorrentino, P. (2015), *Youth*, Italy, UK, France and Switzerland: Indigo Film.

Sorrentino, P. (2016a), *Gli aspetti irrilevanti (The Irrelevant Aspects)*, Milan: Mondadori.

Sorrentino, P.(2016b), *The Young Pope (2016–17)*, USA: HBO Home Entertainment.

Sorrentino, P. (2017), *Il peso di Dio. Il Vangelo di Lanny Belardo (God's Weight. Lenny Belardo's Gospel)*, Torino: Einaudi.

Sorrentino, P. (2018a), *Loro 1*, Italy, France: Indigo Film, Pathé Production, France 2 Cinéma.

Sorrentino, P. (2018b), *Loro 2*, Italy, France: Indigo Film, Pathé Production, France 2 Cinéma.

Sorrentino, P. (2020),*The New Pope (2019–2020)*, USA: HBO Home Entertainment.

PART ONE

EXAMINING AND DECONSTRUCTING SORRENTINO'S ETHOS

Foto di Gianni Fiorito © WILDSIDE/SKY ITALIA/HAUT ET COURT TV/HOME BOX OFFICE, INC./MEDIAPRO.

1

Private Pain/Public Places: Sights, Sightings and Sounds of Nostalgia in *Youth* and *The Young Pope*

Ellen Nerenberg

Wesleyan University

Che cosa avete contro la 'nostalgia, eh'? È l'unico svago per chi è diffidente verso il futuro, l'unico![1]

– *The Great Beauty* (Sorrentino 2013: n.pag.)

The nostalgic directs his gaze not only backward but sideways, and expresses himself in elegiac poems and ironic fragments, not in philosophical or scientific treatises. Nostalgia remains unsystematic and unsynthesizable: it seduces rather than convinces.

– Svetlana Boym, *The Future of Nostalgia* (2001: 13)

Personal Reasons: Restoration, Reform and Reflection

As starting premise for a detailed comparative analysis, a scene each from *The Young Pope* (HBO-Sky, 2016) and *Youth* (2015).

1. Episode 9 of Paolo Sorrentino's *The Young Pope* opens, with credits rolling, on the title prelate, Lenny Belardo (Jude Law), seated on the steps leading to the altar in a majestic, empty Sistine Chapel. In pristine white papal raiment, Lenny launches his fierce anti-reproductive choice campaign. He recites verses

from *Exodus* 21 and extols, minutely, sombrely, by rote, centuries of Church teachings on the sanctity of life. His mentor, Michael Cardinal Spencer (James Cromwell) is the only other presence in this monumental location. From his wheelchair, dressed in a priest's regular black cassock, Spencer counters each point in the pope's argument with different theologians' meditations. Marshalling evidence in support of his argument, the pope ambulates in the cavernous, still space. The immobilized cardinal, on the other hand, exhorts his one-time pupil to adopt a more contemporary outlook and pleads for papal compassion, empathy and a woman's right to choose. He admonishes Lenny for not recalling the lessons of Saint Alphonsus (1696–1787), who, as concerned abortion, 'found everyone guilty except for the woman'. Making his way to the exit, Belardo pauses to gaze upon the shrouded skeleton in the lower left quadrant of Michelangelo's simulated *Last Judgement*. What, he asks Spencer, if in all things everyone was guilty except for the woman? When Spencer asks if Lenny is referring to his mother, the Pope replies, 'Who else could I be talking about?'

2. The conclusion of the penultimate sequence in Sorrentino's 2015 film *Youth* is punctuated by a long shot of an exterior we know is in Venice. The camera closes in to frame a window frame, which itself frames a woman's face. She is Melanie (Sonia Gessner), Fred Ballinger's (Michael Caine) wife, the film's absent presence until this late scene. During Fred's visit, she is shown only in an extreme oblique angle, which robs us of a view of her face. As she sits in her wheelchair, gazing out at the canal below, she gives the impression of preferring not to regard Fred as he speaks to her. The mobile camera tracks smoothly past her wheelchair to exit the slightly open window before stopping abruptly. The static, medium-long, reverse angle shot that replaces it gazes back on where we have just come from to frame the woman at the window. Mouth sagging horribly open, Melanie stares vacantly. The repeated framing devices (the frame of a frame) signify Fred's efforts to contain the pain caused by seeing her.[2]

These two scenes announce different kinds of nostalgia. While Sorrentino's screen projects are rife with nostalgic moments and manifestations, nostalgia as a concept is neither monolithic nor naive. Rather, nostalgia in Sorrentino's *oeuvre* is a complex idea plied variously across different texts in different ways. In sometimes sweeping, transverse gestures, it portends of politics and epistemologies, while at other times it manifests in a more personalized, intimate and psychological vein. This essay centres on nostalgia in two screen texts from Sorrentino's midcareer in order to tease out these complexities.[3]

Each scene ushers in the project's nostalgic operations that span categories ranging from 'restorative' to 'reflective' (about which more directly), and which are brought together by concerns for reform. Michelangelo's simulated *memento mori* in *The Young Pope* 1: 9 closes the sequence (Figure 1.1) and comments – albeit mutely – on Belardo's aim to restore the Roman Catholic Church to a purer state. Fusing sight with sound, a sure link is forged between the Young Pope's personal history, the inconsolable nostalgia he feels for the parents that abandoned him and their family idyll, and his public campaign as primate of the Catholic Church. In *Youth*, Melanie functions much like Michelangelo's shrouded figure and performs a mute tableau vivant of regret and nostalgia. She is 'the personal reason', as Fred informs the Queen's abashed Emissary (Alex Macqueen), for which he cannot publicly perform 'Simple Song #3' at the royal birthday celebration. Insensate (from a much earlier stroke, we presume), Melanie is quite the opposite of the youth the title promises, and yet, as Fred reminds her during this visit, she lies at the heart of the 'Simple Song', the command performance of which impels the ironically titled *Youth* forward to its conclusion (Figure 1.2).

FIGURE 1.1: Michelangelo Buonarotti, detail, Sistine Chapel, *The Young Pope*, Episode 9. Personal reasons, public spaces, global consequences.

FIGURE 1.2: 'For personal reasons'. Melanie Ballinger, *Youth*.

Recalling Romano's words from *The Great Beauty*, offered in epigraph at the beginning of this chapter, Sorrentino observed at the Cannes premiere, 'The film's idea is how we think about future, how the future always offers a possibility of liberty, and liberty is a state inherent to youth' (Zorich 2015: n.pag.). This dual, sometimes contradictory pulsation of nostalgia distinguishes it from 'memory'. As Walter Benjamin described Klee's *Angelus novus*, the angel of history gazes backward to memory and the past. Nostalgia, on the other hand, casts its gaze also towards the future.[4]

Youth tells the story of two decades-long, now septuagenarian, friends Fred Ballinger and Mick Boyle (Harvey Keitel) on holiday at a spa near Davos, Switzerland.[5] While Fred, a retired composer and orchestra director, suffers from 'apathy', Mick maintains a vigorous creative practice, working energetically – one might say 'youthfully' – each day (between curative spa sessions for a series of normal, age-related maladies) with a cadre of young screenwriters on the script of 'Life's Last Day', his cinematic 'testament'. Fred's lone complaint, 'apathy', leads him to eschew any public display of or recognition for his musical compositions. During their sojourn, Fred and Mick, accompanied by Fred's daughter Lena (Rachel Weisz) encounter a host of characters at the hotel: a Diego Maradona stand-in (The South American, Roly Serrano), a young Method actor, Jimmy Tree (Paul Dano) and Miss Universe (Mădălina Ghenea).[6] When Mick's long-time leading lady, Brenda Morel (Jane Fonda) tells him she is opting out of 'Life's Last Day' for a television series and that his last good movie was three films ago, she takes the wind from his sails. Deanimated and undone, he jumps off a balcony to his death. *Youth* ends with Fred who, having shaken off his apathetical coil, directs the orchestra in playing his *Simple Song* at the performance he had declared himself unable to participate in.

The Young Pope, a 10-episode prestige serial drama follows the youthful American of the title, Lenny Belardo (Jude Law), in the first stormy months of his iconoclastic papacy as he tries to 'correct' the direction of the Catholic Church. None of the Vatican's political operators, including Belardo's mentor Cardinal Spencer (James Cromwell) and especially the Vatican Secretary of State Cardinal Voiello (Silvio Orlando) had sufficiently intelligenced this dark horse candidate during the conclave. Lenny takes his papal office by storm, striving to redeem the Church from modernity and modern relativism, and return it to a nearly pre-Lutheran theology. Although he speaks to the faithful in a number of public addresses, he refuses to show himself in public and rejects every attempt to reproduce or monetize his image. He appoints the nun who raised him in an orphanage, Sister Mary (Diane Keaton), as his personal assistant and advisor. His calls for a return to godliness and centuries-old doctrine are catalysed by his orphaned past. He looks everywhere for the parents who abandoned him and until he 'buries two empty coffins in Venice', as Spencer counsels in Episode 8 with reference to his parents, he will not win back the faithful and his papacy will be without a future.

The pervasive theme of nostalgia in Paolo Sorrentino's body of work has received broad commentary in both the popular press and academic scholarship.[7] Such attention is deserved, given the extent to which nostalgia as theme, topic and modality has recurred in the director's screen texts. Nostalgia appeared from Sorrentino's earliest efforts and gives every indication of a continued robust presence midcareer. Sorrentino's nostalgic key prevails from its manifestation as the reminiscent (but never repentant) Tony Pisapia in *L'uomo in più (One Man Up)* (2001), to the homesick Titta Di Girolamo in *Le conseguenze d'amore (The Conseguenze of Love)* (2004) (both played by Toni Servillo), to the depressive man-boy goth rocker Cheyenne (Sean Penn) floundering in the quagmire of arrested development in *This Must be the Place* (2011). *La grande bellezza (The Great Beauty)* (2013) is itself a paean to the nostalgia that saturates the film thematically and across numerous visual and acoustic motifs. The expression of nostalgia in *Youth* (2015) activates similar mechanisms, and, in the longer narrative that serial drama provides, *The Young Pope* (2016) generates still others. To be sure, Sorrentino's films are frequently 'about' nostalgia, memory and about remembering.[8]

Although catalyst of plot and story, Sorrentino's uses of nostalgia are not limited to narrative. Rather, nostalgia is a *modus faciendi pelliculas,* manifesting at every semiotic level. Reading Boym's description of the nostalgic, offered epigraphically here, one might as easily be reading a review of *The Great Beauty*, perhaps the acme (so far) of Sorrentinian nostalgia: elegiac poems and ironic fragments? Check. Unsystematic? Check. Sideways and backwards? If one thinks that Luca Bigazzi's many sinuous tracking shots provide evidence for this, then, yes, check. If one finds such evidence insufficient, then perhaps remembering, with Hennessy, Jep Gambardella's (Toni Servillo) direct address to the camera will persuade more conclusively (Hennessy 2017: 453). Sorrentino's nostalgia makes for good box office, especially abroad, to judge from recent studies parsing the top Italian audiovisual exports worldwide in the 2007–16 period.[9] Nostalgia sells, and nostalgia about Italy sells well, especially to global audiences.[10]

Yet however steeped in memory and nostalgia Sorrentino's films may be (or appear to be), nostalgia itself is not a monolithic category nor does it always signify the same things or in the same ways.[11] Indeed, nostalgia as a concept can vary in type quite substantially. In an attempt to historicize the fairly general concept of 'longing for home' and linking it, with Starobinski, to accelerated transportation and the movement of peoples in the modern age that resulted, Hutcheon indicates a shift from the spatial to the temporal, noting that '[t]ime, unlike space, cannot be returned to – ever; time is irreversible. And nostalgia becomes the reaction to

that sad fact' (Hutcheon 1998-2000: 19; see also Starobinski 1966: 90). Stewart
has called nostalgia a 'social disease', describing it as 'the repetition that mourns
the inauthenticity of all repetition' (Stewart 1984: 23). However much an individual might suffer from nostalgia, it was not limited in scope to the personal.
As Boym remarks, in her influential 2001 study *The Future of Nostalgia*, at the
close of seventeenth and in the early eighteenth centuries, when it was first becoming medicalized, nostalgia was 'not merely an individual anxiety but a public
threat that revealed the contradictions of modernity and acquired greater political importance' (Boym 2001: 5). For Boym nostalgia prevailingly takes on two
rather distinct forms: 'restorative' and 'reflective'. 'Restorative nostalgia', Boym
observes, 'puts emphasis on *nostos* [home] and proposes to build the lost home
and patch up memory gaps' (Boym 2001: 41). Pushed towards more allegorical
lines of interpretation, restorative memory becomes associated with a conservative
(often politically conservative) posture and might be thought of as 'public' tending
for its dynamic role in the crafting of historical narrative.[12] The second, 'reflective' kind of nostalgia, 'dwells in *algia* [pain], in longing and loss, the imperfect
process of remembrance' (Boym 2001: 41). While reflective nostalgia appears more
inward-turning, its symptoms, when monetized by media practices (production,
marketing, etc.) and platforms (cinema, narrow and broadcasting platforms) can
produce material effects in very public cultural industries (e.g. cinema, media and
entertainment; tourism). As Hutcheon and others have clarified, nostalgia lends
significant purchase on the social for the ways it performs longing and feelings of
loss for a time outside of history that never was but is always imagined, desired,
deferred and mourned.

Whereas nostalgia in *The Great Beauty* has justifiably received broad attention, the 'young' dyad that followed Sorrentino's Academy Award-winning 2013
film, *Youth* and *The Young Pope*, benefits from supplementary contemplation in
this regard. Indeed, these two screen texts offer classic, textbook, nearly literalized
examples of pathological nostalgia. Although recent scholarship has tended to
group *The Young Pope* with *Il Divo* and *Loro* in Sorrentino's 'Trilogy on Power',
a significant number of shared attributes invite us to consider the ways *Youth* and
The Young Pope reciprocally and mutually entail.[13] Most obviously, both screen
texts predicate on 'youth', something self-evident beginning with their titles and
developed thematically throughout, particularly as concerns masculinity, reformation, deformation and remorse. In addition, the texts' principal locations – *Youth's*
spa and *The Young Pope*'s transnational Vatican – are 'extra' Italian, close to
Italy yet significantly not 'of' it. These quasi non-spaces are Anglophone, part of
Sorrentino's 'internationalist' filmic cosmos. The other significant aspect regarding location and which brings the texts into adjacency is the way in which Venice
recurs in each.[14] What is more, the texts' close production calendars draw them

into temporal proximity.[15] *Youth* began filming in Switzerland in May 2014 and debuted at the May 2015 edition of the Cannes Film Festival.[16] Though Sorrentino had been thinking of it since 2012, *The Young Pope* began production in August 2015; it was first broadcast in Italy and throughout Europe and the United Kingdom in October 2016 after its Venice Film Festival debut a month prior.[17] Unstintingly, Sorrentino's screen texts are *about* nostalgia, not naively nostalgic. The exploration in these pages of nostalgias present in the dyad *Youth* and *The Young Pope* aims to show the evolving, varied constitution of 'longing for home'.

Forget about It, It's…. Switzerland: Literalizing Pathological Nostalgia

A recurring location in Sorrentino's works, Switzerland, and the Swiss, hold a prominent position in the history and etiology of nostalgia. The term 'nostalgia' was coined in 1688 by the Swiss physician Johanes Hofer when he diagnosed a condition principally afflicting Swiss and German mercenary soldiers and the Papal Guard. Those suffering from the painful 'longing for home', or 'nostalgia', as Hofer called it, experienced lack of appetite, indifference, mental confusion and an inability to distinguish past from present, hallucinations and the sighting of spectral figures, and apathy, which is Fred's diagnosis in *Youth*, the static state from which he is awakened by the film's concluding performance.

The remarkable Swiss protection of privacy so characteristic of its banking industry makes for an ideal location for Titta's money laundering in *The Consequences of Love*, set in the canton of Ticino.[18] *Youth*, for its part, foregrounds Switzerland's reputable spas and medical establishments. What has been said of the space the spa occupies in the film might function just as well for Switzerland's general relation to Italy, both so near and yet behind the Alpine curtain; the spa 'serves as a "transitional space" – Donald Winnicott's idea that there exists a potential space between the self and other within which one can navigate between the inner and outer worlds' (Chahal 2017: 14).

In *Youth*, nostalgia is everywhere visualized, somatized and gendered. Mick the movie director, frequently scoping images as though he were filming them, is deployed to ensure that the visualization motif registers. High in the mountains, Mick and his screenwriters stand on the observation deck of a lodge, looking across the Alpine landscape. Like a sort of manual cinema, Mick remarkably re-enacts the forward and backward motion of nostalgia, performing it and making it visual. Using the telescopic binoculars set in place for sightseers, he shows the Girl Screenwriter (Chloe Pirrie) the mountains as they appear close in distance. This is the future when you are young, Mick tells her (Figure 1.3). Flipping the apparatus, he tells her that what she now sees in the distance is 'youth' as seen through the focal length of older age (Figure 1.4).

FIGURE 1.3: The nearness of youth and the future. *Youth*.

FIGURE 1.4: Scoping the past. *Youth*.

In another scene, the South American engages in a similar re-enactment of nostalgia's dual motions. From the balcony of his room, his gaze on the hotel garden below, he watches in reverie (as we do) a young midfielder wearing Maradona's number 10 standing ready on the soccer pitch. When his wife (Loredana Cannata) asks him what he is looking at, he replies, as he screens his past self, 'El futuro'.

The self-care setting of the Davos spa calls sharply to mind Thomas Mann's *Magic Mountain*, where Hans Castorp begins his journey of formation in the tradition of self-knowledge constitutive of the Bildungsroman Mann's novel epitomizes. At Sorrentino's spa, though, formation yields to deformation. As a shrewd student of human behaviour, Jimmy, the Method actor, transforms into an older Hitler, a deformation he rejects. Like the South American, Mick, too, is a somatic vector of nostalgia. While Fred's 'apathy', as complaints go, is affective, Mick's varied conditions are physiological: unlike Mick, Fred has no prescriptions to fill at the pharmacy. Fading into the asexuality of the elderly, his expanding prostate, as Sorrentino informs us relentlessly, impedes urination and sexual functionality. Defiant in her anti-nostalgia, Brenda is eager to 'call a spade a spade' during their conversation and lets Mick know that his future is all used up and that only shit movies are left in him. The shot-reverse shot rhythm of this sequence bolsters the opposition in the scene between Mick and Brenda as well as the gendered inversion of their positions. Ballsy Brenda has taken the lead from her director. Not only this, but the shot-reverse shot rhythm mimics the give and go of nostalgia as it toggles between the past and the future.

If Sorrentino deploys Mick in the visualization of nostalgia, Fred safeguards its hearing in ways that draw suspiciously close to textbook examples of pathological nostalgia. Homesick mercenaries and the Swiss Papal Guard appeared to long for things from afar that those who were actually in the longed-for place took for granted or were oblivious to. In his *Dictionary of Music*, Jean-Jacques Rousseau 'talks about the effects of cowbells, the rustic sounds that excite in the Swiss the joys of life and youth and a bitter sorrow at having lost them' (Boym 2001: 4). Music is everywhere for Fred: from the rustle of the candy wrapper that so handily dispatches the Queen's Emissary at the abrupt close of their first encounter to the 'rustic cantilena' of the cowbells as he sits in a pasture conducting the herd.[19] The screenplay for *Youth* is instructive about the undercurrents this scene is meant to capture:

He listens to the discordant layers of sound: cowbells, cicadas, bird.

At this point, Fred concentrates and closes his eyes. Very gently he starts to move one hand just like a conductor and, as if he had conjured a spell, several of the cowbells fall silent. Others are still ringing; they no longer create an anarchy of sound, but rather the notes are rolled out melodically. With another wave of his hand, Fred elegantly stops the remaining cowbells so that only two are left ringing out in alternate notes (Sorrentino 2015) (Figure 1.5).

FIGURE 1.5: The sounds of nostalgia: a 'rustic cantilena'. *Youth*.

10

Music is not just sound but, rather, sound 'in concert' with time, sound at timed intervals. Two of the most revealing of *Youth's* literalizations of nostalgia are offered back-to-back at the film's core. The first, which profoundly engages with the notion of time, takes place in the souvenir shop that Jimmy and Fred visit; the second follows immediately. Just as valuable to an understanding of the film's generation of meaning as the paternal themes made explicit in both scenes is the way they consistently and explicitly literalize nostalgia. The souvenir shop makes nostalgia material and monetized.[20] The *mise en scène* assembles the tourism of Swiss nostalgia. Beneath the heavy cloud of Christmas ornaments on sale even during summer holidays is a wall of cuckoo clocks, the quintessence of Swiss craftsmanship. As Fred, composer and therefore master of time, moves along the wall, he sets each clock to the hour (Figure 1.6).

In succession, they perform their hourly pageant with chime, music, sound and mechanized cogs precisely turning (like proverbial Swiss clockwork). The sound is so noticeable it catches Jimmy's attention. All noise stops, the clocks having concluded their symphony (discernible perhaps only to an avant-garde composer), and, as the acoustical noise disappears, so does the 'visual noise' of the crowded frame fade away, as the camera closes in to focus on the exchange between Jimmy and the Pale Teenager (Emilia Jones) in which she tells him that there was 'a bit of dialogue I really liked'.

The scene that immediately follows (edited for sound to dovetail) is visually and acoustically the counterpoint to the souvenir shop: it is open, airy, light, a 'simple scene' to match the composer's simple song. When Jimmy asks him what he does all day, Fred replies that 'they tell me I am apathetic, so I don't do anything'. He doesn't miss work, Fred reassures the Method actor, though he does miss his wife, Melanie. For an examination of nostalgia and how Sorrentino renders it literally, it could be valuable to note how the scene brings together Melanie, the (now lost) inspiration for the 'Simple Song', Fred's apathy so symptomatic of nostalgia and the ironic fragment all of which appear in taxonomies of nostalgia, described above.

FIGURE 1.6: Time, tourism and nostalgia. *Youth.*

Fred allows himself to be surprised that Jimmy reads Novalis, the Romantic poet of fragments. But it is not just any Novalis (any more than it is 'just any Céline' that Sorrentino reprises at the start of *The Great Beauty*). Jimmy's slightly bowdlerized citation 'I'm always going home, always going to my father's house', has occasioned comment about its relation to fathers and patriarchy.[21] However, the citation is also about 'home'. Home for Fred was Melanie, Melanie was melody and song, and, absent Melanie, there cannot, as Fred explains to the dismayed Emissary of the Queen of Fred's no-longer homeland, be any more song.

There may be one last kind of deformation worth noting in Sorrentino's anti-*Bildungsfilm* set in Nostalgialand.[22] Nostalgia is invoked not only for the youth of the film's title, but also for a certain kind of audio-visual text, cinema of the auteurist ilk, of the sort Sorrentino proposes 'in real life'.[23] To judge by Brenda, cinema is over and television is not only the future, it is the present. Perhaps an even greater 'deformation' of the audio-visual text, though, is Sorrentino's tour de force music video for Paloma Faith's 'I Just Can't Rely on You' that launches like a rocket in Lena's dream. Crammed with gratuitous effects, racing cars, burlesque and conflagration, and ending with the deformed image of Lena's face melting as the sound goes wonky, it, like Faith herself, is the stuff of Lena's nightmares.[24] *Youth's* meditation on art forms allows us to ask questions not only about the cinema of and about nostalgia, of which *Youth* is an arch example, but a nostalgia for the medium of cinema in the era of televised serial supremacy and music videos.

Switzerland as a location has less moment for *The Young Pope*, to which I now turn, than the Swiss themselves. In the non-space, or the 'demilitarized zone' of the Vatican State, the Swiss are represented on both narrative and semiotic levels. The Swiss Papal Guard was, after all, Hofer's 'Patient Zero' for the malady of nostalgia. Voiello sets the comely Ester (Ludivine Saignier), wife of one of the Swiss guards, in Lenny's path, certain that she will distract him from the straight and narrow, cause a scandal and the Young Pope's downfall, a plot he sets in motion in Episode 4. Instead, Ester, 'immaculately' conceives after Lenny's laying on of hands, bringing about one of the miracles for which Sister Mary repeatedly tells him he is 'a saint' and for which he will be canonized. Visually, the Swiss Guard contributes to Sorrentino's Vatican simulacrum: their brightly striped Renaissance uniforms complement the sumptuous, but otherwise largely monochrome, ecclesiastical wardrobe. Like so many figures the Holy See summons to its court, the Swiss Guard contribute to the distinctly non-Italian and international quality to the Vatican, almost the inverse to Titta's *Unheimlich* Ticino in *The Consequences of Love*, which lies just beyond the pale of Italian forces of law and order and where Italian is the official language. Like the religionists who come and go from the Vatican and spread out along the global network of the Catholic Church, the Swiss Guard have, since the beginning of the sixteenth century, become a fixed population in the centre of Rome.

From Deformation to Reformation to Reflection: *The Young Pope* and Nostalgia

If *Youth's* spa denizens slouch towards deformation, in Sorrentino's *Bildungse-rien* (or, serial drama about the formation of its protagonist), Young Pope Belardo charges full throttle towards re-formation. From the viagrous to the vigorous, one sees how the masculinities performed in these two, back-to-back projects suggest something of a 'youthful' diptych of dissimilar, albeit connected, frames.[25] In one panel, we see two figures (Mick and Fred) and watch as they perform (musically, meta-cinematically) their encounters with nostalgia and decrepitude. In the other, we see a single youthful figure wrestling with, by turns, 'Lenny's' feelings of personal loss and 'Pius's' outrage over how much ground his 'public' home (the Church, the Vatican) has lost in a global arena and modern world. This complex portraiture elaborates the alternating, dual nature of nostalgia, which, to review, looks backwards into memory and history and forward into the future. This alternation does not parcel out 'restorative' nostalgia for one text and 'reflective' for the other; rather these strains get nego-tiated in each. Lenny/Pius's arc in *The Young Pope* stretches from, at first, the attempt to 'build the lost home and patch up memory gaps' characteristic of restorative nostalgia to the 'reflective' kind of nostalgia that 'dwells in [....] in longing and loss, the imperfect process of remembrance'. Tracing the develop-ment of the pope's homilies for the general public (Episodes 1, 2 and 10) helps chart this path.

Belardo's drive for purge, and restoration, transforms him into a zealot with an enthusiasm for reform that rivals Martin Luther's. His exhortation to the faithful to return to Christ echoes Luther's disdain for the Reformation-era Holy See, with its corrupt and faithless dealings. The issue that brings Belardo's fictional reform close to the protestant Reformation Luther envisioned is the relationship of the faithful to the godhead, the representability of the sacred, and the commodification of sacraments (e.g. the selling of indulgences). When the pope refuses to exhibit himself, an almost schizoid disconnect of body and voice results, replicating the other private and public 'split' between Lenny and Pius.[26]

The Young Pope begins with a false start and a false first homily. The series opens in a dream. In Venice, before St. Mark's Basilica, out of a horrible pile of computer-generated dead babies a crawling baby emerges, to be replaced by a papal figure, his back to the camera, who continues on the path. From child to man, he is the lucky, chosen 'one' to emerge from the unholy pile (Hennessy 2017). This is the dream from which the pope 'awakes', one eye popping open in an extreme close-up to see an upside-down Christ, the waking dreamer's perspec-tive of the crucifix that hangs above his bed (Figure 1.7).

FIGURE 1.7: The world turned upside down, *The Young Pope,* Episode 1.

If this 'world turned upside down' image does not provide a broad enough hint that we are in a parallel dream world, then the full arsenal of special effects for the next six minutes should do the trick: seamless slo-mo tracking shots, high-ranking church officials standing in painterly stillness, no ambient sound, flickering poltergeist lights and a disorienting low-level throbbing sonic pulse all alert us to the strangeness of this scene. And yet, if viewers had never seen a Sorrentino film, they may think that such a full, Baroque onslaught of cinematic excess is the visualization of a disoriented young pope about to deliver his first address.

And what an address it is. Dream Lenny's first homily is jolly, playful, inviting and warm, everything Pius almost studiously avoids for the next 445 minutes, until his public appearance in Venice in Episode 10. From the way the young pope beatifically lifts the leaden skies, summoning the sunlight, to his overly informal 'Ciao, Rome', tossed to the roaring adoring, this is a pastoral, people-person Pope (Figure 1.8).

Francis-like, Lenny reminds those gathered that the Pope is the servant of God and the faithful. Gathering momentum, he then delivers an iconoclastic bomb, a veritable litany of all the things the Church has forgotten. Beginning with masturbation, he makes his way through the top hot topics worrying the contemporary Catholic Church: contraception and abortion, priestly celibacy, nuns and their relation to the mass, scientifically assisted procreation and assisted suicide, Dream Lenny allows it all. The editing is farcical in rhythm, long shots of the Square punctuated by low-angle medium shots of a bombastic pontiff flanked on either side by monumental pillars reminding viewers of the Duce orating from his Piazza Venezia balcony.

14

FIGURE 1.8: Dream Lenny's parting of the leaden skies: the first false homily. *The Young Pope*, Episode 1.

This is a false start in many ways, since Sorrentino pays out his televised, serial story much more patiently. For the rest of this episode and most of the next, we learn how much more Lenny is like Ratzinger than Bergoglio: his movement from left to right in the stylized slo-mo opening credit sequence is not gratuitous in this regard.[27] The young pope's actual first homily is a waking, nightmare inversion of the first. Lenny dreamed of bringing sunshine to the happy masses, but his actual first homily, at the conclusion of Episode 2 and scheduled for the evening, is dark literally and figuratively. Adopting an identical incipit, he asks again what they have all collectively forgotten. But from that point onward, he tacks in a completely antagonistic direction, upbraiding those gathered, scorning the unbelievers and abjuring the freedom he had proposed in his dream homily and ends with a parodic thunderclap and bolt of lightning. Aerial shots have largely replaced the low-angle perspective but the most striking visual element is the invisible Pope, a barking, angry, backlit silhouette (Figure 1.9).

Pius will not show his face until the final 'reveal' of his Venice address in Episode 10 nor will he allow his likeness to be monetized by Sofia, the Vatican Director of Marketing (Cécile de France). There will be no curios made of the Curia, it appears, no graven likenesses, no money-generating commemorative plates to be sent to foreign heads of state. No tourists in Catholicism for Pius, who will provide no souvenirs. Pius wants the faithful to search for God instead of the man who reigns as pope, whose face he will deprive them of. To recoup in Catholics worldwide a sense of the mystery in – and fear – of the Church, he will increase his distance

FIGURE 1.9: The 'real' first homily: an angry, barking, backlit young pope. *The Young Pope*, Episode 2.

from the faithful. It is back to doctrinal basics for Belardo, with a vengeance. Across Season 1, the young pontiff seeks to empty homosexuals from the ranks of the priesthood, curb flagrant abuses of power from among church officials, either withdraw from or interfere in affairs of state (depending on your perspective) by threatening to issue a papal injunction against political participation ('non expedit'), and declare abortion an unforgiveable sin. At the same time, he sports all papal accoutrements and is turned out in considerable sartorial splendour. Yet once the pontifical tiara is returned to the Vatican it is worn only for cardinals, the prince wearing his crown only for members of his court. And for Sky and HBO subscribers: HBO estimated that each episode of *The Young Pope* drew, across various media platforms, approximately 4.7 million viewers in its 2017 HBO airing.[28]

Pius's reformation hangs on Lenny's formation and Sorrentino's story must deliver the young pope into maturity. Instead of Christmas in Guatemala celebrating the prospect of a new saint, Pius at last accepts the advice of his mentor, now dead, and heads to Venice to 'bury' his parents so that he can get on with being the Pope. The past cannot simply remain memory, it must, like nostalgia, turn to the future: his papacy depends upon it. In the full light of day, the Pope quotes at length from the soon to be canonized Blessed Juana. The answer of the future saint to a long list of dichotomized questions ('are we men or are we women? Are we fools or are we smart? Are we rich or are we poor? Are we happy or are we blind?', and so forth), Pius tells those gathered, is that 'God smiles'. It is at this point that Young Pope Belardo embraces 'reflective nostalgia', the type that dwells in 'pain, in longing and loss, the imperfect process of remembrance'. The passage from restorative to reflective is not easy and it is not simple to knit together Juana's long list of either-or terms, in the same way that it is not simple to bring together body and voice, past and future, Lenny and Pius. The pontiff takes the telescope, Gutierrez's (Javier Camara) gift, and, much like Mick Boyle on the observation deck of the Swiss lodge, gazes in the distance (Figure 1.10).

Looking among the crowd for a 'manifestation' of his parents (as he phrased it in Episode 7), he gazes out on the present and finds the past. Panning left to right, the camera finds two unsmiling onlookers who, when the camera pans back, have morphed into Lenny's younger hippy parents (Figures 1.11 and 1.12). When

FIGURE 1.10: Pius XIII seeking out his parents in the San Marco crowd. *The Young Pope,* Episode 10.

FIGURE 1.11: The present and the future of nostalgia. *The Young Pope,* Episode 10.

17

FIGURE 1.12: The past and the future of nostalgia: private pain in public places. *The Young Pope*, Episode 10.

they turn their backs on him again, it is too much for Lenny/Pius to bear and, concluding his homily, he collapses.

Paolo Sorrentino's screen texts are frequently about nostalgia, but, as this chapter has illustrated, neither naïve about the nostalgias they present nor monolithic in their representations. On the contrary, the use of nostalgia in the filmmaker's screen projects reveals a wide range of visual techniques and narrative tactics that perform complicated processes of semiotic signification which have implications for the industrial conditions of the production of screen texts for filmmakers (Italian and otherwise) interested in Italian settings and contexts. Both *Youth* and *The Young Pope*, which share a number of attributes, reveal an almost academic interest in and depiction of varied types of nostalgia, arraying them along visual and auditory motifs. The performers in these midcareer screen texts (whether musicians, conductors, actors, soccer players or prelates) negotiate the limitations of nostalgic memory as they look to the futures of their art forms.

NOTES

1. *What's wrong with feeling nostalgic? It's the only distraction for anyone sceptical about the future. The only one!* All translations are my own, unless otherwise noted.
2. Kilbourn observes that Melanie functions as a mask in this scene and traces the evolution from the 'gaze' and its objectification, to 'the stare'. See Kilbourn (2019: 387). See also Swinnen (2019: 168–69).

3. When the film and the serial drama are referred to collective, it shall be as 'screen texts', a broad enough category to capture both at once.

4. For Benjamin, see Steiner (2010: 165–73).

5. *Youth* was mostly filmed in the Waldhaus Flims in the Swiss alps. See Hooten (2016: n.pag.).

6. The visual extravaganza of the spa (not to mention its setting and cabaret offerings), in league with the aura of reminiscence, and touches of magic thrown in (like the levitating monk) have evoked Fellini's *8½* for more than a few viewers. For a rundown of some of the Fellinian elements, see So (2013: n.pag.) and Killough's response in Killough (2013: n.pag.).

7. So associated with nostalgia is the director that a Boolean search for 'Paolo AND Sorrentino AND nostalgia' returned 1,690,000 references in 'about' 55 seconds.

8. Nostalgia, as outlined presently in the body of this essay, is not interchangeable with memory, though they share characteristics. For Sorrentino and memory, see Cangiano (2019). On the elaboration of melancholy in *The Great Beauty*, with reference to other texts in Sorrentino's *oeuvre*, see Mecchia (2018) and Bouchard (2016).

9. See International Circulation of Italian Cinema (2018: n.pag.). This infographic shows the top ten Italian films in terms of box office receipts in the 2007–16 period. In first place is Woody Allen's *To Rome with Love*, with 7.9 million admissions in 39 global markets. *Youth* is in second place, with 2.9 million admissions in 40 markets globally, with *The Great Beauty* a close third with 2.5 in the same number of markets (and probably identical markets). See also Fadda and Garofalo (2018).

10. For a review of the recent 'vintage' and 'retro' commodity inclinations and creation of taste in the Italian context, see Leone (2015: 10–13). For nostalgia precisely as concerns its role in Italian cinema up until approximately 2003, see Celli (2003). Celli documents the cachet of the Italian 'retro' movie for worldwide audiences interested in a nostalgic view of Italy that inclines towards the sentimentalized and 'Orientalized'. The present essay is the point of departure for a second, forthcoming examination centring on another 'youthful' reformer in Italian screen studies, *Il giovane Montalbano* (RAI, 2012–15), the prequel to RAI's long-running *Commissario Montalbano (Inspector Montalbano)*, which explores the relation of nostalgia in Italian screen texts to international markets and nation-branding.

11. Sorrentino's *oeuvre* is roughly coeval with debates within the academy, unfolding roughly beginning in 2007, concerning the presence and function of 'nostalgia' in the Italian film industry and attached culture industries (including higher education) both in and outside of Italy. See, generally, O'Rawe (2008) and Renga (2014).

12. 'Nostalgia' in Italian cinema, especially the kind that could be seen as relating to either Italian Neorealist cinema, or, like Sorrentino's body of work, to auteurist cinema in a Fellinian vein, produced what could be thought of as a sort of 'allergic' reaction.

13. Nostalgia is indubitably deployed for political leverage. In addition to the frightening contemporary rise of populisms of the political across the globe, we might fruitfully consider the category of 'Ostalgie', or the longing for the East, in which varied cultural articulations post-1989, particularly in Germany, glorified the Communist-era GDR. On 'Ostalgie' see esp. Cooke (2005) and Castillo (2009). I am grateful to R. Glynn for her observations on this count.

19

14. This is not to suggest that groupings for the purpose of analysis are mutually exclusive nor is it an 'either-or' situation encouraging a flattened-out exercise of interpretation so as to fit taxonomies that preclude study.

15. *Youth's* paracinematic context is particularly ironic (or misleading), since one of the several official publicity stills with Michael Caine tiny and alone in the middle of Piazza San Marco in a nocturnal Venice makes it seem as though the city will be a common location in this film, in other words, that Venice would have, in *Youth*, the kind of protagonism Rome enjoyed in *The Great Beauty*. While a key location, Venice lives briefly, albeit memorably, in *Youth's* frames. As K. Zorich has observed, the most 'tumblr'd' image around the time of the film's release showed the line of spa clients lying in a row in one of the thermal baths. Both images are here: https://www.telegraph.co.uk/travel/destinations/europe/switzerland/articles/Inside-the-eccentric-Swiss-hotel-where-Michael-Caine-looks-back-on-his-Youth/ (accessed 10 July 2020), https://dbmoviesblog.wordpress.com/2018/03/17/youth-review/. See Zorich (2015).

16. Vivarelli, who covers Italian audio-visual media for *Variety*, remarked that Sorrentino and his production team worked 'dual fronts' in 2015, referring to work on both *Youth* and *The Young Pope* in a common time frame. See Vivarelli (2015).

17. The film's Cannes premier was 20 May 2015, with the title 'Youth'; the film was released in Italy the same day with what appears to be a bewildering variety of names: *Il futuro, Youth – La giovinezza*, and *The Youth*. See Imdb.pro, https://pro.imdb.com/title/tt3312830/details, and Lyman (2014).

18. Concerning the 'trilogy of power', see, in this collection, Chapter 11 by N. Marini Maio. See also Minuz (2018), Canova (2017), Iannotta (2016) and Mariani (2020).

19. For Titta's psychology as it relates to Switzerland, see Renga (2013) and Comand (2006: 189, 193).

20. The locution 'rustic cantilena' is Boym's (Boym 2001: 4).

21. On the relation of the souvenir shop and collection to nostalgia generally, see Stewart (1984). Bartoletti is particularly relevant on the point of the Alpine souvenirs and especially the nostalgic recreations of 'Heidiland' and 'Heididorf'. See Bartoletti (2010).

22. The patriarchal elements are thickly overlaid in Jimmy's misremembered fragment from Novalis's poem from 1800, 'Longing for Death'. See Kilbourn (2020:101).

23. 'Nostalgialand' is not a gratuitous, 'cute' locution. Rather, I take my cue from Bartoletti's exploration of Heidiland and its relation to the material practices of tourism. See note 20.

24. Concerning 'meta-' and retro cinema, nostalgia, and other auteurs like Moretti and Woody Allen, see Celli (2003).

25. Suffice it to say that the *mise-en-abyme* video in *Youth* differs radically from the official music video for 'I Just Can't Rely on You'. See https://youtu.be/imi9SmktcI, accessed 20 July 2020.

26. In a review of *Youth* for *The Guardian*, Bradshaw referred to 'Viagra cinema', citing also 'sagging' action stars like Dolph Lundgren, Sylvester Stallone and Arnold Schwarzenegger.

See Bradshaw (2016). I am not suggesting that *Youth* and *The Young Pope* fit together as a diptych in the ways of Sorrentino's *Loro* I and II, addressed elsewhere in this collection. Conventionally, painting diptychs frequently (though not exclusively) feature in one panel, the subject, and in the attached or related panel, the patron(s) of the commission. See, for example, the famed Melun Diptych by Jean Fouqet. See https://www.smb.museum/en/exhibitions/detail/jean-fouquet-das-diptychon-von-melun.html, accessed 10 October 2019. Other conventional pairings are linked by a common religious theme (saints in one panel, the Madonna in another). Contemporary artists expanded the composition of the diptych, to bind together two considerably different, even disparate images. On this count, see for example Richard Hamilton's 'The Citizen' series from 1981 to 1983, https://www.tate.org.uk/art/artworks/hamilton-the-citizen-t03980, accessed 14 October 2019. Diptychs are rarely unalike in their dimensions, something that cautions against designating as a diptych *Youth*, which Sorrentino and editor Cristiano Travaglioli kept to a rather conventional 124 minutes, and *The Young Pope*, which totals 546 minutes across 10 episodes. Nonetheless, as I have been suggesting throughout, the two texts entail and dovetail, they are not equivalents.

27. This split presents clearly in the second iteration (if not season) of *The Young Pope*, *The New Pope* (premier 13 January 2020, following the conclusion of the drafting of this essay), not to mention the Netflix-produced *The Two Popes*, which aired 27 November 2019 in the United States, with the UK release two days after.

28. For a reading of this sequence, see R. Kilbourn, '*The Young Pope*'s Credit Sequence: A Postsecular Allegory in Ten Paintings', Chapter 12 in this collection.

29. Nielsen line-ratings were lower, approximately 1.7 million per episode. See Josef Adalian (2017: n.pag.).

REFERENCES

Adalian, J. (2017), 'Why *The Young Pope* was an unexpected victory for HBO', *Vulture*, 14 February, https://www.vulture.com/2017/02/hbo-young-pope-unexpected-victory-for-the-network.html. Accessed 10 November 2019.

Bartoletti, R. (2010), 'Memory tourism and the commodification of nostalgia', in P. Burns, C. Palmer and J. Lester (eds), *Tourism and Visual Culture*, vol. 1, Oxford, UK-Cambridge, MA:CAB International, pp. 26–33.

Bouchard, F. (2016), 'Mélancolique passion: le cinéma de Paolo Sorrentino', *Cinés-Bulles*, 54:1, pp. 22–27.

Boym, S. (2001), *The Future of Nostalgia*, New York: Basic Books.

Bradshaw, P. (2016), 'Dirty grandpa and the return of viagra cinema', *The Guardian*, 18 January, https://www.theguardian.com/film/2016/jan/18/peter-bradshaw-michael-caine-youth-robert-de-niro-viagra-cinema. Accessed 10 November 2019.

Cangiano, M. (2019), 'Against postmodernism: Paolo Sorrentino and the search for authenticity', *The Journal of Italian Cinema and Media Studies*, 7:3, pp. 339–49.

Canova, G. (2017), 'Divi duci guitti papi caimani: L'immaginario del potere nel cinema italiano, da Rossellini a *The Young Pope*', Milano: Bietti Heterotopia, pp. 73–96.

Castillo, G. (2008), 'East as true west: Redeeming bourgeois culture, from socialist realism to ostalgie', *Kritika: Explorations in Russian and Eurasian History*, 9:4, pp. 747–68.

Celli, C. (2003), 'The nostalgia current in Italian cinema', in A. Vitti (ed.), *Incontri con il cinema italiano*, Rome: Sciascia, pp. 277–87.

Chahal, K. (2017), 'Integrity versus despair as illustrated in the film *Youth*', *The American Journal of Psychiatry Residents' Journal*, September, 14.

Comand, M. (2006), 'La matematica del mistero: Sorrentino narratore', in V. Zagarrio (ed.), *Nuovo Cinema Italiano*, Venice: Marsilio editore, pp. 189–95.

Cooke, P. (2005), *From Colonization to Nostalgia: Representing East Germany Since Unification*, Oxford: Berg.

Crowdus, G. (2014), 'In search of the Great Beauty: An interview with Paolo Sorrentino', *Cineaste,* Spring, pp. 8–13.

Fadda, M. and Garofalo D. (2018), 'The distribution of contemporary Italian cinema in the United States: The films of Luca Guadagnino and Paolo Sorrentino', *Comunicazioni Sociali*, 3, pp. 369–83.

Hennessy, B. (2017), 'Reel simulations: CGI and special effects in two films by Paolo Sorrentino', *The Italianist*, 37:3, pp. 449–63.

Hooten C. (2016), 'Paolo Sorrentino's *Youth* and the hotel as a character', https://www.independent.co.uk/arts-entertainment/films/features/youth-film-hotel-switzerland-paul-sorrentino-a6836786.html. Accessed 14 June 2020.

Hutcheon, L. (1998-2000), 'Irony, nostalgia, and the postmodern: A dialogue', *Poligrafías*, 3:19, pp. 18–41.

Iannotta, A. (2016), 'Le immagini del potere: Note sull'identità italiana nel cinema di Paolo Sorrentino', *California Italian Studies*, 6:2, pp. 1–17.

International Circulation of Italian Cinema (2018), 'Italian cinema globally', 13 June, https://www.italiancinema.it/the-global-circulation-of-italian-cinema/. Accessed 10 July 2020.

Kilbourn, R. (2019), 'The "primal scene": Memory, redemption and "woman" in the films of Paolo Sorrentino', *The Journal of Italian Cinema and Media Studies*, 7:3, pp. 377–94.

Kilbourn, R. (2020), *The Cinema of Paolo Sorrentino: Commitment to Style*, New York: Columbia University Press.

Killough, J. (2013), 'Why Paolo Sorrentino is and isn't the new Fellini', *PFC*, 10 December, https://www.purefilmcreative.com/killough-chronicles/why-paolo-sorrentino-is-and-isnt-the-new-fellini.html. Accessed 10 July 2020.

Leone, M. (2015), 'Longing for the past: A semiotic reading of the role of nostalgia in present day consumption trends', *Social Semiotics*, 5:1, pp. 1–15.

Lyman, E. (2014), 'Paolo Sorrentino's "The Early Years" begins shooting, storyline revealed', *The Hollywood Reporter*, 12 May, https://www.hollywoodreporter.com/news/paulo-sorrentinos-early-years-begins-703233. Accessed 10 July 2020.

Mariani, A. (2020), 'Viral (Per)Versions of Power in Paolo Sorrentino's Diptych Loro,' *Modern Italy*, Cambridge University Press, pp. 1–17.

Mecchia, G. (2018), 'Birds in the Roman sky: Shooting for the sublime in *La Grande Bellezza*', *Forum Italicum*, 50:1, pp. 183–93.

Minuz, A. (2018), 'Com'è il fosco potere raccontato dal cinema italiano', *Il Foglio*, 5 February, https://www.ilfoglio.it/cinema/2018/02/05/news/cinema-sono-tornato-sorrentino-fosco-potere-176959. Accessed 10 July 2020.

O'Rawe, C. (2008), '"I padri e i maestri": Genre, auteurs, and absences in Italian film studies', *Italian Studies*, 63:2, pp. 173–94.

Renga, D. (2013), *Unfinished Business: Screening the Italian Mafia in the New Millenium*, Toronto: University of Toronto Press.

Renga, D. (2014), 'Introduction', *The Italianist*, 34:2, pp. 235–37.

So, J. (2013), 'The new Fellini: Paolo Sorrentino's the Great Beauty', *The Daily Beast*, 18 November, https://www.thedailybeast.com/the-new-fellini-paolo-sorrentinos-the-great-beauty. Accessed 10 July 2020.

Sorrentino, P. (2001), *One Man Up*, San Rafael, CA: DVD, Indigo Film.

Sorrentino, P. (2004), *The Consequences of Love*, San Rafael, CA: DVD, Indigo Film.

Sorrentino, P. (2011), *This Must Be the Place*, San Rafael, CA: DVD, Indigo Film.

Sorrentino, P. (2013), *The Great Beauty*, DVD, Irvington, NY: The Criterion Collection.

Sorrentino, P. (2015), *Youth*, Italy, France: Indigo Film, C-Films AG, Number 9, Pathé Production, France 2 Cinéma.

Sorrentino, P. (2015), *Youth* (trans. N.S.Thompson), New York: Quercus (electronic).

Sorrentino, P. (2016), *The Young Pope*, Italy, France, Spain, UK, USA: Wildside, Haut et Court TV, Mediapro, Sky Italia, HBO, Canal +.

Starobinski, J. (1966), 'The idea of nostalgia', *Diogenes*, 54, pp. 81–103.

Steiner, U. (2010), *Walter Benjamin: An Introduction to His Work and Thought* (trans. M. Winkler), Chicago: University of Chicago Press.

Stewart, S. (1984), *On Longing: Narrative of the Miniature, the Gigantic, the Souvenir, the Collection*, Baltimore, MD: Johns Hopkins University Press.

Swinnen, A. (2017), 'The roses are long gone but the chrysanthemums are magnificent: Late-life creativity in Quartet and Youth', 14:2, pp. 162–78.

Vivarelli, N. (2015), 'Sorrentino and crew work on dual fronts', *Variety*, 15 December, 330, p. 10.

Zorich, K. (2015), 'On Paolo Sorrentino's latest film, *Youth*, and its place among earlier works', https://medium.com/@katiazoritch/paolo-sorrentino-perhaps-youth-depends-on-a-walk-around-the-lake-dc077f088cd2. Accessed 10 July 2020.

2

Against Postmodernism: Paolo Sorrentino and the Search for Authenticity

Mimmo Cangiano

Colgate University

Introduction

'You are nobody', said a child to Jep Gambardella in *The Great Beauty* (Sorrentino, 2013). The protagonist of Paolo Sorrentino's masterpiece chose to live a life without establishing his own identity. His decisions have driven him to an existence with no firm points of reference, in which he is continuously modifying his own identity and points of view and refuses to establish a strong and centripetal Self from which to interpret reality. Now old, this lifestyle is tormenting him: in fact, the entire movie will focus on his attempt to regain the Self that he abandoned. The dialectic between a life lived without any points of reference and the search for an identity, for an *ubi consistam*, is central to all of Sorrentino's films.

My article retraces this dialectic in Sorrentino's cinema, clarifying how the search for a stable identity (as a soccer coach, as an actor, as father or son, as a writer) exemplifies both Sorrentino's characters and *Weltanschauung*. The search for an identity is ultimately what allows Sorrentino's characters to overcome the superficiality and frivolousness of an existence without any goals. Only when the character gains her/his own identity, life and reality itself become meaningful, and only then, reality stops being a fluid heap of unrelated facts (a 'spectacle', in a Debaurdian sense), and turns into something that can be interpreted and judged.

Although Sorrentino's cinema has been consistently labelled as exemplarily postmodernist, his characters' search for an identity (a classical modernist topos) reveals how the Neapolitan director has instead repeatedly used postmodernist

24

tools to criticize postmodernist ideology. Undoubtedly, the phenomenic world in which his characters act is dominated by a postmodernist way of thinking and living, by transient sensations, desires and stimuli; however, beyond that world, the character's desire for a strong point of reference remains present. The aspiration to this firm point, which is one and the same as the aspiration to define herself/himself, criticizes their lifestyles and the postmodernist system of values behind them, revealing Sorrentino's cinema as exemplary modernist art.

Postmodernist Cinema?

Paolo Sorrentino's cinema has been repeatedly classified as postmodern. Michael Sicinski has even argued that '*The Great Beauty* is textbook postmodernism'.[1] Certain stylistic and thematic choices, beginning with his insistence on spectacularizing (in a Debaurdian sense) these social relations, allow Sorrentino's poetics to be placed within a cultural framework of the ideological dematerialization of truth and objectivity. Without these concepts, the life of an individual has no foundation, no centre, from which to select and organize the vast quantity of data created by reality. When a unitary hierarchy of values disappears, the subject can no longer master these incoming data. Life becomes a *spectacle*, without a stable referent used to give value and meaning to life itself. Monica Facchini aptly wrote that 'the spectacular reality Sorrentino presents in his film is that of a society in which, according to Guy Debord, "the spectacle is integrated"' (2017: 182).

In Sorrentino's cinema, this existential situation produces four types of reactions. At one end of the existential spectrum lies the need, simultaneously tragic and neurotic, to seize protean reality by force, to interpret reality through a rigid ideological scheme in which everything can be explained and catalogued. In this scheme, extraneous data are expelled (the *sin*) because they do not fit into the initial assumptions of the ideological framework. This is obviously the case for Lenny Belardo, the Pope of the 2016 television series *The Young Pope* (2016). This is a far more prevalent typology in modernist artistic production than in postmodernist production (consider Henrik Ibsen's *Brand* [1866] or Elias Canetti's Peter Kien, the protagonist of *Auto-da-Fé* [1935]).

At the other end of the existential spectrum lie those characters who establish 'superficiality' as a lifestyle and live with no ideological framework: they simply follow the impulse of sensations and moods, and their continuous travelling is a metaphor for the absence of roots and standpoints from which to interpret reality.[2] In this sense, the exemplar case is Valerio Di Girolamo, the brother of the protagonist Titta in *The Consequences of Love* (Sorrentino, 2004). He mistakenly believes that the Maldives, where he is going, are in the Caribbean, thus demonstrating that his only *modus vivendi* is one centred around the journey itself, around continuous movement, and not around a destination. Not coincidentally, Titta judges his brother as superficial, and denies him even his status as a man: he is an element still being formed. He has no identity but superficiality itself (which is absence of an identity): 'You were always a superficial man. You're not even a man. You're just a boy'. Moreover, this interpretative framework is reinforced by the man with the bow tie (the actor Rolando Ravello), who the protagonist describes as 'frivolous'. This reiterates the joint function of superficiality and frivolousness in Sorrentino's cinema, where they always appear in opposition to the protagonist's attempt to acquire a stable identity, from which standpoint he can judge reality: 'I see [...] only a frivolous man. I am not a frivolous man'. The concept of *Frivolität* is also a recurring topic in modernist literature and philosophy (consider Otto Weininger or György Lukács), and one that usually implies a condemnation of the character to a partial vision of reality; the incapacity to connect the particularity of the contingent data to the understanding of overall reality, and the consequent value equivalency of everything reality contains.

At the centre of the behavioural spectrum we find the majority of Sorrentino's characters and his 'heroes', whose specific qualities (another eminently modernist motif) elevate them to a higher plane than the mass of other characters. These qualities are not necessarily positive, but they are always exceptional, and it is this that makes them heroes, protagonists. This trait varies enormously: the extreme sensitivity of Antonio Pisapia, the vitality of Tony Pisapia or the musicality of Fred Ballinger. Among these men, Jep Gambardella naturally stands out since his main characteristic is his consciousness of his own situation. By this, I mean the conflict within Sorrentino's filmography itself, between a society of inconsistency and a man who, in seeking his own identity, tries to create meaning from his own contingent situation. This makes him the archetypical figure in Sorrentino's cinema. Jep Gambardella is aware of the 'spectacle', and understands the impossibility of creating value in a society dominated by nihilism: 'They've been asking me for years why I don't write another novel. But look at these people. This wildlife! This is my life and it's nothing'. His journey from this cynical position to the creation of value (the work of art) is therefore the *mise en abyme* of the director's entire poetics.

All of Sorrentino's characters, not only his heroes, share the same purpose: to present their own identity as a self-contained entity that allows them to interpret reality correctly. One clear example is Stefania's discourse (Galatea Ranzi) in *The Great Beauty* (2013a). Her presentation of her own life and civil commitment (therefore of her own Self: 'As a young girl, in the occupied Arts Faculty, I oozed civil vocation') is harshly deconstructed by the protagonist, precisely by referring to the *Frivolität* of the existence that they all lead. Yet, this behaviour involves an incredibly large number of characters (simply consider Viola's insistence, in the same movie, on informing everyone that she does not own a television), and Sorrentino has also transposed it on the literary level with the volume *Gli aspetti irrilevanti* (*The Irrelevant Aspects*), where the many characters' identities are continually pulled into the sphere of irrelevance.

The behaviour of minor characters always serves a purpose for Sorrentino, evoking pity even as they are caricatures. This sense of pity for them arises from the knowledge that they are experiencing a situation similar to the protagonist's: the caricature stems from these characters' ignorance of the irrelevance of their attempts to develop and demonstrate a stable and compact identity.

These behavioural patterns (and the implied poetics) help us to understand that Sorrentino's cinema is simultaneously postmodern cinema and cinema against postmodernism. The first term refers to the social structure related to late capitalism and the second to the ideology based on this structure according to George Calinescu and Fredric Jameson (cf. Calinescu 1987; Jameson 1991). Sorrentino does not avoid confronting the social and ideological elements that emerge from the postmodern structure, but then he interprets his artistic work (another modernist trait) as a language that can re-establish the shattered totality.

Central to this way of thinking is the concept of identity, obviously, a concept strictly connected to that of 'truth'. Consider Friedrich Nietzsche, whose philosophy is widely known to be the foundation of postmodernist ideology; the death of God (meaning the death of what may give meaning to the contingency of our existence) implies the inevitable death of the subject (of the Self), who, having lost the possibility of defining himself in relation to something that transcends him, loses the ability to define reality.

The postmodernist answer to this situation is based on an exacerbation of the characteristics related to the loss of a fixed identity, where the interpretation of reality as a spectacle guarantees the subject the possibility of establishing a new identity based on a radical difference:

> If identity is not a compact and immobile sphere like the well-rounded Truth of Parmenides, if identity is instead something that must be continuously 'negotiated' [...] with time and with others, it means that all the processes related to the formation of an identity are also 'metabolic' processes of transformation, of alteration [...]. The process of reproduction of an identity reveals the intrinsic character of otherness.
>
> (Remotti 2012: 63)

Sorrentino accepts this point of view but, modernistically, turns it around. Social oppression is not founded on the immobilization of a fixed identity, but on the dialectics that society has put in place between a wholly inconsistent identity and a neurotic search for it. In a society that reformulates social relations and

individual goals on the basis of completely inconsistent values, thereby transforming individuals' attempts to form an identity into a neurotic irrelevance, the answer
(definitely a Romantic one) consists of discovering one's own identity. This alone
will allow the interpretation of reality outside inconsistency (frivolousness) that
reduces the search for value to caricature. The success of Sorrentino's protagonists
in this search connects Sorrentino's poetics more strongly to the modernist than
to the postmodernist.

Furthermore, what allows the subject to define himself and give himself meaning (and therefore a meaning of reality) centres on the immanent substitutes for
this transcendent dead God: the father and mother. The absence of instruments
for interpreting reality will therefore be analysed (as is the case in *This Must be the
Place* (2011) and in the novel *Everybody's Right*, which ends with the protagonist
dreaming of himself as a child with his parents) through the absence of a figure
that teaches us how to interpret reality itself.

In Search of an Identity

It is no accident that Sorrentino set his first film *One Man Up* (2001) in the 1980s,
the decade that revealed the 'spectacularization' of human and social relations
that had previously created and then irreversibly destroyed the social fabric that
was still cohesive in the 1970s. Sorrentino stated in an interview that his favourite
themes are nostalgia, melancholy and memory, and yet the 1980s are the antithesis
of these: a life reduced to a bare present, to enjoyment of the contingent moment.
The 1980s are the counterpart to the reformulation of social relationships, and so
of individual existences, when deprived of their permanent and/or symbolic values.
Tony Pisapia, the man who declares the will to exist in the *hic et nunc* through his
every action and word, is apparently their prophet.

Moreover, while describing the 1980s in another interview, Sorrentino explicitly referenced the concept of *kitsch*: 'When you see photos of the time, you are
struck by how ugly the hairstyles or clothes were, you are struck by the absurd
clash of colours. It was the triumph of kitsch' (in Furxhi 2003: 8–9). Again we
find ourselves in a modernist framework: in using the term kitsch, Sorrentino
was referring to the 'absence of values' that the concept implies, as described by
Hermann Brock.

One Man Up is the film in which Sorrentino most clearly focuses on the issue of
identity (starting with the concept of *doppelgänger*) (cf. Sorrentino in Ceretto and
Chiesi 2006: 44).[3] The decaying process of the two protagonists comes precisely
from a denied identity that coincides with their professional lives: soccer coach
for Antonio, singer for Tony. This is a recurring theme in Sorrentino's cinema.

28

Antonio reaches the peak of his career at the moment he starts to speak as a coach for the first time (in the locker room, when he scores his most beautiful goal). He has refused to throw the game and tells his teammates, 'I'll become a coach'. However, the identity that he is seeking will be negated (the *Subbuteo* that he uses to test out tactical strategies is a sarcastic surrogate of it), and his new identity as an insurer only keeps him further from his true identity. The manager of his former team tells him, yet again, that there is no role for him there, adding, '[i]f you are concerned about the vouchers, I'll issue whatever you need'. It is this which angers Antonio: it is not a matter of vouchers or money because what is at stake is the possibility (or the impossibility) of defining himself and his role in the world, as reiterated in the dialogue with the anchorman (a dialogue that shortly precedes Antonio's suicide):

- I decided to become a coach.
- Are you a coach now?
- No.

Antonio recovers his identity a moment before dying (on a soccer field), declaring to a taxi driver: 'I have to go to Holland to evaluate a player'.

In contrast, Tony lives a specular life. The portrait permanently in view in his living room, showing him as a singer, represents that lost identity pattern. Stuck like his doppelgänger in a process of decay, Tony also tries to create a new identity for himself (as a chef). Nevertheless, Antonio's death allows Tony to realize the shift that is the main characteristic of Sorrentino's protagonists (and what always makes his works *Bildungs*-movies): a shift that in this case is also physically underlined by shaving his head because of a cyst (Iannotta 2016: 4). Vengeance (the murder of the manager of the soccer team) (cf. Vigni 2012: 54)[4] first causes a complete transformation of Tony's character (e.g., waking up early in the morning), and then allows him to reclaim his lost identity, symbolically represented by singing on the boat while fleeing from the police, and then by the applause that he receives from his cell mates.

The Consequences of Love also focuses on a stolen identity. The Mafia has denied the protagonist his identity as an accountant, father and husband. During the movie, the protagonist constantly repeats 'I am Titta di Girolamo', underlining with those words his lost identity (the mirrors that constantly surround and reflect him are part of this). He lacks any agency, and is stuck in the role of spectator and in several non-places (the cellar, the hotel[5]), places that, according to Marc Augé, are worlds devoted to 'lonely individuality, to the provisory and to the ephemeral' (2000: 74), dominated by the absence of memory and by the eternity of a moment deprived of any meaning (Augé 2000: 95). This leads Titta to mentally react by establishing a space full of meaning that coincides with the era of childhood ('We should never break the ties with our childhood'), and through which elements of absolute meaning emerge: 'Dino Giuffré is my best friend, full stop'. He is stuck in the eternal repetition of a present devoid of meaning since there is no room for Titta's identity in this present (he is just the *object* and not the subject of his actions). He therefore retrieves his identity through the same act that will lead to his death: refusing to return the money-filled suitcase to the Mafia: 'You stole my life. I'm stealing your suitcase'. The moment of death becomes a privileged standpoint that leads his life to judgement, to meaning. At the moment of his death (symbolized at the beginning of the movie by a passing hearse) the eternal insignificance disappears and a space opposed to this is activated, the space of memory (the same space that in *The Great Beauty* and *Youth* [2015] is dedicated to art). At the moment of his death, his life gains meaning. Titta ends his existence with an absolute truth ('Only one thing's certain [...]'), Dino Giuffré, who now looks through the camera in complete solitude on a mountainside, is his best friend.

In *This Must be the Place*, and generally in Sorrentino's later works, the process that leads to the formation of an identity is inextricably linked to the relationship with the paternal figure. Even in *The Family Friend* (2006) we see Geremia de' Geremei, the man who 'does not consider God', obsessed with reaching the same professional status as his father, and then with becoming a father in his own right.[6] In *This Must be the Place*, continuing his father's work (punishing a former Nazi who humiliated him in a concentration camp) will allow Cheyenne (another singer who cannot sing) to heal his psychological fractures (exemplified by his new abilities to travel by plane and smoke) through gaining a scheme of values, Jewish identity included, which allows for the interpretation of reality.

Yet, it is in *Youth* that the connection between identity and the role of the paternal figure become central themes, particularly in the character of Hollywood actor Jimmy Tree (Paul Dano). Sorrentino sets the movie in the mountains of Davos, in a place of relaxation and healing that immediately highlights a connection with modernist literature (Thomas Mann, James Joyce, etc.). This connection is reinforced through the link with Romanticism that Jimmy Tree makes explicit through the (false) quotation from Novalis: 'I'm always going home. Always going to my father's house'. It is actually a *pastiche* that merges a verse of the *Hymns to the Night* (Novalis 1960) (where the house of the Father is the house of God) and the notorious imperative of *Heinrich von Ofterdingen* ('we are always going home') (Novalis 2005). It is a *pastiche* that already existed in this form in the volume *The Roots of Romanticism* by Isaiah Berlin: 'I am always going home, always to my father's house' (2013: 104). The false quotation aims to connect the paternal figure (who transmits the value system required to read reality), the image of the home (of the *Heimat*) as the place where everything has meaning and the Christian image of the House of the Father, which encompasses both. Once again, Sorrentino is using a postmodernist tool (the *pastiche*) to attack postmodernism.

Jimmy Tree, who tries to establish a father-son relationship with Ballinger, is experiencing an identity crisis. In this case, the actor is famous for his one and only blockbuster, which encloses him in a false identity. Significantly, the process that leads him to renounce his next acting role (as Hitler) and return to his real identity begins when he meets a young girl who quotes a line from one of his auteur films about the difficulty of being a father. Sorrentino had never before so clearly formulated the connection between identity, the paternal figure and the production of meaning (in this case, as in *The Great Beauty*, related to artistic production).

The situation of Jimmy Tree mirrors, in both a positive and a negative way, the two central characters of the movie: the retired composer Ballinger (Michael Caine) and the elderly director Mick Boyle (Harvey Keitel). However, the situation is also represented on a smaller scale by the other characters in the movie, such as Maradona, who no longer looks like the image connected with his own identity, and is glad when Jimmy Tree tells him 'everyone knows you're left-handed' because that means that everyone knows his real identity.

Mick Boyle's goal is to direct his final movie, a movie that he describes as his testament and the only movie that has any meaning for him. It will be the movie in which he will express himself completely before dying (its title is *The Last Day of Life*). Through his movie, Mick Boyle intends to use the same mechanism as we see with Titta Di Girolamo: the moment of death is the moment in which life attains meaning. The impossibility of directing the movie leads to his suicide: the absence of a final moment means that there is no identity-related reality. Ballinger's journey is the opposite. He begins from a position of complete apathy; having recognized he has lived his life selfishly, worshipping art alone, Ballinger holds a final concert to affirm his belief in the superiority of art over life, of art as the only way to find meaning in life. It is the reaffirmation of his own identity and, paradoxically, a homage to his wife (the *Simple Songs* were composed for her). Through the *Simple Songs*, his wife's life (she is in a vegetative state, and thus deprived of a meaningful existence) will also find meaning.

'Do You Know Why I Only Eat Roots?'

Memory (as seen in *The Consequences of Love*) and art (as seen in *Youth*), which are devoted to rebuilding identity and the possibility of finding meaning in empirical life, overlap in *The Great Beauty*. They overlap (and here we see modernism again) through the name of the author to whom this technique is iconically related: Marcel Proust.

Proust is mentioned three times in Sorrentino's masterpiece. The first time this figure is completely commodified ('Proust is my favourite writer! Along with Ammaniti') and dragged into the *Frivolität* of the nihilist context of the party where the protagonist appears for the first time. In this context, as Jep himself will affirm, creating a work of art is absolutely impossible (if Flaubert's attempt to write a novel over nothingness failed, he cannot succeed). The value that art expresses here is subjugated by the total insignificance of the context.

The second time Proust is quoted is by Andrea (Luca Marinelli) to Jep, and is directly related to the topic of death: 'Proust says that death may come to us this afternoon'. Jep tries to mock the dramatic affirmation of the boy ('What should I take seriously then? – Nothing, apart from the menu, of course'), but nevertheless Andrea is able to deconstruct the cynicism that allows Jep to avoid becoming conscious of his existence, of the values hidden under the 'blah blah blah': 'Just because you don't understand doesn't mean nobody can'. Andrea's death is a decisive moment in Jep's formative process, a process that, as always, coincides with regaining his lost identity as a writer. In fact, it is while preparing for Andrea's funeral that Jep reaches the height of his own cynicism, listing off to Ramona the mundane rules of proper behaviour for that kind of social event. In doing so, he is trying to force even death into the insignificant realm of worldliness and 'spectacle' ('You must never forget that at a funeral you are appearing on stage') (cf. Facchini 2017: 187).[7] However, in front of Andrea's coffin Jep breaks those very rules, showing the irreversibility of the process under way.

Proust indirectly appears a third time in relation to the central theme of the movie: the interruption of Jep's creativity. To the question '[w]hy didn't you write another book?' the protagonist answers, '[b]ecause I went out too much at night', which is a clear reference to the first sentence of *In Search of Lost Times*: 'For a long time, I went to bed early'.[8] Proust's lost time is connected to irrelevant activities in the period before starting to write the work that will redeem that very time. While Jep's lost time is related to other irrelevant activities, both deal with time stolen from the creative process that can redeem existence.

Many critics have compared *The Great Beauty* and Federico Fellini's *La Dolce Vita*, highlighting the presentation of Rome's mundane life. Yet Sorrentino's Rome, as the view of a nearly empty Via Veneto demonstrates, is void of its mundane life, which has moved into private spaces. The real connection with Fellini's work is made through the transition of the two protagonists through different, but both insignificant, *modi vivendi* (of which worldliness is only one). Finally, in Jep's case, the reactivation of memory (his youthful encounter with Elisa De Santis) allows the reactivation of the creative impulse, a clear reference to Fellini's *8½* (1963) (cf. Crowdus 2014: 10).[9] For Sorrentino then, as always, this formative process equates to the retrieval of the protagonist's lost identity, as underlined by the exhibition by Ron Sweet, which appears to touch Jep deeply. The exhibition focuses on the mechanism of memory (one picture a day, from childhood), which is clearly connected to the persistence of identity itself.[10]

In this movie, the protagonist takes many wrong turns while searching for his identity, exemplified by his attempt to gain a new identity (one meant to distance him from old age, and therefore death itself) through Botox. The studio of Alfio Bracco (Massimo Popolizio) is actually the physical setting for a collective post-modernist ritual to defend the continuation of *Frivolität*. In this nihilist temple, nostalgia, or memory, itself is degraded – as happened to Proust at the party – to a commodified element: 'Want to go back 30 years, to when it rained at the end of August? Done. That's 700 euros'.

It is with identity, after all, that Jep's story begins; an identity that, immediately juxtaposed with the mundane world of the party, is even presented as fate, as destiny: 'I was destined for sensibility. I was destined to become a writer'. Retrieving this destiny will lead Jep (who feels close to death: 'The most important thing I discovered a few days after turning 65 is that I can't waste any more time doing things I don't want to do') through all the spaces occupied by insignificance, all the existential and ideological places unable to elevate life to meaning, from Talia Concept's art to Cardinale Bellucci's recipes.[11] His redemption begins following the encounter with Elisa De Santis' husband and the news of her death. Jep realizes that Elisa preserved his memory her whole life ('Elisa only ever loved one man'), turning this memory – almost her whole diary is about him – into the centre of her existence, which gave her life meaning.

After learning this, Jep begins to change his habits, to the shock and consternation of the people around him, those same characters who are part of the nihilist universe of *Frivolität* (the conga lines that 'do not go anywhere'). When Jep cites (again referencing identity) the 'who am I?' of the novel *Nadja* (1928) by André Breton, he receives from Trumeau, who is fully aware of the postmodernist cultural logic, the answer 'And of course in the book there's no reply'. The protagonist's entire story is instead a demonstration of a possible answer. This is intertwined with the identity of Rome itself, through the two characters who symbolize the city through their very names: Romano and Ramona. Romano gains consciousness of himself ('I am so ordinary') through a theatre show purposefully dedicated to the theme of nostalgia (memory), while Ramona's death is the decisive event that pushes Jep towards regaining his identity. With Ramona, after all, Jep saw the sea appear on his bedroom ceiling, the same sea that is always in the background in the memories of his encounter with Elisa De Santis (cf. Salvestroni 2017: 23).[12]

The last confrontation, with Sister Maria 'the Saint' (Giusi Merli), completes Jep's formative journey with an invitation to go back to his roots (once again a reference to Proust). For Jep, these are represented by the cliffs by the sea where he and Elisa made love: the place that redeems his existence and gives it meaning. It is not a transcendent or religious solution (the intercutting montage of Jep and Sister Maria climbing the Scala Santa towards the Crucifix simply expresses her standpoint, not his), and the 'beyond' is explicitly rejected: 'Beyond there is what lies beyond. I don't deal with what lies beyond' (cf. Sorrentino 2012a: 45).[13] What gives meaning to existence comes, for Jep, from immanent reality. The novel that he will begin to write will rise above 'the chitter chatter and the noise', the Heideggerian gossip that hides the elements related to the real values of life (cf. Heidegger 2002). In the same way, the missed opportunity to procreate with Elisa (to 'be a father') that emerges in the first dialogue with her husband ('Did you have children? – No. I couldn't. – But I could') is transposed to the birth of the novel (another eminently modernist topic). The final image of the sea, in the scene with the end credits, is mirrored in the image of the Tiber that crosses Rome on its way towards its final destination.[14]

Jep Gambardella's path represents the self-consciousness of the entirety of Sorrentino's poetics. The contrast between empirical reality and meaning is constantly presented as a contrast between identity and absence of identity, and through, as metaphorical figures and corollaries of meaning itself, the topics of death, childhood and parental figures. The moment (always artistic or mnemonic: for Sorrentino art is, first and foremost, memory) that lend value and meaning to the flow of life, allowing for the interpretation of life itself through the re-appropriation of identity, is the moment in which authenticity becomes possible.

NOTES

1. Cf. Sicinski (2016).
2. In *The Great Beauty*, Sorrentino rejects the metaphor of the journey through the opening quotation from Céline, presenting travelling not as movement without destination, but as a rediscovery of the Self. The journey will become the movement 'from life to death', and we shall see how death is a fundamental element in forming characters' identities.
3. 'It was the concept of *doppelgänger*, a complex topic that fascinates me'.
4. 'An overlapping with his own *doppelgänger*, giving back to him what he had been robbed of'.
5. The opening scene, with an errand boy dragging the suitcase on a carousel in a gloomy place, is naturally a homage to *The Graduate* by Mike Nichols, another movie centred on the recovery of an identity and of the related agency.
6. In this movie there is also a character who fully expresses the process that we are analysing. Tesauro (Elia Schilton), the illegitimate child of an aristocrat, attempts to merge with the father identity, thereby conquering identity, by buying a title of nobility.

7. '[…] it is the protagonist's encounters with death that force him and his spectators to raise the veil of society's artificiality and question its nature'.

8. The similarity of the two sentences is not clear in English. In Italian the juxtaposition is blatant. Proust: 'Per molto tempo sono andato a letto presto la sera'; Gambardella: 'So' uscito troppo spesso la sera'.

9. '*The Great Beauty* is at its core a film about the nature of the creative process'.

10. Also in *The Great Beauty,* the loss of identity leads to desperation. A clear example of this is when the countess Colonna di Reggio (Sonia Gessner) goes to the palace that she once owned to listen to the recording that describes her past life.

11. Through the Cardinal, Jep seeks a spiritual answer to his situation, but he becomes progressively conscious that the Cardinal, a fully fledged part of the *Frivolität*, of 'lost time', does not have such an answer, as sarcastically demonstrated by his use of the evangelic expression *Ecce Homo* when explaining a recipe: 'Ecce coniglio alla ligure' (this has also been lost in the English translation, becoming 'you have Ligurian-style rabbit!').

12. '[…] the protagonist lays down and, before sleeping, projects through imagination a calm, bright, blue sea on the ceiling. […] It is an *other* dimension, beyond his everyday mundane life'.

13. 'One always thinks that a more relevant "beyond" exists, instead it does not exist.'

14. Among other things, at the beginning of the final sequence of the movie, we can see a boy diving into the Tiber, clearly a homage to Pier Paolo Pasolini's *Accattone*.

REFERENCES

Antonello, P. (2012), 'Di crisi in meglio. Realismo, impegno postmoderno e cinema politico nell'italia degli anni zero: Da Nanni Moretti a Paolo Sorrentino', *Italian Studies*, 67:2, pp. 169–87.

Augé, M. (2000), *Non-Places: Introduction to an Anthropology of Supermodernity*, London: Verso.

Berlin, I. (2013), *The Roots of Romanticism*, Princeton: Princeton University Press.

Bonsaver, G. (2013), 'Dall'uomo Al Divo: Un'intervista Con Paolo Sorrentino', *The Italianist*, 29:2, pp. 325–37.

Calinescu, M. (1987), *Five Faces of Modernity*, Durham: Duke University Press.

Canetti, E. (1973), *Auto Da Fè*, Harmondsworth: Penguin Books.

Ceretto, L. and Chiesi, R. (eds) (2006), *Una distanza estranea: Il cinema di Emanuele Crialese, Matteo Garrone e Paolo Sorrentino*, Torre Bordone: Edizioni di Cineforum.

Crowdus, G. (2014), 'In search of *The Great Beauty*: An interview with Paolo Sorrentino', *Cineaste*, 39:2, pp. 8–10.

Debord, G. (2014), *The Society of the Spectacle*, Berkeley: Bureau of Public Secrets.

Facchini, M. (2017), 'A journey from death to life: Spectacular realism and the "unamendability" of reality in Paolo Sorrentino's *The Great Beauty*', in L. di Martino and P. Verdicchio (eds), *Encounters with the Real in Contemporary Italian Literature and Cinema*, Newcastle upon Tyne: Cambridge Scholars Publishing, pp. 181–204.

Furxhi, L. (ed.) (2003), *L'uomo in più di Paolo Sorrentino*, Turin: Atace FAICinema.

Heidegger, M. (2002), *On Time and Being* (trans. Joan Stambaugh), Chicago: University of Chicago Press.

Iannotta, A. (2016), 'Le immagini del potere: Note sull'identità italiana nel cinema di Paolo Sorrentino', *California Italian Studies*, 6:2, pp. 1–17.

Ibsen, H. (1997), *Brand*, Minneapolis: University of Minnesota Press.

Jameson, F. (1991), *Postmodernism, or the Cultural Logic of Late Capitalism*, London: Verso.

Lukács, G. (1995), 'Aesthetic culture', in A. Kadarky (ed.), *The Lukács Reader*, Oxford: Blackwell, pp. 156–70.

Nichols, M. (2007), *The Graduate*, USA: Twentieth Century Fox Home Entertainment.

Novalis (1960), *Hymns to the Night*, New York: Liberal Art Press.

Novalis (2005), *Heinrich von Ofterdingen: A Romance*, New York: Dover Publication.

Proust, M. (2013), *In Search of Lost Time*, New Haven: Yale University Press.

Remotti, F. (2012), *Contro l'identità*, Rome: Laterza.

Salvestroni, S. (2017), *La grande bellezza e il cinema di Paolo Sorrentino*, Bologna: Archetipolibri.

Sanctis, P. De, Monetti, D. and Pallanch, L. (2010), *Divi e antidivi: Il cinema di Paolo Sorrentino*, Rome: Laboratorio Gutenberg.

Sicinski, M. (2016), 'Paolo Sorrentino: A medium talent', Cinema Scope, September, http://cinema-scope.com/features/paolo-sorrentino-medium-talent/. Accessed 18 April 2019.

Sorrentino, P. (2001), *L'uomo in più (One Man Up)*, Italy: Medusa Video.

Sorrentino, P. (2004), *Le conseguenze dell'amore (The Consequences of Love)*, Italy: Medusa Video.

Sorrentino, P. (2006), *L'amico di famiglia (A Family Friend)*, Italy: Medusa Video.

Sorrentino, P. (2011), *This Must be the Place*, Italy: Medusa Film.

Sorrentino, P. (2012), *Tony Pagoda e i suoi amici*, Milan: Feltrinelli.

Sorrentino, P. (2013a), *La grande bellezza*, Italy: Medusa Video.

Sorrentino, P. (2013b), *Everybody's Right* (trans. Howard Curtis), London: Vintage Books.

Sorrentino, P. (2013c), *Hanno tutti ragione*, Milan: Feltrinelli.

Sorrentino, P. (2016), *Youth*, USA: Twentieth Century Fox Home Entertainment.

Sorrentino, P. (2017), *Il peso di Dio: il vangelo di Lenny Belardo*, Turin: Einaudi.

The Young Pope (2016, USA: HBO Home Entertainment).

Vigni, F. (2012), *La maschera, il potere, la solitudine: il cinema di Paolo Sorrentino*, Firenze: Aska.

3

A Journey from Death to Life: Spectacular Realism and the 'Unamendability' of Reality in Paolo Sorrentino's *The Great Beauty*

Monica Facchini

Colgate University

The Spectacle and the Mask

Disappearing giraffes, knife throwers, garish, middle-aged women jumping out of birthday cakes, crazed parties, toothless centenarian saints and hundreds of flamingos magically alighted on a Roman terrace: nothing seems further from reality than the great circus-like spectacle that Paolo Sorrentino offers to his disoriented spectators in his Academy Award–winning film, *The Great Beauty* (2013). And yet, Sorrentino's 'visionary way ... to observe reality' (Zagarrio 2016: 8)[1] reveals contemporary society in its most ambiguous forms, highlighting on the one side the reality of the society of the spectacle and on the other one the inescapable inner reality of human existence with its uneasiness and weaknesses.

In a world in which reality is more and more mediated through television, Internet, social media, reality shows and homemade videos widely distributed on the Internet, there is no unique common perception of what is real. As Federico Montanari has highlighted in *Il campo intrecciato del reale*, the concept of reality today is complicated by the use of multiple media and new technologies, so that '[...] we find ourselves dealing with literally a myriad of meaningful *pictures* expressed through technologies (big and small screens) that contribute to "edit" and organize our perceptive-informative and cognitive reality, but also and above all our affective-emotional one' (Montanari 2009: 22). It is not surprising, then, that in response to questions about a possible relationship between contemporary cinema and Neorealism, young Italian film directors point out the impossibility of a comparison between themselves and the post-war generation, given the different historical, social and political context today. This is a context in which, as Emanuele Crialese states, 'Television employs reality in an absolutely perverse way, passing off as real images that are anything but real' (Taviani-Vicari 2008: 62).[2]

The 'spectacular reality' Sorrentino presents in his film is that of a society in which, according to Guy Débord, 'the spectacle is integrated' (Débord 1990: 8), and, as Maurizio Ferraris suggests in *Manifesto of New Realism*, reality is no longer distinguishable from *reality shows* and becomes 'realitism' (Ferraris 2014: 15). Sorrentino translates on the big screen a 'reality' with which his spectators, greedy TV consumers, are very familiar. It will not surprise then that, against Gary Crowdus's anticipation that the film would not appeal to a younger crowd, given its aged characters and a nostalgic tone (Crowdus 2014: 10), *The Great Beauty* has had a great impact on young generations, who recognized in the film a world they experience everyday through television, Internet and social networks, along with its emptiness and inanity.

'The real world has certainly become a tale or, rather … it became a reality show', states Ferraris (Ferraris 2014: 3) and cinema cannot but mirror it, devising new 'effects of reality' on its screen. This is, after all, not a new technique. Not only was the 'aesthetic of reality' in Neorealist cinema, in André Bazin's words, 'a triumphant evolution of the language of cinema, an extension of its stylistic' (2005: 26), which confirmed that 'every realism in art [is] first profoundly aesthetic' (2005: 25), it was also the case that the realist techniques employed by political film directors in the 1960s – such as Francesco Rosi and Gillo Pontecorvo – aimed at mimicking a certain 'reality' conveyed by the media. The use of black and white instead of colours and grainy photography instead of a clean and refined image re-created on the big screen that effect of 'truth' that their spectators associated with the poor quality and aesthetic of newsreels. Likewise, Sorrentino's use of glossy images in his film mirrors a 'reality' that, though artificially constructed by tabloids and TV programs, conveys to his spectators the same familiar feeling as the images of Rosi's *Salvatore Giuliano* (1961) representing the corpse of the bandit in the same fashion of the newspapers of the time. However, the *mise en scène* of media-constructed reality in both Rosi's and Sorrentino's films is accompanied by a demystification of that very construction, an unmasking of its artificiality made possible by specific stylistic choices such as a peculiar use of camera angles, a non-linear fragmented editing and the intermingling of public, mass-mediated scenes and more private, intimate situations. In particular, Sorrentino's hyperbolic camera movements, rapid montage, obtrusive editing, dazzling lighting and elaborate set design create a sense of awareness of the medium in the spectator, showing, as Vito Zagarrio argues, '*the great beauty* of cinema' (Zagarrio 2016: 7; *la grande bellezza* del cinema), but also demanding a critical approach towards its subject: 'It's true: rather than the "message", Sorrentino is more interested in the *mise en scène*, framing, camera movements. But his aesthetics becomes ethic too, like the old neorealist school' (Zagarrio 2012: 105). In this regard, drawing on Bill Nichols' affirmation that 'meta-narrative can become a fundamental realist agent' (Nichols 1991: 175), Pierpaolo Antonello re-evaluates the political role of the 'constructive' dimension in the work of art that urges the spectator to be critical towards the various mechanisms of reality (Antonello 2012: 178). Sorrentino's 'postmodern stylistic virtuosity' (Marcus 2010: 248) questions the mass-mediated reality of the world of the spectacle, inviting the spectator to reflect on the medium and on the different layers of meaning that compose the narrative text.[3]

When asked to define realism, the literary critic and novelist, Walter Siti, replied that the first image that comes to his mind is that of the frescoes of the *Legend of Saint Francis* (1292–96) in the Upper Church of the Basilica of San Francesco in Assisi. More specifically, Siti refers to a detail of the frescoes attributed to Giotto, in which it is possible to catch sight of the back of a crucifix. A completely revolutionary element, states the critic, the Giotto's crucifix challenged all cultural and artistic codes of the time, becoming 'an emblem of realism: seeing things from a different point of view, catching reality from behind' (Siti et al. 2013: 8). Something similar seems to happen in Sorrentino's film as well. In *The Great Beauty* reality is caught in all its squalor and beauty only from 'behind' the great spectacle of modern society and the masks of its most exuberant, vulgar and miserable characters. As Jep himself suggests in a confrontation with his friend Stefania, the mask helps them eschew the most hurtful reality of their life; it is a necessary lie to survive their uneasiness and fragility. And yet, he will eventually tear away the veil of the spectacle to face his own weaknesses and reveal the 'trick' behind an inauthentic world of parties and excesses.

The double reality of the spectacle, the shiny apparent one and the uncomfortable hidden one, portrayed in Sorrentino's film reminds the spectacle of a certain Rome as depicted more than 40 years earlier by Federico Fellini:

> Through the news, often inaccurate or deliberately distorted in daily newspapers and weekly magazines, it can be understood that one of the things I want to do with *La dolce vita* is describe a certain milieu, a certain world. Directly or indirectly, we all know it, don't we? The world of Via Veneto and Cinecittà, the big international hotels and aristocratic salons (blood or money, old money or new, it doesn't matter) [...] I would like to portray in images the *inauthenticity of this world, its disintegration and, above all, its fundamental anxiety*.
>
> (Minuz 2015: 66)

With these words in December 1958, Federico Fellini explained his intentions in realizing a film like *La dolce vita* (1960), in which the portrayal of the glossy world of Via Veneto and Cinecittà would unveil its artificiality and 'its fundamental anxiety'. Sorrentino's film has been widely compared to Fellini's cinema and style, and the double vision on the spectacular reality he portrays confirms his similarities to the great Italian master. The representation of the anxiety that the society of the spectacle effects on people is even further elaborated and complicated in Sorrentino's film. Here a more intimate, dramatic and fragile reality shines through the lights of the great spectacle, a reality that shows the inanity of this spectacle and its consequences for the life of the individual human being. As Roy Menarini has pointed out, in Sorrentino's cinema, 'the discourse on Italian society ... shows something deeper than what is merely suggested by the "literal" themes set in front of us: the loneliness, uncertainty, fragility of easily influenced characters' (Menarini 2009: 49–50).[4] The Felliniesque spectacle staged in Sorrentino's film betrays, indeed, its Pirandellian nature, both in its humoristic tableaux, in which laughter is always accompanied by the 'feeling of the opposite' (Pirandello 1986: 135) as a form of cognition and compassion, and in the unveiling of the mask that people wear in society to hide their true identity. Indeed, all the major characters in the film hide their own failures and fragilities behind a mask of excesses and vulgarity. However, it is in these hidden aspects of their personalities, in their fears and weaknesses, that the director finds their authentic beauty, 'a hidden beauty, at times invisible' (Sorrentino 2013: 10).

One character among the others seems to epitomize the Pirandellian mask in the film: Ramona, the stripper. Ramona is introduced in the film during one of her performances in her father's club. Here she meets Jep Gambardella and, after her initial defensive and diffident approach, the two become friends. Although Ramona's strong Romanesque accent, brutal sincerity and gaudy outfits provoke the scandalized and fierce comments of Jep's elitist friends, her diffident behaviour and flashy appearance are a mask to hide her fragile nature and sensibility. Her shiny dress, too tight and revealing for the art soirée organized by one of Jep's friends, contrasts with her 'purity' and 'clear-eyed gaze' (Sorrentino and Monda 2014) when, attending the painting performance of a little girl, she is moved to tears by the girl's fury and pain. The fragility of Ramona's inner identity is emphasized by her secret illness, whose nature is never revealed in the film and from which she eventually dies. Like that of all the characters in the film, Ramona's mask is her only shield against a world that has disappointed her, a screen behind which she can hide her weaknesses and vulnerability. She is the most evident example of the film's dual vision of reality, divided between its more spectacular and intimate aspects. However, this is a vision that involves all the characters, including the protagonist, Jep, who, unlike his friends, though, is aware of the 'trick', the mask that everybody wears in society. Therefore, when his friend, Stefania, attempts to assert her own 'mask', priding herself for her alleged life accomplishments and disparaging the shallowness of those around her, Jep unmasks her, harshly, with a list of all her weaknesses and failures:

> all this boasting, all this earnest showing off, all this 'me, me, me' and all these sweeping condemnations hide a certain fragility and unease and above all a whole series of untruths. We care about you, and we know our own untruths, and that's why, unlike you, we end up talking about inane nonsense, because we have no intention of facing our own pettiness.[5]

By exposing Stefania's lies, Jep reveals the true nature of the illusory reality that he and his friends have created to hide the emptiness of their lives and to escape from their own fears and weaknesses.

When accused of not being realistic, Sorrentino replied that what is real in his film are the feelings portrayed through his characters and their general sense of uneasiness in contemporary society (Sorrentino and Soria 2014). The need to give voice to authentic feelings in art is expressed by the main character, Jep Gambardella, when, at the umpteenth attempt of his dear friend Romano to adapt Gabriele D'Annunzio's work to the theatre, he candidly responds that 'intellectual acrobatics' would not help him attain dignity, and that he should instead 'try and write something truly [his] own about a feeling, or sorrow'. His words echo Giovanna Taviani's considerations on Italian contemporary cinema, in which directors are no longer afraid to portray genuine emotions and feelings and rather approach reality as 'lived experience', overcoming a postmodern 'emotional anaesthetization' (Taviani 2008: 85, 87). In Sorrentino's film, the protagonist himself will eventually have to face the reality of his life, reconsidering his own past, with its sorrows and failures.

In Sorrentino's previous film, *Il Divo* (2008), on the *Spectacular Life of Giulio Andreotti*, Millicent Marcus argues that the way the protagonist faces the reality behind the spectacle of his (and Italy's) life is through irony, an attitude which 'allows him the intellectual distance to step back and to think dispassionately about his own existence as it rushes toward its mortal end' (Marcus 2010: 245). It is again irony that, according to Marcus, 'opens the breach between the filmmakers' spectacular formal values and their denunciation of social ills' (Marcus 2010: 246–47), thereby reinstating the ethical value of the formal aspects of cinema. If in *Il Divo* irony is the vehicle through which the director (and with him the spectator) can go beyond the spectacle and unveil a less spectacular reality, in *The Great Beauty*, it is the protagonist's encounters with death that force him and his spectators to raise the veil of society's artificiality and question its nature. In the film, the death of those nearest to Jep is always accompanied by a fading of the loud noises of the spectacle towards an apparent introspective calm, which subverts the precarious balance of the protagonist's inner life: a *Quiet Chaos*, as Sandro Veronesi describes the effects of death on a widower in his 2008 film. Death in *The Great Beauty* constitutes what Ferraris calls 'the unamendability' of reality, something that ultimately forces us to take distance from the ever-present time of 'realitism' and come to terms with reality (Ferraris 2014: 19).

If in the society of the integrated spectacle, we live in an *eternal present*, which, according to Débord, 'wants to forget the past and no longer seems to believe in future' (Débord 1990: 13) in contrast with the idea of time as 'the sphere of human development' (Débord 1994: 110), death reinstates depth and meaning in the ever-present world of appearance, or with Ferraris, 'realitism'. In an article for *La repubblica*, titled 'Benvenuti nel realitysmo', Ferraris points out how realitism discards and goes beyond the reality principle in the name of the pleasure principle. 'In doing so, it circumvents many things we do not like, such as death and what comes before it, ageing' (Ferraris 2011).

The pursuit of pleasure, represented in Sorrentino's film with over-the-top parties, loud music, easy illusory fame, superficial talk, in few words, all the 'blah, blah, blah, blah' as Jep calls it, represents the characters' desperate attempt to escape any thought of death and to chase a dream of eternal youth. The 'spectacular time' (Débord 1994: 110–17) of contemporary society disavows the cyclical rhythm of ancient eras, immobilizing its *spectators* 'at the distorted centre of the movement of its world' so that the consciousness of the spectator can have no sense of an individual life moving towards self-realization, or towards death. Someone who has given up the idea of living life will surely never be able to embrace death (Débord 1994: 115).

In this society of appearances, ageing is forbidden and there is no place for death. Yet 'the social absence of death is one with the social absence of life' (Débord 1994: 115), and no matter how hard we try to create an illusory carefree reality, 'at a certain point, something resists us', something 'unamendable' that ultimately forces us to discern reality from dreams and, eventually, pursue a more authentic life (Ferraris 2014: 19). I argue that death in *The Great Beauty* serves as that unamendable element of reality, which prompts the protagonist to look at life with different eyes and with a renovated awareness of its meaningfulness.

Sorrentino's use of fictional characters and story in his film responds to a need to create a paradigmatic portrayal of the universal aspects of human life, with its beauty and fragility, and to depict the uneasiness of today's society, whose lights and noises only highlight the loneliness of its 'spectators'. A fictional story offers a better model than a true story, claims Siti, 'because it can educate and clarify things lying in the personal and collective unconscious … Fiction narration provides us with a universe and not a chaos, a controllable and determined reality' (Siti 2013: 26–27). Siti's idea of a fictional narrative that can transform chaos into a 'controlled and determined reality' seems to echo Pier Paolo Pasolini's concept of death that, like a montage of life, chooses and orders its truly significant moments, to finally give them a stable and unchangeable meaning.[6]

> *So long as we live we have no meaning*, and the language of our lives ... is untranslatable: a *chaos of possibilities*, a search for relations and meanings without resolution. *Death effects an instantaneous montage of our lives* ..., transforming an infinite, unstable, and uncertain – and therefore linguistically not describable – present into a *clear, stable, certain and therefore describable past.*
>
> (Pasolini 1988: 236–37)

Like a fictional story or film montage, for Pasolini, death is that element that can restore meaning to life, making it understandable and describable. Even though Sorrentino's protagonist does not die (at least not on a literal reading of the film), his encounters with the death of a previous lover and of his dearest friends will drive him back to his past, 'a clear, stable and therefore describable past', devoid of the lies and tricks of his present life. It is only through his confrontation with the past that Jep himself will again be able to write about 'something truly [his] own, about a feeling, or sorrow', breaking the veil of the spectacle and facing the essence of his life, with its fears and beauties.

Jep's reconciliation with his past and the 'unmasked' reality of his life is achieved through a journey across his own past and present, a journey that is his life and his novel, as the opening quote from Louis-Ferdinand Céline's *Journey to the End of the Night* (1932) reveals:

> Our journey is entirely imaginary.
> That is its strength.
> It goes from life to death. ...
> *It's a novel, just a fictitious narrative.* ...
> It's on the other side of life.[7]

With this quote, Sorrentino introduces his spectators to Jep's journey that is also a journey through Rome, through its breath-taking panoramas and ancient palaces and its decadent and corrupted realities. Through an analysis of Sorrentino's cinematic style and the film's references to religious symbolisms, I propose a reading of the film as an 'inverted' journey, one that goes not 'from life to death', as Céline would have it, but from death to life. More specifically, I contend that the unamendability of death in this film effects an epiphanic revelation that induces the disenchanted Jep to remove his mask and face a more authentic reality. It is through this journey that he finally makes sense of his own existence and brings forth his 'novel(/)life'.

Spectacle and Death

As Antonio Monda has remarked, *The Great Beauty* develops along two axes: 'on the one hand, the corruption, decadence, debauchery, and rottenness of a certain segment of Rome and the world and, on the other hand, grace, or at least the search for grace' (Sorrentino and Monda 2014). Indeed, the film not only lines up decadent situations with moments of beauty and unexpected grace, it ultimately merges both. Corrupted high-society and kind-hearted strippers, ostentatious artists and genuine artwork, sex and love, hypocritical religiosity and spirituality, the myth of youth and the unexpected charms of old age – each of these themes is presented in its pettiness and, at the same time, with a grace that unveils human weaknesses and fragility. In this context, even death appears in its twofold nature – a vulgar taboo in the high society and a source of grace for those who live at the margins of such society. Elisa, Jep's first and probably only love, Andrea, a young boy afflicted by a mental disorder and the great questions of life, and Ramona, a forty-year-old stripper suffering from an unknown illness: these characters, who live outside Jep's circle of shallow and miserable friends, are the people 'to whom he attributes the greatest purity', reveals Sorrentino (Sorrentino and Monda 2014). That is why their death has a strong impact on his life, forcing him to put down his mask as the 'king of high society' and come to terms with a reality of failures and uncertainties. As already mentioned, Jep's encounter with death (that of his closest friends but also the projection of his own) will effect in him what Pasolini calls a 'montage of life' (Pasolini 1988: 236), selecting and ordering the most meaningful moments of his past life, which will ultimately result in a renovated impulse to write and, therefore, to live.[8]

'La commare secca', as Pasolini referred to death in one of his film treatments,[9] makes its first appearance already in the opening scene of *The Great Beauty*. Seemingly unrelated to the rest of the story, this scene and the events it portrays establish the atmosphere of the film and offer a key to the cinematic journey that we as spectators are about to undertake. As Sorrentino explains in a video for the *New York Times*, this scene allows him to establish a defining image of Rome as a city in which beauty and decadence, sacredness and profanity, are inseparable (Sorrentino 2013). The smooth shot of the steadicam translates the idleness of the Roman inhabitants that the scene portrays, while leading the spectator through the most touristic sites of the holy city. Its movement is also a reference to and a preview of Jep's indolent wandering between the city's frivolous and decadent parties and its most popular and hidden highlights. The images of Rome's apathetic citizens – leaning languidly on precious ancient busts, falling asleep on benches, and bathing in the monumental fountains of the city – establish a counterpoint to the dramatic image of a Japanese tourist who, overcome by the exceptional beauty of Rome's artistic and natural panoramas, dies from 'a standard case of Stendhal syndrome' (Sorrentino 2013). The death of the Japanese man is accompanied by a choir who sing a sacred song – *I Lie* by David Lang. The events on the screen are narrated through a contrapuntal structure that heightens the spectators' awareness of the medium and a critical approach to the events represented on the screen. Indeed, while the sound image seems to mourn the death of the man, the visual image of an emotionless tourist guide and an annoyed bus driver reveals their insensitivity and indifference to death. All of this happens in the setting of Rome, which, in the director's words, stands 'there in the background, still and sun-drenched, monumental and ravishing. And insensitive' (Sorrentino and Contarello 2013: 12). Sorrentino's words seem to echo a very similar description of Rome as portrayed by Pier Paolo Pasolini in *Mamma Roma* (1962), when, in front of Ettore's death and Mamma Roma's desperation, ' … Roman landscape, with its tall buildings and misty fields, spreads out, vast and indifferent under the sun' (Pasolini 2001: 263). Like fifty years ago, death is regarded with indifference by the holy city and today, like then, only music can restore the dead body to its sacredness.[10]

Music is not the only technical element in this scene that can be connected to the tragic event. As R. W. Gray notes, a series of close-ups addressing the camera directly in the opening sequence of the film seem to be connected to the death of the Japanese man, creating a technically uniform narrative (Gray 2015). The first close-up, which is also the opening shot of the film, reveals the mouth of a cannon that fires right into the camera. Although its function is to announce the time (specifically noon), the fire seems to foretell and metaphorically cause the death of the Japanese tourist a few minutes later. In a similar fashion, the close-up of the leading chorister looking straight into the camera in a melancholic ecstasy stands as both an omen of and a mourning cry for the tourist's death. The quiet atmosphere is abruptly interrupted by a sudden off-screen sound of a loud scream, which introduces the spectators to a very different setting in the following scene. The terrible cry accompanying the last images of the crowd surrounding the dead body of the tourist would at first sound like a ghastly expression of mourning for his death. However, the following close-up of the face of an eccentric woman screaming directly into the camera reveals that, far from being a manifestation of mourning, her scream is a celebration of Jep's 65th birthday and is followed by a loud and sensual music. 'A broad sample of humanity' (Sorrentino and Contarello 2013: 13) is presented on the screen, people dancing, drinking and flirting. In this bedlam of bodies and lust, we are introduced to the birthday man, Jep Gambardella, first surrounded by women who wait to kiss him happy birthday, and then dreamily dancing while the camera frames him upside down in the dizzy and frenzied atmosphere of the party.

The two contiguous scenes – one portraying the death of a Japanese tourist and the other Jep's birthday party – mirror each other in contrapuntal fashion, whose point of contact is precisely the ambiguous scream of the woman. The old monuments of Rome are replaced by dancing podiums and bars, the poised Japanese tourists captivated by the city's beauty give way to ostentatious Roman people, who unlike the apathetic citizens of the first scene are now portrayed dancing on frenetic rhythms. The juxtaposition of these two scenes not only suggests the coexistence of two realities in Rome, the sacred and the profane, as in the intentions of the director (Sorrentino 2013), but also reflects the response of the society of the spectacle in front of death, intended as a 'setback' (Sorrentino 2013: 12), a hindrance to repress. This is especially expressed through the contrasting use of music in the two scenes, in which the sacred music of the a cappella *I Lie* elevates and sacralizes the tourist's death, while the deafening and superficial music of the party rather aims at suffocating any thought of death or sacredness.

Later in the film, Jep Gambardella, in a sort of reflection-confession to one of his female friends, will state, gloating, that 'the conga lines at our parties are the best in Rome... because they don't go anywhere'. These dances are the expression of the futility of the life led by Jep and his friends, of their wandering in circle without aim or goal, and of their loud happiness that is only an illusion. In an interview with Lilli Gruber, Toni Servillo, who plays the role of Jep in the film, interpreted those conga dances as the desire of its characters to continuously evade the important questions of spirituality and identity with which the main character seems, instead, to struggle. 'This is the reason why this film looks at the emptiness', claims Servillo, 'because these questions remain unanswered and these conga lines replace them' (Servillo et al. 2013). And yet, despite the characters' attempt to escape any thoughts of death with their frantic vain dances, the director seems to recall the tragic death of the tourist of the previous scene with a metanarrative gesture. In the middle of an excited group dancing on the notes of *La Colita*, the loud music is suddenly muffled and the unbridled dancing is turned into slow motion. On Jep's face a sardonic smile gives way to a melancholy frown, while he steps out from the crowd and walks towards the camera. A final close-up on his face looking straight into the camera relates his gaze to the previous close-ups of the mouth of the cannon, the chorister and the scream of the woman at the party. As argued before, these close-ups are somehow connected to the Japanese tourist's death and, although Jep is not a 'literal' witness of that tragic event, his melancholy gaze into the camera and his reflections on his past life, establish a technical-metaphorical connection with the tourist's death. This first technical 'encounter' between Jep and death will lead him to interrupt the spectacle of his life, slowing down its frenetic rhythm, and prodding him to start his 'novel'.

Through Jep's direct addressing to a virtual spectator, Sorrentino invites his own spectators to participate emotionally and critically in the actions presented on the screen. This is a clear example of what Francesco Casetti calls 'a gesture of inter-pellation – that is the recognition of someone, who in turn is expected to recognize himself as the immediate interlocutor' (Casetti 1998: 16). As Casetti notes, such procedure has its risks and represents a provocative infraction of traditional narrative rules. The look and voice addressing the camera question the canonical proportion and the 'proper' functioning of representation and filmic narrative. Interpellation, indeed, reveals what is usually concealed (the camera and its work) and opens an off-screen space that is 'other' and can never be on-screen. But above all, interpellations 'tear apart the fabric of the fiction by provoking the emergence of a metalinguistic consciousness …, which by unveiling the game, destroys it. As such, these moments forcibly exhibit what is ordinarily masked, and in this sense they are truly ardent' (Casetti 1998: 17). Jep's address to the film's spectators unveils the 'tricks' of the medium, destroying, on the one hand, its cinematic game and, more importantly, the 'reality' it depicts, i.e. the spectacle of contemporary society. It is not by chance that it is precisely through an interpellation that Jep will start his 'novel', as the use of the voice-over and the literary and almost poetic quality of his monologue confirms.[11] Like the narrative device clearly described by Casetti, Jep's novel too functions to 'tear apart the fabric of the fiction', the mask behind which authentic life lies. This is confirmed by the very first words spoken by Jep, who at his narrative's beginning, tells the story of when he was a little kid and, unlike his fellow friends who were already fascinated by the mysteries of sex, he was attracted by 'the smell of people's houses'. These words, pronounced in a slow and reflective tone in the hubbub of the party, contrast with the images of his friends, who desperately eschew the idea of their old age, pursuing the myth of the eternal youth and flirting with much younger women. But Jep 'was destined to be a *sensitive type*. [He] was destined to become a *writer*. [He] was destined to become Jep Gambardella'. At these words, the camera pans out, and a very long shot of the sky above the party terrace shows the slow appearance of the words, *La grande bellezza*, which stand as the title of Sorrentino's film as well as of Jep's novel, whose incipit he has just narrated.

Though seemingly fragmented and disconnected, the montage and the use of camera angles employed by the director in this sequence constructs a uniform narrative that moves from the death of the tourist through the extravagances of a birthday party to Jep's reflections on his past and present life. Through the tech-nical and stylistic elements of the cinematographic medium, the tourist's death in front of the beauty of Rome acts as a revealing moment, one that compels the protagonist to slow down the hectic pace of his present life and quietly re-consider its meaning behind the mask of spectacle.

The Old Man and the Sea

If Jep's first encounter with death seems to be constructed by technical elements, the second encounter occurs, instead, in the narrative context of the film, when Jep meets Alfredo for the first time. The scene opens with a low-angle shot at the foot of the stairs, conveying a feeling of disorientation and dizziness. At the top of the staircase, Alfredo is waiting in front of Jep's apartment. Jep greets him with the same disenchanted irony with which he wanders through Rome and life. When Alfredo is revealed as the husband of Jep's first girlfriend, Elisa, Jep impassively asks whether they had any children. At Alfredo's mention of his infertility, Jep replies that he, instead, could have had children. With this affirmation, Jep consciously asserts himself and at the same time nostalgically returns to his past with Elisa to contemplate what might have happened had the two not parted so many years earlier. It is only when Alfredo tells him that Elisa died a few days earlier that Jep for the first time loses his composure and lapses into a heartfelt sobbing. As in the film's first sequence, here again the news of death is accompanied by contrasting sound and visual images. Whereas the sacred music of the first scene was replaced in the second one by the scream of the woman at the party, in this scene the image of the two men silently crying is contrapuntally followed by the loud off-screen sound of a nun's ghastly laugh. As in the first sequence, the unexpected sound functions here as a transition to the next scene, where we find Jep and Alfredo caught in a summer storm. Despite the parallels in the technical and stylistic choices between these sequences, the unexpected sound bridge in this scene accomplishes a new and different task. If in the previous scene the presence of loud music enables Jep and his friends to exorcise and mute their weaknesses and fears, including those of growing old and dying, in this scene, the grotesque laughter of the nun morbidly emphasizes death, the thought of which Jep can no longer evade. The news of Elisa's death is for Jep a sudden moment of revelation about his life through a reconsideration of his past, in view of a possible change. This seems to be confirmed by the presence of the rain in this scene.

The repeated presence of water in this film, indeed, conveys the double nature of this element as a symbol both of death and of purification and resurrection. In particular, it is often accompanied by news (Elisa's death), thoughts (Jep's memory of himself almost drowning in the sea as a young boy) or premonitions of death (the sea on the ceiling right before Ramona's death). As the Romanian historian of religion, Mircea Eliade, claims, in the aquatic symbolism 'the waters ... are *fons et origo*, "spring and origin", the reservoir of all the possibilities of existence; they precede every form and *support* every creation' (Eliade 1959: 130). While immersion in water signifies regression and the dissolution of all forms, emersion repeats the cosmogonic act of formal manifestation. This is why, states Eliade, the symbolism of the waters implies both death and rebirth: 'Contact with water always brings a regeneration, on the one hand because dissolution is followed by a new birth, on the other because immersion fertilizes and multiplies the potential of life' (Eliade 1959: 130). On a human level, the immersion is equivalent to death and, on a cosmological level, to the catastrophe (the flood), but 'both on the cosmological and the anthropological planes, immersion in the waters is equivalent not to a final extinction but to a temporary reincorporation into the indistinct, followed by a new creation, a new life, or a "new man", according to whether the moment involved is cosmic, biological, or soteriological' (Eliade 1959: 130–31). The presence of water in this scene, therefore, appears to suggest that the news of Elisa's death results, for Jep, in an immersion into his past, a dissolution of his present form in view of a regeneration. The symbolic function of water is further complicated by the following scene, in which water is the crucial element in Jep's memories of his youth.

As argued before, the technical-stylistic 'encounter' with the death of the tourist prompts Jep to plunge into his past in a reconsideration of his childhood, which in turn brings him to a re-evaluation of his identity and present life. The news of Elisa's death will take him again back to a distant past, and precisely to his youth in Naples and their love story. Jep's memory opens with a low-angle shot of the sea, crossed by a yacht. In contrast with the previous image of Jep shot upside down at the party, in this scene the point-of-view shot of Jep, lying half-naked on his bed, reveals the upside down projection of his memories on the ceiling of his bedroom. Both shots seem to recall Siti's reflection on realism, emblematically identified by the Italian critic with Giotto's untraditional depiction of the back of a crucifix highlighting a different point of view on reality. Indeed, if during the party scene the overturned shot of Jep's face emphasizes the artificiality of the reality of the spectacle (or 'realitism' in Ferraris's words), in this scene the upside-down projection of the sea on Jep's bedroom ceiling reveals an unusual perspective, one which 'catches the [spectator's] mental encyclopaedia by surprise'[12] and points to a re-appropriation of the gaze by the protagonist, who is no more an object of the spectacle but the subject of his own life.

Despite the fact that Jep's memories are focused around his love story with Elisa, they do not indulge in the happy moments of their relationship but are rather haunted by the protagonist's fears as a 65-year-old man. Indeed, while the scene narrates the episode of an 18-year-old Jep who is about to be run over by a yacht, the close-up is not that of Jep's young face, but that of his old one. In order to avoid the yacht, the old Jep plunges into the water and only after narrowly escaping death, he re-emerges to show his young smile at 18 years old. The images of Jep's immersion and emersion from the water of his memories translate the words of Chrysostom to the screen:

> The 'old man' dies by immersion in the water and gives birth to a new regenerated being. This symbolism is admirably expressed by John Chrysostom (*Homil. in Joh.*, xxv, 2) who, speaking of the symbolic multivalency of baptism, writes: 'It represents death and entombment, life and resurrection... When we plunge our head into water, as into a sepulchre, the old man is immersed, altogether buried; when we come out of the water, the new man simultaneously appears.
>
> (Eliade 1959: 132–33)

At the news of Elisa's death, Jep must face his old fear of dying, which, besides being a source of anxiety, will trigger a process of regeneration, as the interaction of the character and water suggests.

Jep's 'rebirth' starts with a journey through his inner self. The water, in fact, is not only a symbol of death and life, but, according to the German psychiatrist Carl Jung, is also a symbol of the unconscious. According to Jung, looking into the mirror of water means dealing with one's own image, and going toward that image results in a brave confrontation with oneself. 'The mirror does not flatter', says Jung, 'it faithfully shows whatever looks into it; namely, the face we never show to the world because we cover it with the persona, the mask of the actor' (Jung 1969: 20). Abandoning his theatrical, sardonic mask and, metaphorically and literally, his 'stage' clothes (he is shown here wearing only an unbuttoned shirt and his underwear), Jep indulges in the memories of his youth, confronting his most intimate fears and drawing his present self into a nostalgic pursuit of innocence. As Sorrentino remarked in an interview with Jean Gili, 'the years go by and Gambardella's major source of despair is the consequences of aging [...] All he has left is the relationship between nostalgia and innocence' (Sorrentino and Gili 2013).

A Novel Life

'But something happened', Romano claims at the news of Jep's return to writing, because, he explains, 'if you want to write again after all these years, something happened'. The news of Elisa's death has forced Jep to a painful introspection and a confrontation with his past and present. These, in turn, result in a renewed impulse to create, to make sense of a journey that is the novel of life. Narrated in the first person by Jep, the film is a reflection of him as a writer, the cinematographic real-ization of his new novel, a discussion of that *Human Apparatus*, as reads the title of his first novel, with its weaknesses and eternal fear of dying. At the end of the film, we realize that we are at the beginning of the novel, or better, at Jep's initial conception of it.

'It always ends like that, with death', says Jep in the closing scenes. But, as a matter of fact, everything started with death. The film itself opens with the death of the Japanese tourist and Jep's introspective journey is triggered by the death of Elisa.[13] Echoing Pasolini's conception of death, according to which the 'language' of our life is unintelligible until we live and only death can give it a stable mean-ing, Jep's voice-over acknowledges the inscrutability of the life hidden beneath an indiscernible 'blah blah blah blah'. Like Pasolini's concept of death as the montage of our lives, the encounter with death leads Jep to select and order the most impor-tant moments of his life, interrupting with his 'novel' the spectacle of his staged life and showing the reality behind the mask. Through it, he tears away the veil of the society of the spectacle with the same irony and melancholy with which he unmasked Stefania's lies, ultimately disclosing the loneliness and emptiness of such a world. As Ferraris notes, indeed, the 'realitism' of contemporary society is a form of solipsism,

> that is of the idea that the external world does not exist, that it is a mere representa-tion, perhaps even at your disposal. At first it seems like a moment of great libera-tion: the weight of the real is lifted and we can be the makers of our own world. ... [T]hen the prevailing mood will be melancholy or rather what we could define as a bipolar syndrome oscillating between a sense of omnipotence and the feeling of the pointlessness of everything. In the end one feels lonely.
>
> (Ferraris 2014: 16–17)

Jep, the 'king of high society', who cannot be content to be a party-goer but 'wanted to have the power to make the parties fail', behind the mask is simply a lonely man, victim of that same high society he tried to conquer, afflicted by the feeling of pointlessness, emblematically expressed by the best conga lines of his parties. Only through the encounter with the unamendability of death, he can see beyond the mask and face reality writing his new novel.

Therefore, when at the end of the film Jep's voice announces, 'let the novel begin', his words are just 'a trick', a montage trick. As spectators, indeed, we had already been listening to his novel and watching its development since Jep's very first appear-ance at the party, when amidst the loud noises of life he began the tale of his own life, with his fears and his regeneration. '*The Great Beauty* is at its core a film about the nature of the creative process', writes Gary Crowdus, 'in particular the artistic belief that reality and truth are best conveyed through imagination and invention' (Crowdus 2014: 10). Not only truth is best conveyed through imagination, but it is only through a renovated creative impulse to 'write' his new book that Jep can come to terms with his real life and stop falsifying it: 'because this fictional story, for some unknown reason, offers a better example than real stories' (Siti 2013: 26).

Jep's voice-over and the autobiographical nature of his narration contribute to blur the distinction between that which is real and that which is 'just a trick'. As Walter Siti explains, the narrator elected as the protagonist of a novel is not a witness of truth: s/he is a *'trickster'* (Siti 2013: 65; in English in the original). And yet, continues Siti, s/he does not wear a mask anymore – her/his voice cracks with anguish or exaltation (Siti 2013: 75). In the fictional dreamlike narration of Sorrentino's film, the spectators is asked to unravel the intricate succession of sometime unlikely events, only to witness the universal truth of human weakness, with its failures and unfulfilled desires. As Riccardo Guerrini, Giacomo Tagliani and Francesco Zucconi state in the introduction of *Lo spazio del reale nel cinema italiano contemporaneo*,

> it is exactly in the imperceptible intersection between reality and representation that the cinematic reinvention of reality is no more a falsification; it rather effects 'a *self-unmasking*, a demystification of the medium and the *mise en scène*, which in turn spurs and produces the *unmasking* effected by the spectator ... who acquires new operative and deconstructive tools and can develop a specific duplicity in the perceptive-interpretational processing'.
>
> (Guerrini et al. 2009: 11–12)

In *The Great Beauty*, stylistic and technical virtuosities and sudden narrative breaks contribute at the unmasking of the medium's own artificiality, creating a distance between the spectators and the events portrayed on the screen, and consequently urging a critical approach towards them and the external reality they represent.

Reality in *The Great Beauty* is never mimetic. Instead, the film engages in an investigation that, according to Giovanna Taviani, distinguishes contemporary Italian cinema, which aims at 'exploring reality but also its cracks, its interruptions; investigating under reality and revealing its absurdity, in the sudden glares of the repressed' (Taviani 2008: 90).[14] The dazzling spectacle of high society in Sorrentino's film is repeatedly interrupted by its own 'king' and his novel/life, whose reflections on the meaning of life are the expression of what that society has so strenuously tried to repress: the fear of ageing and the unamendability of death.

The closing scenes of the film alternate between images of the old nun, Suor Maria, climbing on her knees up the steps of St. John's Church, and of Jep, crossing the sea on a yacht to reach the isle of his youth and his romance with Elisa. The alternation of these two very different journeys evokes two different spiritual experiences in what Sorrentino calls the 'hard work of living' (Sorrentino and Monda 2014), that is the difficulty of giving meaning to life, and that, according to the director, is where the great beauty of life resides. These two journeys portray, on the one hand, the nun's pursuit of the indulgence in the afterlife afforded by the Scala Sancta, and, on the other, Jep's journey across the water to reconnect with this life, buried beneath the hubbub and the noise, and 'the awkward predicament of existing in this world'. Jep's journey is also a narrative one, a *montage* of his most meaningful past events, ordered in a novel that will lead him to his future life. His final gesture of interpellation to his readers-spectators unmasks once again the 'trick' of his narration ('It's just a trick', as his last words reveal), and in so doing, invites them to look behind the shiny mask of the spectacle, at the 'wretched squalor and human misery' but also at the beauty of life. As the 'king of high society', he indeed had the power to make the never-ending party of the society of the spectacle fail.

While he recalls the image of Elisa unbuttoning her blouse in front of him, the face of young Jep becomes again the face of a 65-year-old man, a counterpoint and conclusion to the episode that began with his first memory of her. The old man has faced the sea to confront his true self and has come to terms with his own death. His novel can finally begin.

NOTES

1. All translations from Italian in this essay are mine, unless otherwise stated.
2. On the same note, Vincenzo Marra warns that it is impossible to talk about a relationship with past cinema, without considering how new technologies have affected the power of images (Taviani-Vicari 2008: 68). See also Pierpaolo Antonello's reflection on what reality is today when our access to it is never direct, but distorted by the mass media and their intrinsic '*embeddedness*' (Antonello 2012: 177).
3. On the demystifying, critical and political use of the image in Sorrentino's cinema, see De Sanctis (2010), Guerrini et al. (2009) and Vigni (2012).
4. With these words, Menarini describes not only Sorrentino, but also Matteo Garrone's cinema.
5. Translations from the Italian dialogues in the film are taken from the subtitles in *The Great Beauty*, DVD, directed by Paolo Sorrentino (2014).
6. This connection is not surprising, given Siti's broad knowledge of Pasolini's works as the editor of his complete works for Mondadori and renowned Pasolini's scholar.
7. To Gary Crowdus's question on the influence Céline's novel with its misanthropic black humour had in his film, Sorrentino replies that the French novel has had a big influence on

him, not so much for its misanthropic aspects as for its author's 'morbid obsession with getting to know human beings' and for that disenchantment and irony that are also major aspects of Sorrentino's art (Crowdus 2014: 11). As the scriptwriter Umberto Contarello, who worked on the script with Sorrentino, states, the books that most influenced the film were those by Raffaele LaCapria and Goffredo Parise, especially in connection with that 'disenchanted lightness' that is the main characteristic of Jep Gambardella and his behaviour towards Rome and life. (Contarello and Monda 2014: It is an interview on DVD. Also, the only verbatim quotation is 'disenchanted lightness.').

8. In this perspective, it is significant that of all the extravagant artistic performances Jep attends for his job, he is genuinely moved by the least artificial and unpretentious one, i.e. a man's exhibition of all the pictures of himself that, first his father and, then, he himself took on a daily basis. The long display of the man's portraits visually narrates a stable and therefore describable story, whose authentic nature touches the inner soul of the 'king of society'.

9. Pasolini borrowed the expression from one of Giuseppe Gioacchino Belli's Roman sonnets, 'Er tisico' (1833). The film was then realized by Bernardo Bertolucci, with the title *La commare secca* (*The Grim Reaper*) in 1962.

10. In Pasolini's film, Ettore's death is mourned by Antonio Vivaldi's *Concerto in D minor*, which is the 'death motif' in the film (Magrelli 1977: 50–51).

11. As Carlotta Fonzi-Kliemann noted, 'Jep's voice-over monologues resonate with a marked literary, even poetic quality, whereas in the colloquial spoken language his dry irony prevails' (Fonzi-Kliemann 2014: it is a quotation from a webpage, there are no page indications.).

12. As Siti states, realism means 'cogliere l'enciclopedia mentale del lettore in contropiede' (catching the readers' mental encyclopaedia by surprise) (Siti 2013: 20).

13. As already noted above, during the film the loss of others who are dear to him affects Jep profoundly, as with Andrea and Ramona's death and Romano's departure from Rome.

14. As Paolo Sorrentino puts it in an interview at Cannes Film Festival, 'Luckily, or maybe unluckily, it's reality. It's a world which is reinvented and revisited through the tools that we have at our disposal but, still, it's reality' (Sorrentino and Jahn 2013: it is a quotation from a webpage, there are no page indications).

REFERENCES

Antonello, P. (2012), 'Di crisi in meglio: Realismo, impegno postmoderno e cinema politico nell'Italia degli anni zero: da Nanni Moretti a Paolo Sorrentino', *Italian Studies*, 67:2, pp. 169–87.

Bazin, A. (2005), *What Is Cinema?* vol. 2 (trans. H. Gray), Berkley and Los Angeles, CA: University of California Press.

Casetti, F. (1998), *Inside the Gaze: The Fiction Film and Its Spectator* (trans. N. Andrew and C. O'Brien, Bloomington, IN: Indiana University Press.

Contarello, U. and Monda, A. (2014), '*Umberto Contarello on* The Great Beauty', Disc 2, *The Great Beauty*, DVD, Criterion Collection, USA.

Crowdus, G. (2014), 'In search of *The Great Beauty*: An interview with Paolo Sorrentino', *Cineaste*, 39:2, pp. 8–13.

De Sanctis, P. (2010), 'Forme della sensualità. Il cinema di Paolo Sorrentino', In P. De Sanctis, D. Monetti and L. Pallanch (eds),*Divi e antidivi: Il cinema di Paolo Sorrentino*, Roma: Laboratorio Gutenberg, pp. 23–37.

Débord, G. (1990), *Comments on the Society of the Spectacle* (trans. M. Imrie), London: Verso.

Débord, G. (1994), *The Society of the Spectacle* (trans. D. Nicholson-Smith), New York: Zone Books.

Eliade, M. (1959), *The Sacred and the Profane: The Nature of Religion* (trans.W. R. Trask), New York: Harcourt, Brace & World.

Ferraris, M. (2011), 'Benvenuti nel realitysmo', *La repubblica*, 29 January, http://ricerca. repubblica.it/repubblica/archivio/repubblica/2011/01/29/benvenuti-nel-realitysmo.html. Accessed 11 July 2020.

Ferraris, M (2014), *Manifesto of New Realism* (trans. S. De Sanctis), Albany, NY: SUNY Press.

Fonzi-Kliemann, C. (2014), 'Cultural and political exhaustion in Paolo Sorrentino's *The Great Beauty*', *Senses of Cinema*, 70, http://sensesofcinema.com/2014/feature-articles/ cultural-and-political-exhaustion-in-paolo-sorrentinos-the-great-beauty/. Accessed 11 July 2020.

Gray, R. W. (2015), 'Beauty, travel, and death in Paolo Sorrentino's *The Great Beauty*', *Numéro Cinq*, 6:2, http://numerocinqmagazine.com/2015/02/14/numero-cinq-at-the-movies-beauty-travel-and-death-in-paolo-sorrentinos-the-great-beauty/. Accessed 11 July 2020.

Guerrini, R., Tagliani, G. and Zucconi F. (eds) (2009), *Lo spazio del reale nel cinema italiano contemporaneo*, Recco (GE): Le Mani.

Jung, C. (1969), *The Archetypes and the Collective Unconscious. Vol.9 of Collected Works of C.G. Jung* (trans. R. F. C. Hull), Princeton, NJ: Princeton University Press. Print.

Magrelli, E. (ed.) (1977), *Con Pier Paolo Pasolini*, Roma: Bulzoni. Print.

Marcus, M. (2010), 'The ironist and the auteur: Post-realism in Paolo Sorrentino's Il Divo', *The Italianist*, 30, pp. 245–57.

Menarini, R. (2009), 'Generi nascosti ed espliciti nel recente cinema italiano', in R. Guerini, G. Tagliani and F. Zucconi (eds), *Lo spazio del reale nel cinema italiano contemporaneo*, Recco (GE): Le Mani, pp. 42–50.

Minuz, A. (2015), *Political Fellini: Journey to the End of Italy*, New York: Berghahn. Print.

Montanari, F. (2009), 'Il campo intrecciato del reale,' in R. Guerrini, G. Tagliani and F. Zucconi (eds), *Lo spazio del reale nel cinema italiano contemporaneo*, Recco (GE): Le Mani, pp. 16–26.

Nichols, B. (1991), *Representing Reality: Issues and Concepts in Documentary*, Bloomington, IN: Bloomington University Press.

Pasolini, P. P. (1988), *Heretical Empiricism* (trans. B. Lawton and L. K. Barnett), Bloomington, IN: Indiana University Press.

Pasolini, P. P. (2001), *Mamma Roma*, in W. Siti and F. Zabagli (eds), *Pier Paolo Pasolini. Per il cinema*, Milano: Mondadori.

Pirandello, L. (1986), *L'umorismo*, Milano: Mondadori.

Servillo, T., Sorrentino, P. and Gruber, L. (2013), 'Servillo-Sorrentino: una coppia italiana', *Otto e mezzo*, 7 June, http://www.la7.it/otto-e-mezzo/rivedila7/sorrentino-servillo-una-coppia-italiana-03-03-2014-127692. Accessed 11 July 2020.

Siti, W. (2013), *Il realismo è l'impossibile*, Roma: Nottetempo.

Siti, W., Cervini, A. and Dottorini, D. (2013), 'L'inganno della realtà: Conversazione con Walter Siti', *Fata Morgana*, 21, pp. 7–18.

Sorrentino, P. (2013), 'Anatomy of a scene: *The Great Beauty*', *New York Times*, 13 November, http://www.nytimes.com/video/movies/100000002550148/anatomy-of-a-scene-the-great-beauty.html, Accessed 11 July 2020.

Sorrentino, P. (2014), *The Great Beauty*, DVD, Irvington, NY: The Criterion Collection.

Sorrentino, P. and Contarello, U. (2013), *La grande bellezza*, Milano: Skira.

Sorrentino, P. and Gili, J. (2013), 'Interview with Paolo Sorrentino', Paris-Rome, April, http://www.pathefilms.ch/libraries.files/GrandeBellezza_PK_CHe.pdf. Accessed 11 July 2020.

Sorrentino, P. and Jahn, P. (2013), '*The Great Beauty*: Interview with Paolo Sorrentino', *Electric Sheep*, 5 September, http://www.electricsheepmagazine.co.uk/features/2013/09/05/the-great-beauty-interview-with-paolo-sorrentino/. Accessed 11 July 2020.

Sorrentino, P. and Monda, A. (2014), 'Paolo Sorrentino in conversation with Antonio Monda', *Disc 2, The Great Beauty, DVD*, Irvington, NY: The Criterion Collection.

Sorrentino, P. and Soria L. (2014), *L'Espresso*, 3 March, http://espresso.repubblica.it/visioni/2014/03/03/news/paolo-sorrentino-abbandonatevi-al-mio-film-ne-resterete-coinvolti-1.155422. Accessed 11 July 2020.

Taviani, G. (2008), 'Inventare il vero. Il rischio del reale nel nuovo cinema italiano', *Allegoria*, 57, pp. 82–93.

Taviani, G. and Vicari, D. (eds) (2008), 'La realtà torna al cinema: Sette interviste a registi e sceneggiatori italiani', *Allegoria*, 57, pp. 55–73.

Vigni, F. (2012), 'La maschera, il potere, la solitudine', *Il cinema di Paolo Sorrentino*, Firenze: Aska.

Zagarrio, V. (2012), 'L'eredità del neorealismo nel New-new Italian Cinema', *Annali d'Italianistica*, 30, pp. 95–112.

Zagarrio, V. (2016), 'Una certa tendenza del cinema italiano', *Fulgor*, 5:1, pp. 1–8.

4

Paolo Sorrentino's Cinematic Excess

Lydia Tuan

Yale University

When Paolo Sorrentino was awarded the Academy Award for Foreign Language Film in 2014 for *La grande bellezza* (*The Great Beauty*) (2013), he thanked Federico Fellini, amongst other directors, to little surprise (Oscars 2014). As his Academy Award-winning feature has often been compared to Fellini's *La dolce vita* (1960) and *8½* (1963), critics have noted, both in enduring praise and harsh criticism, that Sorrentino's portrayal of Rome merely updates Fellini's vision of Rome to reflect the Berlusconi era of near-present day – or that it has fallen short of imitating Fellini by pandering to Roman cultural stereotypes to assuage American mainstream audiences (Kliemann 2014).

With the internationally acclaimed *The Great Beauty*, and *The Young Pope* (2016) as his first foray into episodic television, Sorrentino continues to attract critical attention as a director and is becoming an increasingly popular reference for contemporary Italian cinema, which has accumulated considerable debate on the originality of his directorial style. Select observant viewers, for example, have parodied Sorrentino's flair for dramatic slow-motion and excessively theatrical lines in a fan-made video entitled 'Ogni Maledetto Natale (secondo i registi italiani)' ('Every damn Christmas [According to Italian directors]') (2014), which speculates how Sorrentino would have filmed a 'cinepanettone', the genre of Italian farcical films typically released during the Christmas holiday season starting from the 1980s. The video's protagonist ominously and sarcastically deadpans via voice-over while the party ebbs and flows around him in slow motion, 'I didn't just want to participate in the Christmas Tombola game [an Italian bingo-like board game that is traditionally played during Christmas time]. I wanted the power to make it fail'[1] ('The Jackal 2014) – a parody of protagonist Jep Gambardella's dramatically communicated desire to dominate the elite Roman social scene in *The Great Beauty*, 'I didn't just want to go to the parties. I wanted to have the power to make them fail!'. This fan parody picks up on Sorrentino's remarkable style, and this article will pursue an exploration of that signature style through Sorrentino's formal treatment of time and space primarily in *The Great Beauty*, with occasional glances at his other works, namely, *L'uomo in più* (*One Man Up*) (Sorrentino, 2001), *Il divo* (Sorrentino, 2008) and *The Young Pope*.

Locating the distinctiveness in Sorrentino's style, Alex Marlow-Mann observed that Sorrentino writes protagonists that are difficult for viewers to identify with:

> One of the most immediately obvious characteristics of his work is a penchant for ambiguous or downright unsympathetic protagonists [...]. The extent to which the spectator is, or is not, encouraged to 'identify' with such atypical protagonists constitutes one of the most unusual and distinctive elements of Sorrentino's films, particularly *Le conseguenze dell'amore* and *L'amico di famiglia*.
>
> (2010: 162)

Even after 2010, in films such as *The Great Beauty* and *Youth* (2015), Sorrentino has continued largely in the same vein with *The Young Pope*. Its protagonist Lenny Belardo (Jude Law) alienates not only the show's viewers but also its supporting characters. The conflicts in each episode arise from the growing rift between Lenny and the other cardinals, who are collectively perplexed by the ideological conservatism of the youngest pope in Catholic history. Irrespective of whether Sorrentino encourages or dissuades viewers from identifying with his protagonists or not, the development of the protagonist remains central for Sorrentino; he may not be explicitly vying for the empathy of his viewers, but he does convey the protagonist's character and his inner emotional toils audiovisually rather than through dialogue. Explorations of these unlikeable, morally flawed protagonists' personalities, behaviours, motives and enigmatic histories are visually rendered with careful attention to cinematic formal properties. The topic of identity search generally motivates Sorrentino's narratives; his films approach their conclusion when the protagonists uncover a revelation about themselves or reveal a secret from their past. Usually male and at least middle aged, these protagonists are in a constant state of suspension, professionally and emotionally detached as they overly indulge in activities that stray away from their professions, which they find to be draining and exhausting their private selves. The two protagonists in *One Man Up*, both named Antonio Pisapia, lose their jobs as a singer (Toni Servillo) and athlete (Andrea Renzi), respectively, leading Servillo's Pisapia to prolonged unemployment and driving Renzi's Pisapia to suicide. *The Great Beauty*'s Jep Gambardella, a novelist who has self-imposed a hiatus on his writing career after the success of his alleged magnum opus, *The Human Apparatus*, 40 years ago, now spends his evenings wandering from party to party. The commonality amongst these protagonists is clear; even though they *have* professions, they are not working *in* them – and the peculiarity of this shared isolation from their careers, physical environments and social settings, for example, is interestingly reflected in the films' visual tone, specifically through formal treatments of cinematic time and space that, through frequency, integrate into Sorrentino's unique cinematic grammar.

This article considers how Sorrentino employs a distinctive cinematic style that is linked to theories of cinematic excess, particularly those posited by Kristin Thompson. It will begin, first, by discussing style and its relation to excess, given that both terms have often been understood by preceding scholarship to be in opposition. Departing from the oft-discussed role of excess in cinematic content (i.e., narrative), I then delve into a consideration of the potential role of excess in cinematic form, particularly in time and space as previously mentioned. This effort will be carried out in two sections. Analysing four of Sorrentino's films that prolifically represent his filmography, the first section attends to Sorrentino's formal treatment of cinematic time and the second to space. Employing Elizabeth Freeman's notion of chronobiopolitics (2010), I argue that Sorrentino frequently slows down or speeds up time to portray his protagonists' thoughts, memories and flashbacks in a way that parallels their suspended states. The second section addresses Sorrentino's treatment of cinematic spaces, proposing that frequent presenting and re-presenting of previously viewed spaces is demonstrative of spatial excess, a style that is apparent within the particularity behind Sorrentino's use of daytime and night time spaces in *The Great Beauty* and within the mobility (and immobility) of Sorrentino's protagonists that reflect their characters through the accessibility of spaces to viewers. Drawing on Henri Lefebvre's attribution of capital production to the creation of space in *The Production of Space* (1991), this second half communicates the importance of Sorrentino's walking protagonists, who, through their physical mobility, construct an identity of themselves in relation to their physical surroundings. Altogether, this venture of ascribing Sorrentino with a style could, in effect, distinguish him from his Italian predecessors, namely Federico Fellini, and hopefully shed light on and prompt further enquiry of novel formal approaches within contemporary Italian cinema.

Excess as Style

To inclusively acknowledge the vast scholarship on cinematic style and excess would be no small feat; as such, this section will discuss select perspectives that build the foundation for my proposed formulation of Sorrentino's style as excess. David Bordwell notes that style 'simply names the film's systematic use of cinematic devices', in which recognition of film's technical use of formal devices cues viewers to construct a story from the film that they see (1985: 50). In contrast, John David Rhodes suggests that style is not a characteristic of a work but is labour itself:

> When we 'see' style, we see the mark of human labor, a density, an opacity in the image/work/text. Style, when we 'see' it, is something we cannot see through. We stare at it, but not through it. It is the material register – the substratum – of the work. It is no less material than other parts of the work's surface that do not strike us (as style), but unlike those parts of the work's surface, the part that 'is' style (that is marked as style) returns us to the materiality of the work.
>
> Style gathers together and separates and is, moreover, the name of this gathering and separation. It is a kind of effortful activity, perhaps a kind of labor. Style is repetition.
>
> (2012: 49)

Rhodes' treatment of labour is not Marxist but derives from Hannah Arendt's perception of labour to form the basis of his argument for style as the mark of human labour. If identities are conceived through repetition of certain behaviours and attitudes that consolidate into one identity, this would underscore what we mean when we say that someone *has style* and suggest that identity and style are both marks of human labour. The proposition that *style is labour* would thus be fundamental in grasping Sorrentino's beautiful and stylish aesthetic. The repetitive characteristic of style that echoes the repetitive nature of labour suggests how repeated formal choices constitute a director's style. Style becomes identified as a form of labour that does not and cannot alienate labourers from their work because it is labour that constructs identity – here recognized as the work itself.

Interestingly, Sorrentino's own formal choices strive for aesthetic perfection as Sorrentino tends to prefer placing viewer attention towards the centremost part of the frame and symmetrically framing his shots. This centre-framing is accentuated by manipulations of time and space around the protagonist that often work to frame him. For example, when we are first introduced to Jep Gambardella's emotionally conflicted character in *The Great Beauty*, he lights a cigarette in the middle of a vibrant dance sequence with an emotionally removed expression as people dance on his left and right. Two temporalities are visible in this sequence: the dancers', whose movements are exaggeratedly slowed down, and Jep's, whose movements progress at an untampered pace. This temporal split – and aural isolation, as the sound of the party is more muted and broken down in harmony with the temporal change to underscore the sound of Jep's movements – between Jep and his party guests function as centre-framing, as viewers continue to identify with the movements that are happening in real time; the slower temporality of his surroundings highlights Jep as the central focus of this scene. Spatially, the dancers' symmetrical positions flank Jep, crowding and shrinking his stature into the narrow divide in the centre of the profilmic event both visually and diegetically. Altogether, Sorrentino creates a personal moment in this scene between the spectator and the protagonist; by playing with temporalities audio-visually and spatially framing his protagonist into the centre, Sorrentino depicts his protagonists' psychological states through a kind of first-person storytelling that always places the protagonist, formally and diegetically, in the centre of the shot. Sorrentino's effort in directing viewer attention collectively to the centre of the frame exemplifies an attempt to produce a collective subjectivity for viewers. However meticulously crafted, Sorrentino's style induces a viewing practice that is interestingly not as meticulous; viewers who pick up on Sorrentino's style will know to look at the centre of the screen.

As mentioned previously, style and excess have been treated as contrasting terms, making the notion of *excess as style* a relatively undiscussed formulation, and frequent uses of the term 'excess' in film criticism have often referred to the film's narrative content and genre rather than its form. For example, excess has been linked to the genre of extreme cinema, where graphically explicit themes of terror, violence and sex appear for shock value. Pier Paolo Pasolini's *Salò e le 120 giornate di Sodoma (120 Days of Sodomy)* (1975) is one such example that utilizes extreme horror and sexual violence (Curti and La Selva 2007: 246–47), and Italian genre films such as *mondo* documentaries of the 1960s and the 1970s have additionally been acknowledged as excess films. Linda Williams points out that the excess genres of pornography, horror and melodrama use the body as a medium to excessively heighten elements of pleasure, fear and pain, respectively; their label as excess genres derives from acts of spectacular violence often made towards or on the body (1991: 7). Considering excess as a formal element, Kristin Thompson distinguishes style from excess by proposing that style is 'the use of repeated techniques which become *characteristic* of the work' whereas cinematic excess constitutes the other non-characteristic elements that do not follow the remarked style, creating discordance in the unity of the work:

> Excess does not equal style, but the two are closely linked because they both involve the material aspects of the film. Excess forms no specific patterns which we could say are characteristic of the work. But the formal organization provided by style does not exhaust the material of the filmic techniques, and a spectator's attention to style might as well lead to a noticing of excess as well.
>
> (Thompson 1977: 55–56)

61

Similar to Rhodes, Thompson agrees that style involves repetition: the repetition of techniques that leads to its recognition as style. But what if excess similarly involves repetition at such a frequency that it, too, becomes the style? Thompson dissociates excess from style when she notes that 'excess forms no specific patterns', implying that excess cannot be style as it is already the term that denotes aspects that do not play a unifying role in the film's materiality. Excess also encapsulates filmic elements that are 'problematic or unclear' (1977: 60–61), such as when settings or objects are visually presented incompletely, and, even more simply, anachronistic errors that have been overlooked in the finalization of the film. Excess, for Thompson, thus holds as much hermeneutic importance as style does; in fact, noticing the tensions between style and excess is often the departing point for salient criticisms.

Not fully in accordance with Thompson, however, the definition of excess treated in this article borrows a more literal meaning of the term – in the sense of considering excess as extra, overflow, surplus, 'more than' an anticipated quantity – to argue that Sorrentino employs a style that relies on techniques (such as centre-framing) used to an excessive amount, formulating the notion of *excess as style*. The consequences of this style, in addition to its intense aestheticism, impact how viewers understand the inner turmoil of Sorrentino's protagonists, which, as I will demonstrate, is visually conveyed through excessive treatments of time and space. Therefore, this article will step away from Thompson's understanding of excess to consider the term more literally and propose that excess can be stylistic of a film or even its director.

Temporal Excess

Two ways in which Sorrentino manipulates time in his style of excess are through an excessive use of slow motion and flashbacks. Other stylistic elements, however, also include Sorrentino's penchant for lengthy establishing shots in which Sorrentino sets the scene and gauges the tone of the atmosphere, more than needed merely to establish the shot. For the sake of inclusivity, I will mention it here with brevity. At two-and-a-half hours' duration, *The Great Beauty* opens with a party sequence that begins with five minutes of fleeting close-ups of a few partygoers' faces and then pulls back via crane shot to establish the scene as a party before Jep's face appears around the ten-minute mark – a literal signification of cinematic excess that pulls viewers out of the narrative to question directorial intent, making long establishing shots one of the key excessive qualities in Sorrentino's aesthetics.[2] Despite Sorrentino's interesting usage of lengthy establishing shots, this section will now focus on only two of his techniques, namely slow motion and flashbacks, as time-related indicators for his style of cinematic excess.

Manipulations of time have, of course, appeared in film's engagements with labour and modernity such as Fritz Lang's *Metropolis* (1927) and Dziga Vertov's *Man with a Movie Camera* (1929), where labour is organized by time through speeding up cinematic time to depict the technological advances of modernity. In contrast, Sorrentino never uses fast motion, and, in favour of slow motion, depicts slowness by prompting spectators to engage slowly with the concept of decline. In *Il divo*, the entrance of each member of Giulio Andreotti's faction, *la corrente andreottiana* ('Andreotti's party wing'),[3] near the beginning of the film is presented in slightly exaggerated slow motion to depict the danger and corruption of the faction and to heighten intimidation in viewers and anticipation of what is to come. Presented dramatically, the slowness of the scene is accentuated by the non-diegetic music that layers more suspense onto the scene, contributing to the slowness of its pace with the occasional whistling that is timed to indicate the introduction of a new member. In a later scene when the paparazzi take photos of Andreotti's seventh government, Sorrentino slows down time again (and even slows down diegetic sound before fading it out) to allow for Andreotti's narration of his emotions in voice-over, a technique that explicitly gives viewers access to Andreotti's thoughts.

In *The Great Beauty*, Sorrentino slows down time to elongate it and to represent decay and decline with respect to Jep's career and age. Elongation of time visually exaggerates the temporality of the labour process, dramatizing construction as it does with decay to allow for sensuous engagements with the rapidity of passing time. The slowing down of time in *The Great Beauty* draws attention to the biological timelines of the characters as we consume them in cinematic time. Revisiting the introduction of Jep's character in *The Great Beauty*, this time with greater clarity, we may consider that Sorrentino's introduction of Jep's emotional state of distress occurs when the festivities of the party are slowed down. As Jep exits the synchronized dance around him, he steps into the space in between to light a cigarette, and as the camera slowly inches towards him, we see a close-up of his exhausted face (see Figures 4.1 and 4.2).

The camera lingers on Jep's fatigued expression while diegetic sound fades away to welcome Jep's voice-over, producing the impression that amidst wild festivity, Jep is an outlier to not only the pace of the party, as evidenced by the contrasting timelines, but also, in a formal aspect, as Jep, not dancing, has taken repose as the dancers symmetrically frame him on both sides. As already mentioned, the employment of slow-motion here highlights two timelines: the glacial movement of the dancers and Jep's. The two timelines actualize Elizabeth Freeman's notion of chronobiopolitics, which uses Foucauldian biopolitics to propose that the importance of labour lies in its organization by time:

In a chronobiological society, the state and other institutions, including representational apparatuses, link properly temporalized bodies to narratives of movement and change. These are teleological schemes of events or strategies for living such as marriage, accumulation of health, and wealth for the future, reproduction, childrearing, and death and its attendant rituals. [...] In the eyes of the state, this sequence of socioeconomically 'productive' moments is what it means to have a life at all.

(Freeman 2010: 5)

From Freeman's perspective, progress is defined by the production of material labour (or in Arendt's terms, 'work'); to have worked – or to have produced a

FIGURE 4.1: *Dancers frame Jep (Toni Servillo) from both sides. Paolo Sorrentino (dir.)*, The Great Beauty, *2013*.

FIGURE 4.2: *Close-up of Jep's (Toni Servillo) face highlighting his exhaustion and distinguishing him from his surroundings. Paolo Sorrentino (dir.)*, The Great Beauty, *2013*.

work – is what it means to have a life. Labour, in this sense, is done to produce work, and so labouring without the production of work would be unproductive; Marx's notion of unproductive labour agrees with this reasoning. Chronobiopolitics, Freeman argues, is also inherently cyclical; it depends on repetition over time, which also characterizes labour and style within Sorrentino, who conveys Jep's chronobiological crisis by playing with screen time – specifically slow motion. In this introductory birthday party sequence in *The Great Beauty*, Jep's timeline is not 'synchronized', to apply Freeman's terminology, with everyone else's – the 'larger temporal schemae' – so Jep does not 'experience belonging itself as natural' (2010: 5). The slower movements of the dancers around Jep frame his central position by underscoring his faster timeline and deliberately give us access to his thoughts. Sorrentino does not use the slow or long take to capture the natural stillness of the everyday, as in, say, Michelangelo Frammartino's *Le quattre volte* (*The Four Times*) (2010) (see Galt 2013: 54). Rather, he employs the long take with slow motion to frame the protagonist as the primary object of viewer attention, exemplifying Sigfried Kracauer's description that 'slow-motion shots parallel regular close-ups; they are, so to speak, temporal close-ups, achieving in time what the close-up proper is achieving in space' (1997: 53).

Freeman's idea that '[c]hronobiopolitics harnesses not only sequence but also cycle, the dialectical companion to sequence, for the idea of time as cyclical stabilizes its forward movement, promising renewal rather than rupture' (2010: 5) is critical to understanding Sorrentino's protagonists. Their shared state of not working unites them in professional stasis and, consequently, plays a formative role in shaping their identities, which we similarly perceive to be as slow in development or as static as they are described. Sorrentino's use of slow motion in *The Great Beauty* allows viewers to not only visualize the temporal process of decay but to also experience it optically, in the sense that the slowness of the scene relaxes viewer attention to parallel the slow progression of Jep's professional and biological decline. In other words, to convey the feeling of his protagonists' professional suspension, Sorrentino suspends the very act of engaging with the scene, drawing out the length of the shot to strain viewer concentration. *Sight and Sound* editor Nick James' critique of slow cinema's ability to '[lull] its viewers into complacency by asking them to dwell excessively in an image [...] squander[s] "great swathes of our precious time to achieve quite fleeting and slender aesthetic and political effects"' and is applicable here (Schoonover 2012: 66). Although Sorrentino's film is not slow cinema, his use of slow motion shows some affinity with it. Karl Schoonover calls this engagement with the long take 'a more active and politically present viewing practice – an engagement commended for the intensity of its perception' (2012: 66). Sorrentino builds his protagonists on the idea that they are suspended only because they do not have a solid understanding of their own identities. It is only by viewing the film in the same way – suspended from understanding the identities of protagonists who do not yet know themselves and are, therefore, suspended characters – that we come to understand their identities, histories and the effects of their actions.

As much as Sorrentino's manipulation of time produces the effect of decay and decline, it also has the effect of preservation, especially in flashback sequences. Like Sorrentino's slow motion, flashbacks disrupt the teleology of cinematic time, but dissimilar to slow motion, they manipulate diegetic time during the disruption. Jep frequently recalls his first love, Elisa de Santis, after learning about her death, and his memory of her is slowly pieced together and clarified through repetition until *The Great Beauty* concludes with its full reconstruction (see Figure 4.3).

In the first flashback to the memory, Jep is swimming in the sea, and as a boat approaches him, he ducks underwater. When he rises back to the surface, we see a younger Jep, confirming that we are in a flashback. Jep's relationship with Elisa is explicated in a consequent flashback when we learn that Jep lost his virginity to her on that very beach. Sorrentino portrays this memory via the multiple flashbacks scattered throughout his film, and its piecemeal presentation eggs viewers to reconstruct the memory together with Jep. Flashbacks create temporal excess in the sense that we are repeatedly pulled out of the main cinematic timeline and thrust back to an earlier moment in the protagonist's personal timeline. Altogether, the conflation of timelines in this film indicates how Sorrentino's cinematic excess is articulated temporally.

Sorrentino's employment of flashbacks in this film recalls their appearance in his debut, *One Man Up*, as Toni Servillo's Tony Pisapia recalls a memory on the beach with his mother and brother in three flashback moments. Details of the memory are slowly revealed over the three flashbacks; in the second, we learn that the woman

FIGURE 4.3: *Jep's (Toni Servillo) flashback of the beach with Elisa. Paolo Sorrentino (dir.),* The Great Beauty, *2013.*

in the cloak who passes Tony at first is his mother, and in the third flashback, we learn that the man in diving gear in front of Tony is his brother, the athletic Pisapia. Alternatively, Sorrentino's use of flashbacks in *The Young Pope* takes place in dreams and communicates idealization. Lenny recurrently dreams about his parents' abandonment of him (to preserve that memory) and the future moment when he might meet his parents in his adult life (to idealize the perfect meeting). Flashbacks themselves are not unusual filmic devices: the *excessive* element lies in Sorrentino's preference to allude repeatedly to one memory in flashback sequences, which places viewers into the protagonists' perspective and tasks them similarly with recall. Sorrentino's employment of flashbacks thus affixes an oneiric quality to his temporal excess, which may find precedent in the Freudian perspective of dreaming as a laborious act in what he called 'dreamwork', in which the cyclical task of recollection and memory preservation requires a routine effort that recalls the repetitive demands of labour.[4]

As a whole, the effect produced by Sorrentino's manipulation of cinematic time is affect. For a director to have an affective style, the film's formal arrangements need to disrupt the cerebral hermeneutics of viewing; in other words, it needs to draw attention to its own odd arrangement for affect to be triggered. We could argue that Sorrentino is invested in building an affect of confusion and uncertainty in his viewers by breaking conventional temporal arrangements and spatial coordinates signal to viewers that such conventions have indeed been broken. Confronted with Sorrentino's nonlinear temporalities, the spectator seems to be expected to piece together the temporal sequences of events in a sensible fashion to understand the development of the protagonist, which is often the main narrative source itself, as Sorrentino builds his narratives around people, specifically his protagonist, rather than the events that take place around him.[5] We now turn to his complementary excessive use of space.

Spatial Excess

In the opening of *The Great Beauty*, Sorrentino immerses viewers into a sublime state of imagination and wonder through fast, sweeping camera movements that invite them to survey the city and be overwhelmed by an expansiveness of Rome that the camera cannot capture. The Janiculum scene at the beginning of this film closes on a collapsed tourist, and as the camera tightens on the man, viewers are barred from accessing the outward cityscape, entrapped by the very camera that was just moments before dynamically soaring through a portion of Rome. This scene interestingly reduces Rome into three stereotypical archetypes: the chorus that stands for Rome's sanctity, the Japanese tourists who represent Rome's tourism and the sculptures that reflect the city's historical importance. Space, in this sense, is not maximized and minimized like it is in *The Great Beauty*'s night-time parties. Instead, the façade of Rome as the seraphic, historically and culturally rich Italian capital resonates. Its diversity is communicated in one space and one shot, although this image abruptly vanishes with the rough-cut transporting us to night-time Rome.

Sorrentino's portrayal of Rome at night and day produces contrasting depictions of the spaces in the city, but even his night-time scenes of Rome are inconsistent. Sorrentino's Rome seems purer in the day and more grotesque at night (but only during parties), as if to portray a city that exposes its true form after sunset. Within the theatrical staginess of *The Great Beauty*'s parties, rawness underpins these festivities, exemplified by the escalating sexual tension bordering on bestial eroticism. Despite the seemingly precise nature of the choreography in the scene's synchronized dances, Sorrentino couples it with the mariachi players and screaming women who disrupt the dominant house music and physically interfere in the profilmic space, contributing towards a cacophony that audibly and optically disrupts the aesthetic modalities of the shot. The night-time party scenes, along with Jep's slow and languid nightly stroll across the city (which are not grotesque but rather awe-some), present Rome's complexities as a city when its saintly façade has faded. Contrastingly, in *Il divo*, Giulio Andreotti languishes across town in a domineering way that highlights him as the source of political decay and corruption infecting the streets of Rome. Also in *The Young Pope*, Lenny strives to be an invisible pope, giving his homily while shrouded in darkness and exploring Vatican City only at night and on foot.

This section considers Sorrentino's spatial excess from two approaches: first, to ruminate on the repetition of previously introduced spaces as spatial cinematic excess that is often executed through frequent maximizations and minimizations of spaces, and second, to consider how the excessive frequency of walking scenes in Sorrentino's films gives life to spaces and defines the characters walking through or standing in them. The latter approach also argues that walking scenes, which one may assume to be establishing or transition scenes, actually serve a salient diegetic function.

Sorrentino presents space by maximizing and minimizing it. To understand where these spatial arrangements occur demands a return to Jep's birthday scene in *The Great Beauty*. The continued exchange of close-ups and wide shots, of zooming in on certain characters and then zooming out to capture everyone collectively, repeatedly minimizes and expands space. The extensive screen time spent establishing the scene prior to introducing Jep demonstrates not only temporal excess, as noted before, but also spatial excess. But how do we view Sorrentino's formal decisions in this scene as spatially excessive in the same way that they are temporally excessive? What we see here is not the expansion of space relative to other spaces that we see within the film but, perhaps, an increase in the importance that we attribute to that space. This would imply that the amount of screen time given to a space corresponds to its importance relative to other spaces in the film. Spatial excess, prompted by temporal excess (or the large swathes of time that Sorrentino gives to establishing location), thus makes us reconsider the roles of surplus value and functional value when considering the value of spaces in *The Great Beauty*.

Spatial excess infers that repetition of space can multiply narrative possibilities. Close-ups of Jep's friends allow us to take on different subject perspectives as we search for potential protagonists to follow, offering the possibility that any of the characters we see in close-up might be the protagonist or another important character. Most pertinent to the idea of spatial excess, however, is the impression of space being 'doubled' or 'tripled' as we re-view spaces that have been filmed before; such is to claim that spatial repetition creates a surplus of space. Access to multiple perspectives offers the advantage of reconstructing or reconfiguring the spatial logics of a given setting. Sorrentino does not present the space as one might physically traverse it but, instead, disorients viewers who are left to reconfigure spaces through their own visual interpretation. Claudio Bisoni, arguing that Sorrentino's staging of space is his trademark style, notes that Sorrentino always begins with an extreme close-up and then slowly expands the space by subsequently pulling back to allow viewers to associate that object with its surroundings, which slowly come into view. An example can be found in the opening scene of *One Man Up*; Sorrentino begins with a close-up of the coach emptying his pockets on a nearby table, jump cuts to a sweating footballer shaking nervously across the room and then jumps back to a close-up of the coach, tracking the jacket that he angrily swings at the wall. Pulling back from that wall, Sorrentino reveals the locker room setting, associating the coach as the central figure (or the subject) of the space (and, coincidentally, the cinematic frame) as he admonishes his team. Second, Bisoni notes, Sorrentino films space in fragments rather than as a whole. This staging evinces Sorrentino's self-conscious effort to locate

> his work in a 'post-realist' dimension. [...] his critics would nevertheless contend that he has a smug and self-affirming style that is ultimately vacant, incapable of presenting a precise image of, and more interested in visual originality than in narrative and thematic consistency.
>
> (Bisoni 2016: 253–54)

By beginning with the close-up and then pulling back, we associate the subject of the close-up (usually a character or an object) with the space that Sorrentino consequently expands. In other words, Sorrentino's staging spatially frames the object into the centre of the shot – diegetically, although not always aesthetically in the viewer's spectatorial sensorium. Starting with a close-up, Sorrentino films in fragments; he opens a scene with a 'fragment' of the space – the subject of the close-up – before expanding it. This technique recalls Thompson's definition of excess, where she associates partially visible settings with excess because they confound understanding of spatial relations. While the close-up of the coach emptying his pockets in *One Man Up* does not explicitly *confound* the scene's spatial relations, it certainly influences it as viewers recognize the action as comprising of one aspect of the setting. Beginning the scene with a close-up also creates surplus space through minimization (by the close-up) and maximization (by pulling back). Surplus space and fragmented spaces disrupt spatial unity and require attentive observation from the spectator, who is charged with arranging spatial cohesion and predicting the setting until it is completely revealed.

Walking scenes in Sorrentino's films also underscore his style of excess in two ways: frequency and duration. The protagonists do not always walk to a destination, and they are often seen walking alone. In his seminal text *The Production of Space*, Henri Lefebvre offers a definition of space as 'not a thing among other things, nor a product among other products: rather, it subsumes things produced, and encompasses their interrelationships in their coexistence and simultaneity – their (relative) order and/or (relative) disorder' (1991: 73). The title of his text – the *production* of spaces – underscores the ways in which space is produced from the perspective of Marxist capital production and labour. What does it mean to labour in a space? If walking in a space constitutes *labouring*, then we could argue that Sorrentino's protagonists construct their surroundings by walking. Along with objects, the protagonists' footsteps are part of the subject of the shot, centrally framed (in a diegetic sense) by their surroundings as they walk. If walking can form the walker's identity and rewrite his surroundings, then walking should constitute a form of labour, much as verbal speech acts constitute a development of identity. If the footsteps of Sorrentino's protagonists can produce their identity, then the role of these walking scenes offers access to characters' thoughts, much like how Sorrentino's employment of slow-motion functions as a spatially mediated close-up of the character's interiority.

According to Matthew Flanagan, the popularity of walking scenes began in European modernist cinema during the 1950s and the 1960s, developing a 'cinema of walking', wherein

> emotional restraint began to suppress dramatic incident and the themes of alienation, isolation and boredom usurped the weight of familiar conflict. As aesthetic of slow exaggerates tendency toward de-dramatisation, draining emotional distance and narrative obfuscation even further by extending the stretches of *temps mort* and subordinating non-events to extended duration within the shot.
>
> (2008)

While Sorrentino's employment of walking scenes does not make him a filmmaker of the 'cinema of walking' that Flanagan describes (as he considers cinema of walking to be a precursor to the development of slow cinema), it is still worthwhile to observe how the role of walking scenes functions differently in Sorrentino. Other films with prominent walking scenes include Michelangelo Antonioni's *L'avventura* (1960) and *La notte* (1961), where his female protagonists' languid strolls underscore the slowness of Antonioni's long take. In *L'avventura*, walking scenes are justified with a purpose; the female characters are often seen walking to a destination or walking with a motivation. Sorrentino's male protagonists, on the other hand, do not walk with the same incentive. Jep wanders the streets of Rome aimlessly after his parties, promenading to delay his journey home or to seek other sources of entertainment along his path. In *Il divo*, Andreotti's slow, gliding walk suggests that he, too, wanders, even though, as a political leader, he covertly dominates the streets that he walks on. Walking, in both films, carries a leisurely undertone, but it also 'produces' in the Lefebvrian sense, actualizing and livening the spaces in which they walk. Walking, for Sorrentino, is no longer about de-dramatizing; instead, walking *is* the source of dramatization.

In *Il divo*, Andreotti prowls through the narrow streets of Rome with a line of patrol cars and armed officers that trail behind and around him as he heads to early morning mass, framing his body as the central subject of the shot (see Figure 4.4). In the first occurrence of Andreotti's walking scenes, Sorrentino does not maximize and minimize space like he does in *The Great Beauty*'s nighttime party scenes. Andreotti is shot against a wall, the slow camera paralleling his slow movements. Accompanied by soft, lulling music, the scene attempts to attach a sense of serenity to Andreotti's stroll, although the placement of cars and officers

FIGURE 4.4: *Andreotti (Toni Servillo) walking while framed by patrol cars and armed men. Paolo Sorrentino (dir.)*, Il divo, *2008.*

around Andreotti shielding him from every conceivable angle of danger contradicts the serenity that the scene tries to achieve with the languidness of the shot and its assuasive non-diegetic music. Positioning Andreotti against a wall should put his stature to scale against the wall, making him appear petite and negligible against the city that overshadows over him. But such is not the case. When Andreotti spots 'Massacres and conspiracies bear the signatures of Craxi and Andreotti' graffitied on the wall, he halts, and the camera zooms in slightly on Andreotti's face before swerving behind him to display the words from his perspective. As the camera rises above his head, the space of the street is minimized and narrowed, reducing the depth of the city. Here, the minimization of space is not only created by the angle of Sorrentino's camera but also by Andreotti himself, who is stealthily in complete control of his surroundings. His expressionless features convey to viewers that he is unperturbed, as the towering angle of the shot makes Andreotti loom over the message and slyly control it – and the city – with his power and clout. Here, Andreotti's domination is explicitly conveyed through a manipulation of space: Rome shrinks around him as he walks.

Alternatively, in the walking scenes of *The Great Beauty*, Sorrentino's protagonist harmoniously integrates into the ambience and scenery of a more expansive Rome. Before Jep meets Ramona for the first time, we see him strolling along Via Veneto in solitude after a party. This scene does not begin with a close-up; instead, Sorrentino starts by showing Jep crossing a sparsely populated section of Via Veneto, foregrounding how the street, once portrayed as the vibrant 'epicenter of social life in Fellini's *La dolce vita*', is nearly desolate at night time.[6] This desolate, defamiliarized view of Via Veneto further emphasizes the oneiric and detached aspects of Sorrentino's night-time Rome in *The Great Beauty*. The camera then swerves to capture Jep as he is nearly hit by a limousine while crossing. Looking into the car's dashboard, he spots a woman staring blankly, her face blanched from a night of excessive leisure. In contrast to Andreotti's glacial yet assertive gait, Jep seemingly blends into Via Veneto as he ambles across it; he is nearly run over by a car as if he were invisible, and the fact that Sorrentino does not begin with a close-up of him makes him less central to the scene. Despite blending into the street, however, Jep is still central to his walk because the camera never rises above or lowers below Jep's line of sight. Although Sorrentino's camera distances from Jep at moments to capture his movements from interior spaces as he walks on the street, it still tracks him at eye level, expanding space according to his pedestrian movements. Jep, unlike Andreotti, does not impose himself onto the space; his footsteps in this scene, and in *The Great Beauty* generally, unveil Rome's diversity and underscore his lack of individuality within Rome.

Drawing on Michel de Certeau's notion of the concept city, in which walking constructs a lived experience from a unique pedestrian perspective, Alessia Martini similarly argues that Sorrentino's Rome in *The Great Beauty* is a city narrated and unveiled through the footsteps of its characters. Through the protagonists' movements and manner of moving, Martini claims, Sorrentino rewrites Rome into themes of decadence and decline, disassociating from its historical, real-life connotations (2015: 110). De Certeau's notion of the concept city follows from the idea that walking brings the city to life, allowing it to be understood 'from below'. He writes:

> There is a rhetoric of walking. The art of 'turning' phrases finds an equivalent in an art of composing a path (*tourner un parcours*). Like ordinary language, this art implies and combines styles and uses. Style specifies 'a linguistic structure that manifests on the symbolic level [...] an individual's fundamental way of being in the world'; it connotes a singular. [...] Style and use both have to do with a 'way of operating' (of speaking, walking, etc.), but style involves a peculiar processing of the symbolic, while use refers to elements of a code. They intersect to form a style of use, a way of being and a way of operating.
>
> (de Certeau 1984: 100)

Sorrentino's dream-like Rome seems disjointed from Rome in real life (much like in *La dolce vita*), and, as observed in *The Great Beauty* and *Il divo*, Jep and Andreotti's pedestrian movements offer two visions of Rome that bring to the fore two identities and two relationships with the streets. For de Certeau, walking in a certain way or direction and picking one path over another are 'pedestrian speech acts' that reflect the walker's style. Thus, style is equated with the selection of routes that one chooses to take when walking through the city, and a selected combination of any trajectory would be considered a styled arrangement of spatial organization reflective of the walker's identity. Considering the role and manipulations of spaces in Sorrentino is thus useful because, as de Certeau proposes, 'it is assumed that practices of space also correspond to manipulations of the basic elements of a constructed order' (1984: 100). Walking thus produces the protagonist's identity by associating the character with the space, but simultaneously, the protagonist's footsteps also responsively redefine the space in which he walks. Exposure to Rome in *The Great Beauty*, for example, is largely conveyed through Jep's pedestrian perspective.

Let us now turn to a daytime example to comprehend how spatial excess differs in the day and how a walker's immobility may even contributively define space and character. Even though Sorrentino portrays a Rome that is arguably dissociated from the actual city, he borrows real events and places to address the film's themes of cultural decay and institutional corruption. Near the beginning of the film, Dadina asks Jep to revive his writing career by reporting on the Costa

Concordia disaster, but Jep refuses. However, after Ramona's death, he visits the harbour where the Costa Concordia is shipwrecked in a seascape beyond Rome. Jep's immobility in this scene is as remarkable as his movement in the walking scenes; the stillness of his stance as he gazes at the ship symbolizes the stillness of his professional ambitions and his lack of biopolitical synchrony. Space, here, is not opened by footsteps but rather by the ship and its own stasis, which comprise the important motif. Similarly 'wrecked', Jep sees himself in the Costa Concordia; this diegetically pivotal scene is his visual confrontation with his state of non-work and decadent lifestyle.

The ship's placement might seem out of place to viewers at first as it does not diegetically follow the established sequence of events, but it bears a clear contemporary meaning of decay and disaster, and it draws connections between its significance in Italian politics and Jep's declining character.[7] Jep's stasis, along with the relatively static shots in the scene, reflects the cessation of Rome as a city and, to a larger extent, Italy as a country. Sorrentino's inclusion of an actual incident and footage in his portrayal of Rome in *The Great Beauty* contradicts claims that *The Great Beauty*'s Rome is completely ostracized from Italy in actuality.[8] As *The Great Beauty*'s Rome presents a pessimistic yet parodic vision of a state of disarray, it is not nearly 'dreamlike' enough to be dissociated from the actual city (and country).

Walking not only navigates space but also creates it, and excess is recognized as style when the characters take paths that transform the meanings of the space. The chance to think about spatial excess as part of Sorrentino's style is offered by pedestrians who mobilize access through these once inaccessible spaces. A striking example of this is when Jep takes Ramona on a tour of Rome's most beautiful and hidden palaces; the exclusivity of his access actualizes a publicly inaccessible space. As Jep and Ramona walk through this secret space, the busts, statues and paintings come into view very dimly, and she comments, '[h]ave you seen it? It seemed enormous, but it's actually really small' (Sorrentino, 2013). While Jep and Ramona walk through this space, the placement of objects in darkness leaves spectators literally and figuratively in the dark and prevents them from mapping a topology of the space, as Sorrentino presents this inaccessible space as negative or 'surplus' space. The fact that we see only portions of the space at *night* makes us doubt their existence. Similarly in *The Young Pope*, Lenny's insistence on delivering his first homily without any lighting makes him an 'unclear element'. His strong desire to be invisible leads him to embody excess and, as he preaches to his audience that they should see God before they see him, he turns himself into negative space by standing in the shadows. Lenny objectifies himself as 'surplus space' even though he is the subject of his own address (see Figure 4.5).

FIGURE 4.5: *Lenny (Jude Law) embodies negative space in this homily scene. Paolo Sorrentino (dir.)*, The Young Pope, 2016.

Conclusion

Sorrentino's style of cinematic excess, which I have demonstrated through observations of his manipulations of space, is inextricably linked to his manipulations of time. Through extended establishing shots and presentations of nonlinear cinematic timelines, Sorrentino's temporal excess and spatial excess produce each other, allowing viewers to formally engage with the idea of decay and slow destruction, which mirrors the slowness of personal decay felt by Sorrentino's protagonists through their estrangements from their professional lives. As argued by Marlow-Mann, Sorrentino tends to create protagonists that estrange viewers, but this article has attempted to show that even though Sorrentino may not directly ask viewers to identify with his protagonists, their plight and emotional turmoil are visually conveyed via Sorrentino's strong attention to cinema's formal properties (particularly through time and space), allowing viewers to not only visualize his protagonists' strife but to also affectively engage with it through the process of viewing.

In anticipation of the theoretical afterlife of cinematic excess as a term, there is clearly much potential for further interpretations of Sorrentino's excess, particularly pertaining to his excessive use of theatrical imagery and language in his films, and for applications beyond Sorrentino's films. Either considera-tion would contribute towards establishing a genre of excessive cinema, reject-ing the subordinate role of excess in extreme cinema within familiar genres such as horror, pornography and melodrama; instead, the terminology that I have proposed encourages further rumination on the potential for extreme cinema to exist as a subgenre within excessive cinema, where excess may exist as its own aesthetic style.

NOTES

1. Unless otherwise indicated, all translations from the original Italian are mine.
2. The average shot length in contemporary film is under two seconds (see Bordwell 2002: 16–28).
3. Giulio Andreotti was an influential and controversial Italian politician affiliated with the now-defunct Christian Democracy party in the 1970s. He served as minister and prime minister under multiple governments during the First Republic, defined as the post-war political period after the overthrow of Mussolini's fascist regime and the instauration of the Italian Republic in 1946 until the collapse of its party system due to corruption scandals, which led to the Italian general election in 1994. The First Republic was characterized by the dominating Christian Democracy political party and its opposition, the Italian Communist Party.
4. Consult Freud's (1922) essay 'Beyond the pleasure principle' on the repetition of dreams as an effect of trauma.
5. In a response to an interview question about his creative process, Sorrentino admits that he usually begins with a character rather than a storyline (see Zambardino 2014).
6. On the significance of Via Veneto's presence in *The Great Beauty*, see Paulicelli (2016: 189).
7. On the shipwreck as a metaphor for Italy's political history, see Povoledo (2012).
8. Refer to Martini (2015) for claims that Sorrentino's Rome does not reflect Rome's contemporary state.

REFERENCES

Arendt, Hannah (1998), *The Human Condition*, 2nd ed., Chicago, IL: University of Chicago Press.

Bisoni, Claudio (2016), 'Paolo Sorrentino: Between engagement and *savoir faire*', in C. Uva and G. Lombardi (eds), *Italian Political Cinema: Public Life, Imaginary, and Identity in Contemporary Italian Film*, Bern: Peter Lang, pp. 251–62.

Bordwell, David (1985), *Narration in the Fiction Film*, Madison: University of Wisconsin Press.

Bordwell, David (2002), 'Intensified continuity: Visual style in American film', *Film Quarterly*, 55:3, pp. 16–28.

Certeau, Michel de (1984), *The Practice of Everyday Life* (trans. S. F. Rendall), Berkeley: University of California Press.

Curti, Roberto and La Selva, Tommaso (2007), *Sex and Violence: Percorsi nel cinema estremo*, Turin: Edizioni Lindau.

Flanagan, Matthew (2008), 'Towards an aesthetic of slow in contemporary cinema', 16:9, http://www.16-9.dk/2008-11/side11_inenglish.htm. Accessed 1 June 2017.

Freeman, Elizabeth (2010), *Time Binds: Queer Temporalities, Queer Histories*, Durham: Duke University Press.

Freud, Sigmund (1922), *Beyond the Pleasure Principle* (trans. C. J. M. Hubback), London and Vienna: International Psycho-Analytical.

Galt, Rosalind (2013), 'The prettiness of Italian cinema', in L. Bayman and S. Rigoletto (eds), *Popular Italian Cinema*, London: Palgrave Macmillan, pp. 52–68.

Kliemann, Carlotta Fonzi (2014), 'Cultural and political exhaustion in Paolo Sorrentino's *The Great Beauty*', *Senses of Cinema*, 19 March, http://sensesofcinema.com/2014/feature-articles/cultural-and-political-exhaustion-in-paolo-sorrentinos-the-great-beauty/. Accessed 22 March 2017.

Kracauer, Siegfried (1997), *Theory of Film: The Redemption of Physical Reality*, Princeton: Princeton University Press.

Lefebvre, Henri (1991), *The Production of Space* (trans. D. Nicholson-Smith), Malden: Blackwell Publishing.

Marlow-Mann, Alex (2010), 'Character engagement and alienation in the cinema of Paolo Sorrentino', in W. Hope (ed.), *Italian Film Directors in the New Millennium*, Newcastle upon Tyne: Cambridge Scholars Press, pp. 161–73.

Martini, Alessia (2015), 'Concept city: Roma ri-vista e vissuta ne *La dolce vita* e *La grande bellezza*', *Carte Italiane*, 2:10, pp. 107–19.

Oscars (2014), '*The Great Beauty* wins foreign language film: 2014 Oscars', YouTube, 11 March, https://www.youtube.com/watch?v=Zdu-Tqa2udk. Accessed 8 February 2017.

Paulicelli, Eugenia (2016), 'After *La dolce vita*: *La grande bellezza*', in *Italian Style: Fashion & Film from Early Cinema to the Digital Age*, London: Bloomsbury Academic, pp. 185–93.

Povoledo, Elisabetta (2012), 'Italy finds a heroic foil for its scorned captain', *New York Times*, 19 January, http://www.nytimes.com/2012/01/20/world/europe/italians-embrace-a-hero-after-cruise-ship-accident.html. Accessed 28 May 2017.

Rhodes, John David (2012), 'Belabored: Style as work', *Framework: The Journal of Cinema and Media*, 53:1, pp. 47–64, https://core.ac.uk/download/pdf/9551728.pdf. Accessed 27 April 2017.

Schoonover, Karl (2012), 'Wastrels of time: Slow cinema's labouring body, the political spectator, and the queer', *Framework: The Journal of Cinema and Media*, 53:1, pp. 65–78, http://www.jstor.org/stable/pdf/41552300.pdf. Accessed 27 April 2017.

Sorrentino, Paolo (2001), *L'uomo in più (One Man Up)*, Italy: Key Films and Indigo Film in collaboration with TELE+.

Sorrentino, Paolo (2008), *Il divo*, Italy: Indigo Film, Parco Film, Babe Films, Studio Canal with the contribution of MiBACT and the Film Commission Regione Campania in collaboration with Sky Cinema, Arte France Cinéma, Eurimages and Centre National du Cinéma et de l'Image Animée.

Sorrentino, Paolo (2013), *La grande bellezza (The Great Beauty)*, Italy: Indigo Film, Medusa Film, Babe Films and Pathé.

The Jackal (2014), 'The Jackalshit, "OGNI MALEDETTO NATALE (secondo i registi italiani)"' ('The Jackalshit, "Every Damn Christmas [According to Italian Directors]"'), YouTube, https://www.youtube.com/watch?v=1GIVz5cPgHc. Accessed 22 December 2016.

The Young Pope (2016, USA: HBO).

Thompson, Kristin (1997), 'The concept of cinematic excess', *Ciné-Tracts: A Journal of Film, Communications, Culture, and Politics*, 1:2, pp. 54–64.

Williams, Linda (1991), 'Film bodies: Gender, genre, and excess', *Film Quarterly*, 44:4, pp. 2–13.

Zambardino, Vittorio (2014), 'L'uomo che ha riportato l'Oscar in Italia: Intervista a Paolo Sorrentino', Wired.it, 3 March, https://www.wired.it/attualita/2014/03/03/luomo-che-ha-riportato-loscar-italia-intervista-paolo-sorrentino/. Accessed 12 January 2019.

PART TWO

SORRENTINO'S REAL AND SYMBOLIC SPACES

Foto di Gianni Fiorito © WILDSIDE/SKY ITALIA/HAUT ET COURT TV/HOME
BOX OFFICE, INC./MEDIAPRO.

5

Posthuman Sorrentino:
Youth and *The Great Beauty* as Ecocinema

Matteo Gilebbi

Dartmouth College

With the term 'ecocinema' I define a cinema that intersects with ecology and reveals a biosphere that exists together with and beyond the human, particularly beyond human understanding and control.[1] Ecocinema also critically explores human-animal interactions, calls into question *homo sapiens*' exceptionalism and aims to 'challenge the conventionally humanist and anthropocentric parameters' of our world-views (Pick and Narraway 2013: 6–7). As emphasized by James Leo Cahill through his reading of the influential French theorist André Bazin, 'cinema has the virtue of producing unheimlich, unhommely [*sic*], home-less perspectives, displaced from the sheltering confidence of anthropocentrism' (2013: 76). In my interpretation, ecocinema privileges these uncanny territories and traverses them with an approach that leaves behind the human/non-human, culture/nature, sacred/profane, known/unknown dualisms, to more freely explore 'the profound and wonderful openness and intimacy of the mesh' (Morton 2010: 104) that is the entangled connections between creatures, objects, environments, perceptions and ideas. Ecocinema explores this entanglement and celebrates not only its familiarity but also its ambiguity, reproduces not only its power but also its vulnerability and exposes the revised role that humans have inside this mesh, especially in their relationship with non-humans.

In sum, ecocinema disseminates cultural and philosophical posthumanism by representing different aspects of the posthuman condition. As theorized by Rosi Braidotti, in this posthuman condition 'the binary opposition between the given and the constructed is [...] replaced by a non-dualistic understanding of nature-culture interaction' (2013: 2–3). This means that from a posthuman perspective, the boundary between human beings and animals and the differentiation between artificial and natural are 'ontologically and normatively untenable' (Calarco 2017: 237). It follows that anthropological differences, hierarchical views of existence, human exceptionalism, speciesism and anthropo-centric normativity – positions that are dominant and too often undisputed inside the western philosophical tradition – become compromised. While continuing to develop this radical and iconoclastic *pars destruens* of posthumanism is impera-tive, it is also essential for posthuman thought to develop alternative logics, ethics and ontologies, namely, outlooks able to envision and acknowledge a unified *natureculture*.[2] The rejection of the humanist model that divides society and nature needs to be accompanied by ideas and practices on which this radical repositioning of the anthroposphere can stand secure. For instance, imagining and represent-ing the posthuman condition carries an epistemological and political function: an alternative way of seeing the world and the position of humans in it can inspire an alternative way of interacting with this world, and a different form of valuing and taking part in that interaction.

The natural question here is, what will happen to traditional moral and political practices when we envision the environment as a continuum in which *anthropos* is a human-animal, that is, just one life form among many others? Our under-standing of concepts such as subjectivity, agency and responsibility must then be reconsidered. This anthropological shift depends not only on alternative ways of inhabiting the world but also on new ways of depicting it. Paolo Sorrentino's films *La grande bellezza* (*The Great Beauty*) (2013) and *Youth* (2015) possess the ability of representing this anthropological shift; therefore they can help us envision and understand *natureculture* and the role of the human-animal in it, especially when, in these films, a posthuman condition informs the interaction between the characters and their undivided natural and cultural environments. Often in Sorrentino's films the separation between the natural and the cultural spheres narrows and becomes fragile, until, at times, it even disappears. When this happens, the *cultural–human* transitions into a *more-than-human* subject belonging to an anthropological and ontological condition that reaches beyond the fallacy of the culture/nature and human/animal dichotomies. In these films, the *being natural* of the humans, their intimate entanglement with the biosphere that leaves behind the dualistic interpretation of their relationship with the environ-ment, also leaves behind the false construct of humans' complete understanding and dominance over that environment. *Anthropos* becomes just a piece of the puzzle; s/he is not the puzzle solver anymore. In *The Great Beauty* and *Youth* we can find representations of this kind of posthuman subjectivity, that is, the condition of an *anthropos* entangled with an enigmatic biosphere that exposes the restrictions and the fragility of the human condition. As pointed out by Walter Liguori, 'in front of a fragmented, inaccessible, indecipherable reality, Sorrentino's filmmaking means to raise doubts, produce ambiguity' (2017: 169). In these two films in particular, Sorrentino portrays the human facing an opaque and uncharted natureculture, looking for a way to find kinship with the complexity, the fascination and the ambiguity of an alternative ontological condition: the posthuman condition.

Youth: *The Fragility of Everything*

Seasoned director Mick Boyle (Harvey Keitel) is coming to terms with the fact that his film testament will not be completed. The female lead protagonist has just pulled out of the project, determining its failure. At a remote train station on the Swiss Alps, while waiting for a train that will take the co-authors of his screenplay home, Boyle is discussing the fiasco with them. After one shot/countershot, the camera frames the group from the front, the characters perfectly aligned from left to right, sitting, with Boyle in the middle, speaking. He is the focus of the shot, and he is also the mastermind, the person (once) in control, the great director who was working on crafting a masterpiece. However, he declares about his privileged, superior status: 'It doesn't make a difference. Men, artists, animals, plants. We are all just extras'. The camera work and the cinematographic metaphor convey an utterly straightforward idea: being at the centre, in control, as master of nature or as origin of culture, is just an illusion, a made-up dogma. Being human 'doesn't make a difference' because humans exist in an undifferentiated ecosphere where all living beings are 'just extras'. Sorrentino presents the idea of a world without protagonists, without someone at the top of the great chain of life, contesting the humanistic endorsement of human exceptionalism. This traditional humanistic view is expressed in the same scene by the lines of dialogue of Boyle's collaborators. They insist that the work of their mentor is exceptional and extremely valuable; it is the work of a great artist, the product of someone who exists above the others. According to them, he is the human demiurge who rightfully deserves the spot at the centre of creation.

But the scene closes with a long shot that includes the arrival of a train entering the frame from the left; the collaborators stand up and move away to board the train, taking with them their anthropocentric views. They are silenced and forgotten. The only person left, still at the centre of the frame, is Boyle, now alone, contemplating the consequences of his renunciation of human exceptionalism. These consequences are particularly dire for him because his identity as film director, as someone constantly and necessarily in control of his microcosm, suddenly disappears without giving him any alternative. The *pars destruens* of posthumanism might enter the territory of existential nihilism: if 'we are all just extras' then we might infer that nothing matters, while from a thorough posthuman perspective it means that *everything matters* and that no one matters more than anybody else. Sorrentino elaborates on this nihilistic risk of a misinterpreted posthuman condition in the final part of this sequence and later in the film, when Boyle commits suicide, unable to find his role in a world devoid of hierarchies and human privileges. In the final part of this sequence, Sorrentino again films Boyle alone, at the centre of the frame, surrounded by all the female characters he had ever directed, staring at him from a green slope – the visual metaphor of a natureculture where even human representations are entangled with the biosphere – asking Boyle how they should act their scenes. The camera gets closer to the director and, in a medium shot, he is depicted as staring speechless at his actresses and then looking down, dismayed, realizing his inadequacy inside his new decentred position. Nihilism is subverting the fertile outcomes of human dethroning.

This long sequence in which Boyle is trying to grasp his posthuman condition occurs almost at the end of the film, and so this realization that humans are neither special beings, nor in control of their world, is part of the film's conclusion and one of its objectives. The entire film is directed towards this final understanding of the anthropological condition, and it reaches this conclusion through a long and complex meditation on human vulnerability, and through its representation. *Youth* is, in fact, a film about human physical and psychological fragility, where 'the absurd existential experience is highlighted [...] through focusing on the experiences of its physically declining protagonists' (Simor and Sorfa 2017: 205). In *Youth*, recognizing and accepting this fragility becomes a step towards entering a posthuman condition tarnished by nihilism, but also open to interspecies solidarity.

Sorrentino, especially at the beginning of the film, strongly emphasizes the fragility of the human body, focusing especially on its decay due to old age. The camera constantly frames old bodies, the lens lingering on wrinkled skin, protruding bellies, impeded movements, often juxtaposed with images of beautiful and agile young bodies. Sorrentino indulges in extreme close-ups of Fred Ballinger's (Michael Caine) withered hand playing with a candy wrapper; he then cuts to two frail old ladies smoking cigarettes, one of them sporting a large eye patch. This is followed by three more cuts to different-aged people relaxing, exercising or meditating inside the luxury spa that is the main set of the film. Later on, Sorrentino employs a stylish overhead tracking shot to portray the fragility of soccer legend Diego Armando Maradona (Roly Serrano), emphasizing his enlarged body size, his encumbered movements and his constant need for an oxygen mask. He has become a pathetic caricature of his former glory; once legendary, his athletic skills are now almost non-existent. Sorrentino's rendering of Maradona is another example of his attempt at dismantling human pre-eminence and arrogance. Once the archetype of mastery and success, now Maradona's body is irreversibly made weak and vulnerable by time and entropy. Constantly showing the fragility of these bodies and the fundamental immanence of their existence strips them of their supposed superiority over other living beings and therefore infers a displacement of humans from the centre to the periphery.

Hence human fragility should prompt humility and become the cornerstone used to build kinship with other fragile beings instead of dominating them. Recognizing that the same frailty that we often perceive in non-human animals also resides in us should help us recognize the bond with those creatures with whom we share the same, universal decay of the body.[3] This is emphasized by Sorrentino in a scene with Ballinger, who, when alone on an alpine pasture, recognizes and directs the orphic and ethereal music played by the bells of grazing cows and the beaks of woodpeckers. Ballinger had just refused to direct an orchestra and perform in front of a human audience, but now he has no trouble playing music with other animals who have become companions that, to him, are emotionally and socially closer than his fellow humans. Old age and vulnerability is presented as an essential condition for reaching a connection and building a dialogue with animal otherness.

Another instance of Sorrentino's attempt at decentring the dominant human subject through the emphasis of decaying bodies is present in the character of Jimmy Tree (Paul Dano). Jimmy Tree is an actor staying at the luxury spa to study and develop his portrayal of Adolf Hitler for an upcoming movie. Sorrentino slowly discloses throughout *Youth* the fact that Tree is in fact learning to portray an old, tired and vulnerable Hitler by discreetly studying the movements and gestures of the elderly resort guests. Tree spends almost an entire day staying in character, living among the resort guests as Adolf Hitler. In a specific scene, the camera follows Tree/Hitler from behind while he slowly limps towards the dining hall. Sorrentino then shoots him from different angles while sitting at the table alone, observed with extreme curiosity by the other guests. There, in the still silence of the dining room, 'Hitler' eats, blows his nose, coughs, suddenly gets angry and bangs his fist on the table. This anger seems to be connected to the realization that he is brought to by his coughing, by his sniffing, by his limping and by his lowliness. Tree is embodying a tyrant who is powerless not because of a defeat in war, but because he is an old and fragile man. Even the most powerful human is nothing more – and nothing less – than another vulnerable creature submitted to the havoc that time unleashes on the materiality of his/her human body, on the materiality of any body, actually: human bodies, animal bodies, fictional bodies. Fragility is the ultimate levelling and unifying force, a factor that should make humans reconsider their anthropocentric hubris.

This connection between vulnerability, decay and human decentring reappears constantly throughout *Youth*. For instance, many dialogues between Ballinger and

Boyle revolve around their diseases, such as their prostate problems, their impressive life goals reduced to the success or failure of bodily functions. Their memories start to fail them, a topic that is discussed often by the two characters, until Ballinger concludes – his sorrowful face entrapped in one of Sorrentino's tighter close-ups – 'tremendous effort made, with a modest result'. This represents the confession of the most definitive human vulnerability, the corrosion of the *cogito*, the atrophy of that rational thinking and of those memories that more than anything else helped humans establish themselves at the top of the hierarchical chain of life.

Finally, Sorrentino throws a direct blow to anthropocentrism when, with a seven-second-long single shot, he attacks the quintessential representation of man as the measure of all things: the Vitruvian Man. As Rosi Braidotti reminds us, Da Vinci's Vitruvian Man renewed Protagoras's idea of the human subject as a universal measuring scale, as the centre of creation and as an example of perfection. The Vitruvian Man still represents a powerful humanistic universal model that, even if deconstructed many times by anti-humanistic perspectives, 'rises over and over again from his ashes [and] continues to uphold universal standards and to exercise a fatal attraction' (2013: 132). Sorrentino deconstructs this fundamental humanistic iconography by building a scene where the perfection of the Vitruvian male body is replaced by the fragility of an old female body. In the shot a naked elderly woman floats at the centre of a small circular pool, with her head, hands and feet intersecting its circumference, matching almost to perfection many features of Da Vinci's drawing. But in Sorrentino's posthuman deconstruction of this image, everything is in opposition to the original. The body is framed upside-down, in a dark space lit by a gloomy greenish light, barely visible, and it is the body of an ageing woman. The ideal, perfect, radiant male body through which everything was measured is replaced by a real, imperfect and shadowed female body. This kind of body appears to be the standard human body for Sorrentino, and therefore the body through which we should reconsider the human position in the world. This scene, therefore, represents Sorrentino's more radical rejection of the humanist model through its subversion, and it appears to be his most explicit endorsement of a posthumanistic view. Sorrentino's posthumanism takes as its focus the decentring of the human subject by depicting how its fragility is actually one of its most defining features, and above all the inspiration to transform a nihilistic view of human decay into a stimulus for humility and interspecies compassion: as pointed out by Anat Pick, 'the relationship between vulnerability, existence, and beauty necessarily applies across the species divide and so delivers us beyond the domain of the human' (2011: 3). Finally, this emphasis on vulnerability can be interpreted as an antidote to the arrogance of that Vitruvian model that has been fuelling the anthropocentric paradigm.

The Great Beauty: *The Human, the Animal, the City*

The re-evaluation of anthropocentrism present in *Youth* changes viewers' perception of our presumed dominance over a separated natural sphere. A consequence of this re-evaluation emerges in *The Great Beauty*, where Sorrentino echoes what Bruno Latour means when he says that 'we have never been modern' (Latour 1993: 46): we have never been separated from nature, nor have we ever been in control of it. This understanding induces the posthuman subjectivity of being one of the many beings existing inside an uncontrollable and incomprehensible environment. Maybe what Jep Gambardella (Toni Servillo) is relentlessly looking for in *The Great Beauty* is this form of posthuman subjectivity: the search for the great beauty can be interpreted as the search for a new ontological paradigm that allows humans to reach beyond the fallacy of the culture/nature dichotomy. Therefore, Sorrentino's film is staging a sort of coming-of-age of the *anthropos* towards a posthuman condition, namely towards a human subjectivity intimately and inextricably intertwined with the entire ecosphere. The human is exposed as a posthuman subject who, for instance, is portrayed as living in a city that has never been artificial, that is never truly outside of nature. In fact, Rome is filmed as a living entity, and the life of its people is represented as entangled with the city, with each other, with the public memory of a celebrated historical past and with the private memory of Jep's unspoken nostalgic love. This is exemplified in the opening sequence of the film, when the people visiting Janiculum Park are pictured as native animals who have settled there, sharing the space with the indigenous bird species and bathing in the water of the Acqua Paola fountain like wild animals would do in a pond. Almost reminiscent of a National Geographic documentary, Sorrentino composes this one-minute-long sequence through eleven fluid tracking shots that scan the environment looking for human beings who are investigated as live zoological specimens. The Janiculum is an historic landmark and a notable cultural space, and is represented simultaneously as an ecosystem collectively inhabited by human and non-human animals.

By synecdoche, the city of Rome itself is not an artificial space separated, excluded or emancipated from nature. Actually, the categories of 'cultural' and 'natural' become obsolete when applied to the representation of Rome in *The Great Beauty*. There is no separation between these two spaces because these two spaces never existed a priori. Only a single, undifferentiated, whole space exists where different creatures, objects, ontologies and modes of existence interact and intersect with each other. As pointed out by Simonetta Salvestroni 'the film opens and closes with Rome as its protagonist. It is a set that have been offering itself to the gaze of spectators for centuries. Humans are those who make this set alive, vibrant, or degraded' (Salvestroni 2017: 10). An example of Rome as an undifferentiated set shaped by the gaze of the spectator can be found in the scene of Jep's dawn walk after a party, when he is filmed slowly strolling down Aventine Hill, until he stops for a few moments to observe the novices at the Basilica of Santa Sabina. One novice is standing on a wooden ladder in her white tunic, picking fruit from a tree, her upper body – her human identity – partly disappearing inside the tree canopy. She is literally and metaphorically *inside* the tree; she has easily crossed a fictitious boundary and has entered a hybrid but undivided space. This idea is then reinforced by the subsequent shot, when for just a few seconds the camera follows the movement of Jep's gaze moving up, towards the sky, and from his point of view we witness a flock of starlings flying against a sky streaked with the trails of airplane exhaust. This time the undifferentiated space is this sky shared by both birds and machines.

A final example of Sorrentino's interest in the intersection between the natural and the artificial, and their mutual disappearance, can be found in the brief shot of the wreck of the *Costa Concordia* cruise ship. In 2012, this cruise ship partially sank after striking an underwater rock off Giglio Island. Sorrentino films Jep standing on a cliff looking at something, and with a tracking shot from the back he moves over Jep's left shoulder to reveal the cruise ship capsized, a human artefact that has become part of the landscape. It appears as though the island has absorbed the ship, or that the ship had penetrated the shoreline, transforming itself into an unusual rock formation. It is not difficult to imagine that, over time, that ship will become just a thin layer on the island sedimentary strata, marked as an oddity on the notebooks of future geologists. No human product, not even a very large and very complex product like this ship, really exists outside of nature.

The human exceptionalism that perpetuates the conviction of existing either outside of nature or above it, and the 'botched synchronicity between internal and external world' (Brogi 2013: 5) is defined as 'a trick' and 'an illusion' by Sorrentino in several scenes, the most eloquent being the one filmed at Caracalla's baths. Jep is visiting the ruins, and there he finds himself staring at a giraffe standing right in the middle of the archaeological complex. Jep takes his hat off, an emphatic gesture that appears to be an act of respect for the magnificence of the animal. Sorrentino employs another one of his signature tracking shots, moving from bottom to top, following Jep's gaze and emphasizing the size and the beauty of the specimen. Jep is then welcomed by Arturo (Vernon Dobtcheff), a magician who explains to him that the giraffe is part of his show and that he will make the animal disappear. Arturo embodies human control over a subordinate nature: the animal is there because Arturo placed it there, its only purpose is to serve as entertainment and Arturo can make it disappear at will. But Sorrentino inserts a few lines of dialogue that complexify Arturo's role and therefore problematize human control over nature: when Jep asks Arturo if he can make Jep disappear,

Arturo answers that it is impossible to really make someone or something disappear, that what he is doing is simply performing a circus game and that his control over the animal 'is just a trick'. As Arturo's power is just a deception, so is human exceptionalism simply an illusion, dominance over nature a ludicrous belief, and separation between natural and artificial is a false construct.

In addition to visualizing Rome throughout the film as a unified and unifying living being, overriding the modern separation between man and nature, and after exposing the illusion of human control, Sorrentino also presents another aspect of posthuman subjectivity, namely the awareness of belonging to an ecosphere that we cannot dominate because we can never fully comprehend it. As already mentioned, posthumanism provokes us to reconsider how humans are simply one of the many parts that constitutes the ecosphere, and it compels us to recognize that some of these parts cannot be comprehended through a humanistic paradigm. When we leave behind the humanistic illusion of comprehension and control, non-human things and non-human animals appear anew as magical, miraculous and sacred, and the ecosphere becomes re-enchanted. From a world conceptualized as something to understand and control, it becomes a world to respect and enjoy in awe, not necessarily one to understand. As emphasized by Mircea Eliade in his comment on Rudolf Otto's *The Idea of the Holy* (1925), 'the sacred always manifests itself as a reality of a wholly different order from "natural" realities' (1987: 9), and it is always channelled through irrational and overwhelming experiences. These experiences put the human in the presence of the 'numinous', that is, a transcendental element intrinsically different from anything else; it is 'nothing like human or cosmic; confronted with it, man senses his profound nothingness, feels that he is only a creature' (Eliade 1987: 10). Eliade calls these mysterious manifestations of the sacred 'hierophanies' (a combination of the Greek verb ['to reveal'] and the adjective ['holy']) and underlines how hierophanies possess the power to show us 'a reality that does not belong to our world' by manifesting themselves 'in objects that are an integral part of our natural "profane" world' (1987: 11).

In *The Great Beauty*, these manifestations of the sacred, these hierophanies, do not happen through objects, but through humans and other animals, specifically, pink flamingos. Jep hosts in his luxurious Roman loft an old missionary nun, Suor Maria (Giusi Merli), who is considered a saint by her devotees. When they meet at dawn on Jep's balcony, they witness a marvellous event: a flock of flamingos has landed on the balcony to momentarily rest along their migration route. In front of the resting flamingos, Suor Maria questions Jep about his writer's block; he answers: 'I was looking for the great beauty ... but ... I never found it'. He is unaware of the great beauty in front of him, embodied by the quiet piety of a decrepit but foresighted woman, and manifested in the image of the magnificent flamingos flying towards the grandiose cityscape of Rome. It seems that only later on Jep recognizes the hierophany of the encounter with Suor Maria and the flamingos through the voice-over monologue right before the film's conclusion. In it, he states that 'hidden beneath the blah blah blah' he was able to see 'life' and the 'fleeting and sporadic flashes of beauty'; these rare, ineffable moments of vitality and beauty correspond to Eliade's irrational and overwhelming manifestation of the sacred. Suor Maria's holiness, paired with the magnificence of the flamingos and of the cityscape, make Jep realize that the element of grace and purity that he has been searching for does not 'lie beyond', but materializes itself in the interaction between humans, non-human creatures and the material space they inhabit. He finally recognizes that this physical environment can be an enchanted one, and that the human can barely grasp its beauty and sacredness.

Sorrentino explores this sacred, enchanted reality by filming the earthly interaction between human and non-human animals. In doing so, he proposes a communal creaturely condition and represents it as a hierophany. In the same scene mentioned above, the close-up of Jep's face focused on the flamingos reveals his pleasant surprise at this close encounter with nature, an enchanted nature that seems incorporated into the life of both the city and the characters. Here, Sorrentino inserts a brief but extremely crucial exchange between Jep and Suor Maria, after they had briefly discussed Jep's search for the 'great beauty' for the book that he never wrote. During this exchange, Suor Maria makes a strangely surprising reference to her diet based only on roots – roots that carry both a literal and a metaphorical meaning. 'Roots are important', says Suor Maria, because these roots represent, in a metaphorical sense, human historical origin and identity, but they also refer to physical roots, a simple food that reminds humans of being at the same time – and without distinction – biologically animals and culturally gatherers. Suor Maria's holiness resides in being able to see and point out such awareness, the understanding that humans come from a nature they will never leave. The close-up of Suor Maria's face reveals the bliss that comes from this profound awareness of a simple truth: the truth that 'roots are important', that this primordial food still feeds the human-animals who delude themselves into thinking that they are above all other beings. The great beauty is ultimately the understanding, or rather the recollection, that humans – now a planetary force – have always been just creatures like all others enmeshed in the 'unity of all matter', together with roots, flamingos, other people, a vast ancient city and an entire planet. 'Roots are important' should be the mantra of posthuman subjectivity.

In his seminal work *About Looking*, art critic John Berger spends an entire chapter attempting to answer the question: 'Why look at animals?'. He points out that the disenchantment of the relationship between humans, non-humans and their environment has been predominantly caused by a process of separation of humans and animals triggered by modern science and capitalism, two processes that have broken 'every tradition which has previously mediated between man and nature' (Berger 1991: 3). In addition, Berger underlines that 'in the last two centuries, animals have gradually disappeared. Today we live without them. And in this solitude, anthropomorphism makes us doubly uneasy' (1991: 11). Sorrentino is clearly aware of this uneasiness produced by the separation between humans and non-humans, and he seeks to reduce this separation by reproducing in this film a re-enchanted human-ecosystem bond. He uses the language of cinema to reproduce for humans an enchanted reality characterized by a less lonely, less self-ish, less anthropomorphic and less anthropocentric relationship with the world, particularly its creatures. This capacity to make visible and comprehensible a re-enchanted relationship between human and non-human animals is one of the most significant ecocinematic qualities of *The Great Beauty*.

Sorrentino's Ecocinema

Sorrentino's *Youth* and *The Great Beauty* possess several of the key features of ecocinema: the *unheimlich* exposure of human fragility that deflates our hubris and opens the possibility of connecting humans with other vulnerable creatures with whom we share this ecosphere; the reassessment of the anthropological condition of dominance over the environment; the challenge of the Vitruvian paradigm; the erosion of the culture/nature boundary; and the replacement of a confident under-standing of the world with a cautious look at a re-enchanted cosmos inhabited by miraculous creatures.

In addition to critically examining the interaction between humans and the ecosystem, Sorrentino's ecocinema also transforms this interaction and influences viewers' perceptions of the effect that humans have on the environment in the film and beyond. This ecocinema produces a sort of revelation, a form of epiphany that transforms viewers' understanding of the world and the way they act in it. For this reason, these films bring ecological awareness and represent a form of political cinema, particularly now, as we are living in a time where the capacity of humans to transform the environment has made us a global geological force. While some-times a force for good, our actions can often result in global degradation: with human activity has come mass animal extinction, global warming, ocean acidi-fication, drought and famine, environmental migration and refugee crises. This is why this epoch of negative impact is now fittingly called the 'Anthropocene'.

Then, what is the role of ecocinema inside this epoch of dramatic man-made global transformation? As pointed out by Jedediah Purdy, the role of representa-tion and therefore of filmic imagination becomes political in the Anthropocene: 'Imagination also enables us to do things together politically: a new way of seeing the world can be a way of valuing it – a map of things worth saving, or of a future worth creating' (2015: 7). Sorrentino's films, therefore, become ecocinematic and political any time they offer us an alternative representation of the anthropological condition. As we have seen, although constantly focusing on the human subject, Sorrentino presents a narrative that destabilizes the anthropocentric model, replaces it with a non-dualistic posthuman perspective, offers material to discuss possible ways to move past anthropocentrism without leaving the human behind and imagines alternative subjectivities that do not privilege the human-animal. In sum, Sorrentino definitely is a 'visionary anthropologist' (Liguori 2017: 167) whose cinema produces a posthuman imagination that could help us reconsider the ethical and political role that we have in the geological epoch that we are giving shape to.

NOTES

1. For more on ecocinema, see MacDonald (2004), who focuses on the capacity of cinema to document the disappearance of fragile ecosystems and also to preserve their memory; Ivakhiv (2013), who explores, through an ecophilosophical approach, the influence of cinema on the relationship between humans and the environment; and Rust et al. (2016), whose collection of essays use an ecocritical approach to analyse the entanglement between mass media and the environment.
2. This term is borrowed from Donna Haraway's *The Companion Species Manifesto* (2003).
3. This consideration is inspired by the theory of *painism* expressed by Peter Singer in *Animal Liberation* (1975) and by Richard Ryder in *Speciesism, Painism and Happiness* (2011).

REFERENCES

Berger, J. (1991), *About Looking*, New York: Vintage International.

Braidotti, R. (2013), *The Posthuman*, Cambridge: Polity Press.

Brogi, D. (2013), '*La grande bellezza* (P. Sorrentino, 2013)', *Between*, III:5, pp. 1–9, http://ojs. unica.it/index.php/between/article/view/1001/753. Accessed 29 March 2019.

Burt, J. (2002), *Animals in Film*, London: Reaktion Books.

Cahill, J. L. (2013), 'Anthropomorphism and its vicissitudes: Reflections on *homme*-sick cinema', in A. Pick and G. Narraway (eds), *Screening Nature: Cinema Beyond the Human*, New York: Berghahn Books, pp. 73–90.

Calarco, M. (2017), 'Revisiting the anthropological difference', in S. Iovino and S. Oppermann (eds), *Environmental Humanities: Voices from the Anthropocene*, London and New York: Rowman & Littlefield International, pp. 237–54.

Eliade, M. (1987), *The Sacred and the Profane: The Nature of Religion*, San Diego: Harcourt Books.

Haraway, D. (2003), *The Companion Species Manifesto*, Chicago: Prickly Paradigm Press.

Ivakhiv, A. J. (2013), *Ecologies of the Moving Image: Cinema, Affect, Nature*, Waterloo: WLU Press.

Latour, B. (1993), *We Have Never Been Modern*, Cambridge: Harvard University Press.

Liguori, W. (2017), *Da Teatri Uniti ai Film di Paolo Sorrentino: Nuove Tendenze del Cinema Italiano*, Napoli: Liguori.

MacDonald, S. (2004), 'Toward an eco-cinema', *Interdisciplinary Studies in Literature and the Environment*, 11:2, pp. 107–32.

Morton, T. (2010), *The Ecological Thought*, Cambridge: Harvard University Press.

Pick, A. (2011), *Creaturely Poetics: Animality and Vulnerability in Literature and Film*, New York: Columbia University Press.

Pick, A. and Narraway, G. (2013), 'Intersecting ecology and film', in A. Pick and G. Narraway (eds), *Screening Nature: Cinema Beyond the Human*, New York: Berghahn Books, pp. 1–18.

Purdy, J. (2015), *After Nature: A Politics for the Anthropocene*, Cambridge: Harvard University Press.

Rust, S., Monani, S. and Cubit, S. (2016), *Ecomedia: Key Issues*, London and New York: Routledge.

Ryder, R. (2011), *Speciesism, Painism and Happiness*, Charlottesville: Societas.

Salvestroni, S. (2017), *La grande bellezza e il cinema di Paolo Sorrentino*, Bologna: Clueb.

Simor, E. and Sorfa, D. (2017), 'Irony, sexism and magic in Paolo Sorrentino's films', *Studies in European Cinema*, 14:3, pp. 200–15.

Singer, P. (1975), *Animal Liberation: A New Ethics for Our Treatment of Animals*, New York: Random House.

Sorrentino, P. (2013), *The Great Beauty*, Italy: Indigo Film.

Sorrentino, P. (2015), *Youth*, Italy: Indigo Film.

6

Interpolating the 'blah, blah, blah': *The Great Beauty*'s Vocal Rome

Alex Gammon

Florida State University

Introduction

Rome has a voice. It is a city saturated with legend and serves as a vault of memory made tangible and vocal to us through its architecture. Rome's identity in the west is that of the *caput mundi*, or 'head of the world', and this is not without good reason: Rome, more than a city, is an existential *environment* which harbours a distinct spirit of place and a comprehensive tapestry of architecture, which runs the temporal gamut from antiquity to today. Freud succinctly recognizes the spirit of Rome by comparing it to 'a psychical entity [...] in which nothing that has once come into existence will have passed away and all the earlier phases of development continue to exist alongside the latest one' (1962: 17). Much of this classification as an entity is a consequence of the city's timeline materialized in its structure.

In his seminal book, *Genius Loci: A Phenomenology of Architecture*, Christian Norberg-Schulz reinvigorates the notion of *genius loci*, or 'spirit of place', in architectural terms. Drawing from Martin Heiddeger's works in phenomenology, Norberg-Schulz states that architecture 'represents a means to give [one] an "existential foothold"' (1980: 5). He defines the Heiddegerrean concept of 'dwelling' as 'when [one] can orientate [one]self within and identify [one]self with an environment', and affirms that this is the very purpose of architecture (Norberg-Schulz 1980: 5). Regarding Rome in particular, Norberg-Schulz takes as obvious its eternal quality and accredits this to the city's 'very strong, perhaps unique, quality of self-renewal' (1980: 138).

This quality – and in general, Rome's richness of place – has tirelessly inspired the Italian cinematic tradition. Indeed, as the home of Cinecittà, Rome is just as much a historic epicentre for Italian film as it is for the nation at large. Depictions of the Eternal City in cinema are motley, and certainly, its architecture came to the fore in the suffocating urbanism of post-war *neorealismo*. However, when Rome's physical environment receives special consideration through the medium of film, it evolves into a character all its own and consequently, when characters confront their architecture, interaction becomes dialogue. This has especially been the case with the films of Federico Fellini and more recently, Neapolitan filmmaker Paolo Sorrentino.

In summarizing the mutual pressure for architectural/cinematic interplay from preeminent architects and filmmakers such as Le Corbusier, Georges Méliès and Robert Mallet-Stevens, architectural historian Anthony Vidler asserts that 'the obvious role of architecture in the construction of sets [...] and the equally obvious ability of film to "construct" its own architecture in light and shade, scale and movement [...] allowed for a mutual intersection of these two "spatial arts"' (1993: 46). For Rome in particular, that eminent scholar of Italian cinema, Peter Bondanella, contends, 'the impact of Roman mythology upon the cinema [...] has been important enough to constitute a specific genre with recognizable stylistic traits and content' (1987: 207).

These include 'sumptuous sets', being the 'center of sexual escapades' and a focus on a 'time of crisis, the birth of an empire, and its eventual destruction [...]' (Bondanella 1987: 208–13). These themes are still regnant in Rome today as a cinematic setting and this is chiefly due to the city being the historical axis of western civilization and Freud's apt comparison of the layered ruins of Rome to the human psyche itself (Bondanella 1987: 237; cf. Freud 1962: 16).

As film is thus inextricably linked to the architecture of its setting, it is imperative that those directors who acknowledge and call attention to this marriage of forms be studied, especially those dealing in a behemoth such as Rome. Such a marriage of forms finds its ideal in Paolo Sorrentino's film *La grande bellezza (The Great Beauty)* (2013). In Sorrentino's film, the city of Rome gains a newfound importance and appears as a truly vocal entity relaying a message of beauty. The narrative follows Jep Gambardella, a 65-year-old former novelist who whittles away the small hours of the morning in a swirl of parties, art exhibitions and romances set against the backdrop of historic Rome. Sorrentino's film knowingly invokes Federico Fellini's *La dolce vita* (1960), wherein photojournalist Marcello Rubini indulges in the sweet life of Italy's economic miracle years while still yearning for spiritual deliverance. However, both films portray the physical city of Rome differently to converse with their protagonists, and Sorrentino has revitalized Fellini's Rome to reflect his conception of the city's role towards its people. In the wake of Sorrentino's film, there is a need to revisit the figuration of architectural Rome in the filmic language as a vocal entity that encourages rebirth and ascension beyond worldly, material matters.

Scholars and critics alike have taken a broad, but measured interest in Sorrentino's celebration of Rome's physical presence. In *A History of Italian Cinema*, Bondanella and Federico Pacchioni contend that part of *The Great Beauty*'s strength lays, 'precisely in the bounty and intensity of its mise-en-scène and untiring panoramic gaze, both in terms of Rome itself as a physical place, and of the citizens who inhabit this ancient mythic site' (Bondanella and Pacchioni 2017: 575). Sorrentino's treatment of architecture is likewise described as a 'neo-baroque sensibility [which] summons reflective participation' with regards to Italy's national and cinematic history (Picarelli 2015: 10). However, the architectural preoccupation of the film is often treated as a general aspect, serving as one half of the sacred/profane binary.

Rome's sublimity in *The Great Beauty* has occasionally been treated as a conversational object wherein it, 'functions as an *interruption* of the grotesque and the comical, and competes for the attention of Gambardella and of the spectator [...]' (Mecchia 2016: 189, emphasis added). More pertinently, Alessia Martini interprets Sorrentino and Fellini's Rome as the consummate example of Michel De Certeau's Concept City, and by way of this theoretical framework, Jep's perambulations and Marcello's drives through the Eternal City function as a '*pedestrian speech act* [which] is a spatial expression of place in the same way as verbal speech is an acoustic expression of language' (2015: 108, original emphasis).[1] However, the architecture's agency remains overlooked, particularly in the anthropomorphized vocal sense, and there remains a need for investigation into the city's structures.

For Fellini and Sorrentino, Rome is the mouthpiece of a cautionary tale and an eternal beauty, respectively. While the Rome of *La dolce vita* crumbles as a portentous mirror of Marcello's deteriorating spirituality, *The Great Beauty* mindfully presents an idealized and immortal Rome to confront the blight of Jep's ageing and his ostensibly bygone career as a writer. It is the focus of this article to reveal these contrasting yet complementary treatments of Roman architecture in the abovementioned films of Fellini and Sorrentino by way of cinematography, décor, sound and of course, location. Examining the intersection of film and architecture in the very city that effectuates both to the highest degree will illuminate the symbiotic relationship between the two mediums and demonstrate how, for *The Great Beauty* in particular, place can factor into film as a vehicle for meaning and as a *sui generis* character.

Revealing Rome

Both *The Great Beauty* and *La dolce vita* concern themselves with architecture from the outset as a means to immediately provision a platform for Rome's vocalism and characterize the tone of discourse to come. It is the tone itself that differs so distinctly between the films, and much of what distinguishes the respective opening scenes derives from the auteurs' cinematographic choices and, in Sorrentino's case, aural dynamics.

La dolce vita's Rome is one in which post-war trends and modern vices begin stripping away the divine and eternal fulfilment characteristic of the city: St. Peter's Basilica is blasphemed by Sylvia, the prancing pinup; the Baths of Caracalla are rendered a hellish nightclub; and Via Veneto, in all its blasé vanity, is now the hallmark attraction of Rome. Marcello is well on his way to the same personal disavowal of spirit as he opts more for the wastefulness of the socialite than for the empowerment of the writer he so yearns to realize. Sorrentino's approach is even more painstakingly architectural. However, his revelation of Rome is, in his own words, concerned with 'softness' (Sorrentino 2013a). Its elegance is such that it warrants a delicacy in its capturing, which is precisely why the Steadicam is used (Sorrentino 2013a). Rome greets the viewer as a pristine yet august presence of monumentality, and from this introduction, it is clear to the viewer that the city is eponymous to the film's title.

We are launched into *The Great Beauty* by a Steadicam hurling out of the Janiculum cannon's barrel to softly brush over a parapet of applauding tourists. With this, Sorrentino has immediately established his Rome and his film at large: the jarring will confront the gentle, the local the cosmopolitan and the people their architecture. The monuments, fountains and statues are captured with what can only be described as an expression of sacred geometry through the camera: an unblemished, symmetrical style, which is utilized outright to cement physical Rome as the principal and most immediate 'beauty' in the film. Selecting the Janiculum as the location of this weaponized inauguration is fitting, as it is not a party to the Seven Hills of Rome, but rather lies west of the Tiber as an onlooker of the city. It is therefore the ideal location by which to be shot into conversation with Rome, and Sorrentino's sonically startling introduction is somewhat mediated by allowing Rome to geographically settle into its core.[2]

Sorrentino wastes no time in exercising his geometrical treatment of architecture when the Steadicam begins rigidly tracing the edge of the Fontana dell'Acqua Paola. In his analysis of Rome, Norberg-Schulz contends that 'axially ordered enclosure [...] may be considered *the basic element* of Roman architecture' (1980: 149, original emphasis), which Sorrentino captures perfectly in the fountain's semi-circular basin. The shot runs faithfully along the outline, bending with the curve of the stone while slowly absorbing into the frame every glinting drop of water. This procession soon comes to an exact centring of the vocalists overlooking the fountain's balustrade and, upon completion of the shot, the monument has been elevated to perfection by the undisturbed linearity of Sorrentino's cinematography.

The opening scene of *La dolce vita* is considerably less sleek, and with it, there is no beauty to be internalized, but rather an architecturally conveyed warning about the state of Marcello's spiritual affairs. The story of Rome's crumbling is told through its architecture in *La dolce vita* from the beginning: a statue of Christ the Labourer is flown beside a segmented Aqua Claudia and into a neighbourhood of serial tower blocks. With this, the second coming is welcomed by the sights of both an imperial structure in rupture and the isotropic march of modern architecture towards the defenceless city. This architecture will reappear to the man in the helicopter, Marcello, when he utilizes the seediness of the prostitute's flooded flat later in the film as a sexualized venue – a flat resembling these which we see in the opening scene.

Unlike Sorrentino's undisturbed camerawork from his opening scene, Fellini's is constituted by the imperfections of a human perspective from the ground and inside the helicopter, replete with panning point-of-view low angles and aerial shots. The encroaching towers are, in this way, both suffocating the viewer and lying below the viewer for inspection, resulting in the city's premonitory voice of its own doom. Fellini does not divulge his first image of Rome with reverence and, as becomes the norm, Marcello follows his city's architectural tone in tandem – here by catcalling the sunbathing women from the very helicopter in which he is to oversee the delivery of Christ.

But for Sorrentino, the thread of architectural sublimity is unspooled to an even hyperbolic note when, to finalize the opening scene, a Japanese tourist collapses after gazing over the hill at the Eternal City. David Lang's 'I Lie' (2001) rings from the mouths of the choir, harmonizing with the rushing of water as the shot glides out of the fountain and perches to unveil the same breathtaking city that has just proven lethal in its marvelousness.[3] The tranquillity is dismantled, however, when a drunken shriek drowns out the flowing water, Bob Sinclair's 'Far l'amore' (2011) out-sings Lang's composition and a neon-lit dance floor razes the cityscape of Rome. This marks the transition to Jep's portion of the dialogue: his extravagant birthday party. All previous fluidity and softness is lost in choppy cuts, an inverted shot of Jep dancing and the ensuing isolation of Dadina, who, waking up to a deserted terrace, calls uselessly for the friends who have abandoned her – striking, considering how the collapsed man's fellow tourists from the previous scene so readily flocked to his aid. The scenes are in clear opposition, drawing a contrast between the perfection of Rome, the city, and the profanity of Rome, the people. However Rome's structural beauty is not bested. If anything, it takes precedence as a character itself before the film even introduces Jep. Rather, Rome will converse with Jep's mortality and languorous lifestyle throughout the film, hiding under his nose as the symbol to aspire to in his search for the great beauty.

Architecture Talks

It is important to the purposes of this article that Rome's voice is not merely figuratively heard in *The Great Beauty* and *La dolce vita* but in a strict, literal sense as well. It is often in the use of diegetic sound that the intersection of film and architecture becomes manifest in these films. Sorrentino and Fellini use architecture as tools for storytelling and as a vocal character proper. What results are scenes in which characters speak through the architecture by way of the conduits for sound naturally present within the structure. The figurative aspect of dialogue is also in play, however, as not all manifestations of Rome's voice can be conveyed so plainly. Fellini's proclivity for the spiritual and dreamlike lends *La dolce vita*'s Rome to communicate with Marcello more phantasmagorically, but Sorrentino explores methods of the human subject responding in kind to Rome by adopting one's own architectural language.

Marcello's descent into the self-indulgence of post-war Rome is perhaps best architecturally mirrored by the decline of the aristocracy's estate in the sixth episode.[4] The castle of the royal family is no longer a house of order, but a venue for carousal. The villa behind it is no longer a statement of power, but rather a weakened, ruinous dwelling for ghosts (an apt representation of the haunt of bygone aristocratic vigour which seeks its return). The heir, Giulio, asks: 'What should I do, father?' when discussing the 'crumbling' state of their property. Nico, Giulio's lover, dons an old casque and jeers, 'I am your ancestor, Giulio'. The royal bloodline and its estate are shown to be so crippled as to become objects of mockery. To highlight this, a medium summons a spirit from the villa, which inhabits one of the partygoers. In a paroxysm, the possessed woman cries, 'I want life!' and asks to speak with Giulio specifically. The architecture is thus mediated to evoke a vocal representative of an ancestor, or just as likely the villa's very spirit of place, to bemoan its tarnished pedigree. Marcello is similarly in ruin by infidelity and his desire to replace a lost Maddalena with yet another woman: Jane, the American painter. It is thus no coincidence on Fellini's part that the ruins are suggested to be turned into a brothel. Just as Marcello makes no effort to reclaim his stability with his girlfriend, Emma, or his integrity as an artist, the aristocracy would rather cavort and shirk their duties (for none of them work) instead of reclaiming any of the stability and integrity once possessed by their forebears.[5]

The architecture is truly conversant in this episode as Marcello finds himself in a confession-like discussion with Maddalena through the castle's basin duct on the floor above. This same architectural scenario of a detached confessional via sound-channeling structures is repeated in *The Great Beauty* when Jep peers through a lattice in Bramante's *tempietto* and hears a runaway girl tell him he is 'nobody'. In both scenes, the architecture becomes a conduit for truth in the protagonists' identity. Maddalena tells Marcello through the castle that 'one cannot have things both ways', and though this is directed towards herself, it is equally true for Marcello. He can no longer straddle the line between writer and journalist, nor spiritual fulfilment and empty sensuality. In Jep's case, he is without rebuttal when, through the temple, he is informed that his identity is as imaginary as Louise-Ferdinand Céline's quote at the beginning of the film would suggest it is.[6] For Marcello, Rome is echoing his downfall as a warning of what will become of him should he not choose a path apart from nightlife, sex and glamour. For Jep, however, the dialogue is one that deliberately instils in him a void so as to be flushed of his pettiness and misgivings and be filled by the sublimity of existential freedom. Although neither protagonist truly comprehends the message, Rome continues to be in discourse.

While not as outwardly aural as the *tempietto* or the villa, *The Great Beauty* also includes an artist's exhibit in *Villa Giulia*, which is profoundly moving to Jep and acts as an intonation for life through architecture. Taken as a strictly architectural entity, the rear of the villa's casino is bordered by a hemispherical portico surrounding a courtyard. The ceiling inside is painted over with renaissance frescoes, and the walls, a series of murals. The artist chooses to exhibit an autobiography of photographs – one for each day of his life since boyhood – which he plasters in chronological order around the walls of the portico. What is worth noting is that the photographs are placed so as to maintain the architectural integrity of the structure. The photographs are simply overlaid on top of the wall murals, effectively substituting them for a more humanizing, individualistic expression while leaving alone the austere doric colonnade and keeping the structure open to the courtyard. This is deliberate, for in the architecture's semi-circular nature, the curve of the portico allows all of the murals to stretch, turn and face the viewer as they stand from the courtyard, allowing the spectator to absorb the whole façade from one peripheral locus of vision to its opposite. As such, when the artist's ageing portraits replace the murals, it allows all of his life to be visible via this enveloping nature of the portico.

What this scene and exhibition represents for *The Great Beauty* at large is perhaps the singular, most forthright example of the people of Rome speaking back to their architecture. Just as Rome has utilized actual, sensorial sound in its structures – that is, taking the initiative to speak to the human characters in their own language – now Sorrentino presents us with an artist who is unafraid to speak the language of architecture back to Rome by embedding his life as murals in the portico-covered walls of this courtyard. There is no doubt that the exhibition prompts a visceral emotional response in consuming an entire life told through the myriad animations of the face; it is all of human experience writ small. Indeed, Sorrentino capitalizes the experience with a zooming close-up of Jep moved to the verge of tears immediately before another zooming close-up of the artist standing stoically, these two lives becoming captured in photographs of their own and juxtaposed against one another. However, Sorrentino does well not to end the scene on this predictable filmic note. Instead, the final frame is Jep standing in the shadows of the columns, dwarfed by the distended portico and the many faces it now bears on its walls: the human subject alone to converse with his architecture.

The Churches

Much of *The Great Beauty*'s treatment of the Catholic Church is explored by way of character. The cardinal, a garrulous culinary aficionado, and Sister Maria, the sage centenarian, are indicative of how the Church is capable of oscillating between quotidian triviality and profound spirituality respectively. Still, there is a noteworthy architectural aspect to the treatment of religion as a pathway to spiritual fulfilment in both films, and this occurs in Sorrentino's brief glimpses of churches and convents and Fellini's famous scene in St. Peter's Basilica. For both directors, the juncture of film and architecture meets with the camera and the staircase.

Our first introduction to a church proper in *The Great Beauty* is the Sant'Agnese in Agone, a seventeeth-century Baroque church, which at first glance is shrouded in shadow in the Piazza Navona. It is here that Orietta, one of Jep's late-night romances, lives 'when [she] come[s] to Rome'. After going to bed with her, Jep's voice-over states that the most important thing he has learned after turning 65 is that he cannot waste any more time doing things that he does not want to do, referring to staying the night with Orietta. Sorrentino shoots Jep enjoying a cigarette by the window from a low angle outside of the monument, which divulges more of the façade of the church: its concavity, wispy ornamentation and jumbled pilasters. The centre of the church is heavily darkened whereas a street-lamp illuminates the window in which Jep stands, architecturally framed, basking in the afterglow of his libertinism. When Orietta returns to find Jep gone, we are then granted a wide shot of the church in its entirety, looming upon the viewer as a monolith of Baroque craftsmanship. Sant'Agnese in Agone remains standing as a triumph of spiritual inspiration given physical form, but even this is triumphed over in the shot by the small window in the lower left corner of the frame wherein Orietta steps to the balustrade, forsaken and alone. When Sorrentino reveals the entirety of the monument to the viewer, the introduction of character movement distracts and draws the eye to the confining window where Jep has callously left behind his encounter. This effectively interrupts the architecture's voice of spiritual grandeur with a mere interjection of womanizing, to which we instead give our attention due to Sorrentino's filmic sleight of hand.

Within Marcello's discourse with Rome's architecture, Fellini shows superficiality as distancing to Christian and salvational values (Bondanella 1987: 238). Sylvia's excursion in Rome highlights several structures that Fellini renders conciliatory with her superficiality. Her first stop at St. Peter's Basilica depicts an exhausting chase in which Marcello struggles to trail Sylvia as she prances about the church and bolts up the staircase. Instead of the sublime monument of spiritual power that the basilica typically represents, it is here depicted as a playground for tourism and vapid journalism. Sylvia, mockingly garbed in a nun's habit, desires only to write her name on the church walls (as several other tourists have) and ascend to the top balcony. This foretells the useless and isolating qualities of height in the Gothic spire comment later in the film.[7] In a structure that is sacredly bound to Christian virtue – itself a testament to the spiritual qualities of artwork – there is an irreverence of vapidity that comes with speeding along the Basilica's stairway. Sylvia is determined to climb to the top, conquering the sacrosanct structure with her reckless free spirit, and Marcello follows out of lust. On the balcony, at a spire's height, they have achieved nothing in the way of salvation.[8]

What better way to respond to Fellini's scene of rapid ascension and conquest of St. Peter's Basilica than Sister Maria of *The Great Beauty* laboriously crawling to the top of the Scala Sancta ('Holy Stairs')? This scene comes at the end of the film, and the nun's ascension of the staircase serves as a microcosm of pilgrimage, which is mirrored by Jep, who is in sequence making his pilgrimage back to the site of his first love. Sorrentino uses the filmic language of angle and character placement to elicit Rome's voice to the viewer: Sister Maria is shown to have only ascended to the halfway point of the staircase and is looked upon from the first step with an acute low angle as she beholds the fresco of the crucifixion. Christian Norberg-Schulz's preoccupation with architectural movement is illuminating for the purposes of analysing the scene in question: '[…] life is "movement" and as such it possesses "rhythm". The path is therefore a fundamental existential symbol which concretizes the dimension of time'. Regarding the Christian basilica in particular: 'path (nave) and goal (altar) are united to symbolize the "Path of Salvation" of Christian doctrine' (Norberg-Schulz 1980: 56). Sister Maria's ascension via the staircase's architectural expression of path is a parallel to Jep's path of ascension to human connection and wonderment. It is thus a slight in the spiritual sense to the architecture of the basilica in *La dolce vita* when Sylvia asks, '[w]hy doesn't the elevator come all the way up here?'.

Noteworthy is the fact that Sister Maria has not entirely reached the 'Path of Salvation', nor has Jep written his second book. Sorrentino cuts away from the nun at the very step before the landing. It is the staircase here that harnesses Rome's vocalism. Just as Sister Maria looks up at the domed fresco of Christ from her staircase, so too does Jep look up at Elisa from the bottom of the stone stairs leading back to the Tyrrhenian Sea at Giglio Island. Elisa and Christ are thus correlated as objects of spiritual ascension and the conduit for such is the architectural path of the staircase. The spirit of Rome beckons through this architectural appendage, and the great beauty lies above the protagonist of the film and the viewer by incorporating the low angle. The use of stairs as Rome's mouthpiece is apt, for Jep says, 'let this novel begin'. The stone stairs stretch before him to the lighthouse, his journey made clear to him symbolically through the architecture. Elisa sits on a rock along the way, for Jep will set out to write his book – ascending the spiritual staircase – with Elisa's memory alongside him.

Décor

Volumes are spoken through these holistic structures, but furthermore, the peculiar innards of each monument and building speak just as loudly through the décor and statuary. Diegesis and setting are encouraged to comingle in an environment such as Rome and, expectedly, Sorrentino indulges, taking us into Rome's interior as somewhat of a reprised revelation of the city. The scale narrows from the monument-as-unit approach and affords the viewer a new way to experience the spirit of place. Fellini likewise weaves through the interior of Rome: Steiner's flat, the hotel during Sylvia's interview and the modern villa just outside Rome, which plays venue to the orgiastic festivities. In *La dolce vita*, the interior of Rome is domestic and sterile. *The Great Beauty*, contrastingly, chooses to explore museums, which vociferate to Jep vivacity and encouragement.

Most notably, the voice of Rome is reduced to a decorative outlet by way of busts. From these truncated sculptures, we are left with a historical countenance that observes the people of Rome, at times with scrutiny and at times with desperation. In the aforementioned episode of *La dolce vita*, Marcello is first introduced to the cavalier aristocrats in a drawing room, which is positively beleaguered by stone-faced busts of emperors. They cast consternation on a castle, which is no longer a statement of their power, but rather a venue for carousal. The powerful leaders that once oversaw the heyday of Roman culture and the strength of its empire are now witnesses to the degeneration of Italy's noble progeny. Indeed, before leaving the room, Fellini's camera glimpses one bust draped by a party-goer's stole, relegating these likenesses of authority to nothing more than clothes hangers for the outfits flaunted on Via Veneto.

In the cosmetic clinic of *The Great Beauty*, the portraiture bears no imperial affiliation, but rather an immaculate beauty to be sought after by the patrons. Peering from atop a round lobby sofa, a particularly large bust of a muse reigns above the company of socialites as a veritable overseer of physical perfection. Sorrentino reveals a nefarious circus of wealth and vanity: the men and women line the golden furniture of the cosmetic clinic, clutching touchscreens and pocketbooks as they await the 'professor' to call their number and administer his botulinum toxin injection. Each patron wears black, with the exception of Jep. He is visually distinguished by costume, and rightfully so, for he is the only one looking on with bewilderment at the uncanny ritual. While it is true that Jep is confronted by the structural beauty of Rome and besought to inherit its beauty, the busts and décor of the cosmetic clinic speak to him a narcissism that he responds to in the scene's final shot: a close-up of his frowning disappointment and shame as his number is called. The clinic evokes a fleeting superficial beauty, whereas the physical city of Rome possesses an eternal inner beauty, one which Jep begins to realize is far more worthy of being harnessed.

Sculptures reappear alongside paintings as component voices of architecture when Stefano guides Jep and Ramona through their tour of 'Rome's most beautiful buildings'. A far cry from her diaphanous unitard worn earlier in the evening, Ramona treads the palaces and galleries in a ruffed cloak, reminiscent of the woman in the derelict villa scene of *La dolce vita* – notably the only employed partygoer among the group. As this woman and Marcello stroll through the ruins, her royal garb is at odds with both the extinct dynamism of the crumbling villa and her occupation as a secretary. Ramona's costume is in dialogue with the buildings as a similar contradiction where under the regal display lays a gaudy truth: the sumptuous and revealing outfit sheathed in a show of modesty. The plane of reverence is broken when she outstretches her unitard's flashy, golden arms past the austere cloak to capture the perfect picture of the Villa Medici gardens instead of becoming present first-hand in its splendour.

Jep, on the other hand, is thrust yet again into the position of an interlocutor with Rome, immediately confronting Marforio, one of the six 'speaking statues', at the start of the tour (Claridge et al. 1998: 380).[9] The busts in the corridors and the statues of the galleries leer at Jep collectively, giving face to Rome's distress, pain and yet even still, its serenity. These stone expressions relate a plea for the forfeiture of deceitful extravagance and are a call to arms for the likes of Jep, one who can bear the torch for the revival of the city's truthful beauty in himself and in the novel he must no longer neglect to write.

Marforio bears a specific message, as does Raphael's painting, *La Fornarina*, which Jep confronts on the museum tour as well. These works portray the sea god, Oceanus, and Raphael's young lover, respectively (Musei Capitolini Official Website 2017; Oberhuber 1999: 208). The film reiterates Jep's longing for the sea visualized in his bedroom ceiling and his first love, Elisa, with whom he shared an intimate moment by this same sea. Here, the physical Rome attempts to usher him towards his 'roots', to borrow a word from Sister Maria later in the film. Again, Sorrentino individually positions the softly lit Raphael painting and a smiling Jep in rigid centre-frame to extract the same true and tender beauty from Jep's first romance as from Rome's geometrics.

Baths of Caracalla

The two films have in common one monument that is indispensable to Rome's message: the Baths of Caracalla. The Baths were originally constructed as a lavish public attraction for ritual cleansing, intellectual edification and leisure (Claridge et al. 1998: 54, 319–28). Their ruins are now a tourist destination, and while Fellini envisions the Baths as a chthonic playground, Sorrentino has embraced the notion of Rome repurposing architecture from function to spectacle. In fact, Sorrentino utilizes the Baths as yet another means of architecture vocalizing existential freedom to Jep.

For *La dolce vita*, the site's history as an emperor's baths is given in a passing remark by a visitor to call attention to the symbolic weight held by Rome's structural narrative. To briefly mention the historicity of the monument makes it all the more confusing to the viewer when it has been appropriated into a nightclub. In this way, the narrative is redrawn and the people of Rome are beginning to heap upon their city a new one: a narrative of horrific abandon to carnality.

Sylvia's actor friend, Frankie, calls for a rock and roll song and proceeds to fulfil the role of the mythological satyr by securing his nymph (Sylvia) and eliciting from her a celebration of the body through dance.[10] Fellini captures an infernal mood, panning by flaming horse head torches and tilting his camera upwards to show the viewer only blackness, as if the nightclub were a fiery pit. The aqueduct that fed the baths has since fallen into disuse and consequently, any notion of salvation – namely baptismal water – has been replaced in the architecture with fire and an arid aesthetic to play host to Frankie and Sylvia's hellish debauchery. Marcello watches the circular dance, the gyre of Sylvia's spinning body under the satyr's hands, and is still deaf to how Rome's descent into frolicking lust mirrors his own.

Jep's visit to the Baths, however, is the seed to his awakening. Following Ramona's death and his sombre contemplation of the capsized *Costa Concordia*,[11] Jep strolls into the Baths and is confronted with a giraffe and a magician who claims he can make the animal vanish. But the magician confesses that the feat is an illusion. It is here that the film's flagship phrase is delivered: 'It's just a trick'. That the giraffe itself is not real, but rather a computer-generated rendering of one, is no coincidence given the magician's words. This is the filmic equivalent of a 'trick': a graphical image that is both illusory yet still grounded in reality, as can be said of Sorrentino's film and Jep's journey. The magician's words reverberate off the walls of the Baths, resulting in an echo directly from the architecture of Rome itself. It would seem the Baths are still retentive of their anointing waters for Jep, and ironically, he receives them in the figurative shoes of a tourist. As Jep says earlier in the film, '[t]he best people in Rome are the tourists', because they see everything with a freshness and vivacity now lost to the jaded locals of the city. Instead of hearing his mantra of enlightenment from an intimate friend in a private setting, he hears it from a magician acquaintance that entertains the visitors of a tourist hotspot. In this moment, Jep relinquishes his world-weariness and sees Rome – and his life – with the virginal eyes of a newcomer.

Conclusion

Though *La dolce vita* and *The Great Beauty* offer radically different portrayals of the Eternal City, these portrayals are mutually accomplished through architecture. More specifically, it is how this architecture gains a vocal quality through the filmic medium that allows Rome to truly interact with the protagonists of both films. As Bondanella thoroughly puts it, *La dolce vita* sees Rome '[…] reduced to a city where life revolves around foolish public relations stunts, meaningless or shallow intellectual debates, and sterile love affairs' (1987: 238). Such decline is mirrored in the crumbling architecture of the city, which is constantly calling for Marcello's attention to recognize the state of affairs and re-evaluate his lifestyle accordingly.

It is *The Great Beauty*, however, which takes the vocalism of the architecture to unprecedented territory. Sorrentino fashions methods for Rome to speak to Jep by channelling sound, exhuming the ruins of his past through museum artwork and approaching him with a signature geometric sublimity, which characterizes the cinematography throughout the film. Sorrentino has given Jep his 'existential foothold' through the architectural dialogue (Norberg-Schulz 1980: 6). The reaction to Rome's voice – its beckoning or outcry – is what determines such disparate fates for Jep and Marcello in the final scenes of both films.

It is unnerving to witness how spiritually deaf Marcello has become in the final moments of *La dolce vita*. While Paola, the Umbrian angel, calls out to him from across the inlet, he not only fails to communicate, but shrugs at his inability to do so, allowing complacency to triumph. Marcello has failed to realize that he has busied himself in the shadow of Rome. All that Rome has suffered throughout the film – the perversion of its churches, castles and monuments by the hands of socialites – has been the suffering of Marcello, but the city's voices met only silence.

Rome, in all its eternal beauty has likewise clashed with Jep as a man whose age is as mortally frightening as his ever-vanishing potential to write another novel. However, the conversation he and Rome maintain throughout *The Great Beauty* is far from taunting; it is affirming. Liberation comes from resurrecting the life hidden beneath the 'blah blah blah', beneath the worldly trivialities that have tricked us into attending to them foremost. Jep comes to see that he and the 'blah, blah, blah' among him are yet another interpolation in the infinite narrative of the ever-ruinous Rome, tracing back to Marcello's ilk and forward to whatever brand of decadence will take the place of the present.

La dolce vita casts a keen eye on the atrophy of its city, but all is not lost if it still bears a certain sweetness of life. In fact, Fellini himself opines that 'decadence is indispensable to rebirth' (Bondanella 1987: 237). For this director, the dissolution of art, morals and ideologies is natural and not 'a sign of the death of civilization but, on the contrary, a sign of its life' (Bondanella 1987: 238). *The Great Beauty* nourishes itself from the same fodder of decadence, but is sure to retain the immaculateness of its architecture. In the final moments of both films, the opposing reaction of these protagonists to Rome's architectural voice results in two poignantly different conclusions: one in which a man stands dumb on a beach, smiled at, and the other, a man who is smiling himself.

NOTES

1. Unless otherwise indicated, all translations from the original Italian/French are mine.
2. The hill also serves as a symbolic vehicle through the invocation of its namesake, Janus: the Roman divinity of beginnings, who was 'always invoked first in every undertaking, even before Jupiter' (Smith and Anthon 1885: 406). The hill's correlation to Janus is especially germane to the theme of architecture as this divinity was the celestial porter – 'the god who opens and shuts' (Smith and Anthon 1885: 406).
3. In Sorrentino's narration of the opening scene with the *New York Times*, he explains that David Lang's song is 'a beautiful example of sacred music' (Sorrentino 2013a).
4. This scene is shot in the *Villa Giustiniani Odescalchi*. For a brief anatomy of the location and how the partygoers navigated the villa, see Canino Info and Mazzuoli (2011).
5. The unemployment of the wealthy enjoys its reprise in *The Great Beauty*. When Jep asks Orietta what she does for a living, she simply replies, '[m]e? I'm rich'.

6. Sorrentino's epigraph for *The Great Beauty* is Céline's own epigraph from his novel *Journey to the End of the Night* (Céline 2006): 'To travel is very useful, it makes the imagination work, the rest is just delusion and pain. Our journey is entirely imaginary, which is its strength'.

7. Steiner, Marcello's friend and arguably his role model, is insulted by a guest at his own party with Marcello present. A poet says he is 'as primitive as a gothic spire [...] so high up that [he's] unable to hear anyone's voice'.

8. Poking fun at the misinformation and architectural consumerism of the tourist, Fellini allows Sylvia to ask, while gazing at the city, where *Giotto's Campanile* is, which Marcello informs her is not even in Rome, but in Florence. The ignorance of Roman architecture returns in the following scene when the visitor to the Baths of Caracalla believes the entire bathing complex was solely for the emperor.

9. For a summary of Marforio's history and its relocation to the Capitoline Hill, see Claridge et al. (1998). Regarding the 'talking statues', Claridge also discusses Pasquin, the most significant of these statues, and its usage as a platform for epigrams (Claridge et al. 1998: 211).

10. For a more detailed physical description of the satyrs and their proclivity for sensual pleasures in Greco-Roman mythology, see Smith and Anthon (1885: 781).

11. The shipwreck is emblematic of rebirth for Fellini. Bondanella quotes Fellini: 'I have already said that I love shipwrecks. So I am happy to be living at a time when everything is capsizing' (1987: 237).

REFERENCES

Bondanella, P. (1987), *The Eternal City: Roman Images in the Modern World*, Chapel Hill, NC and London: The University of North Carolina Press.

Bondanella, P. and Pacchioni, F. (2017), *A History of Italian Cinema*, 2nd ed., New York and London: Bloomsbury Academic.

Canino Info and Mazzuoli, G. (2011), '*La dolce vita* di Fellini', Canino.info, 15 October, http://www.canino.info/inserti/tuscia/luoghi/dolce_vita/index.htm. Accessed 22 July 2016.

Céline, Louis-Ferdinand (2006), *Journey to the End of the Night*, New York: New Directions.

Claridge, A., Toms, J. and Cubberley, T. (1998), *Rome: An Oxford Archaeological Guide*, Oxford: Oxford University Press.

Fellini, F. (1960), *La dolce vita*, Italy: Cineriz.

Freud, S. (1962), *Civilization and Its Discontents* (ed. J. Strachey), New York: W.W. Norton & Company.

Martini, A. (2015), 'Concept city: Roma ri-vista e vissuta ne *La dolce vita* e *La grande bellezza*', *Carte Italiane*, 2:10, pp. 107–19, https://escholarship.org/uc/item/0gk9569v. Accessed 25 January 2018.

Mecchia, G. (2016), 'Birds in the Roman sky: Shooting for the sublime in *La grande bellezza*', *Forum Italicum*, 50:1, pp. 183–93, http://journals.sagepub.com/doi/abs/10.1177/001458 5816637069. Accessed 5 February 2018.

Musei Capitolini Official Website (2017), 'Collossal statue restored as Oceanus: "Marforio"', http://www.museicapitolini.org/en/collezioni/percorsi_per_sale/palazzo_nuovo/cortile/statua_colossale_restaurata_come_oceano_marforio. Accessed 26 April 2016.

Norberg-Schulz, C. (1980), *Genius Loci: Towards a Phenomenology of Architecture*, New York: Rizzoli.

Oberhuber, K. (1999), *Raphael: The Paintings*, Munich: Prestel.

Picarelli, E. (2015), 'The great beauty: Italy's inertia and neo-baroque aestheticism', *JOMEC Journal*, 1:8, pp. 1–17, http://doi.org/10.18573/j.2015.10032.

Smith, W. and Anthon, C. (1885), *A New Classical Dictionary of Greek and Roman Biography, Mythology and Geography*, New York: Harper & Brothers Publishers.

Sorrentino, P. (2013a), 'Anatomy of a scene', interviewed by Mekado Murphy, *New York Times*, 13 November, https://artsbeat.blogs.nytimes.com/2013/11/13/anatomy-of-a-scene-video-of-the-great-beauty/. Accessed 7 January 2016.

Sorrentino, P. (2013b), *La grande bellezza (The Great Beauty)*, Italy: Medusa Film.

Various Artists (2013), *Original Motion Picture Soundtrack: The Great Beauty*, MP3, Rome: Indigo Film S.r.l.

Vidler, A. (1993), 'The explosion of space: Architecture and the filmic imaginary', *Assemblage*, 1:21, August, pp. 44–59, http://www.jstor.org/stable/3171214. Accessed 31 October 2017.

7

The Great Beauty:
A Journey Through Art and Relations
in Search for Beauty

Michela Barisonzi

Monash University

Paolo Sorrentino has often been accused of favouring form over substance in his films. *The Great Beauty* is no exception, epitomizing for many the aesthetic interpretation of Sorrentino's works. As Fonzi Kliemann points out, this movie has been criticized in Italy especially 'for the characters' superficiality and indifference, for the film's formal artistry matched with an uninspiring, depressing content' (2014: 30+).[1] However, as I aim to show, this film is itself a reflection on the very form-substance dichotomy. This chapter explores how and why Sorrentino introduces elements of beauty throughout the film, before promptly tearing them down to reveal their emptiness. While the form is discussed through the critique of the idea of canonical and modern aesthetics, substance is explored through the endless search for true beauty. In this way, the film brings together the two components of this binary, offering a new definition of beauty, to be found in real human relationships.

Postcards from Rome: The Death of the Tourist

In an attempt to create a dialogical discourse on the social nature of aesthetics, the film opens to a panorama of Rome, and its many aesthetic points of attraction, to address and question the function of the artistic gaze and its relation to the viewers' shared notions of *bellezza* (beauty).

In the opening sequence, the cinematic eye initially underlines the idea of an idyllic Eternal City. It plays on the presence of the tourists to reproduce a voyeuristic gaze

109

that embraces with lyrical splendour the monuments and the sprawling city of Rome from the Janiculum terrace, in a cornice of trees, birds and fountains. The scene then plays with John Urry's definition of the places that are 'chosen to be gazed upon' by the tourist, creating an anticipation that 'especially through daydreaming and fantasy, [...] is constructed and sustained through a variety of non-tourist practices, such as [precisely the] film' (2002: 3).[2] However, in a Nietzschean and D'Annunzian reading of the function of sunlight at noon,[3] the hour at which this scene takes place as underlined by the cannon fire, the viewer is soon presented with a reality beyond this idyllic, daydreaming veil. This light 'attraverso una sorta di ubriacatura che riesce ad annebbiare la razionalità [...][è] in grado di mostrare ciò che per lo più è nascosto' (through a sort of intoxication blurring one's rationality [...] [is] able to show what is usually hidden) (Piredda 2014: 45), the truth overcoming appearance, which here is symbolized by the dead body of the tourist.[4] Once the tourist's gaze is removed, the idyllic depiction (or deception) of the city is replaced by a more disenchanted reality brought about through the representation of Rome's inhabitants.

The contrast between the tourist's and the locals' perception of the city is stark. As Urry points out, the tourist's gaze is 'directed to features of the landscape and townscape, which separate them off from everyday experience. Such aspects are viewed because they are taken to be in some sense out of the ordinary' (2002: 3). The same features, however, become ordinary to the everyday Roman and are neglected by the gaze of the local. For this reason, the camera alternates images of a mesmerized tourist contemplating iconic Roman monuments and the landscape,[5] with images that, as Enrica Picarelli points out, glide 'across the gardens, capturing in tracking shots' (2015: 6) aging and otherwise out-of-place people engaging in trivial and somewhat unpleasant-to-the-eye activities. These people are presented smoking, sleeping, reading trashy tabloid newspapers, or washing themselves in the fountains. They are juxtaposed with the classical beauty of the statues representing the makers of Italy's greatness, Italian heroes, underlining how these monuments go unnoticed by the city's inhabitants.

The different ways in which the tourists and the citizens interact with the beauty of the monuments introduce then the first reflection on the form and substance dichotomy of beauty, the object of this study. Form is represented here through the tourist's gaze, and it is contrasted with substance, or lack thereof (when the connections between people and their past and history are lost), which is introduced and criticized through the presence of the Roman citizens. Sorrentino underlined this direction in an interview for the *New York Times*, in which he stated that Rome 'is one of the most beautiful [cities] in the world, built by the Italian people many many years ago. But now the people who are in Italy are not able to replicate that beauty' (Rohter 2014: n.pag.). 'The beauty of the city and the lack of beauty of the people' (Rohter 2014: n.pag.) creates a further motive for reflection on the form-substance dichotomy symbolized by this scene, as it poses the questions of what beauty is, and what function does it retain in current society.

From an aesthetic perspective alone, the opening sequence leaves us with little doubt as to what is and isn't beautiful. Rome's artistic treasures could hardly present a greater contrast against the almost grotesque figures of its inhabitants. However, in order to answer the first question and adequately define beauty, it is important to consider the constant shift of focus that the film offers beyond the canonical definition of beauty, both from the perspective of the arts and the people themselves.

Reproducing the problematic relationship between the past and the present suggested in Fellini's *Roma*, the film challenges the validity of traditional aesthetic values in modern times, while at the same time questioning current notions of art.[6] This is particularly evident through the contrast between Roman and Renaissance masterpieces and modern forms of performative art. This contrast, however, goes beyond the battle for validation between classic and modern, each vying to be considered the true form of art. From a visual perspective, as the camera pans across various beautiful panoramas of Rome, the audience prepares itself for an even more beautiful climax, almost in an attempt to briefly reintroduce the tourist's gaze. However, these scenes invariably end by turning the viewers' expectations upside down, challenging what they thought they would see. The classical postcard-views of Rome and its iconic monuments do not escape what Deleuze defines as the process of 'tearing a real image from clichés' (Deleuze 1989: 21). Rome and its famous landmarks are no longer treated as framed reproductions for a tourist advertisement of the Italian *dolce vita*.[7] The film's images uproot these landmarks, presenting a different reality that questions the very essence of the *dolce vita*. This process is exemplified by the shot panning across the Colosseum from the protagonist's terrace, where the seemingly idyllic sight of the monument at sunset is spoilt by the traffic jam in the very same image. It is also evident as Jep quietly strolls down the Tiber river in the morning light, where the beauty and spirituality of the scene and landmarks are disturbed by a group of swearing joggers. Through these devices, the film leads the viewer to constantly question whether what they are seeing is indeed beauty, through a process of 'dematerialization of truth and objectivity' (Cangiano 2019: 340), challenging the very notion of aesthetic unity and transcendence to the disadvantage of substance, of which instead Sorrentino has been often accused.[8]

Portraits: Beauty Beyond the Glass

Through a similar process to the one applied to the monuments, the landscapes, and the fine art of the classic and contemporary Roman scene, the film questions the idea of human physical beauty, introducing the viewer to a new aspect of contrast.

After the calm opening across Rome, the film abruptly cuts to a loud, fashionable party for the protagonist's 65th birthday, crowded with young girls, sophisticated women, and otherwise beautiful people. However, this is soon converted into a quasi-grotesque satire of the modern concept of beauty and happiness. By sheer accumulation and juxtaposition of antithetical images of bodies, sounds and movements, the scene of the party reaches a sensorial and sensual overload in what Picarelli defines a 'baroque cinematography of contrasting elements that follow each other in an accumulative aesthetics of dazzling effect' (2015: 8). In this carnivalesque parade, music becomes a powerful instrument to challenge the notion of physical beauty. As Sorrentino pointed out in an interview with Sean Hutchinson (2013), the importance of music and its effectiveness rest on its immediate accessibility, as it does not need any form of cultural mediation to convey an emotion in the listener. The disco version of the pop song by Raffaella Carrà, *A far l'amore comincia tu*, intermixed with the music of a Mariachi band, then, conveys the idea of a theatrical and burlesque parade. This is explicitly underlined by the camera angles which suddenly turns the image of the partying people upside-down. Conversely, the music of Arvo Pärt, with its classical and quasi-religious melodies, suddenly appears when the viewer is taken beyond the glass where an artist-stripper is performing, almost unnoticed by the guests of the party. The association of Pärt's music and the images of the stripper, dressed as a burlesque theatre actress, creates an audio-visual shock that once more destabilizes the viewer's notion of beauty. Pärt's music, as is the case for other contemporary composers of classical music that will be discussed later, is used to signify moments of true beauty, in contrast with the superficial and corrupted beauty represented at the party.

The human body and both its classical and modern interpretations in terms of beauty are torn apart in the scene of the party as the perfect bodies of many young model-like and *velina*-style[9] guests are contrasted with the bodies of Dadina (a dwarf), a washed-up former Italian soubrette whose beauty has long faded, and the aforementioned stripper. Initially, the focus seems to be favouring the erotic moves of the first group of guests as they are at the centre of male appreciation, while the imperfect bodies of these other three women are used to create contrast and an almost burlesque effect. However, the body of the dancer/stripper,[10] especially once desexualized through the sacred melody of Pärt's music associated with her dancing, becomes a pure form of art in contrast with the guests, whose dancing is sexually charged, reproducing an animal-like mating ritual.[11] The shift in the music when the view is presented from inside the glass rather than outside, not only underlines the positivity and harmony of the stripper's body, but seems to hint and symbolize the difference between the exteriority-superficiality from beyond the glass, and its substance and serenity from within the glass.

The choice of music, and in particular that of Pärt, Goreki, Martynov and Preisner, therefore, becomes an instrument to underline moments of true beauty and a source of true beauty itself, through which the film regains a sense of aesthetic unity. As Stefano Sfondrini (2019) points out, the title of Martynov's music *The Beatitudes*, containing the word 'beauty', seems to suggest precisely this function of music. In particular, Sfondrini underlines how *The Beatitudes* is played four times during the film, each coinciding precisely with a moment of true beauty. These moments include the brief encounter between Jep and the iconic actress Fanny Ardant, the photographic exhibition of portraits produced by a father and son, the scene in which Countess Colonna looks at her basinet remembering her childhood, and the closing scene that takes the viewer's gaze one more time along the bends of the Tiber river.

In the first case, the actress represents the idealization of beauty, a diva from the past, filtered through the memories of what she represented for a young Jep and his generation. However, youth, both of the actress and of Jep, is here the key aspect of this idea of beauty. This image connects specifically to the idea of a golden age of life, which I will discuss in more detail later in this chapter, and to which also belongs the image and significance of Jep's first love. The scene of Countess Colonna's cradle points to a similar notion of beauty as it connects to another golden age, that of childhood, and introduces the theme of the bond between a parent and a child. Looking back, it is not the expensive works of art that capture her attention, but the humble cradle, with its beauty transcending aesthetics. This is further developed in the scene of the photographic exhibition, where the bond between son and father overcomes the physical appearance of the subject photographed, giving it true meaning. These are not photos of a beautiful person, but rather beautiful photos, born of a real and beautiful relationship. In all these scenes, with the exception of the closing scene along the Tiber, the focus is on relationships. The use of the music seems then to hint to the fact that images of beauty emerging from true relationships surpass any representation of canonical or conventionally accepted beauty. For this reason, relationships and their effect on the perception of beauty become here the focus of attention.

A Socially Human Apparatus

The film's search for contrast rather than a superficial unity does not spare its protagonists, introducing the viewer to a procession of characters whose lives, while superficially perfect and beautiful, hide endless dissatisfaction and an unyielding sense of social degeneration.

The importance and critique of the connection between social relations and beauty, especially of the body, recurs throughout the film and it is synthetized in the title of Jep's only novel, *L'apparato umano*, which made Jep famous, exponentially increasing his social influence to the point of being crowned the king of Roman 'mondanità' (high society). Here, the phrase human apparatus could be interpreted in anatomical terms as the body itself of a human being. However, apparatus can also be used to indicate, in Foucauldian terms, the sum of structures (institutional, physical, knowledge) through which relations of power are exercised within the social body.[12] This hints towards a more social interpretation of such a system, underlining the human connections and relations that constitute it.

This double definition that connotates the phrase 'apparato umano' is then even more evident when we consider that the physical beauty of the characters, or the representation and perception of it, changes throughout the film, following the development of the relationships between the protagonists. For example, when the character of Ramona is introduced, she is described by her own father as too old to be attractive or a sex symbol, despite working as a stripper in a night club. However, as her relationship with Jep progresses, and as she opens up to him, exposing her frailty, her body acquires a newfound beauty. This goes even further when her weaknesses and disease are revealed, as time is no longer a symbol of aging and decay, but her body becomes a tribute to a fully lived life, which Jep and his circle of friends cannot claim to have lived as they are still trapped in their past. In this sense, Ramona's body acquires the same symbolism that Sfondrini attributes to the photographic exhibition showing the face of the artist, photographed daily over 40 years, first by the artist's father and then continued by the artist himself. This exhibition represents human life in its entirety, with all its imperfection, and reveals visually both the love of a father for his son, and the love of a son for his father in continuing his work and making it public. Ramona's body too then becomes a tribute to life.

In contrast to Ramona's naked aging body and its true beauty, the viewer is presented with the perfect body of the artist Talia Concept who damages or pretends to damage her own body as part of her performance, under the guise of art. The body then becomes a means through which the film investigates the embodiment of beauty while challenging the socially imposed codification of the female body as a passive object, meant to give pleasure through static contemplation.[13] Through the female artist who literally damages her statue-like body, the film visualizes the idea of going beyond a passive superficial and canonical beauty, as only when this is 'torn apart' is it possible for the true beauty of emotions and relationships to emerge. In this sense, in line with Mecchia's (2016) definition of sublime in *The Great Beauty*, the viewer must 'face [...] a sudden, shocking encounter [...] an experience [that] is affective, deeply emotional, and potentially truthful in a manner that need not be strictly rational' (Pence 2004: 55). The provocative representation of the artist's puzzling performance and the unjustified applause it receives from the audience creates, at an unconscious level, this type of shock. This prepares the viewer for the following scene of the interview where the substance of Talia Concept's art falls apart, as Jep reveals how in reality it is only 'fuffa' (empty talk) (Sorrentino 2013). During the interview between Jep and Talia Concept, the viewer is presented with her aesthetic vision, the Concept suggested by her own artistic pseudonym, which may suggest Italy's current aesthetic vision (if we identify the world Talia with Italia).[14] However, this aesthetic vision does not eventuate as her performance and its meaning or lack thereof crumbles under Jep's insistence on concrete answers. Jep's interrogation then mirrors Sorrentino's quest for substance, also underlined by the expression 'zoccolo duro' (hard core) (Sorrentino 2013), with which Jep defines the readership for whom he works.

The fallacy behind Talia Concept's performance, highlighted both by the fake walls she hits and her inability to define her art, therefore, represents once more the film's constant tension between appearance and substance, fully and openly revealed to the viewer by the expression 'è solo un trucco' (it's just a trick) (Sorrentino 2013), in the scene with the disappearance of the giraffe.[15] Nevertheless, Sorrentino goes beyond this unmasking process as he seeks to reveal the true meaning of beauty.

Sublime Relationships and Roots

Scholars such as Mecchia (2016) have pointed to the concept of sublime reflected in the gaze of infinite skies and masses of water, as the answer to the film's quest for beauty. While postulating the idea that, in the film, beauty no longer coincides only with forms and objects such as monuments or bodies, I argue that true beauty emerges from relationships. Nevertheless, relationships too must first undergo a process of destruction. The superficial elements of relationships need to be unveiled in order to leave space for new development or the rediscovery of beauty in true relationships. For this reason, using Elena del Río's definition of Jep as an 'aesthetic catalyst' (2017: 19), it is possible to see how Jep becomes the means through which the film unveils true beauty to the spectator through his relationships.

Family and friends are the privileged loci of such relationships. The first is suggested, as we have seen, in the photographic exhibition and in the scene with the cradle of Countess Colonna, as well as being alluded to during Ramona and Jep's first conversation, with the expression 'la famiglia è 'na bella cosa' (family is a beautiful thing) (Sorrentino 2013), where the notions of family and beauty are directly associated. The second is shown through Jep's interactions with Ramona, Romano and Stefania. This is synthetized in Jep's words 'siamo tutti sull'orlo della disperazione, non abbiamo altro rimedio che guardarci in faccia e farci compagnia e pigliarci un poco in giro' (we are all on the verge of desperation, all we can do is look each other in the eyes, keep each other company, and make fun of each other) (Sorrentino 2013). These words draw attention to the human need for affiliation, support and solidarity from others; however, these needs can be satisfied only through genuine relationships.

For this reason, Jep tears apart the clichéd and superficial life of Stefania, as the film did with the postcard-like images of Rome, in order to unmask the fallacies of her apparently perfect life, and establishing a truthful connection with her and her real needs.[16] It is only after his blunt assessment of her life that Jep and Stefania's friendship becomes once again meaningful, producing moments of true happiness and beautiful memories, such as towards the end of the film, in the scene where they are dancing in the garden, reminiscing about their friendship.

Finally, family, friends and the true beauty of relationships are connected and brought together by the concept of roots that Sister Maria presents to Jep towards the end of the film. For the scope of this chapter, roots are seen as the foundation of one's self, one's sense of identity (Cangiano 2019: 339), and are associated with the idea of youth, which in the film is presented at three levels. In the first case youth is filtered through memory, representing one's past, as in the case of Jep's first love or Countess Colonna's infancy. Then, there is youth in its current existence as underlined in the scenes of the children playing in the gardens near Jep's house, and the children eating sweets before the commencement of the art show. Finally, there is youth and roots in terms of one's place of origin, home, underscored in the character of Romano.

The two examples of Jep and Countess Colonna present roots as the individual's past and origins at a temporal level. This youth, however, because it is related to time, is filtered and presented through a process of idealization through which this stage of life is presented as belonging to a mythical past, a golden age of happiness. For Jep, youth and beauty become one and come to coincide with the beauty of a summer holiday spent with friends, the beauty of his first love and the beauty resting in the promises of the life to come. Although the images connected with this idea of one's own past and happiness produce idyllic moments and beautiful memories, and therefore would in general be seen as positive, they are however a crystallized image of the self in the past and cannot deliver real satisfaction and happiness. This discrepancy between the potential-self, contained only in memories, and the actual self, creates a paralysing tension. For this reason, Jep has not and will never find another true love or write a new book, unless the conflict is resolved. This tension between present and past at Jep's personal level seems then to mirror the contrast between the city's artistic and architectural past glories and its current status of decay that I have explored in the first section of this work.

Jep, like Rome and by extension Italy, is unable to live in the present. He is crystallized in a glorified past that is no longer accessible or reproducible. Even his juvenile artistic success functions as an inhibiting factor. He lives off the fame of his past work without producing anything new. Rome and the country seem to be portrayed in the film in a similar inertia.[17] While seizing the fruits of its past artistic splendour, Italy seems unable to produce new cultural and artistic greatness, trapped in a state of profound decay as suggested both by its inhabitants, and Jep's friends, all undergoing personal crisis.

In the second case, with the images of the children playing innocently, the viewer instead is presented with the creative act of making future memories as youth is lived. The life of the children contains both the present and the potential, or in Deleuze's (1989) terms, the virtual future life and selves. However, as the children are presented as innocent, with no externally derived notions of beauty influencing their perception, they are free to experience true beauty in their playful interactions and in their relationships with their surroundings.

Finally, the third case explores youth and roots from the perspective of who you are and where you are from, through the character of Romano. Romano is presented throughout the film as somewhat desperate for love, hanging onto opportunistic and unreciprocated relationships. He is trying to live the life he dreamt of when he was young, represented by his move to Rome, the capital of the 'mondanità'. However, as the film progresses, he finds more moments of happiness when he is true to himself. His writing and performance receive a standing ovation when he composes his own content, instead of rehashing someone else's work. He tells Jep of his relations with a woman from his hometown and talks of her fondly – not in terms of her looks, but as a person. Then, at the conclusion of the film, he tells Jep he is leaving to return home, stating that Rome 'mi ha molto desluso' (has really disappointed me) (Sorrentino 2013), and after 40 years in Rome, the only person who deserved a goodbye was Jep. In this, the viewer sees Romano finally come to terms with the empty farce he has been living and sees him choose to go back to his geographical roots, his village, which symbolizes his authentic self and the genuine relations that come with that, as 'only when the character gains her/his own identity, life and reality itself become meaningful, and only then, reality stops being a fluid heap of unrelated facts (a "spectacle", in a Debaurdian sense)' (Cangiano 2019: 340).

Conclusions

Sorrentino in *The Great Beauty* does not prefer form over substance, but rather explores the very idea of what it means to have substance, presenting aesthetic beauty in order to critique it, and finding true beauty in unconventional places.

Sorrentino shows the viewer how beauty can be found in love, in a true friend, in the games of school children or in the tribute of a father to a son. Beauty is not in objects, but in life conceived as the precarious and ever-changing sum of human fragilities and relationships, or in Simondon's words as a 'milieu densely populated with relations' (Combes 2012: 37).

NOTES

1. See also Picarelli's reflections on the accusations of superficial sensationalism, and the caustic comments, directed to this film by much of the Italian press and critics in the days following the Oscar award ceremony (2015: 1–2).

2. The daydreaming and fantastic atmosphere are here underlined through the use of music, which will be discussed more in detail throughout the chapter.

3. The mention of D'Annunzio refers to his interpretation in *Il trionfo della morte* of Nietzsche's midday light, and its disenchanting function through which Ippolita's idealized beauty is torn down to reveal her true and somewhat imperfect physicality (see Barisonzi 2019).

4. As Jep's voice states at the end of the film 'Finisce sempre così: colla morte. Prima però, c'è stata la vita. Nascosta sotto il blah blah blah…' ('It always ends like this: with death. However, first there is life, hidden under the blah blah blah…') (Sorrentino 2013). Therefore, the death of the tourist becomes necessary to dissipate the 'blah', the superficial appearances that his gaze proposes to the viewer in order to start the quest for true beauty.

5. The film even hints at the possibility that the tourist died because he was overwhelmed by the view.

6. According to Fonzi Kliemann (2014), Sorrentino in the film prefers classical art over modern artistic performances; however, the constant challenging perspective with which the film presents both forms of art shows how in reality this question of validity of one over the other is left unresolved.

7. Johnny Bertolio in a detailed review of the literary sources that, more or less overtly, informed *The Great Beauty*, starkly states that the Rome here depicted is 'neither World War II "open city" of the neo-realist cinema nor the effervescent site of the 1960s economic boom of Federico Fellini's movies. The Rome portrayed by Sorrentino is the sad mirror of a masturbatory society whose only goal is to arrive in decent shape to the next night's party' (2016: 319).

8. Images, music and camera angles are used to underline this contrasting perception of beauty, and create an initial sense of fragmentation that seems to challenge Alain Badiou's (2013) definition of classical cinema as a romantic form that asserts an authorial and aesthetic unity within the two-hour feature format.

9. I refer here to the term as it is used in the famous Italian TV format *Striscia la notizia* to label the main female characters. This programme epitomizes what Picarelli aptly defines

as the 'various forms of light entertainment that invariably foreground charismatic male figures while belittling and overexposing, the (scantly-dressed) female body' (2015: 5). These programs, Picarelli continues, have contributed to the establishment of the so-called phenomenon of *berlusconismo* and its 'pornocratic rule' of aesthetics and cultural inertia (2015: 5–6), which, according to the scholar, is attacked in the film.

10. The contrast is even more striking when you consider that this performer is actually wearing a burlesque-theatre costume.

11. Picarelli points here to the use of the camera that 'pushes through a mass of limbs that move frenetically, mimicking or pursuing copulation' underlining how 'all its flesh in its primary meaning of living matter' and 'excess dominates the scene', to create an even more striking and overwhelming effect of 'sensorial overload' (2015: 8).

12. I refer here to the definition that Clare O'Farrell (2005) gives of apparatus in her work on Foucault, using this term as the official translation of the original French term *dispositif*.

13. Contrary to Danielle Hipkins' considerations on Sorrentino's representation of the female character as a 'fetish object for the narration of male desire' (2008: 213), I consider the representation of the female body in *The Great Beauty* as a means of female affirmation that challenges the stereotypical idea of perfection and aesthetically superficial beauty. This is especially achieved through the characters of Ramona and Talia, as these women defy the social canons of beauty by consciously using their imperfect (aged or injured) bodies as means through which they affirm their independence from male characters.

14. This identification is suggested by the use of the term 'Talia' to indicate Italy in literary works such as Capuana's *Gambalesta*. In this patriotic novel, the Sicilian crowd salutes Garibaldi's arrival with the motto 'Viva la Talia'.

15. Interestingly, Giacomo Boitani points to the way in which the trick of the disappearance of the giraffe as well as the scene of the flamingos on Jep's balcony are used to create a clash between these computer-generated images and the 'impeccable photography of Rome that characterizes the majority of the film' (2014: n.pag.). However, Boitani considers this clash as an awakening for Jep, through which the protagonist manages to 'transcend the artificial, but paralyzing dualism between socially-responsibly creativity and pure aestheticism' (2014: n.pag.). Conversely, I suggest that this clash is used to reinforce the distinction between appearance and substance as the holographic reproduction of the giraffe comes to symbolize the aesthetic form that creates stupor and a superficial initial admiration in the viewer, as it does in Jep, but whose disappearance leaves the viewer questioning the lack of substance.

16. Significantly, the scene in which Jep exposes the façade of Stefania's life is followed by a scene where Stefania is shown swimming underwater naked in her swimming pool and then emerging from under the water's surface in a symbolic rebirth.

17. On the concept of Italy's inertia, see Picarelli (2015: 6–7).

REFERENCES

Badiou, A. (2013), *Cinéma,* Cambridge, UK; Malden, MA: Polity Press.

Barisonzi, M. (2019), *Adultery and Hysteria in the Nineteenth-Century Novel: The Case of Gabriele D'Annunzio,* Leicester, UK: Troubador Publishing Ltd.

Bertolio, J. L. (2016), 'The literary substance of *The Great Beauty* (2013)', *Journal of Italian Cinema and Media Studies,* 4:2, pp. 319-22.

Boitani, G. (2014), 'The Art Conondrum, with a Capital C', *The Mantle,* https://mantlethought. org/arts-and-culture/art-conundrum-capital-c. Accessed 8 August 2019.

Cangiano, M. (2019), 'Against postmodernism: Paolo Sorrentino and the search for authenticity', *Journal of Italian Cinema and Media Studies,* 7:3, pp. 339–49, doi: 10.1386/jicms.7.3.339_1.

Combes, M. (2012), *Gilbert Simondon and the Philosophy of the Transindividual,* Cambridge, MA: MIT Press Ltd.

Del Río, E. (2017), '*The Great Beauty*: Adventures in transindividuality', *NECSUS: European Journal of Media Studies,* 6:2, pp. 19–36, doi: https://doi.org/10.25969/mediarep/3398.

Deleuze, G. (1989), *Cinema 2: The Time-Image,* Minneapolis: University of Minnesota Press.

Fonzi Kliemann, C. (2014), 'Cultural and political exhaustion in Paolo Sorrentino's *The Great Beauty*', *Senses of Cinema,* 70, pp. 30+, EBSCOhost, search.ebscohost.com/login.aspx? direct=true&db=f3h&AN=95292728&site=ehost-live&scope=site. Accessed 18 July 2019.

Hipkins, D. (2008), 'Why Italian film studies needs a second take on gender', *Italian Studies,* 63:2, pp. 213–34.

Hutchinson, S. (2013), 'Sean interviews *The Great Beauty* Director Paolo Sorrentino', *Criterion Cast,* 13 November, http://criterioncast.com/interviews/sean-interviews-the-great-beautydirector-paolo-sorrentino/. Accessed 28 May 2019.

Mecchia, G. (2016), 'Birds in the Roman Sky: Shooting for the sublime in *The Great Beauty*', *Forum Italicum,* 50:1, pp. 183–93.

O'Farrell, C. (2005), *Michel Foucault,* London: Sage.

Pence, J. (2004), 'Cinema of the sublime: Theorizing the ineffable', *Poetics Today,* 25:1, pp. 29–66.

Picarelli, E. (2015), '*The Great Beauty*: Italy's inertia and neo-baroque aestheticism', *JOMEC Journal 8, Italian Cultural Studies* (ed. F. Bernardi), pp. 1–16, http://dx.doi. org/10.18573/j.2015.10032.

Piredda, P. (2014), 'L'etico non si può insegnare', *Studio ermeneutico sull'etica e il linguaggio in Nietzsche e D'Annunzio attraverso la filosofia di Wittgenstein,* Leicester: Troubador Publishing Ltd.

Rohter, L. (2014), 'Paolo Sorrentino on "The Great Beauty" and Italian Alienation', *The New York Times,* 4 December, http://carpetbagger.blogs.nytimes.com/2013/12/04/paolo-sorrentinoon-the-great-beauty-and-italian-alienation/. Accessed 19 May 2019.

Sfondrini, S. (2019), '*The Great Beauty in The Great Beauty*', https://www.academia. edu/12517026/La_grande_bellezza_in_La_grande_bellezza_. Accessed 6 June 2019.

Sorrentino, P. (2013), *The Great Beauty,* Italy: Medusa Video.

Urry, J. (2002), *The Tourist Gaze,* 2nd ed, London: SAGE.

8

The Urban Dimension as Film Character: Rome in *The Great Beauty*[1]

Carla Molinari

Leeds Beckett University

Introduction

> In themselves, the pictures, the phases, the elements of the whole are innocent and indecipherable. The blow is struck only when the elements are juxtaposed into a sequential image [...]. Only the film camera has solved the problem of doing this on a flat surface, but its undoubted ancestor in this capability is architecture.
>
> (Ejzenštejn 1989: 117)

The relationship between cinema and architecture is rich, complex and based on a mutual series of exchanges (Penz and Thomas 1997). Architecture, indeed, is a key element of films – from the construction of sets to the selection of real locations, there is always specific attention in the representation of architectural space in cinema. On the other hand, it is also vital for architects to reflect about and through cinema, and to learn from it. In this sense, there are two main crucial ways to approach films from an architectural perspective: one related to cinematic tools, and how these tools can be adopted in the design process; and the other about the specific use of films as instruments of analysis. Films can be relevant resources to understand and analyse architectural spaces and their cinematic relations, as Bruno Zevi argues:

> The researches of Edison and the Lumière brothers in the 1890's led to the invention of a camera geared to carry film forward continuously, so that a series of exposures could be taken in rapid succession, making it possible for photography to render an illusion of motion. This representation of architectonic space, because properly applied it resolves, in a practical way, almost all the problems posed by the fourth dimension.
>
> (Zevi 1974: 58–59)

From its revolutionary beginning to the more contemporary experimentations, cinema has always had an extremely interesting influence on architecture and, more specifically, on urban spaces. The modern city, in particular, with all its dynamic, swirling, futurist peculiarities, found in cinema a precious ally (Koeck and Roberts 2010). The idea of loss and alienation, inherent in urban industrial size and well expressed by Charles Baudelaire, Walter Benjamin and others, was in part based precisely on the feeling of increased speed and constant bombardment of sounds and images effectively reproducible only through filmic sequences.

> The ability of this new medium to capture images, process them, and then project them to the public contributed substantially to the making of the modern. In the process, cinema became engaged with the city, and vice versa, synchronizing its narrative and representational techniques with the emergence of radically new modern urban conditions.
>
> (AlSayyad 2006: 3)

This strong bond between films and cities, eventually creating what scholars define as 'city-based genres' (Webber and Wilson 2008: 1), provides an important field of investigation for architects and suggests the need to develop a 'focused and rigorous reading of the city on the screen in order to [...] explore the filmic spaces of the past in order to better anticipate the spaces of the future' (Penz 2010: 233).

This chapter aims to define an analytic method to analyse cinematic texts from an architectural perspective, and more specifically the investigation will focus on the filmic techniques used by Paolo Sorrentino in narrating Rome in the film *The Great Beauty* (2013). The in-depth analysis of several scenes of the film will be supported by a comparison with other Sorrentino's works, as well as with other films representing Rome. The final aim is to understand the relevance of Rome and its fictional representation in *The Great Beauty* (Martini 2015), underlining the power of cinema in narrating, and finally transforming, the urban context.

Sorrentino and the City

As argued in other essays of this collection, *The Great Beauty* does not have a singular, clear narrative line; teleological events do not result in a climax. The plot is just about a series of episodes during a specific period of time. This way Sorrentino is able to describe several important themes or situations from everyday life directly providing to the spectator the possibility to reconstruct the narrative line, piece by piece, and possibly the final meaning. Indeed, during the film we assist to a series of episodes related to Jep Gambardella, the main character, and his friends, a group of intellectuals from a tired and bored upper class settled in Rome. Jep, magnificently performed by Toni Servillo, is described as *quite an important* journalist, who once wrote *quite an important* book. Like all his friends, he appears as a person somehow unsatisfied, almost *empty*; he is constantly looking for something, for some kind of great, yet unattainable, beauty (Fiorito 2013; Salvestroni 2017).

Despite the vagueness of the narrative line, one crucial and constant element of the story is Rome. Even if in the majority of Sorrentino's films there is an evident attention to locations, as well as to the camera's techniques used to represent these locations, *The Great Beauty* is his only film in which a city has such an important role (Martini 2015). Rome is also the main location of other important works of Sorrentino, such as *Il Divo* (2008) and *The Young Pope* (2016). However, the role of Rome in *Il Divo* is different to the one in *The Great Beauty*. In *Il Divo*, Rome appears in some specific scenes and with great intensity (Viano 2010), but without occupying a predominant role. Similarly, the Rome of *The Young Pope* provides the perfect environment for the story, eventually highlighting some relevant aspects of the plot through the urban context, but the city is never the subject narrated.

Eventually, one might argue that *The Great Beauty* is probably the only film directed by Sorrentino where the city acts as character. In his other works, the cityscapes as well as landscapes are often used as perfect scenography, until the creation of a strong *'panic'* bound with characters (Mariani 2019), but never becoming more important than them. The location never takes total control of the scenes, as it does in *The Great Beauty*.

Interestingly enough, even in *Rio, I Love You* (Arriaga et al.2014) a film composed by several shorts realized by different directors, Sorrentino does not investigate the city directly. The film is part of a franchise created by Emmanuel Benbihy with the aim of using motion pictures to promote the touristic, economic and cultural development of urban areas. The series started with the films *Paris, je t'aime* (Assayas et al. 2006) and *New York, I Love You* (Akin et al. 2008), and as the titles clearly show these films were all a *love declaration* to a specific city. However, Sorrentino does not really use the city. More specifically, his short about Rio is based on the story of a couple occupying three main scenes. The first scene is on a plane approaching Rio from which we can see the city as a background. The second one is in a private villa surrounded by green hills and few other villas, seeing the sea in long distance. Finally, the last scene is on the beach. There are no constructions, streets, people. There is no city in sight; just sand. Ironically, the city appears only on the t-shirts that the male character wears; as a touristic banal simplification of the urban context, Rio is a vignette.

In a very different way, Rome in *The Great Beauty* has a specific, unique role, and seems to follow a long series of examples of films deeply connected with cities, using the urban context not simply as background, or scenography, but as the main subject. One of these, the *City Symphonies* realized during the 1920s and 1930s represents the great interest that directors often have in filming cities and their dimensions, giving them the main role and developing the rest of the story around it. If we consider then, the 'city-genre' as specific filmic category (Webber and Wilson 2008: 1), this essay argues that the use of Rome in *The Great Beauty* makes this film part of this genre.

> Rome has been a particularly popular location for Italian filmmakers, especially since the years of Neorealism. The fascination for this city is still alive, as demonstrated by the latest film by Paolo Sorrentino, *The Great Beauty* (2013), in which Rome returns to be something more than a scenario, playing almost a leading role.
>
> (Martini 2015: 107)

Considering a first reaction to the scenes filmed in the urban context, Rome in *The Great Beauty* clearly appears as a wonderful, beautiful scenario. It seems that the urban locations have been carefully selected by Sorrentino, and also filmed using specific cinematic methods and techniques. When we watch *The Great Beauty* for the first time, indeed, Rome appears almost as an unreal, enchanted dimension. The director's decision here is very clear, and is based on the will to somehow avoid the complex reality of a contemporary metropolis, with all the problems that we can imagine inside an urban area of almost 3 million of habitants. In the film *Sacro GRA* ('Holy GRA') (2013), released the same year and directed by Gianfranco Rosi, for instance, we see a totally different version on Rome – more realistic and complicated.

> A movie has neither presumptions or obligations to encyclopaedic completeness, and so its choice of fragments and their mode of assembly is relatively unfettered. What is selected for inclusion is often less revealing that what is excluded – lost, as it were, in the interstices between chosen fragments. Rome's enormous social and material complexity and its paradoxical relationship to time (its 'eternal' epithet attests to its ability to change) make the number of possible 'takes' on the city limitless.
>
> (Bass 1997: 84)

In this sense, it seems important to understand and analyse the specific narrative methods and techniques, applied by Sorrentino in *The Great Beauty*.

Methodology

The architecture and planning profession need to better comprehend the mechanisms by which a city can be portrayed on the screen, so that they too can convey
their vision of a future city by means of the moving image. Therefore, new analytical
tools need to be devised.

(Penz 2010: 233)

Following Penz's suggestion, before analysing how Rome has been represented in
The Great Beauty, a specific method of analysis needs to be devised. More specif-
ically, the version used for this analysis is the 137 minutes long film released as
DVD copy by Artificial Eye in January 2014.

First of all, the film has been divided into scenes, for a total of 46. Each scene
is defined as a *narrative unit* in which the temporal frame (but usually also the
location) is constant and gives a clear sense of consistency to the scene. Then, all
the scenes have been examined considering four main aspects: location, music, day
times and finally characters. It is important to underline that, even if the investigation clearly gave complete and precise results for each category, these results have
been summarized in general groups in order to provide meaningful final insights.
For instance, in the case of location, each place and related information (i.e. name,
architect, year, etc.) have been researched and noted, but finally all locations
have been divided into four main groups. This series of simplifications is useful
to develop a more relevant analysis of the results, providing a general conclusion
about the filmic techniques used in the representation of Rome.

The analysis of the locations is evidently the key aspect of this investigation.
These have been divided into groups following the three headings that Thom Anderson defines in his film essay *Los Angeles plays itself* (2003): 'city as background',
'city as character' and, finally, 'city as subject' (Penz 2010). The 'city as background'
is when the urban landscape simply defines where (and eventually when) the scene
is taking place; in this case, there is no specific relationship with the characters,
their actions or emotions. The 'city as character' provides the perfect location for
the scene; in this case, there is a clear and meaningful relation with the characters,
and the urban context acts like one of them. Finally, the 'city as subject' is when the
city is not just directly taking part in the scene, acting as one of the characters, but is
actually the protagonist, transforming the other actors to spectators. Furthermore,
a fourth group has been added to Anderson's headings: 'no Rome', that identifies
the scenes where there is no city (i.e. when the location is not in Rome, or when
there is no evidence that the space represented is actually in Rome).

The category of day times is based on the analysis of having daily or nightly
hours as background for the scenes. In this case, three main groups have been

125

identified: 'day', 'night' and 'no time' (i.e. where the location, usually an indoor space, does not provide any information about the specific time).

As far as music, as previously discussed, all the songs have been identified and then categorized into two main groups: 'classical' and 'no classical' (or other genres). This major distinction has been done following the key role of rhythm in relation to filmic sequences, and how the director seems to carefully select music in a way that operates accordingly to it.

Finally, the category related to characters has been developed in order to better understand and define the role of each specific scene in relation to the general narrative line. In this sense, two main groups have been identified: 'characters with main roles' and 'character with secondary roles'. This simple distinction is based on the consideration previously discussed that *The Great Beauty* is a film composed by a series of episodes, some of which are about Jep and his friends' adventures, and some that do not necessarily have a clear narrative role.

Furthermore, a series of graphic visualizations of the four categories analysed (Figures 8.1, 8.2 and 8.3), as well as a series of basic statistical investigations, have been realized in order to better identify and explain the relationships between categories.

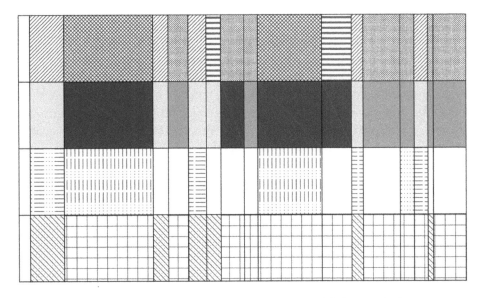

FIGURE 8.1: Scenes from 1 to 16 of *The Great Beauty* analysed following the four categories: locations, day time, music and characters.

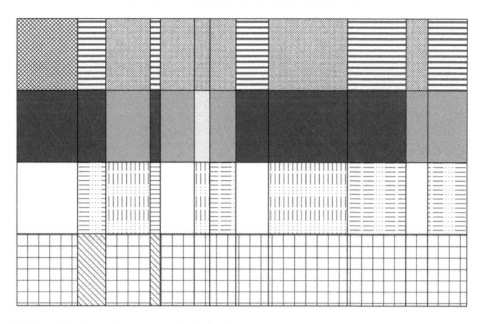

FIGURE 8.2: Scenes from 17 to 29 of *The Great Beauty*.

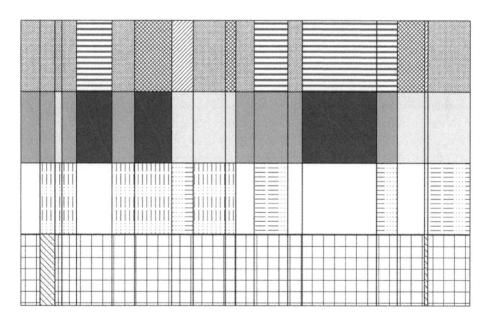

FIGURE 8.3: Scenes from 30 to 46 of *The Great Beauty*.

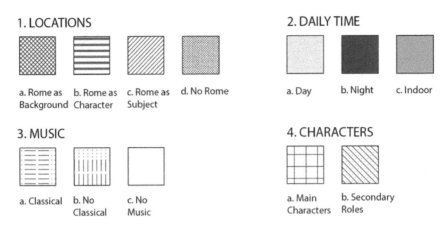

1. LOCATIONS

a. Rome as Background b. Rome as Character c. Rome as Subject d. No Rome

2. DAILY TIME

a. Day b. Night c. Indoor

3. MUSIC

a. Classical b. No Classical c. No Music

4. CHARACTERS

a. Main Characters b. Secondary Roles

FIGURE 8.4: Key to Figures 8.1, 8.2 and 8.3.

Results and Discussion

Several interesting results can be drawn from the analysis conducted, firstly in relation to each specific category selected, and then crossing the data between categories.

The first category explored was that of locations. In over 46 scenes examined, just under half of them do not contain any evidence that the setting is actually Rome: eighteen were filmed in indoor spaces, avoiding any relations with the exterior, and four scenes are set in a different location altogether (i.e. Isola del Giglio). Despite the filmmaker's clear desire to show off Rome, still almost half of the scenes (47.83%) are not related to the city at all. Alternatively, Rome and its urban context are clearly represented in the remaining 24 scenes (almost 52% of those examined). The spectacular cinematography employed in these scenes gives to the city a key role, and creates a sensation of watching a film completely set in Rome. We can separate these 24 scenes into three main groups: one where the 'city is the subject' (seven scenes, 15.22%), one where the 'city is a character' (eight scenes, 17.39%), and one where Rome is 'a background' (nine scenes, 19.57%). Adopting Anderson's categories shows that in *The Great Beauty*, Rome is described and used in a number of different ways, ranging from being the main subject to a simply static and meaningless scenario.

Furthermore, it is interesting to note that the film does not generally show the real, physical passages between different spaces; all the scenes are basically filmed in the same place, or room, before suddenly switching to a different location. Although Jep is constantly walking around Rome (Martini 2015), for example, this cinematic movement is not really used as a method to explore the urban context on any great scale, as it does not consider the relations between places, buildings, streets and so on. In contrast to the famous scenes of Nanni Moretti in *Caro Diario* (*Dear Diary*) (Nanni Moretti, 1993) or of Gregory Peck and Audrey Hepburn in *Roman Holiday* (William Wyler, 1953) on board their Vespa, Rome is not really explored as a whole city in *The Great Beauty*, but as a series of individual sites. However, its characters often move, walk and dance around spaces, although always remaining inside the same main location. In this way, Sorrentino is using the bodies of characters to explore the spaces, to take control of them and to show different inner relations. In fact, in the scenes in which 'Rome is the subject', the movement is usually a key factor: for example, when Jep is visiting the Tempietto del Bramante in Montorio, the fact that the mother is looking for her daughter supports our exploration of the beautiful architectural temple through the camera. Similarly, when Jep is looking at a monastery's garden from his terrace, he sees three children running and playing around in it, giving the camera the chance to reveal the location's geometric design.

> Film follows the geographic course of architectural exploration: it ventures to draw on the multiple viewpoints of a picturesque route. It reinvents this practice in modern ways by allowing a spectatorial body to take unexpected paths of exploration.
>
> (Bruno 2008: 20)

Following Bruno, I would argue that the 'paths of exploration' experienced by the 'spectatorial body' in *The Great Beauty* are based on a specific 'flânerie', focusing on single urban places more than their connections (Bruno 2008: 20). Sorrentino also exploits the characters' bodies and movements in the majority of the scenes where 'Rome is a background', not always clearly shown, and therefore there is no real relation with the city. One example of this is in the several party scenes on Jep's terrace, where the Colosseum is visible, but only in the distance and shrouded in darkness (as we can see the Martini advertising symbol on the roof, during Jep's birthday party). People dance, walk or sit and enjoy the atmosphere in the space of the terrace without really exploring the urban space around it, as Jep says: 'They are nice conga lines we do at parties, aren't they? They are the most beautiful in the world [...] because they don't go anywhere'. If we read this quote from the perspective of considering the representations of the city in the film, we can argue that Jep is reflecting not just on the physical but also the emotional impossibility of him and his friends to really embrace and explore the realities of the city, and of life.

The results in relation to the category about times of day reveal that there is almost an even balance between the scenes shot during day- and night-time hours (fourteen, 30.43%; thirteen, 28.36%), and scenes filmed in interior spaces where it is almost impossible to clearly differentiate the time (nineteen, 41.3%).

Furthermore, there are only two scenes filmed at dawn (counted as day-time scenes), both located at the end of the film: one scene is when 'La Santa' is looking (gathering?) the herons on Jep's terrace, and the other is when there is the last flashback about Jep's first love, on the Isola del Giglio.

Interestingly, every time that the scenes are filmed indoors, there is no real connection with the outdoor space of the city. There are almost no moments in which windows or doors are framing the external urban setting from the inside – just as we are not sure about the time of day, neither are we certain about spatial positioning. One of the few exceptions to this is the scene inside Orietta's flat, when Jep is looking at Piazza Navona from the bedroom's balcony. The darkness, however, covers almost everything.

It is interesting to note that the interior domestic spaces are usually depicted as very banal, impoverished and almost miserable. Alfredo's flat (we actually see only his combined living-dining room) is totally anonymous, with simple and cheap furniture, and even fake flowers on the centre table; Romano's rented room is in a shared flat. Similarly, Jep's indoor space is not very exciting: we see the kitchen, the bathroom and the bedroom, and they all appear as small, simple rooms. Even his bed seems to be a sofa bed, showing all the precariousness and dreariness of life. Orietta's flat, although in an amazing location, is a place not really lived in, with all its contents – except the bed – packed. The only characters with amazing places to live are the Count and Countess Colonna, and Jep's friend Violetta and her son, Andrea. However, the Count and his wife actually live in the basement of their beautiful palace (Palazzo Sacchetti), depicted as a sad and dark museum of their life. In Violetta and Andrea's case, even though their rooms are shown as being huge and richly decorated, the misery of the characters transforms the beauty of the space in surreal inappropriateness.

Taking up the category of music, Sorrentino uses a long series of songs in the film's soundtrack, stating:

> Music is very important in my life and therefore it is also important in my films. I always choose on the basis of what I like to listen to and often it is the screenplay that suggests a certain music, or many times I try different ones and only at the end I choose the one that seems most suitable to me. Other times, instead, a certain music has helped me to write, to imagine a certain scene, and so it is natural that it then becomes the background to the scene itself, and that I play it according to the suggestions of that music. But even in this case I do not spend so much time reasoning; I look around, on the basis of what I like. Then I find that entrusting the entire soundtrack to a single musician is a limiting solution. A screenplay offers such a wide spectrum of sensations that it is difficult for a single musician to express them all.
>
> (Bonsaver 2009: 329)

Several songs on *The Great Beauty* soundtrack were originally created by Lele Marchitelli, while others were selected from the existing works of different artists. In order to simplify the analysis of the results of this category, the songs have been divided into two main groups: 'classical' and 'non-classical'. Although the division here is admittedly generic, it was important to identify the scenes where Sorrentino is using classical music, as usually in these scenes the director uses a slower cinematic rhythm. In total, there are fifteen scenes with 'classical' music (32.61%), twelve scenes with 'non-classical' music (26.09%) and nineteen scenes with no music at all (41.30%). When classical songs are used, the camera movements, as well as the final montage of shots, follow a slower rhythm of long takes and slow-motion scenes. On the other hand, when the music is non-classical, the film has quicker and more agitated sequences, often with a large use of close-ups. For instance, when Jep is visiting the Capitoline Museums with Ramona and Stefano, the classical song played is 'The Beatitudes' written by Vladimir Martynov, and the camera is slowly following the movements of the characters, underlining the process of pleasant discovery of artworks and mainly filming at an eye level. On the other hand, the several parties of Jep and his friends are always supported by very rhythmical songs, and the cinematic tools in these scenes follow the different rhythms, filming the bodies and their dancing movements.

Another important aspect of this category is that music and sound is used several times to create a connection between different scenes. The change of location is not based on the camera following characters moving across places, but rather on songs or dialogue: Jep's voice is sometimes used as *fil rouge* to connect different episodes that are clearly happening in different moments of time, as well as different spaces. His first monologue, for example, along the banks of the Tiber river, actually started at the end of the scene before; when he is looking out across a dark Piazza Navona from the open window of Ombretta's flat, then we follow his voice and the music along the river during the day-time. Sorrentino is using sound as a cinematic tool to maintain a connection between different episodes, avoiding the impression of having totally separate narrative units.

Finally, in the case of the category about characters, we clearly have more scenes featuring the main characters (thirty-five, 76.09%) than ones involving secondary roles (eleven, 23.91%). However, we can argue that having almost a quarter of all scenes focusing only on characters with secondary roles is actually a quite high percentage for a film. In considering those scenes with secondary characters, we have to make a distinction between two variables. On some occasions, we have only unknown characters (as at the beginning of the film, when there are a series of frames showing different people, with no specific roles, around the Gianicolo's area), while on others, we have Jep meandering around the city and meeting unknown people, usually in beautiful spaces (as in the case of the scene around Santa Sabina all'Aventino, where Jep is simply walking and looking at different people, observing their actions inside beautiful urban frames – first a series of Catholic school girls, then a man walking a dog and finally a nun picking oranges from a tree). What is the role of these scenes in relation to the story? If we consider just the characters, and what they are doing, we can argue that without these episodes, the final tale would be exactly the same. In this sense, these scenes are very unique, as they do not contribute to the development of the plot. However, if we consider the city itself as a main character, the argument could be very different, as in these scenes the city of Rome reveals itself and its best locations and their related uses. As the book *Paolo Sorrentino, 'La grande bellezza': Diario del film* clearly testifies, these seven scenes shown in the film are just a small amount compared to the several sequences that have been actually filmed around the eternal city 'in search of faces, ghosts, characters, that rich, sometimes monstrous, fauna that inhabits the great beauty' (Fiorito 2013: 13).

To conclude this analysis of results, it is vital to finally compare the categories with one another. If we look only at the seven scenes where the city is the subject (following the analysis of the category of locations), we can see how all of them have been shot during day-time hours, with classical music as a background (apart from one that has no music at all), and featuring secondary characters. This specific pattern or selection of cinematic tools identifies a series of scenes where Rome is represented as both a beautiful and magical city and an ancient one that is trapped in the past. The daylight helps, in this case, to clearly show the places, allowing viewers to identify and recognize them, while the classical music underlines their solemnity and majesty. The characters in these scenes do not have any specific role or meaning in relation to the main narrative line; we do not know anything about them (apart from their first names, in a few cases) and we do not see them in any other scenes. Such characters include the artist exhibiting at Villa Giulia, all of the nuns, and the children laughing and playing in a number of different scenes. Jep is usually the only character that we know in these scenes, but as the girl hiding in Tempietto di Bramante in Montorio says to him: 'You are nobody.' He is just a spectator to these scenes, as we are, and Rome is the only main character.

In this sense, we can define these specific scenes as 'cartoline', following David Bass's interpretation of films about Rome. In his essay entitled 'Insiders and outsiders' (1997), he defines six categories of films based on their representations of Rome, and only one of these is defined from an outsider's point of view. In the films analysed in this category, the city is both looked at and represented as (almost from a touristic perspective) a series of 'cartoline', as selections of just some of its most famous and beautiful spots. There is a manipulation of time and space in order to create a beautiful and concise portrait. For instance, when Jep is looking down at the garden from his terrace, the real location of that place is actually the Palazzo Sacchetti, about 3.5

kilometres from his flat near the Colosseum. This is an evident manipulation of space, following the need of representing beautiful shots of Rome in a concentrated manner.

On the other hand, Bass names a second category relevant to our discussion, that of 'The insider's view: The metaphoric city'. This category is almost completely based on an analysis of Fellini's films:

> Fellini presents a complex and compromised vision, collaging ancient and modern, sacred and profane, public communication and private incomprehension. [...] Though tourist views, urban contexts, neighbourhoods and the periphery all occur in Fellini's films, his relation to individual locations in Rome is loose. He neither navigates nor jump-cuts knowingly around the city, but presents single scenes in succession which each investigate particular aspects of Rome and its life. Fellini collides his scenes together, like the succession of acts in a circus or variety theatre.
>
> (Bass 1997: 93)

As in Fellini's work, there is a collage of different scenes and episodes, and a range of topics in *The Great Beauty*. The relationship with Rome is 'loose', as there is no real cinematic exploration of urban spaces and relations, as we previously stated, but simply movements *inside* specific locations. However, there seems to be a major difference between how Rome is portrayed in *The Great Beauty* and in Fellini's works, and this is related to the concept of theatre. If Fellini is using the city as a beautiful setting, selecting locations around Rome based on their potential of being the perfect spaces for specific scenes, Sorrentino is instead looking at the city without considering the filmic narrative line. The story does not provide the criteria to find the right places for the scene – if anything, it is the opposite. Rome in *The Great Beauty* is more powerful than narratorial, and simply finds some moments in which it can reveal itself and its perfect 'cartoline', while Sorrentino is transforming all of us into tourists who are looking around the city, just like him:

> But I do not really know the city. Indeed, it is a city that I do not want to know in-depth, because as with all the things that are known in-depth, there is always the risk of being disappointed. Therefore, I just guess it, passing through it every day as a tourist without a return ticket, and I am happy like that. [...] The largest holiday resort in the world. This is Rome for me.
>
> (Sorrentino 2013b: 9–10)

Conclusion

We can argue that Sorrentino describes different cities and different spatial dimensions in the film. Apparently, there is one Rome that is eternal and beautiful, but that is trapped in the past. It is the space of memory, to which everyone is constantly looking, admiring and searching for beauty, represented in the wonderful architecture of Rome, a series of great masterpieces not truly lived in by the characters. This Rome is evident in the scenes that we call the 'cartoline', where the city is the main subject. In contrast, there is the empty, corrupt and soulless world that is the contemporary reality. It is the real dimension of life, where spaces are unclear, undefined, and the city is showing itself through its people and thereby appears similar to every other city. These are the scenes where Rome is not present, or is used as a simple, static and sterile background. However, there are moments of connection in between these two dimensions, in the scenes where Rome itself is a character. In these sequences, the two different worlds seem to encounter each other, and the characters from the real dimension are trying to approach that of the eternal Rome. The lights turn off and they observe this antique world carefully, from a distance. They meander around this beautiful suspended dimension, where everything is mute, by candlelight. Even the people that are part of this other dimension – if there are some – are like ghosts, crystalized presences coming from another time, or another world. It is like the real dimension is constantly looking for the eternal and beautiful one.

Finally, we can argue that one of the key aspects of *The Great Beauty* is closely related to Sorrentino's capacity to manipulate and depict the city in a way that respects its magnificent complexity, but also reflects the 'touristic' imagination of it. On the one hand, therefore, the identification of the urban landscape with the preconceived archetype, conveyed by the 'cartoline' scenes, feeds the sense of belonging to the city. On the other, the imaginative and idealized power of the urban landscape of Rome, captured by the camera in an idyllic vision, translates into experience, and therefore into unique and subjective perception. Rome reveals itself as the Eternal City, where the individual finds space between the repetitiveness of postcard images. When Dickens finally saw the Rome he had imagined, he unhesitatingly wrote: 'Here was Rome indeed at last; and such a Rome as no one can imagine in its full and awful grandeur!' (Dickens 1846: 81). While clearly expressing satisfaction, his words emphasize at the same time that, however prepared you may be, Rome as a whole, in all its greatness, cannot be imagined (Molinari 2018: 149).

NOTE
1. Unless otherwise indicated, all translations from Italian are mine.

REFERENCES
Akin, F., et al. (2008), *New York, I Love You*, United States: Grosvenor Park Media.
AlSayyad, N. (ed.) (2006), *Cinematic Urbanism: A History of the Modern from Reel to Real*, New York: Routledge.

Arriaga, G., et al. (2014), *Rio, I love you*, Brazil: Conspiração Filmes, Warner Bros.

Assayas, O., et al. (2006), *Paris, je t'aime*, France: Canal+.

Bass, D. (1997), 'Insiders and outsiders: Latent urban thinking in movies of modern Rome', in F. Penz and M. Thomas (eds), *Cinema and Architecture: Méliès, Mallet-Stevens, Multimedia*, London: BFI, pp. 84–99.

Bonsaver, G. (2009), 'Dall'uomo al divo: Un'intervista con Paolo Sorrentino,' *The Italianist*, 29:2, pp. 325–37.

Bruno, G. (2007), *Atlas of Emotion: Journeys in Art, Architecture, and Film*, New York: Verso Books.

Bruno, G. (2008), 'Motion and emotion: Film and the urban fabric', in A. Webber and E. Wilson (eds), *Cities in Transition: The Moving Image and the Modern Metropolis*, London: Wallflower Press, pp. 14–28.

Cresti, C. (2001), *Cinema e architettura*, Firenze: Pontecorboli Editore.

Dickens, C. (1846), *Pictures from Italy*, London: Bradbury & Evans.

Ejzenštejn, S. (1989), 'Montage and architecture', *Assemblage*, 10, pp. 110–31.

Fellini, F. (1960), *La dolce vita*, Italy, France: Riama Film, Pathé Consortium Cinéma.

Fellini, F. (1963), *8 e ½*, Italy, France: Cineriz, Francinex.

Fiorito, G. (2013), *Paolo Sorrentino, 'La grande bellezza': Diario del film*, Milano: Feltrinelli.

Iannotta, A. (2016), 'Le immagini del potere: Note sull'identità italiana nel cinema di Paolo Sorrentino', *California Italian Studies*, 6:2, pp. 1–17.

Jeunet, J. (2001), *Amélie*, France, Germany: Canal+, France 3 Cinéma, UGC.

Koeck, R. and Roberts, L. (eds) (2010), *The City and the Moving Image*, London: Palgrave Macmillan.

Licata, A. and Mariani Travi, E. (1985), *La città e il cinema*, Bari: Edizioni Dedalo.

Mariani, A. (2019), 'Experiencing *Panismo* in Sorrentino's *The Great Beauty, Youth*, and *Loro*', *Italica*, 96: 3, pp. 486–510.

Martini, A. (2015), 'Concept city: Roma ri-vista e vissuta ne La dolce vita e La grande bellezza', *Carte Italiane*, 2:10, pp. 107–19.

Mazierka, E. and Rascaroli, L. (eds) (2003), *From Moscow to Madrid: Postmodern Cities, European Cinema*, London: I.B. Tauris & Co.

Molinari, C. (2018), 'Townscapes', in M. Iuliano (ed.), *Rome in RIBA Photographs Collection*, Milano: Skira, pp. 148–49.

Moretti, N. (1993), *Caro diario*, Italy, France: Sacher Film, Banfilm – La Sept Cinéma.

Pallasmaa, J. (1999), *The Architecture of Image: Existential Space in Cinema*, Helsinki: Rakennustieto Publishing.

Penz, F. (2010), 'The real city in the reel city: Towards a methodology through the case of *Amélie*', in R. Koeck and L. Roberts (eds), *The City and the Moving Image*, London: Palgrave Macmillan, pp. 233–52.

Penz, F. (2018), *Cinematic-Aided Design: An Everyday Life Approach to Architecture*, New York: Routledge.

Penz, F. and Thomas, M. (eds) (1997), *Cinema and Architecture: Méliès, Mallet-Stevens, Multimedia*, London: BFI.

Prina, V. (2009), *Cinema architettura composizione*, Santarcangelo di Romagna: Maggioli Editore.

Rosi, G. (2013), *Sacro GRA*, Italy, France: DocLab, La Femme Endormie, Rai Cinema.

Salvestroni, S. (2017), *'La grande bellezza' e il cinema di Paolo Sorrentino*, Bologna: Archetipolibri.

Schaal, H. D. (1996), *Learning from Hollywood: Architecture and Film*, London: Edition Axel Menges.

Sorrentino, P. (2008), *Il Divo*, Italy: Lucky Red.

Sorrentino, P. (2013a), *La grande bellezza*, Italy, France: Indigo Film, Medusa Film, Babe Films, Pathé.

Sorrentino, P. (2013b), 'La grande bellezza', in G. Fiorito (ed.), *Paolo Sorrentino, 'La grande bellezza': Diario del film*, Milano: Feltrinelli, pp. 9–12.

Stiërli, M. (2013), *Learning from Las Vegas in the Rearview Mirror: The City in Theory, Photography and Film*, Los Angeles: The Getty Institute.

Stiërli, M. (2018), *Montage and the Metropolis: Architecture, Modernity and the Representation of Space*, London: Yale University Press.

Tschumi, B. (1983), 'Sequences', *The Princeton Journal: Thematic Studies – Architecture*, 1, pp. 152–68.

Viano, M. (2010), 'Between modernity and eternity: *Il divo* in cinematic Rome', *Annali D'Italianistica*, 28, pp. 341–62.

Vidler, A. (1993), 'The explosion of space: Architecture and the filmic imaginary', *Assemblage*, 21, pp. 44–59.

Webber, A. and Wilson, E. (eds) (2008), *Cities in Transition: The Moving Image and the Modern Metropolis*, London: Wallflower Press.

Wyler, W. (1953), *Roman Holiday*, United States: Paramount Pictures.

Zevi, B. (1974), *Architecture as Space: How to Look at Architecture*, New York: Horizon Press.

PART THREE

A JOURNEY INTO
SORRENTINO'S PSYCHE

Foto di Gianni Fiorito © WILDSIDE/SKY ITALIA/HAUT ET COURT TV/HOME
BOX OFFICE, INC./MEDIAPRO.

9

The 'Primal Scene':
Memory, Redemption and 'Woman'
in the Films of Paolo Sorrentino

Russell J. A. Kilbourn

Wilfrid Laurier University

'[W]e fear the visibility without which we cannot truly live.' — Audre Lorde
(quoted in Garland-Thomson 2009: 59)

Introduction

As 'the Dude' (Jeff Bridges) says of notorious *L.A.* pornographer Jackie Tree-horn (Ben Gazzara) in the Coen Brothers' 1998 film *The Big Lebowski*, 'he treats objects like women'. Taking the joke at face value, to treat an object as a woman is typically treated in our society is to treat it as if it were an *image*. This article examines the representation of gender, beginning from the marginalization and sexualization of the female subject in the films of Paolo Sorrentino – including *Le conseguenze dell'amore* (*The Consequences of Love*) (2004) and *L'amico di famiglia* (*The Family Friend*) (2006), but focusing espe-cially on *La grande bellezza* (*The Great Beauty*) (2013) and *Youth* (2015), and the television series The Young Pope (2016) – to better understand the signifi-cance of 'woman' for the cinematic and mnemic constitution of what I call the Sorrentinian subject. In the process I situate Sorrentino's work in the context of the contemporary transnational art cinema tradition, with a nod to the current rise of prestige television programming. And, in a shift from the desiring and objectifying intra-diegetic gaze to what Rosemarie Garland-Thomson in the context of disability studies calls 'the stare', in the final 'coda' I briefly analyse

Sorrentino's fascination with non-normative identities whose on-screen function as locus of a radical alterity serves in the end to throw an even sharper, more ironic light upon the masculine subject at the centre of each story. From film to film to TV series the treatment of gender grows increasingly complex, particularly with respect to the nexus of memory and whatever secular or post-secular redemption awaits the protagonist.

The sexual and gender politics of Sorrentino's films have been an issue for critics and scholars since the director first came to prominence in Italy, before breaking out internationally with *The Consequences of Love*.[1] My argument begins beyond Milicent Marcus's reading of Sorrentino's 'post-modern *impegno*', in which 'the contemporary vogue for stylistic virtuosity – including the use of pastiche, abundant citation, semiotic playfulness, imagistic saturation, decorative exuberance – can co-exist with an ethics of political engagement in the arts' (2010: 246).[2] This is necessary to appreciate an ongoing sense of political engagement in contemporary Italian film and TV work that is not beholden to a tradition of cinematic realism. I therefore broach a more general appraisal of Sorrentino's ironically dialectical approach, which frequently seems to produce a contradiction between film form and diegetic content. This allows for a reconciliation of the films' typically self-reflexive style with the ethical commitment of a social and political critique conveyed via a spectacular image.[3] A film such as *The Great Beauty* especially harkens back to the 'beautiful *image*' of 1980s European and Hollywood cinema, exemplified by the *cinema du look* in France (Bordwell and Thompson 2009: 582 – 84), by films as diverse as *Diva* (Beineix, 1981) and *Wings of Desire* (Wenders, 1987). As will be seen below, in the transition from his feature films to the long form TV series, Sorrentino's treatment of gender acquires a politically progressive appearance, in which the sheer beauty of the image is tempered or even overpowered by its affective impact within the montage. The thematic shift is occasioned by a modal shift from a transnational art film style towards a hybrid species of postsecular male melodrama.

Sorrentino's ironically dialectical approach becomes most contentious in the representation of gender, especially images of women. (To this extent, I am partaking of what feminist film theory knows as 'images of women' criticism in the most literal sense, but without the attendant assumption of a direct relation between such images and real-world women to which this approach was prone [see: Hipkins 2008: 214].[4] It goes without saying that such images do not bring the actual experience of real women to the screen in any unmediated sense.[5]) This is not merely another instance of a male Italian director indulging in the medium's potential for the exploitation of women's bodies, however.[6] Sorrentino exploits all the resources of narrative cinema to engage critically and self-reflexively with questions of identity, power and representation in a contemporary transnational and – in *The Young Pope* – postsecular context.

The 'primal scene' in my title alludes to Freud and the Oedipal crisis only to the extent that our subjectivities are shaped by the films we watch, especially by certain specific set pieces, recurring character types, visual clichés or iconic images – the iconography of the cultural politics of gender, sexuality, race, class, ability, age or various other categories of individual or collective identity.[7] There is thus an implicit acknowledgement here that such a primal scene is always already culturally-ideologically constructed, the *locus classicus* in occidental culture being that of Adam and Eve in the Garden in Milton's already thoroughly remediated version of the story. (In *Paradise Lost* [Milton 1993], it should be recalled, the figure of woman is already present in all its contradictions, embodying both damnation and the promise of salvation – for the man. Such occidentalist tropes are thus far older than either Sorrentino or, for that matter, Freud; nor are they limited to the Italian context. They therefore fully justify the feminist critique whose most productive form emerged in 1970s film theory.) In my approach here, I invoke neither a psychoanalytic nor a literary-theological model but a theory of cinema as eidetic memory, for, just as we tend to remember films on the basis of single powerful images and set pieces (see e.g. Scorsese 2017), so do we make reference to cinema when we seek to represent memory to ourselves. I will return below to the significance of memory in Sorrentino's cinema. For the moment, I should add that by 'iconic image', I do *not* mean the Russian Orthodox variety, which represents a wholly *other* aesthetic logic.[8] Nor do I primarily refer to Charles Sanders Peirce's semiotic usage, where 'iconic' names the mimetic or imitative dimension of the image that, along with the indexical, accounts for its unique relation to the representation of an extra-filmic reality. The contemporary turn away from psychoanalytic models of film analysis has been balanced by a turn back to the cinematic image as visual-mimetic sign, where the relation between signifier and real-world referent (in a pre-digital sense, at least), is not arbitrary and cannot be ignored. It is largely the advent of digital technology that precipitated this return, ironically, as we begin to mourn the loss of an image that represents a reality that we know unconditionally was there before the camera.[9]

Generally speaking, all of the films since *The Consequences of Love* (and including *The Young Pope*) feature individual shots or whole scenes that may or may not further the narrative but whose sheer beauty arrests the eye. (The latter is largely the result of lighting: director of photography Luca Bigazzi favours placing lights within the shot, indistinguishable from real light sources within the scene. This is one reason why all of Sorrentino's films after *One Man Up* [2001] are more visually pleasing than his first feature.) Many of these iconic set pieces feature secondary (or tertiary) female characters in various stages of *déshabillé*.

These are what I mean by 'primal scenes': compare for instance the spa bath sequence towards the end of *Youth*, featuring Romanian model-turned-actress Madalina Ghenea, to the scene it transmediates: Anita Ekberg in the Trevi fountain in Fellini's *La dolce vita* (1960).

The scene in *Youth* represents a far more egregious instance of objectification than its Fellinian antecedent. It is hard to not see Fellini's influence, however, when Sorrentino includes in a film a sequence involving the objectification of a woman's body. On the other hand, Fellini himself cannot be blamed for inventing but only for perpetuating this convention. Issues of authorial sexism and misogyny aside, the question is: why would a twenty-first-century director like Sorrentino choose to do this? In what ways, if any, do his films succeed in changing the meaning of this kind of generic set piece, inscribing a critique while amplifying the spectacle, the sheer beauty of the image?

By 'subject' or subjectivities here I refer to human types, conventional social roles, performative identity categories and so forth – and only secondarily the subject of Freudian, Lacanian or feminist psychoanalytic theory. Others have analysed *The Great Beauty* from a feminist-psychoanalytic perspective (e.g. Mariani 2017). More broadly, feminist theorists of melodrama in the 1980s and 1990s identified the 'over-valuation of masculinity' as a fundamental problem in North American mainstream culture (Gledhill 1987: 10). My approach here draws equally from this branch of post-structuralist theory and the kind of post-Marxist ideological critique typical of cultural studies. It goes beyond both, however, insofar as the first is too prone to reducing every film narrative

FIGURE 9.1: Madalina Ghenea as 'Miss Universe'. Sorrentino (dir.), *Youth*, 2015.

to an allegory of the Oedipal family romance, and every female body to a cipher for castration anxiety, and the second tends to overlook film form in favour of story content as the basis of an uncritical view of realism that one continues to encounter in cultural analysis and media studies. In film, after all, any so-called 'unconscious' dimension, like everything else, is right on the surface.[10] Throughout film history, even the most intimate moments of subjective interiority, if they are to be made manifest, end up looking much the same as everything else. I use the term 'subject' therefore in a philosophical or narratological sense, as ground for identity or self, as concatenation of attributes or predicates. But by 'subject' I also mean a visual-optical position in space, a mobile point-of-view upon the objective world, upon others, or the Other. Historically, in the occidental tradition on which my argument is necessarily based, this subject is silently but inescapably gendered masculine.

What I call the Sorrentinian subject is embodied in a series of protagonists, all of whom are white, male, heterosexual, mostly (but not always) European and of a certain age or generation (Jude Law's youthful American Pius XIII is an interesting variation). The complement to this recurring type is the enigmatic figure of 'Woman'[11] – the very 'monolithic and transhistorical entity' identified by Molly Haskell in her canonical 1974 text, *Reverence to Rape*.[12] The fact that his films perpetuate even as they appear to critique specific gender-based, sexist (and, for some, misogynistic) stereotypes of femininity, places Sorrentino into a long line of (male) filmmakers for whom the female body is at best a paradox or contradiction and at worst the ultimate reified object of heterosexual-consumerist desire. Sorrentino is hardly the first Italian director to engage in this kind of self-reflexive critique of the male gaze as it tends to manifest in Italian popular culture (see, e.g., Nichetti 1989), a fact that only foregrounds the difficulty of exploiting such images to critique them without on some level appearing to participate in the perpetuation of a whole range of negative connotations. Ultimately, to invoke in any interpretive act the author's gendered identity, coupled with the intentional fallacy implicit in any auteurial approach, risks opening up a critical minefield unless this is balanced with a consideration of as much as possible of the surrounding context.

On the one hand, then, Sorrentino is an Italian auteur working in a transnational cinematic context using the latest technologies to produce stylistically cutting-edge and formally progressive audio-visual narratives. On the other hand, Sorrentino appears to uphold to a significant degree a retrograde point of view on gender difference and the representation of women. The latter is the inevitable complement to the films' elegiac meditation upon what it means to be a no-longer youthful, late-middle aged or even elderly man in twenty-first-century Europe (*The Young Pope*, again, obviously complicates this reading).

Sorrentino and 'the Gaze'

In her classic essay on 'Visual pleasure in narrative cinema', Laura Mulvey argued that:

> [Woman's] visual presence tends to work *against* the development of a story line, to freeze the flow of action in moments of erotic contemplation. [...] A woman performs within the narrative, the gaze of the spectator and that of the male characters in the film are neatly combined without breaking narrative verisimilitude. For a moment the sexual impact of the performing woman takes the film into a no-man's-land outside its own time and space.
>
> (2000: 488)

Rather than re-explore this psychic no-man's-land,[13] and the attendant questions of alleged narrative disruption, however, I want to stay on the surface, on the level of the image as visual signifier. In a subsequent essay, for instance, Mary-Anne Doane does just this:

> The woman's beauty, her very desirability, becomes a function of certain practices of *imaging* – framing, lighting, camera movement, angle. She is thus, as [...] Mulvey has pointed out, more closely associated with the *surface* of the image than its illusory depths, its constructed 3-dimensional space which the man is destined to inhabit and hence control.
>
> (Doane 2000: 497, original emphasis)

Like Mulvey, Doane refers primarily to specific ideological effects of classical Hollywood style; nevertheless, she describes a more or less explicit gendering of the image in its Peircian semiotic dimensions that may be useful in our discussion of Sorrentino. In other words, where 'woman' is aligned with the *surface* of the image in its radical exteriority, the masculine protagonist is associated with the visual and metaphorical *depths* of the image, with the metaphysical depths of memory and with nostalgia as masculine affect.[14] Thus, where woman in this classical view is coterminous with the image itself in its objecthood, the masculine protagonist is the subject of memory, of melancholic or elegiac remembrance (see Mariani 2017: 175),[15] in which the object of nostalgic desire is a woman who as often as not is no longer among the living. This woman, however, despite being dead in the present is very much alive in the protagonist's memory, at least insofar as she represents for him – for his narrative trajectory – the eschatological force of his salvation. She is, in short, his saviour – the feminine embodiment or personification of the salvific force of memory, so to speak. This is the eroto-salvific paradigm so dear to occidental culture; it forms the basis of many famous literary and cinematic narratives, both old and new, from Goethe's *Faust* (1976) and Wagner's *The Flying Dutchman* (1982) to Hitchcock's *Vertigo* (1958) and Michel Gondry's *Eternal Sunshine of the Spotless Mind* (2004). In the cinematic expression of this model, the affective and non-rational dimension of nostalgic or elegiac memory is associated with the masculine; this is the aspect of the image where the illusory force of realism is working its magic, occluding the material basis of the image, and thus representation itself. On the other hand, the image *qua* image is aligned with the feminine, the aspect in which the image stops the narrative in its tracks, drawing the viewer's attention away from the content and onto the form of the film, laying bare its formal operations, the potential source of spectatorial emancipation (see Brecht [1948] 1977; Rancière 2009). To read the iconic images of women in Sorrentino's films this way, is to resist the more doctrinaire reading traceable to Mulvey, in which the very opposite is seen to occur, the viewer's rational response short-circuited by the overpowering affect of the feminine in close-up. It is out of the tension between these two perspectives that the richly ambiguous but troubling meanings of the films arise.

With notable Italian cinematic intertexts such as Fellini's *I vitelloni* (1953), *La dolce vita*, *8½* (1963) and *Roma* (1973), and Antonioni's *La notte* (*The Night*) (1961) and Ettore Scola's *La terrazza* (*The Terrace*) (1980) – *The Great Beauty* positions itself unapologetically in the tradition of filmic explorations of the psycho-emotional life of middle-aged and older heterosexual bourgeois or upper-middle class male intellectuals, epitomized by many of the characters played by Marcello Mastroianni.[16] Protagonist Jep Gambardella (Toni Servillo) represents a significant change in the nature of Italian cinematic masculinity, however, in the transition from post-war to post-millennial. The tone here is generally far more elegiac than in the cinema of the post-war period. His 65th birthday and the news of her death inspire in Jep a melancholic return to memories of Elisa (Annaluisa Capasa), his first love, signalled by flashbacks to their time together 40 years before, off the coast of Naples. Elisa never appears as a character except in flashback, her death at the story's outset the event that precipitates Jep's ultimate epiphany. The concluding scene is structured more conventionally than Jep's earlier flashbacks to his time in southern Italy, which generally begin with him dozing on his bed in Rome, gazing up into the ceiling above, which digitally transmogrifies into the upside-down Mediterranean Sea.

In this final flashback, present tense Jep travels by boat to the same coastal area, the act of putting himself into the same place physically and seeing the same lighthouse triggering the shift back into his own past. 'This is how it always ends', Jep intones in voice-over, on the lighthouse stairs, in place of his younger self, aligned by eyeline match with Elisa above him. Intercut with this mental journey is Suor

Maria (Giusi Merli), 'la Santa', crawling on her knees up *la Scala Sancta di San Giovanni* in Rome, an ascent with Christ as its goal, underlining the irony of this visual and thematic juxtaposition. In this complex flashback, a consummately cinematic memory, the resurrected youthful Elisa appears on the stairs above, baring her breasts to the suddenly youthful Jep, then turning away. The now once-again 65-year-old Jep stands watching her retreating, Eurydice-like. In voice-over, he says: 'Finisce sempre cosi: colla morte. Prima però, c'è stata la vita. Nascosta sotto il blah blah blah... [...] Gli sparuti incostanti sprazzi di bellezza e poi lo squallore disgraziato e l'uomo miserabile. [...] Dunque, che questo romanzo abbia inizio'.[17] Jep is an exorbitant updating of the morally undeserving late-middle-aged man redeemed by the woman from his past – the age-old trope of gender-specific eroto-salvific redemption, the eschatological framework ironically deconstructed ('Altrove c'e l'altrove', he remarks. 'Io non mi occupo [...]'[18]). The reference to a new novel beginning indicates that Jep's salvation will take the form of his rebirth as a writer, here, in memory's primal scene, and that this new novel will tell the very story we have just witnessed.

The Great Beauty treads a fine line here between an unironic nostalgia and a more critically complex position. Historically, discussions of the intersection of film and memory have generally focused on commercial genre films rather than an art cinema tradition (e.g. Erll 2011). Hollywood's conservative nature, for instance, means that it is far more likely than a more 'serious' art cinema to exploit nostalgia unironically. Nostalgia continues to be invoked in popular discourse in a pejorative sense, a reputation that has influenced popular thinking about memory itself. 'Memory is not commonly imagined as a site of possibility for progressive politics', writes Alison Landsberg. 'More often, memory, particularly in the form of *nostalgia*, is condemned for its *solipsistic* nature, for its tendency to draw people into the past instead of the present' (2003: 144). The concluding scene in *The Great Beauty* is saved from falling into cliché,[19] in my view, by the overall structure of the montage: the intercut shots of 'la Santa' crawling penitently up the stairs towards her symbolic and redundant salvation complicate Jep's elegiac flashback, inflecting its meaning in a richly ambiguous direction, a conclusion underscored by Jep's final line in the film: 'É solo un trucco' ('it's just a trick').[20]

In *Youth*, by contrast, the already old men (Michael Caine's Fred Ballinger and Harvey Keitel's Mick Boyle) do not appear to be 'saved' or redeemed by the scopophilic vision of a stark naked 'Miss Universe' in the Swiss hotel spa pool. To Ballinger's question '[w]ho is that'? Boyle responds: 'God' – before correcting himself: 'Miss Universe'. How different is Marcello's response to Sylvia's trespassing in the *La dolce vita* Trevi Fountain scene: 'She's right. I've had it all wrong. We've all had it wrong' – whereupon he joins her, fully clothed, in the fountain.[21] The scene in *Youth* is simultaneously more progressive – the two men, like Miss

Universe, are presumably also naked (their elderly bodies hidden underwater) – and more retrograde: their fixed intra-diegetic gaze is both a parody and an egregious example of Mulvey's male gaze. The *mise en scène* perpetuates the problem in terms of Ghenea's hyperbolically voluptuous body, lit and framed as if for a *Sports Illustrated* photo shoot, the two men looking on in the background, impotent subjects to her youthful and sexually potent object.[22] In *La dolce vita*, by contrast, Sylvia beckons to Marcello, displaying an agency ironically denied her twenty-first-century counterpart in *Youth*. Marcello joins Sylvia in the fountain, their almost-embrace in balanced medium two-shot; the woman remains elusive but with a measure of power over the man, ever withholding herself at the last minute, a projection perhaps of Marcello's shaky post-war masculinity. In this regard as well, the viewer who over-identifies with Marcello will be rewarded with the sophisticated frustration of the post-war art film spectator, and spared the phantasmic satisfactions of Mulvey's ideal masculine consumer.

To the foregoing, we can compare the other primal scene of Italian post-war cinema: Pina's death in Rossellini's *Roma, città aperta* (*Rome, Open City*) (1946), a graphic match of the frontal view of Michelangelo's *Pietá* (1499). The final shot of Don Pietro holding the dead Pina in his arms says as much about Christian iconography as it does about the representation of women in Neorealist film. This comparison transcends post-war Italian cinema, revealing the generic and tropological underpinnings of the Passion narrative as crucial intertext for so much contemporary cultural production. As Lenny remarks to Cardinal Gutierrez (Javiér Camara), in Episode 1 of *The Young Pope*, as they gaze together upon Michelangelo's statue in St. Peter's Basilica: 'It all comes back to this in the end, doesn't it? To the mother'. At the conclusion of Episode 3, moreover, in a high-angle shot that foreshadows his death in the final episode, Lenny faints into the arms of Esther (Ludivine Sagnier), the Swiss guardsman's wife, positioned from the series' start as 'virgin mother' (and counterpart to Sister Mary [Diane Keaton], for all intents and purposes Lenny's foster mother).

Later, in Episode 8, Lenny's birth mother (Olivia Macklin) is seen in an unattributed hallucinatory vision – and perfect graphic match to the foregoing scene – as virgin mother to the young Dussolier (Jack McQuaid), who, as the adult Cardinal (Scott Shepherd), is murdered in Honduras in Episode 7. In scenes such as these, the TV series complicates and, to a certain extent, transcends the more conventional and troubling representation of women in the films. That said, there is still a pronounced tendency for carefully composed, well-lit static shots of young attractive women in various stages of undress – especially in the protagonist's fantasies, dreams and flashback sequences.

A relevant guide to this nexus of passion, pathos and gender – particularly with respect to the character of Lenny Belardo, Pope Pius XIII – is Linda Williams 1990s

FIGURE 9.2: Anita Ekberg as 'Sylvia'. Fellini (dir.), *La dolce vita*, 1960.

FIGURE 9.3: Anna Magnani as 'Pina' and Aldo Fabrizi as 'Don Pietro' in *Rome, Open City*.

FIGURE 9.4: Jude Law as 'Lenny Belardo' and Ludivine Sagnier as 'Esther' in Episode 3 of *The Young Pope* (2016).

FIGURE 9.5: 'Girolamo' (unattributed) in Episode 2 of *The Young Pope* (2016).

work on the centrality of melodramatic narrative to American popular culture. Among the five characteristics of melodrama, Williams singles out the recurrent type of the 'victim-hero', the 'recognition of *virtue* involving a dialectic of *pathos* and *action*', in which gender identity (in cinematic and televisual narratives, at least) is revealed as constructed in relation to a power dynamic in which anyone, regardless of biological sex, 'becomes' a 'woman' when in the position of victim (2001: 28). This is the moral-affective counterpart to the notion (from 1970s feminist film theory) of the 'female gaze'.[23] According to Williams:

> Recognition of *virtue* orchestrates the moral legibility that is key to melodrama's function. [...] The suffering body caught up in paroxysms of mental or physical pain can be male or female, but suffering itself is a form of powerlessness that is coded *feminine*. Of course the transmutation of bodily suffering into virtue is a *topos* of western culture that goes back to Christian iconography.
>
> (2001: 29, original emphasis)[24]

The connection with Christian iconography, especially Renaissance paintings of the crucifixion, is crucial: the spectacle of Christ on the cross, the very moment in the Passion narrative of abject suffering and ecstatic transfiguration. This is also the image par excellence that encapsulates the meaning of divine grace as the promise of forgiveness and redemption at the core of Catholicism. In the twenty-first century, however, it is one thing to be a victim and bear the biological body of a man, while it is another thing altogether to be so in the undeniable, because visually displayed, body of a woman. And there is a third category still: the non-normative body of the disabled person.

From Gazing to Staring

With *The Young Pope*, Sorrentino shifts from the classic secular salvific model of the woman whose death somehow redeems the undeserving artist figure, to an ironic yet openly religious iconographic model of Christ and Mary alike in their redemptive relation to the protagonist. In a sense, both spiritual and erotic salvation are fused in the figure of Sister Mary (both Keaton and Allison Case as the younger version), who also functions as surrogate mother to Lenny – although he seems to be the only character who does not recognize this. It is important to acknowledge the relative complexity of Sorrentino's invocation of these art historical, Christological and narrative tropes. Equally as troubling, arguably, as the exploitation of women's bodies are the occasional inclusion in the films and the TV series of non-normative identities, bodies and faces – although it is arguable that the entrenched normativity of the male body comes in for mild critique in either the elegiacally ageing (Ballinger and Boyle in *Youth*) or melodramatically pathetic (Geremia in *The Family Friend*) male bodies of the protagonists. Here we see Sorrentino moving beyond his Fellinian fascination with grotesque and/or hyperbolic human bodies to something more serious, less susceptible to ironic interpretation.[25] For reasons of space I will touch on only a few brief examples here.

In *Youth*, right after the above-mentioned spa pool scene Boyle learns that Brenda Morel, his long-time lead actress (played by Jane Fonda) has quit his latest and final film. Boyle soon after kills himself out of despair at his failed project, his 'testimony', whereas Ballinger, within the story world, is somehow redeemed, judging by the final scene of his command performance for Queen Elizabeth of his famous, Brittenesque 'Simple Songs'. In the scene immediately before this, Ballinger achieves for himself what appears to be a highly narcissistic form of redemption. Visiting her room in a long-term care facility in Venice for the first time in ten years, he delivers a long monologue ostensibly to his wife, Melanie (Sonia Gessner), who remains silent throughout. The scene is framed so that she is visible in medium shot with her back to the camera as she gazes out the window at Venice. Only at the end of the scene, with Ballinger, after many years of neglect and infidelity, having paid his penance to his wife, do we see the reverse angle of Melanie's grotesque, mask-like visage in medium close-up, staring open-mouthed in a frozen rictus, evidently so ill that it is impossible to know if she heard anything of her husband's confession.

She is not a subject at all but only a face or mask, literally a *persona*, her open mouth a terrible visual mockery of the fact that she was once a gifted soprano for whom Ballinger originally wrote his 'Simple Songs'. What is the larger significance of this penultimate image of his incurably ill wife's mask-like face in Venice? What is the significance of the film's title, 'Youth', with respect to gender difference? To ability? (Her condition is arguably a kind of disability.) To age? The Venetian setting is explained, or rather itself explains in retrospect, an early dream sequence, in which Ballinger, in his conductor's coat and tails, traverses the raised *passerella* down the centre of a beautifully lit, flooded nocturnal Piazza San Marco, encountering the oneiric figure of Miss Universe in full beauty pageant regalia. They pass each other awkwardly on the narrow boardwalk, and, as Miss Universe struts towards the Museo Correr, Ballinger, continuing on towards the Basilica, gradually sinks into the rising *aqua alta*, calling out for his wife: 'Melanie!'.[26] This opening dream scene thus establishes, albeit obliquely, Ballinger's guilt over his wife's condition and his (non-)response to it, while at the same time foreshadowing the film's conclusion, in which he overcomes his psychological impasse and his sense of guilt towards his wife by agreeing to conduct his 'Simple Songs' once more – with a different singer.

On a more ironically metaphorical level, the film's title – *Youth* – foregrounds Sorrentino's abiding concern with a masculinist culture that can never reach adulthood; a generation of perpetually adolescent subjects, kept from ethical and axiological maturity through its ongoing interpellation by advertising, trashy television, crass music videos and, by implication, the Internet, especially social media (in this critique Sorrentino echoes the later Godard[27]). Not incidentally, the latter technologies, such as social media, go unrepresented in this and other projects, Sorrentino's stories focusing instead on characters and situations that seem somewhat out of time, if not downright old-fashioned – or just plain old. (Once again Jude Law's 'young pope' presents a complex variation, being at once prematurely old and perpetually immature.). Generational difference emerges in *Youth* as perhaps the most significant determinant of contemporary identity, in a culture that is also characterized, in Fredric Jameson's perspicacious critique, by a lack of historical consciousness and a consequent over-privileging of the present – a 'presentism' whose *reductio ad absurdum* is a perpetual present moment of consumption (Jameson 1999: ix). This attitude emerges in *Youth* in particular as the unspoken nemesis of any serious person, meaning any *man* of a certain age whose ironic self-understanding in the present is ineluctably tied to his memories of the past. This is not because it is good or necessary to remember specific things, but because in *The Great Beauty* and *The Young Pope* especially remembering per se, even bad or traumatic memories, is prerequisite to the maintenance of a subjectivity determined by an elegiac sensibility that knows itself to be out of date and yet derives an ironically nostalgic pleasure from this critical self-understanding.

The potentially patronizing close-up on Melanie Ballinger in *Youth* demands an analytical model other than a gendered theory of looking. In *Staring: How We Look*, Rosemarie Garland-Thomson elaborates a theory of 'the stare', otherwise known as the 'Baroque stare' or the 'colonizing gaze', in the context of disability studies. While Garland-Thomson's examples of the stare are primarily sociological, the visual basis of 'the stare' justifies the appropriation of this idea into a film studies context, applying it in aesthetic-ideological rather than sociological terms.[28] Translating Garland-Thomson's 'stare' into the terms of a visual structure in specific films helps to illuminate scenes in which a more ideologically based notion of the gaze fails to lead to deeper understanding.[29] In other words, even when stripped of its original feminist-psychoanalytic connotations and applied more straightforwardly as a critique of the process of objectifying ('reifying') another human being, reducing her/him to an object of erotic desire, the 'stare' by contrast reduces the other person to precisely that: an *other* who is the object of either fascination or disgust, or some intermediate but still powerful affective response. Either way, arguably she or he is reduced to something other than fully 'human' in the process:

> Cultural othering in all its forms – the male gaze being just one instance – depends upon looking as an act of domination. The ethnographic or the colonizing look

operates similarly to the gendered look, subordinating its object by enacting a power dynamic. When persons in a position that grants them authority to stare take up that power, staring functions as a form of domination, marking the *staree* as the exotic, outlaw, alien, or other.

(Garland-Thomson 2009: 42)

The stare would seem to be clearly at work in *The Great Beauty*, for instance, in those scenes involving Dadina (Giovanna Vignola), Jep's editor, who is in her own words a 'dwarf' (*una nana*). Dadina is a fully fleshed-out character, however: a successful businesswoman of a certain age with an active sex life (as implied in the dialogue) and a healthy sense of self-irony. In showing Dadina as capable of laughing at herself, Sorrentino appears open-minded while getting away with exploiting the actor's physical appearance for a melancholically humorous effect. This unusual casting choice pays off, as Dadina's scenes with Jep emerge as important because of the light they shed on his character.

An even more glaring example of Sorrentino's exploitation of the stare occurs in The *Young Pope*, Episode 2, when Cardinal Voiello returns to his apartment near the Vatican. Sorrentino structures the scene as one of thwarted voyeurism: the viewer is aligned with Sister Mary as she spies on Voiello at Lenny's behest. The viewer likewise spies on him, perhaps hoping (with Sister Mary) to catch him out in some unpriestly behaviour in the privacy of his home. This is suggested for instance by the fact that, as he carries a box of pastries into the building, he is followed by an attractive young woman in a tight red dress. The framing and *mise en scène* conspire to create this sense, as Mary is able to watch unobserved, *Rear Window*-style, from an adjacent car park, Voiello conveniently visible through the large windows of his lavish apartment. The red dress turns out to be a red herring as from outside we watch Voiello greeting his charge, Girolamo (unnamed in the credits), a young man with a severe physical (and perhaps mental) disability, played by an actor who is clearly authentically disabled.

If nothing else, Sorrentino's casting choices cannot be accused of 'cripface': Hollywood's tendency to cast non-disabled actors in treatments of mental and physical disability. There is something to be said for casting genuinely differently abled actors in disabled roles – although it is important to avoid the uncritical conflation of the role and the person playing it. Generally speaking, the difference of disability trumps that of either gender or age – until, that is, all three identities are merged in the same character. *The Young Pope*'s counter-tendency is announced in the series' opening dream sequence. At one point Lenny says in voice-over over a close-up of a young worshipper with Down syndrome: 'God does not leave anyone behind'. The fact that this occurs within a dream sequence does not alter the scene's exemplary status as instance of Sorrentino's use of non-normative identities as a spectacular way to underline the series' apparent championing of the meek and powerless, the disenfranchised and disabled, while simultaneously complicating the exploitation of women's bodies and faces – all in the service of adding nuance to our understanding of the principal masculine characters.

Coda: The Young Pope *as 'Middle-Brow Melodrama'*

In *The Young Pope* series, as in *The Great Beauty*, memory is foregrounded as the primary metaphysical framework, whether in the form of the burden of an individual's past or the pressure of history upon the present. The former – subjective memory tied to individual character – manifests in these later works in the form of the flashback in which the highly conventional and artificial cinematic rendering of memory has been naturalized. The flashbacks in the TV series are structurally less complex than in *The Great Beauty*, for instance. Undoubtedly, this is in part the result of narrative expediency, but it is worth noting that these scenes culminate in a treatment of memory – in general and specifically in terms of the protagonist – that, if not more sophisticated or complex, appears to me more progressive than the films from the perspective of gender politics.

In one telling example, the conclusion of the penultimate episode of *The Young Pope* represents a thematic and structural inversion of the conclusion of *The Great Beauty*: instead of the dead woman reappearing as her younger self to save the ageing and undeserving protagonist, here the Pope speaks in voice-over the words of his teenage self to his now middle-aged former beloved, the nameless woman who nevertheless receives the revelation of his love as a gift in the present. But this love letter is read over a montage of several other characters from the preceding episodes, each of whom somehow shares in this confession of love.[30] Here the voice-over begins while Esther is in frame, in what appears to be the answering shot to one of Lenny on the beach near her house in Ostia; his eyeline suggests that he is looking at her, whereas by the time she finds his gift (a photo portrait) he is already flying away in the papal helicopter, like the archangel after the annunciation.

It is no coincidence, however, that this voice-over-montage sequence is preceded in the same episode by two deathbed scenes, one within the other. In the first Cardinal Spencer (James Cromwell) succumbs to cancer, ironically, just as his opportunity to assume the papacy is within sight. In the second scene, another flashback, to Lenny's childhood orphanage in upstate New York, the custodian's wife (Ann Carr) lies dying from what appears to be cancer. The two death-bed scenes are ironically juxtaposed as Spencer asks Lenny to confirm the miracle cure he performed on the sick woman decades before, as evidence of his saintly status. Lenny grants Spencer's dying wish, recounting the event and offering him the comfort of knowing that his faith in God has not been in vain.[31] That Lenny does not extend the same favour to his expiring former mentor is an irony muted by the series' wholesale descent (if that's the right word) into a hybrid form of postsecular male melodrama. But this is more a description than a criticism, as the affective intensity of the scene is clearly written into the script, with its highly conventional flashback structure guaranteeing the veracity of the 'miracle' for the viewer as much as the other characters who witness and/or hear of it. Thus, the almost kitschily Christological *mise en scène* – large crucifix and statuette of Mary, anti-naturalist lighting effects, actors staring in wide-eyed wonder – contrasts starkly with the final scene in *The Great Beauty*, analysed above. Again, this scene inverts the one in the film: the man saves the woman who is not dead but dying. Her mask-like visage in this flashback visually echoes Melanie's rigid, open-mouthed expression in the above-mentioned shot in *Youth*. If the youthful Lenny's (Patrick Mitchell) miraculous curing of his friend Billy's mother, his saving her from death, fails to redeem all those other men in Sorrentino's films, this is not just a criticism of Jep or Ballinger as masculine subjects.

By comparison to this scene in *The Young Pope*, there is greater artistic sincerity to the elegiac nostalgia of the final flashback in *The Great Beauty*, just as the lack of closure in the latter and in *Youth* is paradoxically more satisfying than the TV series' melodramatic finale. The resurrected woman's beatific expression invites the viewer to exchange a stare for an awestruck gaze – whether of sentimental wonder or cynical disbelief, as the case may be. Such a female character, however, no matter how marginalized by age, illness or gender, is still recuperable, part of the closed (masculinist) economy of *The Young Pope*'s narrative. She remains in the end a fictional construct, a narrative function. The series' authentically disabled bodies, by contrast, represent identities not susceptible to such melodramatic redemption, the actors' extra-diegetic authenticity translating, paradoxically, into a spectacular image of radical unknowability.

NOTES

1. *The Consequences of Love* was the highest grossing Italian film to date. *Il divo* shared the Jury Prize at Cannes and also secured wide international distribution and coverage in the international press. *The Great Beauty* can be seen as Sorrentino's consecration by the Academy. My thanks to an anonymous reviewer at *JICMS* for this clarification (see also Hipkins 2008, 2013; Mariani 2017; Simor and Sorfa 2017).

2. Marcus invokes the historically important notion of *impegno* in a contemporary context as indicative of not a single, overarching ideological agenda but of a 'diversification' of a generally leftist critical perspective (Antonello and Mussgnug 2009: 3).

3. I owe this reading of Sorrentino's filmic image as 'spectacular' to an anonymous reviewer at Columbia University's Wallflower Press.

4. 'Unfortunately mainstream Italian criticism has only flirted with the basics of this prelimi-
   nary stage, and certainly never moved towards thinking about "images for women". There
   is in fact an uncomfortable degree of overlap between the most basic "images of women"
   criticism and a kind of descriptive criticism that merely celebrates a bevy of female beauties,
   repeatedly fetishizing female stars without analyzing the complex gendered construction
   that constitutes a star'. (Hipkins 2008: 215)

5. The spectacular nature of Sorrentino's images reveal a fictional version of what Jill Godmi-
   low calls 'the pornography of the real' in documentary film: 'the objectifying of a graphic
   image, turning it from a subject into an object, so that the thing or person depicted can be
   commodified, circulated and consumed without regard to its status as a subject' (quoted
   Kraemer 2015: 65 – 66).

6. Danielle Hipkins describes 'the much-lauded recent films of Paolo Sorrentino, in which
   the female is merely a fetish object for the narration of male desire (*The Consequences of
   Love*, 2004; *The Family Friend*, 2006)' (2008: 213).

7. My approach begins from a point beyond psychoanalytic theory if only because it is no
   longer reasonable to read every film made according to a certain set of stylistic parameters
   as an allegory for the history of the psychoanalytic subject, the Oedipal family romance.

8. Although on the level of content – e.g. Madonna and child – this is not irrelevant to my
   reading of Sorrentino's films.

9. By the same token, exploitative and objectified images of human bodies in the digital era
   have only proliferated, in part because they do not depend upon an indexical link to the
   pro-filmic world. In any discussion of such images, however, there is always more at stake
   when one knows that the actor was really there before the camera, a body subject to the
   violence of representation.

10. As Susan Sontag observed, in her essay on Bergman's *Persona*: 'it's in the nature of cinema
    to confer on all events, without indications to the contrary, an equivalent degree of reality:
    everything shown on the screen is "there", present' (2000: 67).

11. For Mulvey: 'the castrated woman' = 'Woman-as-lack' = 'Woman' (2000: 483).

12. Quoted in Hipkins (2008: 215n4).

13. Regarding the latter see, e.g.: 'the viewer suspends disbelief in the fictional world of
    the film, identifies not only with specific characters in the film but more importantly
    with the film's overall ideology through identification with the film's narrative struc-
    ture and visual point of view, and puts into play fantasy structures [...] that derive from
    the viewer's unconscious.' (Cartwright and Sturken 2001: 73). In the Italian context
    this stems from 'the *velina* or television showgirl, who is a standard trope' within the
    '*cinepanettone*' tradition. As Danielle Hipkins (citing Alan O'Leary) reminds us, 'the
    velina's function is most often read as debasing to women, as contaminating the genre
    further through the female actors' origins in the despised medium of television and all
    its associated particular political problems, and with the women's frequently semi-naked
    appearance as object of the male gaze. It is worth remembering that for international

film audiences, however, this particular vision of women is familiar not so much from Italian television, or the '*cinepanettone*', as from Italy's tradition of art-house cinema, such as the opening scene of *La dolce vita*. Such a use of the female body formed, and continues to form, part of the international appeal of Italian cinema, although the growing visual presence of bikini-clad women on Italian television is almost universally deplored.' (Hipkins 2013: 1 – 2).

14. For a different reading of the gendering of these diegetic elements in the context of Italian 'heritage cinema' see O'Leary (2016: 67).

15. Mariani quotes an interview with Sorrentino in which he confesses: 'melancholy is a vital key to the leitmotif in the movie' (2017: 181n28).

16. As early as 1960 'Pauline Kael called this film genre the "come-dressed-as-the-sick-soul-of-Europe party"' (Bradshaw 2013: 3). For Peter Bradshaw, *The Great Beauty* looks like a '"come-dressed-as-the-fantastically-vigorous-and-unrepentant-soul-of-rich-Europe" party' (2013: 3). As Roger Clarke puts it, 'this isn't the 1960s bourgeoisie deliquescing into their own emptiness – this is the vaunting pleasure of the modern "one per cent" reveling in unapologetic wealth' (Bradshaw 2013: n.pag.).

17. 'This is how it always ends: in death. But first there was life, hidden beneath the blah blah blah. [...] The fleeting and sporadic flashes of beauty amid the wretched squalor and human misery. [...] Therefore, let this novel begin.'

18. 'What lies beyond lies beyond. That is not my concern.'

19. For a complementary reading of this scene as a 'parody of men's obsession with female beauty' see Simor and Sorfa (2017: 11).

20. See Hipkins' reading of the film, echoing the terms of my argument but with a different valuation: 'Hailed as part of the "re-birth" of Italian cinema, Sorrentino's intense evocation of Fellini's Rome expresses nostalgia for and an attempted re-instantiation of the same gender dynamic. The female character is, once again, made to carry the burden of corporeal ageing, like the (feminized) body of Rome itself, whilst male ageing is a question of redeeming soul and memory, in which the male melodrama of Jep's suffering, as Catherine O'Rawe describes [...] becomes "the gateway to the sublime"' (Hipkins 2013).

21. Fellini famously based this scene on a real incident in which Pierluigi Praturlon, one of the original paparazzi, photographed Ekberg wading in the Trevi fountain (Levy 2016: 281 – 82).

22. See Simor and Sorfa's reading of this scene's 'excessive style' and parodic 'representation of female beauty' (2017: 11).

23. Cf. Mary Anne Doane: 'The cinematic apparatus inherits a theory of the image which is *not* conceived outside of sexual specifications. And historically, there has always been a certain imbrication of the cinematic image and the representation of the woman. [...] For the female spectator there is a certain *over-presence* of the image – she *is* the image' (2000: 497 – 99).

24. Williams amplifies what she calls melodrama's 'sentimental politics', which often entails a climax that offers 'a feeling for, if not the reality of, justice', in which 'the death of a good

person offers paroxysms of pathos and recognitions of virtue compensating for individual loss of life'; i.e. 'compensation' as *redemption* through 'self-sacrifice', typically on the part of a woman (2001: 31).

25. Regarding Sorrentino's penchant for the Fellinian grotesque see O'Rawe (2012). See Hipkins 2013 regarding Sorrentino's transition from the on-screen objectification of women to the broader exploitation of non-normative bodies and faces, especially but not exclusively those of women. See especially the aging former *'velina'* in *The Great Beauty*'s opening party scene vs her antecedent in Marcello's 'harem' dream in *8 ½* (Hipkins 2013: 2).

26. In a structurally identical dream scene in *The Young Pope*, Episode 7, Lenny's birth mother, emerging from what appears to be an enormous pile of (dead?) babies, proceeds across the Piazza, where she is joined by Lenny's father. Together they move towards him as he, emerging from the depth of the shot just like Ballinger, proceeds open-armed towards them. The dream ends as the three embrace.

27. See e.g. *Éloge de l'amour* (2001).

28. I thank my Ph.D. student Grace McCarthy for drawing my attention to Garland-Thomson's work and for first suggesting the stare as a cinematic and not merely a sociological structure.

29. E.g., R. W. Fassbinder's *Ali: Fear Eats the Soul* (1974), whose characteristic set piece is a highly formalized, artificial scene in which one or more characters stare blatantly at another marked as their ethno-cultural or racial other. In Fassbinder's film this strategy adds a clearly Brechtian resonance to the film's meanings.

30. In a manner reminiscent of what has become a stock musical sequence in contemporary American 'smart' film and television, in which several disparate characters, separate in space, are united in a montage by a piece of music played over top. The famous montage in P. T. Anderson's *Magnolia* (1999), in which all the major characters sing the same song while in separate locations, is the self-reflexive *ne plus ultra* of this technique. Sorrentino's employment of a wide variety of musical styles as a principal source of meaning in his films guarantees the frequency of this technique. Regarding the 'smart' film see Sconce (2002). Thanks to the website 'tunefind', we know that the pop song playing over the final montage is 'Never be like you' by Flume (featuring Kai).

31. Curiously, Spencer's dying words, 'time to die', directly quote replicant Roy Batty's dying words in the original *Blade Runner* (Scott, 1982).

REFERENCES

Anderson, P. T. (1999), *Magnolia*, USA: Ghoulardi Film Company and New Line Cinema.

Anon. (2017), '*La grande bellezza*', The Internet Movie Database, 15 April, http://imdb.com/title/tt2358891/trivia. Accessed 15 April 2017.

Antonello, P. and Mussgnug, F. (eds) (2009), *Postmodern Impegno: Ethics and Commitment in Contemporary Italian Culture*, Oxford: Peter Lang Pub. Inc.

Antonioni, M. (1961), *La notte*, Italy: Nepi Film.

Bazin, A. (2009), 'Cinematic realism and the Italian School of the Liberation', in *What is Cinema?* (trans. and annotated by T. Barnard), Montreal, QC: Caboose, pp. 215–250.

Beineix, J.-J. (1981), *Diva*, France: Les Films Galaxie.

Bergman, I. (1957), *Wild Strawberries*, Sweden: Svensk Filmindustri.

Bondanella, P. (2009), *The History of Italian Cinema*, 3rd ed., New York: Continuum.

Bordwell, D. and Thompson, K. (2009), *Film History: An Introduction*, 3rd ed., Boston: McGraw Hill.

Bradshaw, P. (2013), '*La grande bellezza (The Great Beauty)*', review, *The Guardian*, 5 September, https://theguardian.com/film/2013/sep/05/le-grande-bellezza-great-beauty-review. Accessed 15 April 2017.

Brecht, B. ([1948] 1977), 'A Short Organum for the theatre', in *Brecht on Theatre* (ed. and trans. J Willet), New York: Hill and Wang, pp. 179–208.

Cartwright, L. and Sturken, M. (2001), 'Spectatorship, power, and knowledge', in *Practices of Looking: An Introduction to Visual Culture*, Oxford and New York: Oxford University Press, pp. 72–93.

Clarke, R. (2013), 'Review: *The Great Beauty*', BFI: Film Forever, 6 December, http://bfi.org.uk/news-opinion/sight-sound-magazine/reviews-recommendations/great-beauty. Accessed 15 April 2017.

Coen, Joel and Ethan (1998), *The Big Lebowski*, USA: Polygram Filmed Entertainment.

Davis, L. J. (ed.) (2017), 'Introduction: Disability, normality, and power', in *The Disability Studies Reader*, 5th ed., London and New York: Routledge, pp. 1–16.

Di Lodovico Buonarroti Simoni, M. (1499), *Pietá*, Rome: St. Peter's.

Di Martino, L. and Verdicchio, P. (eds) (2017), *Encounters with the Real in Contemporary Italian Literature and Cinema*, Newcastle upon Tyne: Cambridge Scholars Press.

Doane, M. A. (2000), 'Film and the masquerade: Theorizing the female spectator', in R. Stam and T. Miller (eds), *Film Theory: An Anthology*, Oxford: Blackwell, pp. 495–509.

Erll, A. (2011), *Memory in Culture* (trans. S. B Young), New York: Palgrave Macmillan.

Fassbinder, R. W. (1974), *Ali: Fear Eats the Soul*, West Germany: Filmverlag der Autoren.

Fellini, F. (1953), *I vitelloni*, Italy and France: Cité Films and Peg-Films.

Fellini, F. (1960), *La dolce vita*, Italy and France: Riama, Cinecittà and Pathé Consortium Cinéma.

Fellini, F. (1963), *8½*, Italy and France: Cineriz and Francinex.

Fellini, F. (1973), *Roma*, Italy and France: Ultra Film and Les Productiones Artistes Associés.

Garland-Thomson, R. (2009), *Staring: How We Look*, Oxford and New York: Oxford University Press.

Gledhill, C. (ed.) (1987), 'Melodrama and cinema: The critical problem', in *Home is Where the Heart is*, London: BFI, pp. 5–13.

Godard, J.-L. (2001), *Eloge de l'amour*, France and Switzerland: Avventura Films.

Goethe, J. W. von (1976), *Faust, A Tragedy* (ed. and trans. W. A. Cyrus Hamlin), New York: W.W. Norton & Company.

Gondry, M. (2004), *Eternal Sunshine of the Spotless Mind*, USA: Focus Features.

Grey, T. (ed.) (2000), *Richard Wagner: Der fliegende Holländer*, Cambridge: Cambridge University Press.

Haskell, M. (1974), *Reverence to Rape: The Treatment of Woman in the Movies*, Chicago: University of Chicago Press.

Hipkins, D. (2008), 'Why Italian film studies needs a second take on gender', *Italian Studies*, 63:2, Autumn, pp. 213–34.

Hipkins, D. (2013), 'The showgirl effect: Ageing between great beauties and 'veline di turno'', *Reading Italy*, https://wp.me/p2iDSt-bW. Accessed 15 October 2017.

Hitchcock, A. (1958), *Vertigo*, USA: Paramount Pictures.

Jameson, F. (1999), *Postmodernism, or The Cultural Logic of Late Capitalism*, Durham, NC: Duke University Press.

Kaplan, E. A. (2010), 'Is the gaze male?', in M Furstenau (ed.), *The Film Theory Reader: Debates and Arguments*, London and New York: Routledge, pp. 209–221.

Kilbourn, R. J. A. (2010), *Cinema, Memory, Modernity: The Representation of Memory from the Art Film to Transnational Cinema*, New York and London: Routledge.

Kraemer, J. A. (2015), 'Trauma and representation in the animated documentary', *Journal of Film and Video*, 67:3&4, Fall/Winter, pp. 57–68.

Landsberg, A. (2003), 'Prosthetic memory: The ethics and politics of memory in an age of mass culture', in P Grainge (ed.), *Memory and Popular Film*, New York: Manchester University Press, pp. 144–161.

Levy, S. (2016), *Dolce Vita Confidential: Fellini, Loren, Pucci, Paparazzi and the Swinging High Life of 1950s Rome*, New York and London: Norton.

Marcus, M. (2010), 'The ironist and the auteur: Post-realism in Paolo Sorrentino's Il divo', *The Italianist*, 30, pp. 245–57.

Mariani, A. (2017), 'The empty heterotopic (non-)space of Sorrentino's female characters in The Great Beauty and The Consequences of Love', in S Byer and F Cecchini (eds), *Female Identity and Its Representations in the Arts and Humanities*, Newcastle upon Tyne: Cambridge Scholars Publishing, pp. 168–184.

Milton, J. (1993), *Paradise Lost*, 2nd ed., New York and London: Norton.

Mulvey, L. (2000), 'Visual pleasure and narrative cinema', in P. Stam and T. Miller (eds), *Film Theory: An Anthology*, Oxford: Blackwell, pp. 483–494.

Nichetti, M. (1989), *Ladri di saponette*, Italy: Bambú Cinema e TV and Reteitalia.

O'Leary, A. (2009), 'Marco Tullio Giordana, or the persistence of Impegno', in P. Antonello and F. Mussgnug (eds), *Postmodern Impegno: Ethics and Commitment in Contemporary Italian Culture*, Oxford: Peter Lang, pp. 213–231.

O'Leary, A. (2016), 'Towards world heritage cinema (starting from the negative)', in P. Cooke and R. Stone (eds), *Screening European Heritage*, New York: Palgrave Macmillan, pp. 63–84.

O'Rawe, C. (2012), 'Brothers in arms: Middlebrow Impegno and homosocial relations in the cinema of Petraglia and Rulli', in D. Hipkins (ed.), *Intellectual Communities and Partnerships in Italy and Europe*, Oxford, Bern, Berlin, Brussels, Frankfurt am Main, New York and Vienna: Peter Lang, pp. 149–167.

Rancière, J. (2009), *The Emancipated Spectator* (trans. G Elliott), London and New York: Verso Books.

Rossellini, R. (1946), *Rome, cittá aperta*, Italy: Excelsa Film.

Scola, E. (1980), *La Terrazza*, Italy and France: *Dean Film, International Dean, Les Films Marceau-Cocinor*.

Sconce, J. (2002), 'Irony, nihilism, and the new American "smart" film', *Screen*, 43:4, Winter, pp. 349–369.

Scorsese, M. (2017), 'Standing up for cinema', TLS, 31 May, http://the-tls.co.uk/articles/public/film-making-martin-scorsese/. Accessed 1 June 2017.

Scott, R. (1982), *Blade Runner*, USA: The Ladd Company.

Silverman, K. (1986), 'Suture [excerpts]', in P. Rosen (ed.), *Narrative, Apparatus, Ideology: A Film Theory Reader*, New York: Columbia University Press, pp. 219–234.

Simor, E. and Sorfa, D. (2017), 'Irony, sexism and magic in Paolo Sorrentino's films', *Studies in European Cinema*, 14: 3, pp. 200–215.

Sontag, S. (2000), 'Bergman's Persona', in L Michaels (ed.), *Ingmar Bergman's Persona*, Cambridge: Cambridge University Press, pp. 62–85.

Sontag, S. (2001), *L'uomo in piú (One Man Up)*, Italy: Indigo Film and Key Films.

Sorrentino, P. (2004), *Le conseguenze dell'amore (The Consequences of Love)*, Italy: Fandango, Indigo Film and Medusa Film.

Sorrentino, P. (2006), *L'amico di famiglia (The Family Friend)*, Italy and France: Fandango, Indigo Film and Medusa Film.

Sorrentino, P. (2008), *Il divo*, Italy and France: Indigo Film, Lucky Red and Parco Film.

Sorrentino, P. (2011), *This Must Be the Place*, Italy, France and Ireland: Indigo Film, Lucky Red and Medusa Film.

Sorrentino, P. (2013), *La grande bellezza (The Great Beauty)*, Italy and France: Indigo Film and Medusa Film.

Sorrentino, P. (2015), *Youth*, Italy, France, UK and Switzerland: Indigo Films, Barbary Films and Pathé.

Sorrentino, P. (2016), *The Young Pope* (Italy, France, Spain, UK and USA: Wildside, Haut et Court TV, Mediapro, Sky Italia, HBO and Canal+).

Tunefind (2017), https://tunefind.com/show/the-young-pope/season-1/38422. Accessed 30 October 2017.

Wagner, R. (1982), *Der fliegende Holländer (The Flying Dutchman)* (trans. D Pountney), London: Calder.

Wenders, W. (1987), *Wings of Desire*, West Germany and France: Road Movies Filmproduktion.

Williams, L. (2001), 'The American melodramatic mode', *Playing the Race Card: Melodramas of Black and White from Uncle Tom's Cabin to O.J.Simpson*, Princeton, NJ: Princeton University Press, pp. 10–44.

10

Anxiety (of Influence) and (Absent) Fathers in Sorrentino's English-Language Narratives

Sandra Waters

Rutgers University

Upon the release of Paolo Sorrentino's Oscar-winning film *La grande bellezza (The Great Beauty)* in 2013, critics, scholars and cultural commentators immediately drew comparisons to Federico Fellini's *La dolce vita* (2014) in terms of title, characters, setting, cinematography and storyline, or lack thereof (Donadio 2013; Stille 2014; Sicinski 2013: 20).[1] At least one critic has inferred that *The Great Beauty's* protagonist Jep Gambardella could be an older Marcello Rubini from *La dolce vita* and suggests that *The Great Beauty* could be the continuation of *La dolce vita* (Stille 2014). Sorrentino's much-anticipated next film, *Youth* (2015), was eerily reminiscent of Fellini's *8½* (2001), his own subsequent film to *La dolce vita*.[2] In fact, the following describes the plots of both *8½* and *Youth*: a lauded artist taking refuge at a European spa is goaded to work rather than rest; a most beautiful woman appears as inspiration; dream sequences abound. That Fellini's work influences Sorrentino's films I do not question; the degree to which Fellini represents an artistic father figure to Sorrentino creates a Bloomian key with which to further investigate the younger director's body of work. The existential malaise that permeates Fellini's films is also reflected in those of Sorrentino, but the cause is different for the two eras: the former is caused by a post-war society in rapid flux while the latter's work set in the early twenty-first century depicts a background of decades of poor leadership and stagnation (O'Neill 2016). Although Sorrentino's Italian-speaking characters represent a corrupt or decadent socio-patriarchal system in contemporary Italian society, the director extends this same existential problem to foreign settings (Ireland and the United States for *This Must Be the Place* [2011], and Switzerland in *Youth*) and with English-speaking protagonists (*The Young Pope* [2016]), which signals an additional problem. Fred Ballinger in *Youth* is a deficient father to Lena; Lenny

161

Belardo of *The Young Pope* was abandoned at an orphanage at age 6 by his biological parents; the absent *and* damaged father in *This Must Be the Place* produces a damaged son, Cheyenne. The father figures that appear in these films and television episodes function sometimes as extensions of a failed father, and at other times as correctives to a failed father, and thus serve to illuminate both the anxiety of artistic influence and the broken social patriarchy that Sorrentino depicts on-screen.

This article examines the role of damaged or absent fathers – actual, metaphoric and artistic – as represented in Paolo Sorrentino's works that are filmed in English: *Youth, This Must Be the Place* and *The Young Pope*. Harold Bloom's theory on creative anxiety (1997) is especially helpful when analysing artistic or precursor father figures and speaks to the professional lives of Sorrentino's protagonists. The psychoanalytic thesis of the anal father as developed by Slavoj Žižek (1992a, 1994, 1999) via Jacques Lacan and Sigmund Freud as a postmodern response to Lacan's symbolic father serves as my theoretical structure in analysing the psyche of the uncommon protagonists represented in Sorrentino's English work: a famous and ageing conductor-composer along with his famous and elderly director friend, a reclusive rock star and the Pope. Paired with the uncommon settings represented or suggested in these works (an exclusive Swiss spa, the Holocaust, Vatican City), Sorrentino's common and ideal viewers are presented with a person and place that have very uncommon or surreal qualities, which leads me to a reading of these filmic elements vis-à-vis the symbolic realm and symbolic figures that permeate Lacan's (and thus Žižek's) theories.

For Lacan, the Imaginary is the order of images rather than language, which is relegated to the Symbolic Order; thus, the Imaginary is often utilized when analysing the medium of cinema. The Symbolic is the realm of social reality, which is regulated by laws and rules defined through language; it is the domain of culture, whereas the Imaginary is that of nature. The Real is not reality or the real world, but it is impossible to imagine and thus, impossible to attain, as it resists both symbolization and language. Additionally, there can exist no absence in the Real. As Lacan explains, the Real is '[…] the essential object which is not an object any longer but this something faced with which all words cease and all categories fail, the object of *anxiety* par excellence' (1988: 164, emphasis added). The *objet petit a* is the remnant left over by the introduction of the Symbolic into the Real; it is a surplus of meaning and *jouissance* ('pleasure'); it is the unattainable object of desire (Lacan 1988). To illustrate just some of these ideas and how they connect to Sorrentino's work, I turn to *Youth*, his first post-Oscar film.

Youth

At the beginning of *Youth*, retired classical music composer and conductor Fred (played by Michael Caine) is presented as a failed father in life and in art.

He refuses multiple requests by the Queen of England to conduct his popular and successful 'Simple Songs' accompanied by a world-renown soprano, and he is unable to comfort his daughter Lena (played by Rachel Weisz) when she discovers that her husband is leaving her. In fact, when asked what her job is, Lena replies that she has two jobs: being Fred's daughter, and working as his assistant. Relegating her personal relationship with her father to a professional realm highlights the fact that she does consider it work, something that is perhaps tedious and requires continual effort, something that is not always pleasant, although it is necessary; it also implies that something is amiss with their personal relationship. When Lena and Fred undergo a spa treatment together as a bonding effort, Lena, crying, angrily lists some of the reasons she believes Fred to be a poor husband and father: that he cheated on his wife Melanie with many other women, that he once fell in love with a man, that he never showed Lena any affection when she was a child, but rather called for her silence whenever he was home and, inevitably, working. Once she confronts her own pent-up emotions and Fred's shortcomings as a family man with her vocal and emotional outburst, a general catharsis for many of the film's protagonists ensues. For Fred, the professional and personal realms are necessarily connected, as towards the end of the film he finally reveals that the reason he refuses to conduct 'Simple Songs' is that he wrote them for his beloved wife, who also always performed them when he conducted them. Since Melanie is currently living in a long-term care facility in a non-responsive state, she can no longer perform. Melanie left the Symbolic when she lost the power of language and entered the Real, which is unattainable by everyone else. With the absence of Melanie in Fred's life, she has been replaced and is represented by 'Simple Songs', which becomes the unattainable object of desire in her place, something that Fred initially refuses to share with anyone, seeing as he can no longer communicate with Melanie herself and she cannot perform. The 'Simple Songs' also become a Hitchcockian McGuffin, the filmic object that sets desire, and thus the plot, in motion (Žižek 1992b: 8). They are a written, alternate version of the voice Melanie has lost personally and professionally as she is doubly silenced; she can only begin to regain her voice, in part, by the cathartic 'aria' that Lena 'sings' to Fred. Once Lena speaks to Fred in a language that he understands – music laced with melodrama – he can comprehend a performance of 'Simple Songs' without his wife. Ironically, from Melanie's frustrating silence Lena's therapeutic voice emerges, and Fred is only able to begin to understand his daughter and function as a good father after she has performed her cathartic 'aria' – complete with melodramatic tears for maximum effect – in one long, close-up shot of her face. Once Fred says aloud why he is blocked professionally, he is able to resolve his reluctance to visit his wife. His daughter (who has overheard his 'confession') realizes that he has been a devoted husband after all, since he is professionally blocked by her absence in his personal life. In a quick series of sequences that mark the film's denouement, Fred visits the grave of Igor Stravinsky (his professional father figure), then he visits his catatonic wife for the first time in ten years, and, if we are to believe that the final sequence of the film is not a dream or a fantasy, that he does indeed overcome his professional blockage and performs 'Simple Songs' with a different soprano for the queen and his public.

Melanie's absence is also balanced in the film by the presence of another soprano, Sumi Jo, who is regarded by the queen's emissary as the person who should perform 'Simple Songs' with Fred conducting. Sumi Jo's ability to perform Fred's professional crowning achievement underscores the fact that Melanie is utterly silent. The absence of Melanie, 'Simple Songs' and Sumi Jo throughout most of the film is countered by the impossible presence of all three at its conclusion. The appearance of Sumi Jo presents another complication in that she is not simply a filmic character in the film *Youth*, but also a professional, famous soprano in the real world who plays herself in the film *Youth*. So, just as Melanie's entrance into the unattainable Real has left Fred in the Symbolic realm with his 'Simple Songs' that represent his unattainable object of desire, Sumi Jo straddles both the Imaginary realm of her character in the film that resolves Fred's anxiety and also the real world of director Sorrentino, who has succeeded in representing Fred's *petit objet a* through a surrogate.

This process is echoed in the film by Julian (Lena's husband) replacing his wife with another, Paloma Faith. Faith is not only a filmic character in *Youth* but is also an English pop singer known for her quirky fashion style. Like Sumi Jo, Faith has a small role in *Youth*, playing herself. Unlike Sumi Jo's redemptive role in the film, Faith is represented as a husband-stealer. The few seconds in which the character Faith appears as herself interacting with other protagonists present her as nearly the opposite of her public persona: she is depicted as unrecognizably demure, wearing a white suit and speaking calmly to defend herself. The 'real life', private Faith is unlike her professional, public version, seen in an abbreviated video produced specifically for *Youth* of her song 'Can't Rely on You' (2014), in which, while wearing multiple garish outfits of revealing clothing, she wriggles suggestively on top of a car driven by Julian. At the end of the video segment, Faith appears dressed as Lena, in a dark wig and a demure black dress, but her mouth opens impossibly wide as her figure nears the camera, threatening harm to her viewer.

Whereas here Faith is portrayed as having a negative effect on Lena, Sumi Jo is portrayed as redemptive for Fred, as a close-up shot of her slightly open mouth during the concert is intercut with a shot of Melanie, mouth agape and skin blotchy, in contrast to Sumi Jo's perfect make up and gestures, but similar to Paloma-as-Lena's screaming maw.

FIGURE 10.1: Paloma Faith as Lena. Sorrentino (dir.), *Youth*, 2015.

FIGURE 10.2: Sumi Jo's lower face. Sorrentino (dir.), *Youth*, 2015.

The intrusion of real life personas Paloma Faith and Sumi Jo initially stand as negative figures to Lena and Fred, but while Sumi Jo eventually serves to shake Fred out of his post-retirement slump and acts as the conduit for his wife, Paloma Faith portrays a real threat to Lena's personal well-being. As real intrusions into the Imaginary unreal space of the spa and the oneiric presentation of the concert hall, Sumi Jo and Paloma Faith are successful vocal artists, although their narrative functions as represented by their open mouths differ. Sumi Jo channels Melanie's voice, while Paloma Faith – one wife swapped out for another – appears visually as Lena, and her mouth opens wide to let her emotions out.

FIGURE 10.3: Melanie's vacant stare with open mouth. Sorrentino (dir.), *Youth*, 2015.

Whereas Fred succeeds as a husband, father and conductor at the end of *Youth*, Mick Boyle (played by Harvey Keitel) fails both professionally and personally. The character of film director Mick, good friend to Fred and father-in-law to Lena, is also professionally blocked, and functions as a negative double or alter ego for the character of Fred. Mick and Fred are both famous artists, have been good friends since they were young, have both had great professional success, and once even shared an attraction to the same woman, Gilda Black, representing just one of several unattainable ideals that appear in the film.[3] Although Mick is also staying at the spa, he has undermined the idea of the spa as a place of rest and reinvigoration, having brought his professional realm with him: he and his six acolytes are working on the script for his next film. Unlike Fred, Mick will remain a failed father both to his son, who disregards Mick's advice and has left Lena, and also as a failed father figure to his six disciple-workers. A surprise visit by Brenda Morel (played by Jane Fonda), Mick's recurring lead female star, serves as another real intrusion into the Imaginary spa setting, in both physical presence and content of her dialogue. Although ageing diva Brenda wears expensive clothing and lots of makeup, her facial wrinkles, wig and bright yellow outfit contrast visually with the simply attired younger women who populate the spa, and her presence there is brief. The visit ends with her revealing another real intrusion into Mick's delusion: that his past few movies have been quite bad. Once his producers hear of Brenda's withdrawal from the film, all production of the script is halted and the project dies. Despondent, Mick commits suicide.

Although their endings are quite diverse, the means by which the two lead male characters are inspired to catharsis – one through death and the other through professional continuance – are women acting as their superegos, explaining to them how they have failed. Whereas Fred is confronted by a family member (his daughter) about his personal failings, and he is thus able to eventually work through his personal problems via his professional life, Mick is confronted by Brenda, a colleague, about his professional failings and cannot fathom a life, personal or otherwise, without work. His life *is* his art. Although the spectator hears snippets of Fred's 'Simple Songs' throughout the film and sees a production of them at the film's conclusion, we know virtually nothing about Mick's art except for the working title of his current film project, *Life's Last Day*, which is a titular harbinger of his fate.

In a sense, Mick and Fred function as complementary, polar examples of Bloom's theory on artistic anxiety. Bloom argues that every poet is necessarily influenced by previous, or precursor, poets (1997). Whereas strong poets are eventually able to create original work that will stand the test of time by working through the six ratios that Bloom suggests,[4] weak poets are unable to get over the anxiety that all poets feel when confronted with the importance of precursor poets. Bloom's theory is rife with Freudian constructs regarding the id and superego and the return of the repressed, and is often applied to artistic activity in general, not just poetry. Interpreting the precursor artist as a professional mentor, or father figure, fits well into Bloom's Freudian analysis of struggling to overcome one's forebears. Mick and Fred are seen by their younger peers as precursor artist-fathers with regard to Bloom's analysis, but as they both age, the latter retains his status as a strong artist figure while Mick regresses through Bloom's ratios as he attempts to recreate his previous success as a director, acting as his own precursor artist, but ending his professional life as a weak artist-father. In attempting to surpass his younger artistic self through new methods, aided by his acolytes, he fails and kills his real self instead.

The character of actor Jimmy Tree (played by Paul Dano), who is staying at the spa prior to a new professional project, plays various symbolic roles in the film. As a promising young actor who is most well-known for his role as a robot in the film *Dr. Q*, he looks up to Mick (rather, an earlier version of Mick) as an example of Bloom's strong poet, a predecessor of the film world from whom he can glean artistic inspiration. Fred sees him as a young artist, and possibly as a metaphorical son who needs guidance, never mind that he cannot guide his biological daughter. Jimmy is depicted as an attempted infiltrator of the Fred–Mick dyad: he is much younger than they are, but he sees himself as a wise soul, disdainful of his own work in a commercially successful film. In fact, when Miss Universe approaches him to tell him how much she enjoyed *Dr. Q*, he attempts to show off in front of Fred and Mick by expressing condescension for her tastes, but she proves to be quick witted, and Jimmy looks like a biased cad in thinking that beauty queens cannot be intelligent and beautiful. He still has much to learn from his poet fathers, who look on in amusement at his social faux pas. Whereas Mick and Fred were confronted by women in private, Miss Universe approaches Jimmy in public, which leads to his dressing down in front of his poet-fathers and highlights his need for professional direction.

Unlike the age-specific friendship of Mick and Fred, the women who confront and inspire them span many age groups. In fact, the person who inspires a new professional path in Jimmy is a young teenage girl, Frances. When Frances approaches him to talk about his role in a film, he is astonished to learn that it is not the robot film to which she refers, but to a little-seen film in which Jimmy plays a 'father who never knew his son' (Sorrentino, 2015), and the two recreate the dialogue from a scene regarding the aforementioned father and son. The unexpected maturity in a girl so young lends her an otherworldly presence, but this intrusion into his Symbolic realm also inspires Jimmy to immerse himself in his next role as an aged Adolph Hitler, the quintessential damaged father figure. As he has taken a weak poet (Mick) as one of his damaged father figures, Jimmy makes a poor choice and is in danger of becoming a lesser artist as a result. Jimmy is aware that he seeks direction when he cites Novalis, saying, 'I'm always going home, always going to my father's house' (Sorrentino, 2015), but the fact that he needs to seek a 'father' repeatedly highlights his poor choices. He, like Mick, also attempts to surpass his artistic previous self, ascribed to his role in *Dr. Q*, but fails as his next protagonist of choice is utterly corrupt.

Just after the narrative concludes, an asynchronous brief clip of Mick – who cannot logically take part in the film's denouement – appears on-screen. He looks directly into the camera in close-up, and he frames a shot around one eye with his fingers. This gesture highlights his profession as a film director, and visually recalls the same gesture that the character of Giotto's pupil demonstrates in Pier Paolo Pasolini's *Decameron* (1971). In homage to artists of many kinds, Pasolini cast himself in this role, which indicates straightforward if not simple comparisons between painters and film directors.

FIGURE 10.4: Mick creates a frame. Sorrentino (dir.), *Youth*, 2015.

FIGURE 10.5: Pasolini as Giotto's pupil creates a frame. Pasolini (dir.), *The Decameron*, 1971.

More multi-layered is the figure of Pasolini: he is director, actor and painter, all of which are emphasized in acts of framing in his film. When Giotto's pupil arrives at his worksite, he is filmed from behind. As he contemplates the blank wall where he will create his fresco, a scaffolding structure is wheeled around him, as the film's spectator sees not only the painter's blank surface cut into rectangles for his future work depicting various biblical scenes, but also the actor/director Pasolini framed and enclosed within the scaffolding. Mick is simply framed by the close-up shot he is in, but the shot's emphasis is placed on Mick's framed eye looking directly into the camera, as a direct interpellation of the spectator. Giotto's pupil also looks directly into the camera in close-up, but then he is depicted venturing into the town's marketplace, where he is seen framing certain townsfolk who will appear in future vignettes in the filmic version of the *Decameron*. The spectator of the film sees what he sees: the people he is viewing in long shot, and then his chosen subjects in medium shot. The contrast of the two scenes highlights Pasolini's fame as a realist director who used non-professional actors and natural lighting as opposed to Sorrentino's reliance on cinematic excess, and acknowledgement of the spectator. Nevertheless, it is impossible not to see the director figure of Mick as the director Pasolini, both of whom recall the work that Sorrentino performs as *mise en abyme*.

This nod to the art of filmmaking and beloved filmmakers in *Youth* is directly followed by a black screen upon which appears 'for Francesco Rosi', another one of Italy's most well-known directors of the latter half of the twentieth century. So, at the conclusion of the film, the filmmaker Sorrentino reminds us that he has cast an actor to play a filmmaker who takes his own life but who also acknowledges the camera as the fourth wall, and that his film recalls his artistic fore-bear Pasolini, and is dedicated to one of his recently deceased artistic forebears (Rosi died in January 2015) whose filmmaking style has little resemblance to his own.[5] This is but one instance where the extradiegetic and the diegetic comingle, allowing for a reading in which Sorrentino shows us how he pays homage to and then experiences Bloom's apophrades as he surpasses his artistic influences, the great directors (or, father figures) who have come before him. He also does this through the filmic roles he creates: Fred is a clear reference to Federico Fellini, nominally and visually.

Fred, wearing his dark suit and thick-rimmed glasses, is visually reminiscent of *8½*'s protagonist and filmmaker Guido Anselmi, who was a thinly veiled incarnation of Fellini himself. Sorrentino also pays homage to Fellini through the character of famed director Mick with their shared profession. After Brenda confronts Mick, he imagines many of the women characters he had created over the years on a hilltop near the spa. The stereotypes represented – floozy, housewife, ditzy girl, ballet dancer, nun – are reminiscent of many of the women depicted in the harem scene from Fellini's *8½*. Thus, Mick is also associated with Guido and functioning as Fred's alter-ego, and therefore tied once again to Sorrentino himself. In having the director Mick commit suicide within the film, Sorrentino suggests that perhaps Guido had also committed suicide under the table near the conclusion of *8½*, when the spectator sees him handling a pistol and hears a loud bang. However, in giving Fred, his principal protagonist, a life-long career and catharsis through his eventual post-retirement performance, he goes beyond Guido's surreal and inconclusive circus caused by artistic blockage (and through extension, Mick's similar failures) and gives his film a clear narrative ending and his protagonist Fred a defining purpose in both life and art. In doing so, Sorrentino also answers the critics who call him a simple twentieth century reiteration of Fellini, and carries out Bloom's clinamen ratio: if we accept Sorrentino's interpretation of the auto-biographical *8½*, Fellini's Guido failed professionally, but Sorrentino's Fred – as the flip side of both Guido and Mick – succeeds.

This Must Be the Place

At first glance, Fred is not dissimilar to the protagonist of *This Must Be the Place*, Cheyenne (played by Sean Penn), another famous musician who has withdrawn from professional life for traumatic reasons. Cheyenne is an American expatriate living in Dublin who travels to New York to see his estranged and dying father – a Holocaust survivor – and then hunt down the Nazi who tormented his father at Auschwitz. Visually, Cheyenne adopts the androgynous look of Robert Smith, the singer and guitarist for the alt/goth-rock group the Cure; he has dyed black, teased hair, messy red lipstick and pancake makeup. He has not performed in decades and lives as a recluse because one of his fans committed suicide, and he (and the fan's parents) holds himself responsible. Whereas Cheyenne has not worked in many years, his wife Jane (played by Frances McDormand) works as a firefighter. There is no clear antecedent in Fellini's body of work to which Sorrentino's first English-language film refers, but there are extradiegetic elements that make their way into the diegesis, complicating the relationship between the filmmaker and his creations, his protagonists. Fathers and father figures abound within the film's storyline.

Lacan elaborates on the three types of fathers connected to his three orders; in the Symbolic, the father is identified with the name-of-the-father: the figure of the law that denies pleasure or enjoyment and keeps it all for himself. The Symbolic father is not an actual person, but a position that regulates desire; it is something that dictates what you cannot have; it is somewhat connected to Freud's idea of the superego. The Real father at times becomes the figure who legislates, who lays down the law, but who usually is inadequate or even fraudulent in this regard. The Imaginary father is a fantastic composite of all the father figures that the subject creates: he can be an ideal or a bad father. The ideal father acts like a symbolic father, preaching life through repression and denial of enjoyment, while the anal father is associated with enjoyment, and initially can appear to be the subject's double (Žižek 1992a: 143). Žižek's expansion and elaboration on Lacan here identifies the anal father as the reverse of the ideal father. Theorist Todd McGowan has expanded the idea of the anal father even further; he claims that instead of appearing as a mysterious authority figure who is removed from our lives in the Symbolic, the anal father is very much present, and as such, is a rival for enjoyment while he commands our enjoyment (2004: 46). McGowan would consider Cheyenne's father a conventional, symbolic father, as he '[...] enforces prohibition and acts as a barrier to enjoyment' (2004: 41). When Cheyenne finally does arrive back home in New York, he is too late for a reunion and any possible attempt at reconciliation, as his father has already died, remaining only a removed, symbolic figure for Cheyenne, not unlike Melanie for Fred in *Youth*, an empty shell.

The ex-Nazi Aloise Lang whom Cheyenne hunts down is a twisted figure of authority gone horribly awry, and a punisher to Cheyenne's father. Until the point in the film when he appears on-screen, he has represented an absent, symbolic father for Cheyenne, but when he finally does appear on-screen we see that he is physically decrepit and blind, which is visually contrary to propagandistic images of the all-powerful Nazi regime, but also figuratively mirrors the corrupt regime that he symbolizes and from which he comes. Cheyenne points a gun at him but does not shoot; Lang is physically harmless. Instead, he forces Lang to strip naked and walk outside in the cold winter of Utah, humiliating him, and symbolically castrating this symbolic authority figure on the level of structure by taking away all of his power and capacity of enjoyment (McGowan 2004: 41).

McGowan claims that the postmodern anal father – as opposed to the absent symbolic father – appeals to us because he wants us to enjoy, he seems more approachable, he doesn't necessarily appear to be an authority figure and shows off his incompetence (2004: 49–51). Whereas identifying Cheyenne's father as the absent symbolic father and Aloise Lang as the symbolic castrated father, pinpointing a character in *This Must Be the Place* that represents the anal father proves more difficult. The character of David Byrne displays some traits of the anal father listed above, but he is not incompetent at all. The character of Jane, however, does display more traits of McGowan's anal father.

Jane, like Cheyenne, is an American living in Dublin but, unlike Cheyenne, is content and contributing to society, even though she is not on-screen for most of the film. Gender non-conforming Jane assumes several conventionally masculine characteristics: she works and thus brings a steady income to their household, she expects Cheyenne to do some of the cooking (she comes home after work to ask, '[w]hat's for dinner, honey?') and she is better at sports than Cheyenne is – and regularly lets him win. The fact that she is competitive and duplicitous would give her traits of McGowan's anal father, but the scene that depicts her as transformative in this structure is that in which Cheyenne performs cunnilingus on her. In this scene, she evokes the origins of Lacanian (and Freudian, and Žižekian) theory and sexual pleasure, but instead of compelling the subject – Cheyenne – to enjoyment, she is saying, 'make ME enjoy!'. Thus, she represents the anal father as she takes all of the pleasure and leaves none for Cheyenne, but she also overturns established psychoanalytic theory in reclaiming woman's sexual pleasure. Jane's enjoyment is personal and also extended towards her husband Cheyenne; through this particular kind of sexual pleasure she suggests Cheyenne's lack of pleasure (sexual and otherwise), which propels the plot forward and also points out other lacunae that perform the same function in the film's narrative.

The film's title is also the title of a 1983 Talking Heads song from the album *Speaking in Tongues*, of which there are no less than six versions over the course of the film, diegetically and extradiegetically, none of which are the original recording. At one point in the film, the lead singer of the Talking Heads, David Byrne, appears within the narrative to sing the song on stage,[6] after which Cheyenne and he have a conversation about artistry and anxiety. Later on, a young boy asks Cheyenne to sing 'This Must Be the Place' (2005), by Arcade Fire, an indie rock group whose first full-length album was released in 2004.[7] These scenes scattered throughout the film allow for a Lacanian reading of the film's title, which points out how the original song is absent, it is lacking; here it functions as Lacan's *objet petit a*—the unattainable object of desire, and it becomes a symbol many times over: a title, David Byrne's new version played without his original band members, various remakes heard extradiegetically and a diegetic informal sing along. The original song 'This Must Be the Place' belongs initially to the real world, and for Sorrentino and his protagonist Cheyenne as a Symbolic object rein symbolic father–Cheyenne's...castrates–and terpreted over and over again in this, the Imaginary realm of film. The song functions as but one type of underlying structure that regulates the film, and as Žižek would say about Hitchcock's McGuffin - his example of *objet petit a*–drives the plot forward although or perhaps precisely *because* it is missing, a lack.

In contrast, there is a surplus of the figure of David Byrne in *This Must Be the Place*. His role in the film is similar to Paloma Faith and Sumi Jo in *Youth*. Obscuring representations of the Symbolic and Imaginary is the intrusion of the real world into the film, when the character of the musician-artist David Byrne is played by the actual musician-artist David Byrne. This rupture allows for further bleeding into Sorrentino's films by extradiegetic elements, and an extension of the metaphoric Bloomian father figure to the artist, both protagonist Cheyenne and director Sorrentino.[8] Diegetic David Byrne used to be Cheyenne's contemporary; they wax nostalgic, and after performing the title song he shows Cheyenne one of the other projects he is currently working on: an organ reconfigured with long ropes that emits strange sounds in a vast studio. David Byrne the character has evolved as an artist, but he still looks back upon his previous success. He is like Cheyenne, and is initially presented as his similar, his alter-ego, but whereas Cheyenne is stuck 30 years in the past due to unresolved trauma, David Byrne is continually doing new things. They are not unlike Mick and Fred of *Youth*: contemporaries, good friends, both successful singers in the past, although one of them is blocked professionally.

In sum, the song 'This Must Be the Place' represents a lack, much like 'Simple Songs' do in *Youth*. Because the song is a lack, it also becomes a desired symbol. Ultimately, the songs are what set desire and plot in motion; they are the underlying structures to the films. The same can be said about fathers and father figures: there are two sets of characters in *This Must Be the Place* that represent on one hand the traditional symbolic father–Cheyenne's father who dies and Lang the Nazi who Cheyenne symbolically castrates–and on the other hand the contemporary anal father, Jane, who goes one step further than the patriarchal structures as delineated by Lacan, Žižek, then McGowan by reclaiming her (woman's) power of enjoyment. She represents a transformative female version of the anal father who will share enjoyment, unlike Žižek and McGowan's structures. Jane was present at the beginning of the film, and it is to her that Cheyenne returns at the end of the film. As it turns out, he always had what he needed from the very beginning, but he needed to leave to figure it out. As the Talking Heads' lyrics point out at the beginning of their song 'This Must Be the Place' (1983), 'home is where I want to be, but I guess I'm already there'.

The Young Pope

Unlike *Youth and This Must Be the Place*, which are contained, completed narrative products that are ideally consumed in two-hour time slots in a public theatre, *The Young Pope* is (in the United States) in the medium of a limited series premium cable television show, which necessarily presents and is consumed in a different way than film, with its viewers watching one hour a week throughout the show's initial run.[9] Although the two films discussed here have a normal running time for narrative cinema, the first season of *The Young Pope* comprises ten hour-long episodes, each of which addresses a particular problem, but taken as a whole, also include longer story arcs.[10] *Youth* and *This Must Be the Place* are 'journey' films in which the protagonists are depicted mainly outside of the home, but *The Young Pope* is set where the recently elected (and fictional) Pope Pius XIII will live for the rest of his life. Although the two films boast unusual settings and famous artists as protagonists, in the television programme Sorrentino presents a series of utterly singular people, places and occasions.

In contrast to the unfamiliar yet multiple, recognizable and public places that Cheyenne visits in *This Must Be the Place*, and to the exclusive, nameless Swiss spa where *Youth* unfolds, *The Young Pope* is set in a unique physical space: Vatican City. Separated from the real world by guards, gates and alarms, the Vatican is the only 'real' place depicted in Sorrentino's English *oeuvre*, even though it is the least accessible by the common person.[11] Additionally, in contrast to the spa as a place of relaxation, a refuge from one's daily work routine, Vatican City is a major tourist attraction and the worksite and home of the first American Pope, Lenny Belardo (played by Jude Law). The Pope is one of the most recognizable people in the world, but at the same time, this particular Pope is unrecognizable by the general public because very few know what he looks like. He gives sermons with his back to the audience and covers his face with a veil when he travels to Africa, in accordance with Lenny's desire to remain unknown to his public. For devout Catholics and the media depicted in the television programme, his face becomes the *objet petit a*, what is missing and desired. In a sense, he is defined as an empty shell, a perfect nesting place for the symbolic father. In fact, when he is elected, he becomes the ultimate father figure *and* symbolic father, representing the rules and beliefs of the Catholic Church. All the same, he is a contradictory figure with two selves. He is a void representing an institution as Pope Pius XIII, and Lenny, a person with normal human problems and emotions. He smokes, in defiance of a previous Pope's rules, but does not let anyone else smoke in his presence. Although he is the first American Pope and also quite young, he is extremely conservative, calling for abortion, divorce and homosexuality to have much more severe consequences than his predecessors. It is as though he overcompensates as

Pope for Lenny's shortcomings. Even though he is the ultimate father figure, as the earthly head of the Catholic Church, he himself is not a biological father, and his own biological family rejected him.

Lenny is traumatized by the fact that his parents left him at an orphanage when he was a young boy, and their lack in his life is what propels the entire season's plot forward. He is obsessed with them, with finding them and with objects that are connected to them. We see representations of Lenny in flashbacks with his parents and their bucolic, hippy life; we also see a fraudulent couple who pretend to be his parents in the present, and Lenny's vision of them at his first true public appearance in Venice. Growing up in an orphanage and having sworn himself to a life of celibacy, Lenny acquires and discards a series of substitute family figures who can never be what he is really looking for, the unattainable object of desire.

Lenny grew up under the tutelage of Sister Mary (played by Diane Keaton) who is a surrogate mother whom he embraces and also rejects. Cardinal Michael Spencer (played by James Cromwell) is the closest signifier Lenny has to a father figure, but Spencer is outraged that Lenny was chosen as Pope instead of him, and he rejects his own protégé, refusing to work under him or with him in an advisory role, and dies towards the end of the series, leaving yet another lack in Lenny's life. Like Mick for Fred in *Youth* and David Byrne for Cheyenne in *This Must Be the Place*, Lenny has an alter-ego, the Cardinal Andrew Dussolier (played by Scott Shepherd), with whom Lenny grew up in the orphanage. Sorrentino himself claims that they are opposites: Andrew wants freedom while Lenny represents rules (Sorrentino, 2016). Lenny is the superego to Andrew's id, as the latter over-indulges in liquor and sexual relations with both men and women.

Lenny's relationships with women are intriguing because he is not a father, nor a husband or a lover, and as an orphan, one could argue that he is no longer a son, highlighted by the fact that Lenny hires Sister Mary as his professional advisor, rather than keeping their relationship personal. Lenny is unique among Sorrentino's protagonists in that he does not have sexual relations, even though many of his colleagues–men of God–have lovers. Lenny's sole and very abbrevi-ated romantic relationship followed the rules of medieval courtly love more than late-twentieth-century dating standards: Lenny and his object of desire never made physical contact, but he wrote love letters to her for years and never sent them. Eventually they are published in *The New Yorker*, that twenty-first-century version of literary salons. Lenny delivers the *petit objet a* of his romantic interest–the love letters–not just to her, but to the whole world via a real-world intrusion (*The New Yorker*) into the Imaginary yet very real space of the Vatican. This foreshadows his unveiling of the *petit objet a*–his face–to the public at the conclusion of the series but also underscores the ambiguity of the appearance of Lenny's *petit objet a*–his parents–at the conclusion of the film.

Although the protagonist of *The Young Pope* is not an artist per se, the personal life of the fictional Pope Lenny Belardo reflects Sorrentino's more so than that of the artist protagonists in *Youth* and *This Must Be the Place*, as Sorrentino lost both parents in a car accident when he was quite young. Lenny's search for his missing parents mirrors the familial journeys that both Fred and Cheyenne undertake, but echoes more loudly the trauma that the young Sorrentino must have suffered. Even though it is problematic to compare *mise en scène* to those who produce it, the figure of the auteur (or filmic author) is still gaining momentum.[12] Granted, a simple reduction of director and protagonist as equal accomplishes nothing; it is precisely *because* of the differences between life and art that Sorrentino is able to address his troubling past in his art.

Fred is a damaged, then repaired father figure; damaged son Cheyenne is able to overcome the negative influence of the symbolic father figures through Jane's reclaiming enjoyment in his place and acting as a corrective to his failed father figures; Lenny is initially presented as the ultimate symbolic father, the Pope, but throughout the series his familial shortcomings reveal Lenny's traumatized private side. Any deficiencies, failures or crises depicted by the fathers, sons and father figures on-screen is countered by the success of Sorrentino himself off-screen, as extradiegetic elements make their way into the diegesis, complicating the relationship between the filmmaker and his creations (his protagonists, his progeny), but also his cinematic predecessors with whom he is frequently compared and judged, mainly Fellini, Pasolini and Rosi. Sorrentino also demonstrates that he has run the gamut of Bloom's ratios in the media of film and television and accomplished just as much as his predecessor poet-directors and father figures. Sorrentino leaves Bloom's anxiety of influence to his secondary 'weak' poet-protagonists and damaged father figures (Mick Boyle, Michael Spencer), while he himself becomes a 'strong' poet-director, perhaps even overshadowing his own poetic forerunners. As Bloom says: 'This must be the place' (1997: 157).

NOTES

1. *La dolce vita* was originally released in 1960.
2. *8 ½* was orginally released in 1963.
3. Another would be the repeated appearance—in dreams and in wakeful states—of Miss Universe as an ideal feminine beauty.
4. Bloom's ratios are *clinamen* ('poetic misreading'—in which the artist moves away from a precursor, insinuating that the latter's artistic output was not completely precise; the 'potentially strong poet' corrects that), *tessera* ('completion and antitheses'—in which the artist insinuates that the precursor did not complete his idea, as he [mis]utilizes the precursor's terms in a different sense than the precursor did), *kenosis* ('repetition and

discontinuity'—in which the artist attempts to separate himself from the precursor's work), *daemonization* ('the counter-sublime'—in which the artist rejects the precursor's originality, but swears by his own), *askesis* ('purgation and solipsism'—in which the artist devalues both his and his precursor's works by ridding them of all predecessors and insisting upon their work standing alone, without influences) and *apophrades* ('the return of the dead'—in which the artist displays his work which has gone beyond that of his precursor, read in the latter's terms).

5. Sorrentino thanks Rosi at the end of *Il divo*, as well, and related to an interviewer that Rosi said to him, 'You are not my son, you are not my nephew, but you are a good director' (Crowdus 2009: 37).

6. This gestures to the live version of the Talking Heads from Jonathan Demme's 1984 concert film *Stop Making Sense*, starring the Talking Heads.

7. Arcade Fire's version of the song was performed regularly during their live performances in 2005.

8. Sorrentino thanked the Talking Heads (among others) when accepting his Academy Award for *The Great Beauty*.

9. I should mention that *The Young Pope* was conceived, funded and marketed much differently than the two films I discuss, as it was developed in tandem with Home Box Office. The discussion between television and film alone in Sorrentino's *oeuvre* requires more space and ink than I have here.

10. All the same, Sorrentino himself has said that he believes the series is more similar to a '[...] 10-hour film' (Ma 2017).

11. The surreal setting of Vatican City in *The Young Pope* is in contrast to the unmistakably Roman *mise en scène of The Great Beauty*, Sorrentino's most well-known film; it was filmed in Italian, not English.

12. At least, according to Lucy Fischer's research (2013: 1–2).

REFERENCES

Bloom, H. (1997), *The Anxiety of Influence: A Theory of Poetry*, 2nd ed. , New York: Oxford University Press.

Crowdus, G. (2009), 'Exposing the dark history of Italian political history: An interview with Paolo Sorrentino', *Cineaste*, 34:3, pp. 32–37.

Crowdus, G. (2014), 'In search of The Great Beauty: An interview with Paolo Sorrentino', *Cineaste*, 39:2, pp. 8–13.

Demme, J. (1984), *Stop Making Sense*, USA: Palm Pictures.

Donadio, R. (2013), '*La dolce vita* gone sour (and this time in color): Paolo Sorrentino's *Great Beauty* explores Italy's decline', *New York Times*, 8 September, p. C1.

Fellini, F. (2001), *8½*, Italy: The Criterion Collection.

Fellini, F. (2014), *La dolce vita*, Italy: The Criterion Collection.

Fischer, L. (2013), *Body Double: The Author Incarnate in the Cinema*, New Brunswick: Rutgers University Press.

Lacan, J. (1988), *The Seminar of Jacques Lacan: Book 2: The Ego in Freud's Theory and in the Technique of Psychoanalysis 1954–1955*, Cambridge: Cambridge University Press.

Ma, W. (2017), 'Jude Law sizzles in *The Young Pope*', News. com. au, 18 April, http://news. com. au/entertainment/tv/tv-shows/jude-law-sizzles-in-the-young-pope/news-story/604da24949 e528091c9ea709d6992e38. Accessed 5 February 2018.

McGowan, T. (2004), *The End of Dissatisfaction? Jacques Lacan and the Emerging Society of Enjoyment*, Albany: State University of New York Press.

O'Neill, D. (2016), 'Ageing with style', *The Lancet*, 387:10019, 13 February, p. 639.

Pasolini, P. P. (1971), *The Decameron*, Italy, France and West Germany: Produzioni Europee Associate.

Romney, J. (2012), 'On the road again', *Sight & Sound*, 22:4, pp. 16–20.

Sicinski, M. (2013), 'Paolo Sorrentino: A medium talent', *Cinema Scope*, 58, pp. 17–21.

Sorrentino, P. (2011), *This Must Be the Place*, Italy, France and Ireland: Indigo Film.

Sorrentino, P. (2013), *La grande bellezza*, Italy: Indigo Film.

Sorrentino, P. (2015), *Youth*, Italy, Switzerland, UK and France: Indigo Film.

Sorrentino, P. (2016), 'Inside the episodes', *The Young Pope*, DVD extras, Italy, Spain and France: Home Box Office (HBO).

Stille, A. (2014), 'Dancing to nowhere', *New York Review of Books*, 9 January, http://nybooks. com/daily/2014/01/09/great-beauty-dance-nowhere/. Accessed 3 July 2017.

Talking Heads (1983), 'This Must Be the Place (Naïve Melody)', *Speaking in Tongues*, LP, New York: Rhino and Warner Bros.

The Young Pope (2016), (Italy, Spain and France: Home Box Office [HBO]).

Žižek, S. (1992a), *Enjoy Your Symptom! Jacques Lacan in Hollywood and Out*, New York and London: Routledge.

Žižek, S. (1992b) 'Introduction: Alfred Hitchcock, or, the form and its historical mediation', in S Žižek (ed), *Everything You Always Wanted to Know about Lacan (But Were Afraid to Ask Hitchcock)*, London and New York: Verso, pp. 1–12.

Žižek, S. (1994), *The Metastases of Enjoyment: Six Essays on Woman and Causality*, New York and London: Verso.

Žižek, S. (1999), *The Ticklish Subject: The Absent Centre of Political Ontology*, London and New York: Verso.

11

'È solo l'alito di un vecchio': Obscenity, Exchange Regimes, and the Catastrophe of Aging in *Loro*[1]

Nicoletta Marini-Maio

Dickinson College

Cinema has fashioned many figures from the protean form of Silvio Berlusconi: from Federico Fellini's prophetic *Ginger e Fred* (*Ginger and Fred*) (1986) to Franco Maresco's surreal *Belluscone, una storia siciliana* (*Belluscone, A Sicilian Story*) (2014), 34 films have narrated the personal and political story of the Mediaset founder. In this rich corpus, Berlusconi is at times evoked as the omnipresent symbol of power, often parodied, but for the most part is investigated, damned, deformed, deconstructed, captured, killed (and even frozen) and finally made spectral.[2]

The diptych *Loro 1* and *Loro 2* (2018a, 2018b) allow Paolo Sorrentino to add his own authorial flourish to these manifestations, which are symptomatic of the difficulties in representing a subject as puzzling and polysemous as Berlusconi.

With *Il divo* (2008) and *The Young Pope* (2016), *Loro* duet completes the Neapolitan director's 'trilogy of power', described as 'temporal power, spiritual power, and mediatic power' (Minuz 2018), and is released in a time when Berlusconi's party *Forza Italia* (Go Italy), founded in 1994, is condemned almost to insignificance and its absolute leader is deteriorating both physically and psychologically. As if to parody the enactment of this deterioration, the film centres on the decline of Berlusconi's personal and public life in the 2006–10 period. During this time, the former prime minister, defeated by the Centre Left in the 2006 elections, succeeded clamorously in reacquiring the majority in parliament and returned to govern, corrupting six senators from the opposition party along the way. Subsequently, however, his political position was progressively weakened by the accusations of several young women to whom he promised financial and political benefits in exchange for sexual favours, and by growing international hostility, until ultimately, he was forced to submit a humiliating resignation in 2011.[3] Berlusconi is the ideal subject for Sorrentino. In his recent monograph on Sorrentino's cinema, Russ Kilbourn argues that 'Loro represents the apogee, even the apotheosis, of the Sorrentinian subject in the figure of Silvio Berlusconi' (Kilbourn 2020: 152). Sorrentino's cinema of 'crepuscular aestheticization' (De Gaetano 2018) indulges in decadent settings and failure figures, in particular the undoing of male bodies as they negotiate female erotic capital, topics Sorrentino explored, for example, in The Great Beauty (2013) and Youth (2015). In Loro, these bodies, settings and figures embody the catastrophe of aging and impotence in the symbolic interactions of the regime of the exchange of sex and power, and power for sex. Although it oscillates continually between the political subject Silvio Berlusconi (off-screen for most part of Loro 1) and the materialistic, decadent anthropology of 'Berlusconism' (the 'them' of the title), the leader's body remains symbolically at the film's centre. Around his name, his figure and his simulacra, the bodies of young women refract and multiply, evoking the hedonism and commodification of Italian society of neoliberalism in which, as Roberto De Gaetano has noted, 'power is the practice of the limitless circulation of bodies and desires and the equivalencies of the political operative and the escort' (De Gaetano 2018).

Loro's orgiastic spectacularity brings to the fore private and prohibited sexual behaviours, that is, the 'obscenity' of Berlusconism, giving the film a political valence that has not as yet garnered much critical attention. The film, in fact, offers political mimesis of the collective, of the They or Them, a strategy for 'postmodern engagement'[4] that focuses on the narrative potential of Berlusconism, from which it reproduces both in form and in content the practices and cultural objects. In other words, Loro brings to the representational centre the self-reflexive narration of the private and 'prohibited', which furnishes the narrative key to explore, concurrently, the human and grotesque aspects of Berlusconi as well as Berlusconism and its masks and anthropology.[5] This representational strategy leaves behind, as Il divo did, the investigative concerns and documentary intentions of the cinema d'inchiesta and of realist representation. When asked at the 2017 Cannes Film festival why he had made a film about Berlusconi, Sorrentino replied, 'Because I am Italian and want to make a film about Italians. Berlusconi is an archetype of Italianness that allows you to narrate Italians' (Anon. 2017). Notwithstanding this kind of open avowal, the film has been roundly criticized for the absence of a political dialectic, for its excessive humanization of Berlusconi and for the aestheticized and seductive portrayal of his court (Dominijanni 2018; Morreale 2018b; Scott 2019; Aspden 2019).

This essay seeks to highlight the political dimension of the figurations of Berlusconism overlooked by spectators, even the most critically prepared, who lament consistently the absence of critical distance and social critique. I argue that such disappointment derives from an unwillingness to accept the film's fluid structure, which constitutes a postmodern political allegory whose slippery dramatic centre shifts continuously. Such fluidity confounds sequentiality of events and takes away the heuristic value from the narrative. The film's thematic are undoubtedly political but are marked by fluctuating deictic references (*lui, loro, lei, noi, gli altri*, or him, them, her, us, the others, all of which are as central to the film as the title itself suggests) that produce unstable points of view and mechanisms of identification. A disquieting disorientation can result from such shifting terrain. A disorientation which is political, too.

To illustrate *Loro*'s thematic and narrative fluidity and its political dimension, I examine several of its principal thematic and structural clusters. These include the cumbersome presence of the 'obscene' leader; the representation of the regime of economic exchange that prevails in neoliberal societies like contemporary Italy; the clash between the young women's explosive and the desire of aging, impotent men and the mystic and religious symbolism that subtends the film. These clusters are examined employing textual elements, in particular, the film's structure and deictic articulation. For clarity and legibility, I organize these elements into discrete sections, deconstructing what Sorrentino's film, which resists attempts at categorization and sequential coherence, presents as a synthetic entirety.

Paratext and Structure

Released in Italian theatres in two distinct parts within a period of two weeks, Sorrentino's film reveals its collective positionality from its anonymous, pronominal and plural title. *Loro 1* (104 minutes) was released on 24 April 2018, and *Loro 2* (100 minutes) followed on 10 May 2018. For the international market, a film known simply as *Loro*, an integrated version of 150 minutes, appeared some months later.[6] Homophonically, the *l'oro* (gold) of the title, seems to refer to the exchange of individuals as subjects for commodified bodies. This signifies not only *l'oro* as a symbolic objectification of *loro*, that is, the rich and powerful, but also *l'oro* in exchange for *loro*, that is, the bodies and subjects that, with 'gold', can be bought. The key element of neoliberal society that Berlusconism brought forward in all its force defines the doubled significance of *loro*, which, as Annachiara Mariani observes, collapses the idolatrous incarnation of Berlusconi with the pathological obsession for *l'oro* (Mariani 2019a). Mariani argues that in *Loro*, this pathology gets represented as an actual addiction that, propagating like a virus, takes possession of both mind and body (Mariani 2019a).[7]

To conclude analysis of the paratextual elements, we can also note that the two-act structure with staggered distribution celebrated antecedents like Bertolucci's *Novecento* (*1900*) (1976) and Marco Tullio Giordana's *La meglio gioventù* (*The Best of Youth*) (2003). At the same time, the two-act configuration

181

also recalls the bipartite characteristic of the made for Italian television biograph-
ical miniseries (and we recall that *La meglio gioventù* also began as a miniseries
for television).[8] These references contrast almost parodically, underscoring *Loro's*
difference from both the epic story (*Novecento*) and the historical melodrama
(*La meglio gioventù*) as well as, more generally, the narrative conventions of the
biopic. At the same time, however, these elements seem to underscore the exper-
imental attraction of the serial story, especially if considered in the light of the
productive experience of *The Young Pope* (Sorrentino 2016). Indeed, Sorrentino's recent interest in seriality manifests in various ways in the paratext for *Loro*:
each of the two acts breaks down further into two halves according to thematic,
aesthetic and deictic criteria. I will presently address the indispensable role that
deixis plays in Sorrentino's film, and will say here only that it acts as a semiotic
device that organizes the enunciation by generating progressive semantic shifts:

Loro 1

- *loro*/them (*Loro* 1, from beginning to min. 61.33): carnivalesque introduction
  to the anthropology of Berlusconism, principals Sergio Morra (Riccardo Scar-
  marcio), an entrepreneur from Puglia, and his wife Tamara (Euridice Axen)
  organize a ring of escorts and 'image girls' so as to gain access to Berlusconi,
  increase financial gain and enter into the mechanisms of power;
- *lui*/him and *lei*/her (*Loro 1*, min. 61.33 until the end): Berlusconi (Toni Servillo)
  at Villa Certosa, in full-blown political and personal crisis, during a melancholy confrontation with Veronica Lario (Elena Sofia Ricci). It is at this point
  that the brief story of the mysterious character called *Dio* (God) takes place;

Loro 2

- *lui*/him and *loro*/them (*Loro* 2, from beginning to min. 58): Berlusconi, on
  advice of the financier Ennio Doris, plays the 'salesman of dreams' and corrupts
  six senators to secure the failure of the Centre Left government; escorts and
  'image girls', participate in 'elegant dinners' and put on shows such as the
  erotic *bunga bunga* parties;
- *lui*/him, *lei*/her and *gli altri*/the others: (*Loro* 2, from min. 58 to the end): Berlusconi returns to power; sex scandals unfold; there is an earthquake in Aquila;
  the definitive crisis with Veronica; the disappearance of Berlusconi who leaves
  behind a defeated humanity contemplating the destruction of the earthquake.

These parts are developed not only in chronological order but also in 'modular'
order (Marcus 2010: 250), that is, alternating between sequences of varying length,

some of which could be moved without damaging the narrative integrity of the film.[9] Worth noting here are several elements typical of series, like the combination of several self-contained microstories (for example, the escapade of Sergio Morra, the affair between Santino Recchia and Tamara, the *Dio* character) with the macrostory (and history) of Berlusconi and Berlusconism; *Loro 1*'s lengthy exposition (it takes more than an hour for Berlusconi to actually appear); and finally the cliff-hanger at the end of *Loro 1*, when a suddenly youthful Veronica (Adua Del Vesco), filmed from behind, turns to look directly into the camera and declare her love for Silvio.

The stratification of references alongside the unusual structure makes *Loro* an anomalous biopic that goes beyond the typical interconnections between regimes of truth and spectacular invention.[10] As Millicent Marcus has observed in her analysis of *Il divo*, the defining characteristic of Sorrentino's cinema is the ambiguity (if not contradiction) between these two regimes, something achieved by way of explicit manipulation of mimetic signs typically used to indicate the 'relation to the real' in documentary cinema as well as the 'political' film (Marcus 2010: 250).[11] In *Loro*, this will to manipulate is asserted from the very beginning with the citation of Giorgio Manganelli's *Pinocchio*: 'Tutto documentato. Tutto arbitrario', or, 'Everything is documented. Everything is arbitrary' (Manganelli [1977] 2002). As Annachiara Mariani suggests, the Manganelli quote puts the film in dialogue with the fundamental contradiction of the contemporary world 'dominated by fake news, relativism and subjectivism', in which the links between falsehood and truth are so deep that it has become impossible to assess a politician objectively (Mariani 2019b: 443).

The Obscene Leader

Loro (and *Loro 1* in particular), inundates the viewer with a semiotic surplus of young female bodies on display, sold, bought, prostituted and even inspected for hygiene and security, as Ida Dominijanni has justifiably observed (Dominijanni 2018), or exposed as bodies in a 'butchery', in a 'shameless and lewd chaos at the limit of post-human' (Belpoliti 2018a). For a film made during the time of the #metoo movement, this is a controversial choice. Adopting 'the repugnant character of Berlusconian ethics and aesthetics' can seem like siding with the 'perverse enjoyment' (Dominijanni 2018) of a regime composed of phallocentric figurations incarnated by Berlusconi. Catherine O'Rawe decisively rejects Sorrentino's choice:

> The ultimate effect is of a film that, whether deliberately or not, replicates the film culture that produced it: addicted to the lure of interchangeable young female bodies, and unable to conceive of female points of view or a female address.
>
> (O'Rawe 2018: 152)

Yet it is precisely this self-reflexive strategy that *Loro* puts into motion, one that 'imprints its figurative regime on the grammar of pornography', as Baptiste Roux maintains (Roux 2018: 52), characterizing the film's central aesthetic and epistemic nucleus – that is, the erotization of power relationships typical of neoliberalism that the Berlusconian regime fully unveiled. It is a narrative and aesthetic process akin to Scorsese's approach in *The Wolf of Wall Street* (2013), which, along with Harmony Korine's *Spring Breakers* (2013), is often cited as a stylistic reference for *Loro 1*: both films incorporate 'cultural values and attitudes [...] at both narrative and formal levels' (Salek 2018: 5). This mimetic strategy brings to the fore the 'obscene' condition of Berlusconism which gets translated into an 'injunction to jouissance' so typical of neoliberal society, and the ways it centres on the commodification of the self. The overexposure of bodies and sexual relations reveals its status as a component of power. Typically, private and prohibited sexual behaviours are located *ob-scenely* or, literally, off-screen or offstage. From offstage to centrestage, the obscene becomes the ethical and aesthetic centre of representation. This is a deliberate use of *mise en scène* of the principal element of Berlusconism identified by, among others, Ida Dominijanni, who writes that 'the obscene conquers centrestage, and becomes *the* stage' (Dominijanni 2014: 237). With the rupture of the barrier between public and private, we see

> A radical regime change in terms of enunciability and visibility that reverberates in the complex foundations of the public, political, and mediatic sphere and in the social linkage of individual and collective behaviours.
>
> (Dominijanni 2014: 237)

Starting from a socio-psychoanalytical perspective, Fulvio Carmagnola and Matteo Bonazzi also discuss the question of Berlusconi's obscenity (2011: 15–16). They state that contemporary politics actualizes

> the dismantling of the [on]scene/obscene dialectic, imploding at the crucial point that made it possible. 'Berlusconi' is the full name of this figure of history; he is not the figure of the modern leader anymore that was the point of reference for the masses (the 'unitary trait' of which Freud spoke, the *einziger Zug*) but on the contrary, he is the expression of the singularity of his 'jouissance' that can become ours as well.
>
> (Carmagnola and Bonazzi 2011: 36–37)

The issue of the obscenity of power saturates *Loro* with a symbolic valence that is in open conflict with the tradition of the Italian political film, provoking a significant shift both in the representation of the political narrative and its very content. Gianni Canova observes that in Italian cinema of the post-war period, 'real power is almost always *obscene*: it is exercised – literally – *offstage*, beyond the sphere of the visible' (Canova 2017 41, original emphasis). In the semiosis of power of relational values, discursive formations and cultural objects of Italian society, this obscenity is embodied by the *palazzo* – perhaps the weightiest of political allegories from Guicciardini to Pasolini.[13] The *palazzo*, or the Ministry, is the metaphoric centre of power in which damaging conspiracies are born and where the nation's fate is decided behind closed doors. In this semiosis, the *palazzo* allies with the monumental buildings in which mysterious political manoeuvres unfold. These schemes subtend criminal ends, which often lead to disastrous consequences. To stay within the ambit of Sorrentino's cinema, we could think of the sequence from *Il divo* in which a number of politicians from the House of Representatives are gathered in the *Transatlantico* hallway.[14] Suddenly, a skateboard whizzes down the corridor, passing all of the politicians and lifting off – becoming the bomb that caused the Capaci massacre.[15] This metaphor traces an indubitable link between the mafia and the *palazzo* politicians, who, up until that moment, were plotting an intricate scheme for the selection of the President of the Republic.

The archetypal allegory of the *palazzo* in *Loro* is utterly marginal to the political spaces and acts visualized by the film. The only 'official' political moment in the film is the 2008 ratification of Berlusconi's fourth governing coalition. However, this scene centres on the grotesque performance of the leader as he stands before the President of the Republic petrified by disdain. National and international politics are not mentioned save as elements that serve to characterize Berlusconi's narcissism. There is a clumsy attempt to conspire against Berlusconi on behalf of Minister Santino Recchia (Fabrizio Bentivoglio) and powerful congresswoman Cupa Caiafa (Anna Bonaiuto), both from Berlusconi's party *Forza Italia*. But even this plot is no more than a background element and it was in fact removed from the international release.[16] Berlusconi's encounters with other politicians are limited. One such noteworthy encounter is the conversation with an elderly fictional character that goes by the suggestive name of *Crepuscolo* (Twilight) (Roberto Herlitzka), who seems to personify the arc of Berlusconi's trajectory. The conversation with *Crepuscolo* is similar to Berlusconi's exchanges with his alter ego Ennio Doris (Toni Servillo), as well as with his long-time friend Fedele Confalonieri (Mattia Sbragia), and with retired showman Mike Bongiorno (Ugo Pagliai). These conversations – all involving aged men – focus on issues of public image and behaviour, the foundational elements of Berlusconian power and, more generally, neoliberal ethos: 'selling a dream', as Berlusconi himself affirmed repeatedly.

The rhetoric of 'selling a dream' centres the extended opening sequence of *Loro 2* in a memorable exchange between Doris and Berlusconi (both played by an ineffable Servillo) in which Berlusconi convinces himself to deploy his rhetorical skill as a salesman to corrupt a sufficient number of senators in order to

185

FIGURE 11.1: A frame from the long conversation sequence between Doris and Berlusconi in Villa Certosa. Both characters are staged by Toni Servillo (*Loro 2*).

regain power. This sequence, from a static camera as a long shot, films the two characters in conversation across an elegantly laid table on a wide and luxurious seaside veranda, a clear allusion to the Sardinian Villa Certosa, where part of *Loro 1* unfolds. As noted, the decadent arc of Berlusconism visualized in *Loro 1* takes place, for the most part, outside of the public yet mysterious *palazzo* of politics. Even after Berlusconi's return to power, many of the events take place in private spaces: in the spectacular Villa Certosa, reinvented in an assembly of elements inspired by reality (the freshly mowed lawns, the artificial volcano, the super luxurious architecture) and fictitious details (the futuristic design, the surreal *mise en scène*); in Palazzo Grazioli, Berlusconi's Rome residence while he served as Prime Minister; in private and exclusive nightclubs; at a spa and in salons of the haute bourgeoisie. *Loro* achieves its political valence by staging individual and collective behaviours in these spaces and in their private dimensions (Figure 11.1).

In other words, political allegory in *Loro* changes location and narration, moving from the place of the *palazzo* of politics to the private space of bodies and relations understood as a commodity to be exchanged. As is typical in Sorrentino's cinema, there is a hyper-descriptive allegory centred on appearances, on allusion, and on exaggeration and certainly not on a logical chain of events. In fact, 'Sorrentino does not judge, he exposes, suggests, proposes' (Belpoliti 2018b), and his cinema represents facts, even catastrophic ones, 'from an antiromantic and antinovelistic perspective, that is, without examining its causes, but presenting its manifestations' (Brogi 2013: 6).[17] This is postmodern allegory (or perhaps Mannerist or neo-Baroque, if you will) that produces signifiers that acquire emblematic value on their own from their existence as simulacra.[18]

Shifts in the Deixis: Loro, Lui, Lei, Noi, Gli Altri

The film's thematic and allegorical clusters configure around the deictic ambiguity of the title *Loro*,[19] which produces a disorienting fluctuation of points of view and mechanisms of identification. Who are 'They'? Why employ an anonymous, plural title for a film that should be about 'him', Silvio Berlusconi?

Throughout the film, pronominal references are unstable, even opposed. The first part of *Loro 1* focuses only on *loro*, Them – the group of social climbers made up of Morra, his wife Tamara, Fabrizio Sala (incarnation of the theatrical *impresario* Lele Mora) and the Armada of young women recruited by Berlusconi but with which political opportunists like Recchia and Caiafa are also associated. In brief, in this first part, the deictic pronoun *loro* indicates a collective entity, a kind of sample or specimen of Berlusconian anthropology. The viewers are implicitly invited to detach themselves from *loro* (us versus them) and take an ethical stance.

As already noted, after approximately an hour into *Loro 1*, Berlusconi appears, the obscene leader never identified by name (the name Silvio is uttered twice in the entire film) but alluded to, cited in sottovoce, a mysterious identity recorded on cell phones as *lui*, Him, an almost idolized subject. In this section of the film, *loro* defines, as Morra says himself, the circle of 'those who count' (*Loro 1*). They are politicians, entrepreneurs, producers and directors of film and television linked to Berlusconi's world and who can offer work and well-being to the young women recruited for the boss's pleasure.

A good amount of time in both *Loro 1* and *Loro 2* is spent detailing the melancholic confrontation between Berlusconi and his wife Veronica Lario in discussion about their relationship and the grave responsibilities Berlusconi has as a politician and a man. In these sections of the film, the collective *loro* is no longer the subject and is replaced by *lui*, Him, and *lei*, Her, portrayed within the personalized sphere of their life as a couple. Even the film's aesthetics in these sections changes, adapting to the melancholic tone of the encounters: the editing slows, the effects disappear and the camera allows for relatively long, static shots (at medium distance).

In the second half of *Loro 2*, with the earthquake in Aquila, new subjects materialize in the darkened, nocturnal setting. These are the earthquake survivors who contemplate the ruins of their city in silence. After delivering to an elderly woman from Aquila the grotesque 'dream' she had been promised (a house and a set of new dentures), Berlusconi disappears completely from the film. For the finale, a lengthy, horizontal pan with the superimposed title *Loro* sweeps slowly by a line of firefighters silenced by the destruction the earthquake has left in its wake (Figure 11.2).

Even though they are unmanned by the catastrophe, the firefighters are the new, heroic 'Them' of the title that fully performs its deictic function, that is, designating first the earthquake survivors and then the firefighters in their situational

FIGURE 11.2: The final shot with the line of firefighters in L'Aquila struck by the earthquake. The title *Loro* stays for the entire closing credits, signifying one last semantic shift.

context. The progressive change of referents, from the community of boisterous members of the Berlusconian court to the silent heroes of L'Aquila, produces a sort of symmetry and reversal that has led to some discussion of the film as a kind of palindrome (Anon. 2018).

The fluctuations of the deixis determine a process of disorientation concerning the mechanisms of spectatorial identification that, typical of Sorrentino's cinema, abjures simplicity and linearity.[20] The deixis of the pronoun 'Them' forcefully depends on the situational context in which spectators, present in the 'here and now' of the viewing, are required not only to make choices regarding cinematic narrative logic, but also to become a sort of collective interlocutor. They are invited to situate themselves as a 'we' as opposed to a 'they' that is identified either critically ('we are not like them') or empathetically ('we are like them'). In both cases, there is an ethical 'we' interpellated by the 'vacuum' of meaning in Berlusconism that *Loro* enacts (Belpoliti 2018c).

Above all, the deictic referents of *Loro* are not only constantly in flux, but they are also ubiquitous. They seem to be everywhere, in all the relations and practices of power. They forge a pervasive network of multiple, relational and heterogenous subjects that mirrors the Foucauldian 'microphysics of power' exercised through 'dispositions, manoeuvres, tactics, techniques, functionings' (Foucault 1977: 26–27). In fact, the shifting deixis – alongside the unequal rhythm of cinematography and editing – produces a sense of mobility and 'concatenation', reminding us that, indeed, 'power is everywhere' (Foucault 1978: 92).

The Exchange Regime, Young Women and the Aged Body

The first 60 minutes of *Loro 1*, with Berlusconi physically off-screen, constitute a film within a film. The lengthy preamble presents a true pornography of power that is materialized in a proliferation of overexposed and copulating bodies captured in orgiastic positions and attitudes. They follow the inexorable race to power of Sergio Morra, the incarnation of the mediocre Bari entrepreneur Gianpaolo Tarantini who, following the sex scandals of 2008–09, was tried for promoting prostitution. In the film, Morra rents Villa Morena, a luxurious (and fictitious) home next door to Villa Certosa where he directs the traffic of sex workers and 'image girls' in the hopes of capturing Berlusconi's attention, gaining the politician's favour and possibly winning government contracts and entering into politics. Morra's wife Tamara helps him bring to paroxysm the exchange of money, bodies and sex that dominates *Loro 1* and reaches its apex in the swimming pool scene in which drugs and sex reign supreme (Figure 11.3).

This adrenalin-driven mission is assisted by rapid editing, a camera that is nearly frenzied in its mobility and by an allegorical (most literal and Antonioni-like) explosion of drug pills (Figure 11.4).

The rhythm of the scene alternates between slo-mo and regular speed, rapid zooms, and superimposed images, voice-overs and freeze frames. This, without a doubt, recalls Scorsese's style from both *The Wolf of Wall Street*, which has already been mentioned, but also *Goodfellas* (1990).[21] In addition, the style also imitates television commercials, accentuating the interdependence of style and content.

The orgiastic bedlam of the first half of *Loro 1* is initially unleashed by the vision of Silvio's smirk tattooed on the buttocks of the escort, ironically named Candida (Carolina Binda). The genesis of their relationship – which comes from a potential government contract – is a relatively important plot point that I return to below. This sequence, distinguished by Berlusconi's inviting smirk and Morra's subsequent illumination, is articulated in the three-step unfolding of Morra's gaze. Morra is first filmed in profile in a medium shot. He looks into the camera, inviting viewers (who are necessarily off-screen), with a wink and a nod, to share in his sexual pleasure. As Morra enters Candida from behind, his gaze drops to her

FIGURE 11.3: A still image from the pool party at Villa Morena in *Loro 1*.

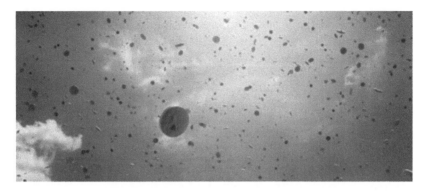

FIGURE 11.4: The explosion of ecstasy pills at the pool party in *Loro 1*.

tattooed buttocks to find Berlusconi's smirking face looking back at him. Morra's insistent gaze moves from the tattoo to contemplate something off-screen that only he can see: his personal dream of power and riches (Figure 11.5).

The obscene body of the boss, physically off-screen or offstage but at the same time phantomatically present in the shape and form of the tattoo, conjures *Lui*, Him, Silvio Berlusconi, in the midst of *Loro*, Them. The monstrous birth of this idea follows the coupling of Morra, pimp and a social climber, and Candida, whose name means 'pure', the irony of which she herself subsequently points out. Silvio's 'appearance' produces an immediate effect in Morra, galvanizing and inspiring him to devise the scheme of the exchange of sex, power and money with the 'obscene' politician. It is significant that Morra's intercourse with Candida is part of the title sequence, in which the title *Loro* compellingly indicates the 'them' of Berlusconi's court.

The obscenity of Berlusconism manifests itself from the film's outset in a semiosis that travels beyond the palaces of power and whose signifiers are bodies or eroticized and eroticizing somatic traces. The chief example of this is Berlusconi's smirk, which 'somatizes' (Ceraolo 2018) a new representation of the political that itself hinges on the express transgression of the Law, something it achieves by sneering at its rituals and figurations. In fact, as Massimo Recalcati has argued, 'there is no sense of the Law disjointed from that of enjoyment' in Berlusconi's world (Recalcati 2010: 13). Berlusconi's smirk on Candida's butt is shown in its obscene location in a colossal extreme close-up (Figure 11.5) and trumpets the regime of exchange. The smirk written on Candida's body is, at the same time, both a concrete 'injunction to jouissance' as well as the grotesque simulacrum of the leader's most identifiable feature – that is his face with its unmistakable, trademark smirk. Although offstage and off-screen, the smirk is nonetheless in reality always located at the centre, at the joining of bodies of those who idolize and imitate him.

Loro's visualization of the hedonism of Berlusconism is rooted in formal mimicry that relies on the aesthetic of the orgy and on the libidinal tension

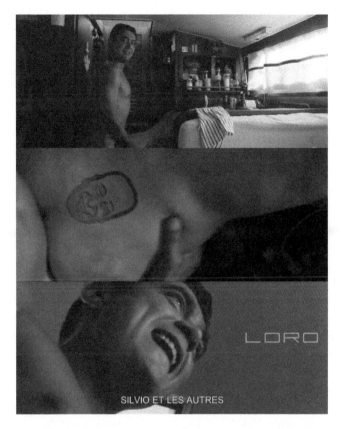

FIGURE 11.5: Still images of Morra's sequence. Morra has an illumination and conceives his plan after seeing Berlusconi's smirk on Candida's back in *Loro 1*.

established between the either aging or aged male body and the young women convened for his pleasure. This visual regime is decidedly phallocentric and objectifies the female body as it executes, almost dogmatically, classic theories of scopophilia. The camera dwells, in long takes, on nude and semi-nude bodies, often in slo-mo, offering the forceful, obsessive projection of male fantasy. Nevertheless, the libidinal investment is filtered by the grotesque mask of the aged male who must reckon with his own drastically diminished, even infantilized virility. As Francesco Ceraolo has observed, the mask of Berlusconi that *Loro* offers is

> orgiastic and ludic, the aging body of a transfigured Servillo that reflects the dynamics of an infantile desire, above all the desire of play and sex, through which the contemporary average (Italian) man understands the real world.

> (Ceraolo 2018: n.pag.)

Together with this aging mask, the young women's bodies occupy the centre, subverting the 'classical idea [...] of politics that believed it was possible to hide inside the home the least presentable aspects of the human condition, those that are closer to the animal nature: bodies, women, sexuality, illness, aging, death' (Melandri 2009). In this sense, the young women of *Loro* are political bodies that shine a light on the fundamental condition of Berlusconism in which the commodification of sexual and personal relations intertwines with the essence of power in neoliberal society. They perform the postfeminist discourse of empowerment, which allows them to *choose* to instrumentalize their own bodies in the pursuit of money and power and, at the same time, to impose a narcissistic vision of themselves 'in which the reifying male gaze is internalized to the point that it constitutes a new disciplinary regime' (Gill 2007: 152).

From the beginning, when Morra monetizes Candida's athletic body, from which he 'extracts' a lucrative government contract, the theme of the relationship of the young female body to the aged male body is presented as a central dynamic. Candida is a gymnast whose agile body, coordination and strength contrasts visibly with the clumsiness and vulnerability of the aging and aged (decrepit, even) men making up Berlusconi's circle. In the sequence already described of Morra and Candida's encounter, Candida appears semi-nude before two men to whom she is exhibiting herself. Filmed first from behind and then frontally, the composition of the image is explicitly phallic (Figure 11.6).

Her energetic, disinhibited sexuality is emphasized also when she encounters Berlusconi's *impresario*, Fabrizio Sala, during a selection of the escorts in Puglia. As an illustration of 'what she can do' (*Loro 1*), Candida does a flip, filmed using multiple (and noticeable) techniques. The flip is first filmed by both anterior and

FIGURE 11.6: Candida shows her athletic abilities to Morra and the politician from the local Puglia government in *Loro 1*.

posterior tracking shots, in a rhythm that alternates between slo-mo and regular speed with a partial point of view shot that shows us Sala's fear of being struck by Candida's vaulting body. Elliptical editing, however, shows Candida's soaring body landing not in Puglia but in Rome where the young woman, now completely nude, lands on the supine body of a middle-aged man lying on a bed in a luxuriously decorated hotel, mounting him as she lands (Figure 11.7).

Candida's sequence inaugurates a series of encounters between young women and aging, older men. In *Loro*, interactions between young female bodies and their aged male counterparts exhibit a broad array of technologies of seduction, from domination to admiration, which place Candida, Tamara, Stella (Alice Pagani), Kira (Kasia Smutniak) and all the other young women presented as nameless in the conditions of a 'double entanglement' (McRobbie 2009: 12): by ensnaring, assaulting or simply caressing the aged male body, these young women accede to a certain level of empowerment, but only in the sense that they self-style themselves as objects of desire in response to the pleasure imperative of the Italian neoliberal society still dominated by men. Rosalind Gill uses the concept of 'sexual subjectification' to define this process, in which women self-discipline themselves as desiring subjects in order to maintain the men's attention and thus ensure financial security to themselves (Gill 2003). It is in this context that we should understand the scene in which Tamara seduces Recchia or the other scenes, especially those we could consider collective or choral.

Loro spends considerable effort and cinematic pyrotechnics in filming these scenes. The scenes with the so-called 'Olgettine'[22] and the young women recruited by Morra are many in number, lengthy, frequently filmed in slo-mo with significant attention to sensual gestures and corporeal aesthetics. The low angle used to film the *bunga bunga* scene in *Loro 2* (Figure 11.8) is meant to imitate the pornographic gaze of the desiring spectator even as the girls concentrate almost obsessively on Berlusconi, the one true spectator of their performance.

Yet Berlusconi hardly seems adequate to the task. Like the man enveloped by Candida in his bed, Berlusconi is a passive spectator to their dance and seems barely able to stay awake following his sexual exertion.

In addition to Veronica, only young Stella shows some awareness of her own position vis-à-vis older men. Her character's plotline delineates a symbolic parable that starts, literally, with the 'luminosity' of postfeminism (McRobbie 2009: 7; Kearney 2015: 264) and ends with the unremarkable 'old man's breath' (*Loro*). She is at the centre of three key sequences: her solo dance beside the pool, her encounter with the mysterious character *Dio* (about which I will have more to say presently) and her rejection of Berlusconi's advances in the bedroom. The pool dance actually fulfils an important narrative function, stitching together the section of *Loro* dominated by Morra with the media magnate's first appearance. In the finale of the party scene, while the others sleep, the camera finds Stella, framing her in a

FIGURE 11.7: Still images from the elliptic montage with Candida's flip in *Loro 1*.

FIGURE 11.8: Still image from the *bunga bunga* sequence in *Loro 2*.

FIGURE 11.9: Berlusconi appears in drag as an odalisque, while contemplating Stella's dance in *Loro 1*.

low-angle medium shot with a luminous sky behind her. She is dancing seductively. The shot that follows is an inversion in many ways: an extreme (continuous) long shot from behind the subject and deep within the scene and from a significantly higher angle until it finally focuses on Berlusconi, the addressee of Stella's sensual promise, also filmed from behind, immobile and unreactive (Figure 11.9).

He is dressed in drag as an odalisque, at the centre of the symbolic null, watching Stella dance from a distance. The camera then follows Berlusconi to Veronica's bedroom, where we see her vision of him: in a close-up, he appears heavily made up, in his ridiculous costume, his customary smirk distinguishable in the 'fixity' of Toni Servillo's interpretation (Belpoliti 2018c) (Figure 11.10).

Stella highlights the mechanism of the 'double entanglement' to which all the young women seem to succumb. In fact, she challenges it by proposing a more complex feminine subject and eventually rejecting it.

FIGURE 11.10: Berlusconi's smirk with his grotesque costume, in *Loro 1*.

In this regard, her encounter with *Dio* in a wellness clinic is significant. The old man, whose face is covered by a hand towel and whose voice is altered by a special microphone, confesses his sexual fragility to the young woman, telling her that she can bring him to climax in '4 seconds' (*Loro 1*). Stella displays unease and disgust throughout the sequence, but in the end succeeds. In a later scene with Berlusconi, Stella's disgust transforms into pity and refusal. At the end of one of the notorious 'elegant dinners' at Villa Certosa, made uneasy by the other young women who snort cocaine and try to please Berlusconi in any way possible, Stella shuts herself up in her room, which is where Berlusconi finds her. Stella's rejection of Berlusconi's advances reveals a chink in the armour of the magnate's power. Rejecting him irrefutably, she says, 'you've got my grandpa's breath. It's not good, it's not bad, it's just an old man's breath' (*Loro 2*). At this point, however, the only thing for Stella to do is exit the scene, something not available to Berlusconi's wife, Veronica. No longer young nor dominated by her husband, Veronica is still nonetheless imprisoned by the circumstances. Despite her tendencies to segregate herself from her husband's court and courtiers, she is shown imprisoned by the hedonistic trappings of Villa Certosa (Figure 11.11), like the trampoline, the merry-go-round, the cable car, the bedroom, the Buddhist temple and the living room.

The Mysticism of the Sacrificial Body

The figurations of the pleasure imperative dictated by the neoliberal society do not exhaust the allegorical representation of Berlusconi's decline in *Loro*. The religious dimension is also particularly relevant throughout the film. It produces a parallel narrative of (de)sacralization of Berlusconi's parable. This is significant, if we consider that the leader and the political message of Berlusconism are themselves constructed on a 'sacro-religious infrastructure' (Chiodi 2007: 95) that

FIGURE 11.11: Veronica Lario on the encased trampoline, in *Loro 1*.

generated religious symbolism and 'manifestations [...] of public resacralization' (Chiodi 2007: 99). Since his debut in politics in 1992, Berlusconi has described himself as the 'new man' fighting for a luminous future for Italy (Parotto 2007: 33–40). According to a heroic narrative attentively elaborated in pamphlets and public speeches, he sacrificed himself, even while fighting cancer, in order to achieve the superior goal of liberating Italy from the danger and hatred of communism (Parotto 2007: 22–40). The religious symbolism of his propaganda has been both implicit and explicit, including, for example, open references to the Bible, the promotion of politics as a fight in the name of love (Parotto 2007: 91) and the claim of being 'the anointed of the Lord' (Marinelli and Matassa 2006: 36), a 'patient victim' and the 'Jesus of politics' (Anon. 2006).

Echoing the religious symbolism constructed by and around the leader, *Loro* presents three sacrificial bodies: a lamb, God, and the deposed Christ which, together, constitute a story arc of sacrifice and failure. Interpretation of the three bodies remains ambiguous. This confirms Sorrentino's allegory is self-validating, in that the incarnation/embodiment of a signifier works to describe, suggest and propose.

The lamb is the protagonist of the film's lengthy establishing sequence, which is about three minutes long. In the centre of the frame in an extreme, low-angle close-up, the lamb appears on the lawn at Villa Certosa. The lamb seems to respond to the strains of the Neapolitan song exhorting it to *Scetate* (*Svegliati*, Wake up). It opens its eyes and turns to move away from the camera. The next shot changes the perspective. The camera frames the lamb, still at the centre, frontally but now within the house. The song, like the lamb, has also 'come inside', and is now inside the diegesis playing at low volume. A sort of mute dialogue begins, with a shot-reverse shot rhythm marking the silent exchange between the lamb and a gigantic television where we see, but do not hear, Mike Bongiorno conducting a game show. The 'dialogue' with inanimate (or non-human) animals continues with a shot-reverse shot exchange with the air conditioner which turns out not to be so inanimate, since, when the temperature plummets to 0, the lamb perishes. The use of deadpan address (an impassive address to the camera) that governs this sequence, with the subject that looks straight into the camera circled and framed by profilmic elements symmetrically arranged, makes the lamb a disquieting subject. As it pivots like a kind of *agnus Dei*, symbol par excellence of ecclesiastical sacrifice, between a surreal, dream-like state and reality, it could refer to the body of Berlusconi, the obscene leader that must be eliminated or the collective malaise of the mediatic society of consumption characteristic of neoliberalism.

With the *Dio* figure, Sorrentino's allegory confirms its insistent focus on the signifier: *Dio*, the godhead whose identity defies specification, greets his female visitors in the sauna at the spa so that they can masturbate him to climax, all with his face hidden and his voice altered (Figure 11.12).

This is the abstraction of the impotence of the aging male body protected from virus or contagion and venerated by the establishment. The sauna that contains *Dio* is also the quintessence of the private and obscene, where nudity and isolation are the norm. In the context of Berlusconism, and in Sorrentino's allegory, the sanitized sauna becomes the quintessence of a *palazzo* emptied of any residual of conventional politics. In this sterile vacuum the Law literally coincides with enjoyment and desire.[23] There is no other option, no other reality but this *palazzo* to protect the decrepit *Dio* from the seductive female bodies and the catastrophe of aging.

FIGURE 11.12: A still image of Stella in the sauna with *Dio*, in *Loro 1*.

The deposed Christ appears in the film's final sequence, transported by a crane which deposits it atop the ruins of L'Aquila after the earthquake (Figure 11.13), a scene that recalls the scene of the flying Christ that blesses Rome from a helicopter in Fellini's *La dolce vita* (1960). Sorrentino's Christ offers no blessing; rather, it is a figure of death and catastrophe that marks Berlusconi's definitive exit from the stage/story/screen. Once again, Sorrentino's allegory does not explain itself, it simply manifests. It suggests. In slo-mo.

Overall, the allegorical trajectory – from the impassive *agnus Dei* to the impotent *Dio* and the dumped Christ – endows the 'obscene' leader's body with a transhuman quality. It adds one more grotesque layer to the phantasmagoria of decadence represented in *Loro*. At the same time, as this essay has discussed, the 'obscene' leader brings to the fore the private and prohibited sexual behaviours that are normally off-screen. Berlusconi himself is literally off-screen for the first half of *Loro 1*, but his spectral presence looms on the court of his adepts, the *them* of the title, all absorbed in the erotization of power relationships. Berlusconi and his aging political peers encounter the 'sexually subjectified' (as Gill would define them) young women who self-submit to their gaze and desire with the intent to achieve financial advantages and power. All these exuberant young women, including the gymnast with the tattoo, bring into play a 'girl-power' attitude that cannot but reaffirm their adherence to the decadent anthropology of 'Berlusconism'. Around 'him' and his idolatrous, grotesque figurations, the young women's bodies evoke the hedonism and commodification of Italian society of neoliberalism. The two exceptions are young Stella and Veronica Lario, who both unveil the vulnerability of Berlusconi's aging body. Stella rejects the 'luminosities' of postfeminism and leaves the scene, while Veronica makes similar attempts but eventually remains physically imprisoned in her husband's luxurious villas.

FIGURE 11.13: The deposed Christ on the ruins of L'Aquila, in *Loro 2*.

In this political mimesis of the collective, where the mechanism of identification shifts continuously because of the fluctuating deictic references (*lui, loro, lei, noi, gli altri,* or him, them, her, us, the others), Berlusconi's body remains symbolically at the film's centre. But it is an awkward body, which emanates fear, disorientation, confusion, self-humiliation and even boredom. Remember when he falls asleep at the *bunga bunga* party? It is in moments like this that the 'obscene' leader reveals the vacuity of its petty universe and the critical distance is re-established. The rest is Sorrentino, baby.

NOTES

1. An unabridged version of this article, in Italian, has been published in the academic journal *L'Avventura*, 1 (2020): 167-186. Please note that I translated into English the original quotations in Italian.

2. The films that centre on, or are inspired by, the figure of Silvio Berlusconi, are now 36 if one considers *Loro 1* and *Loro 2* and the international version *Loro* as two different films. *Quando c'era Silvio* (*When Silvio Was There*) (Oliva, 2005), *Il Caimano* (*The Caiman*) (Moretti, 2006), *La bella addormentata* (*Dormant Beauty*) (Bellocchio, 2015) and many other well-known films are part of this corpus. For a description of the complete corpus, please see my *Berlusconi in Cinema: A Very Seductive Body Politic* (2015).

3. For more detailed information on the declining phase of Berlusconi's last government, see Chiaramonte and D'Alimonte (2012), Mariotti (2011) and the dossier 'Condannato Berlusconi' (2015) published in *Repubblica.it* (2015).

4. See the theoretical discussion of 'postmodern *impegno*' (engagement) in Pierpaolo Antonello and Florian Mussgnug (2009).

5. Roberto De Gaetano (2018) compares *Loro* and *Il caimano* for their representation of 'power as mask', maintaining that both films represent power not through a single character, but in the identification of 'its shared traits'.

6. Note, however, that this film was released in France as *Silvio et les autres* (*Silvio and the Others*), a title that highlights Berlusconi's centrality while suggesting a sense of insignificance or even mediocrity for the 'others'. In this essay, I will use generically the title *Loro*. I will explicitly refer to part 1 or 2 or to the international version in case of specific observations.

7. Mariani points out that this pathology manifests itself in the film through a sort of metallic lightning in the eyes like that, equally symbolic, that strikes the characters of *Bird Box* (2018), the Netflix USA post-apocalyptic thriller (Mariani 2019a). I thank Mariani for sharing her stimulating paper with me.

8. The link between *Loro* and the Italian two-episode biopic for TV is mainly cultural, since *Loro* was not produced for TV. For info on the Italian miniseries, see Grignaffini (2012: 57–59).

9. Millicent Marcus discusses 'modular unites' in regard of *Il divo*, but her analysis sheds light on *Loro* as well.

10. Gianni Canova recently discussed the political biopic in Italian cinema (2017: 73–96), while Giacomo Tagliani analysed *Loro* specifically with reference to the political biopic produced in the United States (2019: 17–35).

11. In her discussion on the use of captions in the opening credits of *Il Divo*, Marcus also discusses about 'referential ambiguity' (Marcus 2010: 253), a characteristic that she attributes to Sorrentino's entire work. It is worth noting that the manipulation of discursive regimes and hybridization of forms are today central in analyses of both narrative film and documentary (Bruzzi 2010).

12. For the concepts of 'obscenity' and 'injunction to jouissance', see Massimo Recalcati's Lacanian discussion of Berlusconism (Recalcati 2012: 15–16), Guido Mori's exploration of Sorrentino's cinema prior to *Loro* (Mori 2018: 77–99) and the philosophical analyses offered by Gianluca Solla (Solla 2011: 129-161) and Lorenzo Bernini, who also uses the trope of the 'catastrophe' as a philosophical concept to discuss the regime of the 'obscene tyrant' 2011: 15–51).

13. Pierpaolo Pasolini first introduced the architectural metaphor of *palazzo* as the place of hegemony in his newspaper article 'Fuori dal Palazzo', published in *Lettere Luterane* (Pasolini 1976: 92–97). His metaphor has become common in journalistic writing as well as everyday language.

14. The *Transatlantico* hallway is located in Montecitorio Palace, headquarters of Italy's House of Representatives. It is an impressive hallway inlaid with polychrome marbles and its décor recalls that of twentieth-century transatlantic ships.

15. The Capaci bombing took place on 23 May 1992 and was orchestrated by mafia boss Salvatore Riina. Anti-mafia magistrates Giuseppe Falcone and Francesca Morvillo, and three police escort agents (Vito Schifani, Rocco Dicillo and Antonio Montinaro) were killed.

16. The characters of *Loro*, including the politicians, typify the anthropology of Berlusconism in a broad sense and it is complicated to match them with real Italian people from Berlusconi's court. For example, because of his passion for composing poems, Santino Recchia is reminiscent of ex-Minister of Culture Sandro Bondi, while, for his flashy shirts (or his 'faggot's shirts', as Cupa Caiafa stigmatizes them), he invites comparison with ex-President of Lombardy Roberto Formigoni. Provocative and coarse, Caiafa recalls former supporter of Berlusconi, Daniela Santanché.

17. In his analysis on the transmediality of *The Young Pope*'s title sequence, Russell Kilbourn argues that Sorrentino's allegory is a dynamic process that acquires its meaning 'in the convergence of [...] viewer and TV show' (Kilbourn 2019). This process, Kilbourn claims, does not remove the arbitrariness of interpretation that is typical of allegoresis, but it makes the literal plan a new form of belief. For a thorough analysis of *The Young Pope*, please see Kilbourn's recent monograph on Sorrentino's cinema, (Kilbourn 2020, 123-149).

18. Speaking of *La grande bellezza* (*The Great Beauty*), Pierpaolo Antonello claims that the terms 'postmodernism', 'mannerism' and 'neo-baroque' are interchangeable for Italian cinema (Antonello 2012: 178).

19. Deixis indicates the quality of some adjectives and pronouns to designate with some precision certain elements in space and time. With regard to personal deixis, in this essay I am referring to John Lyons' theoretical elaboration (1977: 636–702). For deixis in the Italian language, see Vanelli and Renzi (1995: 261–377).

20. In the interview by Marco Belpoliti, Toni Servillo himself speaks of 'disorientation' in *Loro* (Belpoliti 2018b).

21. With regard to Scorsese's style and, more in general, the evolution of narrative continuity in Hollywood cinema, see the second part of David Bordwell's seminal book *The Way Hollywood Tells It: Story and Style in Modern Movies* (2006: 115–90).

22. The belittling label of *Olgettine* comes from the condominium in Via Olgettina 65, Milan, owned by Berlusconi. A number of the escorts and image girls recruited for the parties lived in Via Olgettina on free loan.

23. With regard to the notion of 'sterile masculinity', Berlusconi, and aging, see Lisa Dolasinski (2018).

REFERENCES

Anon. (2006), 'Proposte scritte sull'acqua. Berlusconi attacca Prodi', *Repubblica.it*, 12 febbraio, https://www.repubblica.it/2006/b/sezioni/politica/versoelezioni23/gesuberlu/gesuberlu.html. Accessed 12 September 2019.

Anon. (2015), 'Berlusconi condannato', *Repubblica.it*, 12 April, http://www.repubblica.it/topics/news/processo_mediaset-64029241/. Accessed 12 September 2019.

Anon. (2017), 'Sorrentino, il mio film su Berlusconi', *Ansa.it*, 22 May, http://www.ansa.it/sito/notizie/cultura/cinema/2017/05/22/sorrentino-il-mio-film-su-berlusconi_70885924-abd9-4703-a365-e22152a4d3af.html. Accessed 12 September 2019.

Anon. (2018), '"Loro" pt. 2 e Lui', review, 27 May, https://www.idiavoli.com/it/article/loro-pt-2-lui. Accessed 12 September 2019.

Antonello, P. (2012), 'Di crisi in meglio. Realismo, impegno postmoderno e cinema politico nell'Italia degli anni zero: da Nanni Moretti a Paolo Sorrentino', *Italian Studies*, 67:2.

Antonello, P. and Mussgnug, F. (eds) (2009), *Postmodern Impegno: Ethics and Commitment in Contemporary Italian Culture*, Oxford: Peter Lang.

Aspden, P. (2019), 'How to make a film about Berlusconi? Paolo Sorrentino on a biopic for the fake-news era', FT.com, 18 April, https://www.ft.com/content/9f111a8e-602e-11e9-9300-0becfc937c37. Accessed 12 September 2019.

Bellocchio, M. (2015), *La bella addormentata (Dormant Beauty)*, Italy: Cattleya.

Belpoliti, M. (2018a), 'In quel corpo c'è la seduzione del potere', 24 April, https://ricerca.repubblica.it/repubblica/archivio/repubblica/2018/04/24/in-quel-corpo-ce-la-seduzione-del-potere08.html. Accessed 12 September 2019.

Belpoliti, M. (2018b), 'Servillo: "Servono idee per superare l'ossessione Berlusconi"', Repubblica. it, 12 May, https://rep.repubblica.it/pwa/intervista/2018/05/12/news/_servillo_servono_idee_per_superare_l_ossessione_berlusconi_-196233031/?refresh_ce. Accessed 12 September 2019.

Belpoliti, M. (2018c), 'Sorrentino: Loro 2', review, *Doppiozero*, 14 maggio, https://www.doppiozero.com/materiali/sorrentino-loro-2. Accessed 12 September 2019

Bernini, L. (2011), 'Not in my name. Il corpo osceno del tiranno e la catastrofe della virilità', in A. Chiurco (ed.), *Filosofia di Berlusconi. L'essere e il nulla nell'Italia del cavaliere*, Verona: Ombre corte, pp. 15-51.

Bertolucci, B. (1976), *Novecento (1900)*, Italy, Germany, France: PEA, Artistes Associés, and Artemis Productions.

Bordwell, D. (2006), *The Way Hollywood Tells It: Story and Style in Modern Movies*, Berkeley: University of California Press.

Brogi, D. (2014), 'La memoria e lo sperpero. Su La grande bellezza di Paolo Sorrentino', Le parole e le cose, 3 March, http://www.leparoleelecose.it/?p=34644. Accessed 14 September 2020.

Bruzzi, S. (2010), *New Documentary*, New York: Routledge.

Canova, G. (2017), *Divi duci guitti papi caimani. L'immaginario del potere nel cinema italiano, da Rossellini a The Young Pope*, Milan: Bietti Heterotopia.

Carmagnola, F. and Bonazzi, M. (2011), *Il fantasma della libertà, Inconscio e politica al tempo di Berlusconi*, Milano: Mimesis.

Ceraolo, F. (2018), 'L'archetipo e il simulacro', *Fata Morgana Web*, 24 aprile, https://www.fatamorganaweb.unical.it/index.php/2018/04/24/archetipo-simulacro-loro-1-sorrentino/. Accessed 12 September 2019.

Chiaramonte, A. and D'Alimonte, R. (2012), 'The twilight of the Berlusconi era: Local elections and national referendums in Italy, May and June 2011', *South European Society and Politics*, 17:2, pp. 261-79.

Chiodi, G. M. (2007), 'Postfazione. Risacralizzazioni mimetiche', in G. Parotto, *Sacra officina. La simbolica religiosa di Silvio Berlusconi*, Milano: Franco Angeli, 95-107.

Costa, P. M. and Russo, F. (1887), *Scetate*, Italy: public dominion.

De Gaetano, R. (2018), 'Berlusconi tra Sorrentino e Moretti', review, Fata Morgana Web, 30 April, https://www.fatamorganaweb.unical.it/index.php/2018/04/30/berlusconi-tra-moretti-e-sorrentino/. Accessed 12 September 2019.

Dolasinski, L. (2018), 'Media-ting "sterile masculinity": On male aging, migration, and biopolitics in a (post)Berlusconi Italy', *gender/sexuality/italy*, 5, pp. 80-106, http://www.gender-sexualityitaly.com/5-media-ting-sterile-masculinity-on-male-aging-migration-and-biopolitics-in-a-postberlusconi-italy. Accessed 12 September 2019.

Dominijanni, I. (2014), *Il trucco. Sessualità e biopolitica nella fine di Berlusconi*, Roma: Ediesse.

Dominijanni, I. (2018), 'Loro e noi', review, Internazionale, 24 April, https://www.internazionale.it/opinione/ida-dominijanni/2018/04/24/loro-sorrentino-recensione. Accessed 12 September 2019.

Fellini, F. (1960), *La dolce vita*, Italy and France: Riama Film, Gray Films, Paris, S.N. Pathé Cinema

Foucault, M. (1977), *Discipline and Punish: The Birth of the Prison* (trans. A. Sheridan Smith), London: Allen Lane.

Foucault, M. (1978), *The History of Sexuality* (trans. R. Hurley), New York: Pantheon Books.

Gill, R. (2003), 'From sexual objectification to sexual subjectification: The resexualization of women's bodies in the media', *Feminist Media Studies*, 3.1, 99–106.

Gill, R. (2007), *Gender and the Media*, Cambridge, UK: Polity Press.

Giordana, M. T. (2003a), *La meglio gioventù, Atto I (The Best of Youth, Act I)*, Italy: Rai Fiction.

Giordana, M. T. (2003b), *La meglio gioventù, Atto II (The Best of Youth, Act II)*, Italy: Rai Fiction.

Grignaffini, G. (2012), *I generi televisivi*, Roma: Carocci.

Kearney, M. C. (2015), 'Sparkle: luminosity and post-girl power media', *Continuum*, 29:2, pp. 263-73.

Kilbourn, R. (2019), '*The Young Pope*'s credit sequence: A postsecular allegory in ten paintings', *Global Intersections and Artistic Interconnections in Italian Cinema and Media across Times and Spaces: Journal of Italian Cinema and Media Studies, Second International Conference*, The American University of Rome, 14–15 June.

Kilbourn, R. (2020), *The Cinema of Paolo Sorrentino: Commitment to Style*, New York: Columbia University Press.

Lyons, J. (1977), *Semantics*, vol. 2, Cambridge: Cambridge University Press.

Manganelli, G. ([1977] 2002), *Pinocchio: un libro parallelo*, Torino: Einaudi.

Marcus, M. (2010), 'The ironist and the auteur', *The Italianist*, 30, pp. 245-57.

Maresco, F. (2014), *Belluscone. Una storia siciliana (Belluscone: A Sicilian Story)*, Italy: Rean Mazzone, Zen Zero.

Mariani, A. (2019a), 'Megalomaniac (per)versions of power in Paolo Sorrentino's diptych Loro', *Global Intersections and Artistic Interconnections in Italian Cinema and Media across Times and Spaces: Journal of Italian Cinema and Media Studies, Second International Conference*, The American University of Rome, 14–15 June.

Mariani, A. (2019b), '*Loro 1* and *Loro 2*, Paolo Sorrentino (Dir.) (2018)', review, *Journal of Italian Cinema & Media Studies*, 7:3, pp. 443-45.

Marinelli, G. and Matassa, A. (2006), *Il pensiero politico di Silvio Berlusconi*, Roma: Gremese.

Marini-Maio, N. (2015), *Berlusconi in Cinema: A Very Seductive Body Politic*, Milan: Mimesis.

Mariotti, C. (2011), 'Berlusconism: Some empirical research', *Bulletin of Italian Politics*, 3:1, pp. 35-57.

McRobbie, A. (2009), *The Aftermath of Feminism*, London: Sage.

Melandri, L. (2009), 'Perché "il personale è politico" resta solo uno slogan?' 11 November, http://www.universitadelledonne.it/lea10-11-09.htm. Accessed 12 Septmber 2019.

Minuz, A. (2018), 'Com'è il fosco potere raccontato dal cinema italiano', Il Foglio, 5 February, https://www.ilfoglio.it/cinema/2018/02/05/news/cinema-sono-tornato-sorrentino-fosco-potere-176959. Accessed 12 September 2019.

Moretti, N. (2006), *Il Caimano (The Caiman)*, Italy/France: Sacher/Bac/Stephan/France 3.

Mori, G. (2018), *Del desiderio e del godimento: Viaggio al termine dell'ideologia ne 'La grande bellezza' di Paolo Sorrentino*, Milano: Mimesis.

Morreale, E. (2018a), 'Capitolo 1: Il privato è politico in questo prologo dell'epopea', review, *Repubblica.it*, 23 April, https://rep.repubblica.it/pwa/longform/2018/04/23/news/sorrentino_film_loro_berlusconi-194648810/. Accessed 12 September 2019.

Morreale, E. (2018b), 'Ambizioso e ispirato ma non centra il risultato', review, *Repubblica.it*, 3 May, https://ricerca.repubblica.it/repubblica/archivio/repubblica/2018/05/03/ambizioso-e-ispirato-ma-non-centra-il-risultato38.html?ref=search. Accessed 12 September 2019.

Oliva, R. (2005), *Quando c'era Silvio (When There Was Silvio)*, Italy: Luben.

O'Rawe, C. (2018), 'Editorial: Contemporary Italian film culture in the light of #MeToo', *The Italianist*, 38:2, pp. 151-52.

Parotto, G. (2007), *Sacra officina: La simbolica religiosa di Silvio Berlusconi*, Milano: Franco Angeli.

Pasolini, P. (1976), 'Fuori dal Palazzo', in *Lettere Luterane*, Turin: Einaudi, pp. 92-97.

Recalcati, M. (2010), *L'uomo senza inconscio*, Milano: Raffaello Cortina.

Recalcati, M. (2012), *Ritratti del desiderio*, Milano: Raffaello Cortina.

Roux, B. (2018), '*Silvio et les autres*, Paolo Sorrentino. La complainte du dentier', review, *Positif*, 693, p. 52.

Salek, T. A. (2018), 'Money doesn't talk, it swears: *The Wolf of Wall Street* as a homology for America's ambivalent attitude on financial excess', *Communication Quarterly*, 66:1, pp. 1-19.

Scott, A. O. (2019), '"Loro" review: A corrupt leader, and the people who love him', review, *The New York Times*, 19 September, https://www.nytimes.com/2019/09/19/movies/loro-review.html. Accessed 12 September 2019.

Solla, G. (2011), 'L'osceno: La società immaginaria e la fine dell'esperienza', in A. Chiurco (ed.), *Filosofia di Berlusconi: L'essere e il nulla nell'Italia del cavaliere*, Verona: Ombre corte, pp. 129-61.

Sorrentino, P. (2008), *Il divo*, Italy, France: Indigo Film, Parco Film, Babe Films, StudioCanal, Arte France Cinéma, Sky Cinema.

Sorrentino, P. (2013), *The Great Beauty*, Italy, France: Indigo Film, Babe Films, Pathé Production, France 2 Cinéma.

Sorrentino, P. (2015), *Youth*, Italy, France: Indigo Film, C-Films AG, Number 9, Pathé Production, France 2 Cinéma.

Sorrentino, P. (2016), *The Young Pope*, USA: HBO.

Sorrentino, P. (2018a), *Loro 1*, Italy, France: Indigo Film, Pathé Production, France 2 Cinéma.

Sorrentino, P. (2018b), *Loro 2*, Italy, France: Indigo Film, Pathé Production, France 2 Cinéma.

Tagliani, G. (2019), *Biografie della nazione*, Soveria Mannelli: Rubbettino.

Vanelli, L. and Renzi, L. (1995), 'La deissi', in L. Renzi, G. Salvi, A. Cardinaletti (eds), *Grande grammatica italiana di consultazione*, vol. III, Bologna: Il Mulino, pp. 261-377.

PART FOUR

SORRENTINO'S
POSTSECULAR POPE

Foto di Gianni Fiorito © WILDSIDE/SKY ITALIA/HAUT ET COURT TV/HOME
BOX OFFICE, INC./MEDIAPRO.

12

The Young Pope's Credit Sequence: A Post-secular Allegory in Ten Paintings

Russell J. A. Kilbourn

Wilfrid Laurier University

Preamble

As I was finishing this essay the teaser-trailer dropped for *The New Pope*, Paolo Sorrentino's latest television series and the sequel to 2015's immensely popular *The Young Pope*. By the time this essay appears, the new series will be available to anyone with access to the appropriate platform. At this point, however, the trailer seems to tell us at least two key things about *The New Pope*'s diegetic world: (1) Belardo (Jude Law) did not die at the end of the final episode; and (2) nevertheless, there is a new pope in the Vatican, played by John Malkovich. But there is more that can be gleaned from an initial analysis of the trailer's 1 minute 30 second running time. Structurally, the trailer consists of two crosscut sequences. The first features Law as Belardo, strolling in the foreground in slow-motion along a beach (Venice's Lido?), parallel to the shoreline, passing a number of attractive young women in bikinis, engaged in a variety of activities (including volleyball, a Sorrentino motif), but mainly watching Law's tanned, muscular, blindingly-white-speedo-clad body, as it passes, Devlin's cover of 'All Along the Watchtower' over top. One quickly recognizes the same visual structure, long horizontal tracking shot and editing patterns, as in *The Young Pope*'s now famous credit sequence. A cut to a close-up on Law/Belardo as he turns and looks straight into the camera and then winks, confirms this impression. Finally, the last woman he passes, dressed in the cerulean-blue of a new age Madonna, gazes desirously and faints, falling over on her side, in a direct visual echo of the first series' reproduction of Maurizio Cattelan's sculpture *The Ninth Hour*, a miniaturized Pope John Paul II crushed by a smoking meteorite – a spectacle that will be elaborated upon below. The other

208

trailer sequence, intercut with the foregoing, involves what appears to be the investiture of the new, as yet nameless, pope (Malkovich), as he processes through the papal palace towards the balcony where he will deliver his first address. This sequence recapitulates, shot-for shot, the first of two opening dream sequences, one nested within the other, with which *The Young Pope*'s first episode opens. The fact that the very same scene plays out again, but with a different protagonist played by a different actor, is both uncanny and funny, and is clearly designed, like the scene of Belardo on the otherworldly Lido, to pique the viewer's interest and compel them to watch the new show once it airs on HBO or Sky TV. Whether or not these sequences will make it into the new series is anyone's guess. The 'teaser-trailer' will have done its job.

Introduction

What we now call intermediality is the contemporary expression of a long-standing tendency for inter-art cross-pollination, a feature of cultural production that demands from the analyst a comparable openness to hybridity and impurity. This juxtaposition of modes of production with those of reception or analysis also reflects a long-standing binary best exemplified in this context by the relation between *allegory* as a genre or rhetorical mode, as an approach to organizing a narrative, and *allegoresis*, derived from biblical exegesis, as persistently pervasive mode of reading and interpreting. I invoke allegory not least because of *The Young Pope*'s subject matter, which recounts the fictional story of the first American pope in the Vatican's history, exploring the personal and political behind-the-scenes machinations in the papal palace. In what has been a divisive point in its reception, the series critically analyses the current state of the Catholic Church, examining the nature and value of religious faith in the twenty-first century, focusing on specific hot-button topics, such as abortion or homosexuality and sexual abuse in the priesthood. In a final irony it appears to come down on the side of the validity of faith, insofar as the titular pope performs more than one 'miracle' and, in the end, having proven his 'sainthood', is granted a vision of what at first appears to be the redeeming Christ in the clouds above Venice's Piazza San Marco (see Figure 12.1). That Belardo's ultimate redemption seems meant to be taken literally compels us to consider the implications of Sorrentino's artistic choices. Zusanna Stanska, Silvia Dotto and Sorrentino himself, in their different ways, assert the same idea: that the credit sequence functions as a kind of allegory; given this, it is reasonable to speculate about how best to interpret the meanings contained therein. The allegorical privileging of latent over manifest meaning (which parallels the same hierarchy in Freudian psychoanalysis) also, inevitably, de-privileges the

FIGURE 12.1: Lenny's vision in the clouds, *The Young Pope*, Episode 10.

formal dimension of the text: while most commentators provide contextual and content-based information about each artwork, few to none address the formal, generic or mediatic relations of source text and TV series.

The credit sequence first occurs in Episode 3, then six more times, skipping Episode 9, for a total of seven repetitions. In each instance, Belardo/Pope Pius XIII (Jude Law) traverses an idealized Vatican gallery in a slow-motion left-to-right long-take tableau, with Devlin's instrumental version of Dylan's 'All Along the Watchtower' over top (in the fifth episode, however, 'String Quartet no. 4: V. Meditation' plays instead, bridging from Lenny's dream of losing his parents in a nocturnal Venice[1]). His progress across the shot is mirrored by that of the flying star, which, as it passes in the background from the visual field of one painting to the next, changes to a burning comet and finally to a fiery meteorite. The star/comet/meteorite casts light and shadow according to the logic and physics of 3-D space as it traverses each painting, no matter the artwork's original relationship to visual realism or single-point perspective. The sequence was likely achieved with a combination of live action-green screen filming + digital masking + computer animation, including particle simulation for the shooting star.[2]

In her 2016 *Tesi di Laurea* on the visual arts in Sorrentino's cinematographic image, Dotto offers detailed readings of the series' incorporation of artworks from across history, with a particular focus on the credit sequence. Some of these ten artworks in their subject matter do seem to prefigure specific events or situations in specific episodes. Attending to the relation between the reproduced artworks and

FIGURE 12.2: *The Young Pope* credit sequence.

the series' narrative leads to an enhanced understanding of Belardo's character; it also foregrounds *The Young Pope*'s engagement with Catholic theology, and it clarifies the significance of digital technology for a filmmaker who claims to eschew elaborate or ostentatious digital visual effects.[3] *The Young Pope* is a digital product in at least three different senses: (1) the entire series was filmed with the Red Epic camera, meaning that it is digital from image capture to its reception by the viewer; (2) there are a number of digital visual effects embedded across the series, most of which the average viewer might not remark as such, or even remark at all. These include, for instance, digitally enhanced shots of St. Peter's Square in Episode 1, the second episode's digitally composited kangaroo (Ivie 2017b), and the huge pile of digitally rendered babies in the first episode. In this respect *The Young Pope* aligns itself with much relatively well-financed contemporary prestige television product. Finally, and most obviously: (3) as noted, the opening credit sequence is a thoroughly digitally composited, computer-animated sequence: a series of digital 'events'.

The sequence begins with Gerard van Honthorst's *The Adoration of the Shepherds*, showing a group of shepherds witnessing the birth of Jesus, and ends with Maurizio Cattelan's 1999 sculpture *The Ninth Hour*, a sculpture of a diminutive Pope John Paul II being crushed by a meteorite (see Figure 12.2). The latter is the final manifestation of a shooting star that accompanies the youthful Pope on his walk past the paintings. In the series' most flagrant use of digitally rendered post-production effects, the comet leaps from painting to painting, breathing fiery life into – literally *animating* – each static artwork. I argue here therefore that

Sorrentino's ironic transmediation of the medieval, Renaissance, Baroque, nine-teenth- and twentieth-century artworks reproduced in the credit sequence alle-gorizes the series' engagement with the contradictions of the current post-secular era. All ten artworks together constitute a macro-allegory that illuminates the narrative as a whole and Belardo's trajectory in particular.

While it is likely that some of the individual artworks have been subjected to allegorical readings themselves, independently of their presence in *The Young Pope*'s title sequence, close inspection of each shows that there is no consistent 'micro-allegorical' relation point for point between any one artwork and the corre-spondingly numbered *Young Pope* episode. I therefore offer a few observations on the first nine artworks in terms of not their allegorical as much as their analogical – diegetic, characterological, thematic – connections to *The Young Pope* series and, where relevant, to Sorrentino's canon more generally. As will be elaborated below, each artwork is a digital as much as it is an allegorical 'event', and a few of the paintings seem to bear a less significant relation to the series than others. For instance, the seventh image, Mateo Cerezo's *St. Thomas of Villanueva Distribut-ing Alms (1645):* according to Stanska, 'St. Thomas of Villanova was a Spanish friar of the Order of Saint Augustine who was a noted preacher, ascetic and reli-gious writer of his day. He became an archbishop who was famous for the extent of his care for the poor of his see' (2016). While one could read in this a prefigu-ration of Belardo, the connection seems too general to be of analytic value. More interesting is that the flying star, by now a fiery meteorite, ignites the bouquet of flowers held by an airborne cherub as it passes through the painting, right behind St. Thomas's head. I will therefore key my remarks about the artworks to the fiery ball's progress as the animated visual element that knits the sequence together.

The Artworks

The first instance of the credit sequence occurs immediately after a monologue by Belardo, ending in a close-up on his mouth, in which he confesses (somewhat disingenuously, as it turns out) to Don Tommaso: 'I love myself, more than my neighbor, more than God. I *believe* only in myself. *I* am the Lord omnipotent. Lenny: you have illumined yourself. Fuck!' As noted, the title sequence begins with Honthorst's 1617 rendering of the shepherds bearing witness to the birth of Jesus in Bethlehem. As Stanska observes, this subject is often combined themat-ically with the Adoration of the Magi, 'in which case it is typically just referred to by the latter title' (2016). In the Gospel of Mathew the Magi ('wise men' or also 'astrologers') arrive at the court of King Herod in Jerusalem to tell him of the appearance of a star that heralds the birth of the King of the Jews. Honthorst's painting displays strongly chiaroscuro lighting effects, which are dynamized by the passage of the bright star across the darkness between the angels above and the humans below. As Stanska also notes, Honthorst's work is an early version of a 1622 painting badly damaged in the 1993 Via dei Georgofili bombing, near the Uffizi in Florence, ordered by Totò Riina (2016: 4). This is the very period covered by *Il Divo*, Sorrentino's 2008 biopic of Giulio Andreotti.

The flying star-comet in its course redefines the spatial coordinates of the corridor or gallery along which the pope proceeds, passing as it were 'behind' the intervening wall and re-appearing in the airspace of the second image, Pietro Perugino's *Delivery of the Keys* (1481–82), a painting that hangs in the Vatican's Sistine Chapel. The scene depicted refers to Matthew 16:19, in which the keys to the kingdom of heaven are given to St. Peter. Matthew's, it should be recalled, is the only one of the Gospels to mention the star of Bethlehem in the Nativity story. This handing over of the keys is also of course the mythical origin of the papacy, as Peter was the first pope of the Catholic Church. The two key events (so to speak) – that of Jesus's birth and that of the founding of the Church – are brought together through the star's increasingly fiery intercession.

According to Stanska, the third image, Caravaggio's *Conversion on the Way to Damascus* (1601), 'depicts the moment recounted in Chapter 9 of the Acts of the Apostles when Saul, soon to become the apostle Paul, fell down on the road to Damascus. He heard the Lord say "I am Jesus, whom you persecute, arise and go into the city." The scene shows the very moment Paul is overcome with the spirit of Jesus Christ and has been flung off of his horse' (Stanska 2016: 5). In this one case the fiery star does not appear visibly traversing the space above the figures, but is suggested only by the bright glow (and consequent shadows) it casts in its trajectory from left to right – as if reflecting the fact that in this moment Saul, who here becomes Paul, is momentarily blinded by the light of revelation (Acts 9:13-19). Also, this painting may obliquely reference Cardinal Voiello's (Silvio Orlando) change of heart towards Belardo, in Episode 5 (not 3).

The fourth artwork, *The Council of Nicaea* (eighteenth century), resonates in relation to Belardo's first address to the Cardinals in Episode 5. 'The First Council of Nicaea was a council of Christian bishops convened in the Bithynian city of Nicaea by the Roman Emperor Constantine I in AD 325. This first ecumenical council was the first effort to attain consensus in the Church through an assembly representing all of Christendom' (Stanska 2016: 6). Among other things, the council aimed to settle the Arian Heresy, a non-Trinitarian doctrine regarding the nature of the Son of God and his relationship to God the Father (Dotto 2016: 137). Evidently, Arius himself is visible at the very bottom of the painting (Dotto 2016: 137). Such Trinitarian contradictions are echoed in the first episode, when Spencer asks Belardo: 'Who *are* you, Lenny?'[4] to which he responds, 'I am a contradiction. Like God. One in three and three in one. Like Mary, virgin and mother. Like man, good and evil.' After her arrival at the Vatican, Sister Mary (Diane Keaton) reminds Belardo that as Pope he must now put aside his painful personal memories in order to lead the Church:

> The time has come for you to let your sorrows fade. To become irrelevant, distant, memories…overpowered by the terrible responsibility that God has given you. From now on you are no longer Lenny Belardo, the fatherless, motherless boy. From now on you are Pope Pius XIII, Father and Mother of the entire Catholic Church.

In what is undoubtedly an ironic commentary upon this theological paradox, in more than one episode we see the Pope contemplating a painting not included in the credit sequence, Jusepe de Ribera's 1631 portrait of Magdalena Ventura, a woman who famously grew a long black beard, and who is portrayed with her husband, her breast bared to suckle her infant son. Depending on one's historical viewpoint, she is either a monster or an innovator in gender identity. Also worth noting is that *The Council of Nicaea* was painted in the eighteenth century by an anonymous group of Ukrainian icon painters. Despite its late provenance, the work's style is non-realist, with a radically different perspectival logic from that of the Renaissance, Baroque or nineteenth-century paintings. Most critics who write on the credit sequence provide (as I do here) brief summaries of the historical events captured in the paintings, without actually engaging with the artworks as specific visual-material objects. *The First Council of Nicaea* is a good example, as it is often described as if it were merely illustrative of this historical event, and not first of all a specific artwork in a specific style with a specific provenance in a specific time period (see Figure 12.3). On the other hand, in the context of the credit sequence, this work, like the others, is transformed first and foremost into a digital object, and here the fiery star or comet, as it flies over the heads of the assembled Church fathers, illuminates their faces, as if they existed in three dimensions and not two.

What is now a blazing ball of fire likewise careens over the frozen crowd in the fifth image, Francesco Hayez's 'Peter the Hermit riding a white mule with a crucifix in his hand and circulating through the cities and villages preaching the Crusade' (1827–29). This is one of Hayez's grand historical paintings, depicting Peter the Hermit, a priest of Amiens, said to have been the originator of the First Crusade after Jesus appeared to him and bade him preach the crusade among the paupers. 'Dio lo vuole', Peter claimed, in what becomes here an anticipation of Belardo, arrogating to himself a direct channel to God's will, which in the early episodes he appears to confuse with his own. It is also worthy of note that, while Peter and his followers were in Germany on their first Crusade in 1096, they actively participated in the killing of Jews across the Rhineland. Anti-Semitism

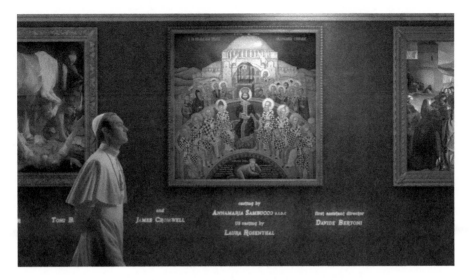

FIGURE 12.3: Jude Law as 'Lenny Belardo/Pope Pius XIII' in *The Young Pope's* credit sequence.

was a not uncommon feature of the Crusades, as many self-professed crusaders felt the need to express their religious zeal well before reaching the Holy Land. (The ninth artwork in the sequence, François Dubois's *The St. Bartholomew's Day Massacre,* like Hayez's much later painting of Peter the Hermit leading the first crusade, is another work whose subject foregrounds the Church's long history of depredations against non-Christians and non-Catholics.)

With Belardo keeping pace, the blazing comet progresses into the digital time-space of the sixth image, Gentile da Fabriano's 'St. Francis Receiving Stigmata' (ca. 1420), actually the back panel of a processional banner, the front showing 'The Coronation of the Virgin'. This is tenuously significant because *The Young Pope* series concerns itself as much with motherhood and the strong Marian aspect in Catholic culture as with more obviously paternal or patriarchist themes, such as masculine identity, fatherhood, maturity and so on. As indicated above, however, the series' treatment of Belardo's character is more invested in the hybridity or fluidity of subject positions that transcend conventionally rigid gender binaries. Finally, the banner's St. Francis aspect – which is all we get to see – with the saint's stigmatized palms, appears to ironically prefigure the Tonino Pettola subplot, which is in Episode 4 (not 6).

Image number 8, Domenico Cresti's *Michelangelo Presenting the Model for the Completion of St Peter's to Pope Pius IV* (1618), represents the founding of the modern Catholic Church in the re-construction of St. Peter's Basilica in Rome, which links this work thematically to the second image in the series, Perugino's *Delivery of the Keys,* from the century before. Also, any painting with another pope in it may be said to prefigure the series' titular character, Pius XIII, who shares his name with this predecessor. The question becomes: what does it mean that the star-cum-comet-cum-meteorite, instead of casting a light, now brings fiery destruction, burning a hole right through the pope's parasol on its way to knock down one of his successors? This general theme is brought home in the ninth and penultimate artwork in the sequence, Francois Dubois's *The St. Bartholomew's Day Massacre* (1584), which depicts the slaughter of French Calvinist Protestants (Huguenots) by French Catholics in Paris in 1572. Now recognized as one of the sixteenth century's worst massacres, borne of religious persecution, it also emblematizes western civilization's long history of religiously inspired mob violence. As Belardo in close-up in the foreground winks self-reflexively at the camera, the flaming meteor sets buildings alight, leaving death and destruction in its wake.

The Digital and the Allegorical 'Event'

Well before the credit sequence's first occurrence in Episode 3, *The Young Pope* begins in a dream, nested within another. The dreamer is Belardo, newly elected pope, the first American, and the youngest on record. The first dream opens with a high angle shot of a mountain of apparently sleeping, new-born babies of all races and colours. Belardo himself appears, in white papal dress, crawling out from beneath the huge pile of digitally rendered infants, in front of the Basilica in Venice's Piazza San Marco, looking across at the Palazzo Correr. It is difficult to not see this as an ironically literal (as opposed to allegorical) reference to Belardo's background as an orphan who emerges as the 'chosen one'. A visual echo of Fred Ballinger's Venetian dream in *Youth* (2015), this brief scene cements in Sorrentino's canon the status of Venice as the locus of the series' themes of birth, love, loss, death and redemption, all channelled through the protagonist's personal trajectory as an American orphan who grows up to become the leader of the Catholic Church and God's representative on earth. The initial dream ends with a straight cut to an extreme close-up on Belardo's eye, looking upward toward the crucifix on the wall above his bed, also in close-up. Christ's head and shoulders appear upside down, as if from Belardo's point of view. A cut to a medium shot of the whole sculpture upside-down from a steep low angle confirms this, since in the next centrally framed shot of Belardo sitting up in bed, the sculpture is right side up. (This scene is recapitulated at the beginning of episode 5, when he awakens from a variant of a recurrent dream of losing his parents in Venice.) Thus begins the series' juxtaposition of the paternal crucifix as masculine signifier and the Virgin Mary as personified maternal principle, between which Belardo's personal drama plays out (see Figure 12.4).

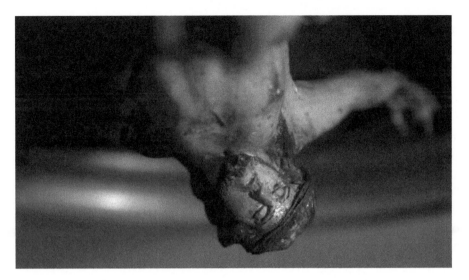

FIGURE 12.4: *The Young Pope*, Episode 1.

My reading of *The Young Pope*'s title sequence connects two different kinds of 'event': allegorical and digital. In his classic study *Allegory: The Theory of a Symbolic Mode*, Angus Fletcher begins with allegory as a rhetorical trope defined, like irony, as saying one thing and meaning another (2012: 2). Allegory derives from the Greek verb *agoreuein*, to speak openly, in the marketplace (*agora*), + *allos*, other. Allegory therefore literally means to speak otherwise openly, in public; to speak openly of that which you cannot speak by speaking otherwise. This is why Fletcher remarks that allegory 'destroys the normal expectation we have about language, that our words "mean what they say"' (2012: 2). Like apophatic irony, allegory is ideally situated to enable the speaking about or representation of things that are otherwise very difficult or impossible to speak or show. Of course post-eighteenth-century allegory is not the allegory of the early modern period any more than it is that of Dante's fourfold model, although the retention of the comprehensive term suggests a general continuity.[5] Fletcher in fact argues for allegory's survival as a necessary or unavoidable structure of thought – and therefore of speech, writing, filmmaking, etc. (2012: 2–3) – involving, in the most comprehensive sense, a certain attitude towards verbal and visual representation, when confronted with an ostensibly ineffable or unrepresentable subject matter or theme. As tropes that say one thing and mean another, allegory shares with rhetorical apophasis and irony a fundamental doubleness. The assertion of allegory is notoriously risky, however, as it always depends as much on interpretive as on compositional knowledge; on expectations brought to the text from outside rather than simply what is manifest there. This typically takes the form of either a purported access to the signifying intention informing the utterance (the actual tropes and locutions associated with these terms), or, more sensibly, a frankly unilateral imputation by the reader/viewer of a doubled semantic structure comprised of both latent and manifest meanings, in which the latent is 'intuitively' privileged over the manifest – a preference of great antiquity, translating into 'a preference for spiritual over carnal readings' (Kermode 1979: 15), symptomatic of the metaphysics of inside-outside, depth-surface and so on. The former (access to signifying intention) originates in the experience of audition: being in the presence of the speaker in the moment of enunciation, like the crowd before the Jesus of the Gospels, of which only a few have the ears to hear the parable's true message. The latter (imputation of latent meaning) is the general situation of the reader of fictional texts, where the designation of 'fiction' implies the potential presence of the markers of ironic discourse. The latent-manifest binary is cognate, moreover, with Roland Barthes' famous distinction between the connotative and denotative levels of discourse typically exploited in mid-twentieth-century advertising.[6] As with any post-medieval example of polysemous textual meaning, what is long since absent – and this is where the continuity breaks down – is the ultimate level of a premodern fourfold model: the anagogical or eschatological. In *The Young Pope*'s post-secular narrative, however, the latent-manifest binary maps onto the anagogical-literal, which in turn maps onto that of the metaphysical vs. the immanent. The 'immanent' side of this meta-binary signifies what is left after the deconstruction of the edifice of western metaphysics that post-structuralism succeeded in dismantling in theory but not in the popular discourse.

In his Afterword to the 2012 re-issue of his classic text, Fletcher asserts that allegory remains as widespread and as significant as ever (2012: 370–71). In Milo Sweedler's reading, Fletcher's assertion of allegory's ongoing ubiquity and significance is no accident but is rather entirely symptomatic of the current moment: allegory, Sweedler argues, 'is the representational mode endemic to multinational capitalism in its advanced stage' (2019: 158). Alongside the persistence of allegory as mode of expression or narration, it is arguable that *allegoresis* – the allegorical mode of interpretation – continues to define the dominant and generally unreflective approach to the consumption of later twentieth- and early twenty-first-century popular culture.[7] The average consumer or viewer would likely not describe their approach to popular cultural narrative as a form of *allegoresis*, however, whose origins are in biblical exegesis, and whose practice reached a height of refinement in Dante's fourfold model of reading and understanding the *Commedia*. Contemporary allegoresis is both more banal and decidedly secular in form, although it undoubtedly conceals an ultimately conservative desire for the kind of under- or over-lying order or meaning that is latent in premodern allegory: whatever takes the place of the anagogical. I speak of the deeply entrenched tendency to read pop cultural texts – especially commercial films – according to received universals or absolutes (what Fletcher calls 'the idolatry of unexamined ideas'; 2012: 374): as pseudo-Christian allegories of human characters compelled to make moral-ethical decisions in a world rigidly structured around the forces of good and evil. As a result, the protagonists of these narratives are reduced to avatars of universal types, representing the human nature we supposedly all share, regardless of superficial differences, like gender, race, belief or economic status. In this, admittedly cynical, outline, the specific story recounted in a given fiction film or television series – not to speak of the formal means of its recounting – while important, is almost always reflexively subordinated to the privileged allegorical level of blandly Manichean universal meaning. None of this of course is contingent on the status of the text in question as bona fide allegory; this is a general template loose enough to fit all of the major commercial film properties since the mid-1970s: *Star Wars*, the *Matrix* trilogy, superhero franchises like the MC universe, *Harry Potter*, *Hunger Games*, *John Wick*, and so on and so forth *ad infinitum*. It is reasonable to assume that all such examples are deliberately constructed as allegories to be understood in this manner.

In the *Cambridge Companion to Allegory*, Lynette Hunter analyses allegory's place in contemporary literature and visual art: 'Allegory has come to be perceived as a rhetorical stance, one that in literature includes the writer, the words and the reader into a reading event called "text" or textuality. It is not a thing but an event that happens' (2010: 266). This is because, as Hunter explains, '[a]ny one piece of writing may be an allegory if the reading constitutes it as such, while at another time [the same text] may be read more generically as utopian or satirical or even realist' (2010: 266). I highlight Hunter's understanding of allegory as not simply a genre, trope or mode but as a dynamic 'event that happens' in the convergence of reader and text – or, in *The Young Pope*'s case, viewer and TV show. In other words, even today allegory depends on the allegorical habit of mind the reader or viewer brings to the text; what literary scholars term *allegoresis*. The allegorical privileging of latent over manifest meaning, and therefore the metaphysical over the immanent dimension of experience, also, inevitably, de-privileges the formal dimension of the text: while most commentators on *The Young Pope*'s credit sequence provide contextual and content-based information about each artwork, few-to-none address the formal, generic or mediatic relations of source text and TV series. I would therefore also cite the ubiquity of digital compositing as a visual effect characteristic of contemporary film and TV production. In the digital era, 'compositing refers to a process wherein a number of different digitized elements, whether captured, synthesized, or applied as algorithmic filters, are assembled from a variety of sources and combined ideally into a perceptually seamless artifact' (Rodowick 2007: 167). David Rodowick refers to the result of digital compositing as not an image proper but rather as a 'digital event'. In any given film or TV series one is now faced with the possibility of a sequence of non-indexical digital 'events' composited together to present an (in some ways) unprecedented modality of visual presentation (much of this, of course, is invisible to the untrained eye)[8]:

> As befits the mathematical basis of information processing, the digital event corresponds less to the duration and movements of the world [i.e. realism] than to the control and variation of discrete numerical elements internal to the computer's memory and logical processes. [...] A digital event...is any discrete alteration of image or sound data at whatever scale internal to the image. Elements may be added, subtracted, or refashioned interactively because the data components retain their separate, modular identities throughout the 'editing' process.
>
> (Rodowick 2007: 166–67)

As suggested, the allegorical and the digital event share a fraught relationship with realism, whether construed as photographic or perceptual or otherwise. According to Lev Manovich, '[t]he achievement of photorealism is the main goal of research in the field of computer graphics' (2002: 150). Photorealism is defined as 'the ability to simulate any object in such a way that its computer image is indistinguishable from its photograph' (1999: 150). The digital continues by and large to be determined by its role in the service of photographic or 'synthetic' realism, emphasizing the surface level of the image, where the 'referent' is no longer outside the image, in 'reality', but is an image itself. For Manovich, '*synthetic* realism' entails a photorealistic image that exists neither in the physical world nor in our minds but only on a screen: 'It is only [the] film-based image that computer graphics technology has learned to simulate' (2002: 150). The questions raised here about the formal properties of the image vis-à-vis its meaning(s) brings the discussion back to allegory. Allegory continues to define itself over against this so-called literal level, emphasizing instead the level or levels of meaning ostensibly conveyed by the image or text but in an as it were hidden or invisible manner. These questions crystallize in *The Young Pope*'s credit sequence's reproduction of these artworks insofar as the paintings are digitally transformed into 3-D tableaux – digital 'events' – with a spatial depth that visually contradicts their provenance as 2-D art objects. Finally, then, Hunter's contention that allegory is a dynamic 'event that happens' draws our attention to its narrative dimension of temporal unfolding. Here Hunter echoes Paul De Man's formulation: 'in the world of allegory, time is the originary constitutive category' (1983: 191). By digitally spatializing these paintings the credit sequence illuminates allegory's essentially temporal nature.

The digital inflection of film form engages with the post-secular, returning us to Gilles Deleuze's famous contention in *Cinema 2* that 'the link between man [sic] and the world has been broken. Henceforth this link must become an object of belief' (1989: 62). For Deleuze, the task of 'modern cinema' is to restore 'our belief in the world' (1989: 62). For John Caruana and Mark Cauchi, the predicament faced by the spectator of post-secular film (or, now, television programming) presents a microcosm of 'precisely what the predicament of belief requires us to do: to make the leap of committing ourselves. Nevertheless, according to this way of thinking about belief, we are beseeched to remain open to the possibility of revising our stances. Thought of in this way, modernity, at its best, demands of each of us to resist the seduction of certainty' (2018: 5). The post-secular therefore names a moment in which the question of belief is balanced between the so-called certainty of the invisible and metaphorical or metaphysical dimension of meaning that one might even refer to as anagogical or eschatological, and the surface layer of things, the literal or denotative level. The signifying dimension of a given sign is always a kind of ideal quantity, dependent on consensus and cultural and historical determination. The literal level of the visual image supports a naïve understanding of photographic realism as a representation of what things look like, calling us to believe not in another but in *this* world in its immanence. Far from being naïve, however, this is the most difficult kind of belief, because it is predicated upon the refusal of any metaphysical, spiritual, anagogical or eschatological dimension. And even if pre-digital, photochemical cinema remains the gold standard for re-presenting the world in which we live (i.e. realism); these days the image is generally not a result of re-presentation but of digital simulation. The question of the ongoing relevance of belief or faith in the twenty-first century therefore links up at this point with both realism and also the mode of reading known as allegoresis As Hunter remarks: '[a]ny one piece of writing may be an allegory if the reading constitutes it as such' (2010: 266). In digitally reconstituting these artworks *The Young Pope* credit sequence therefore foregrounds this question of belief in the banal sense of virtual photo-realistic three-dimensionality that makes no rational sense but that most canny viewers readily accept without question.

In a 2017 interview Sorrentino explains the role and significance of the artworks featured in *The Young Pope*'s title sequence. They are there, he says, to 'tell a story about the Roman Catholic Church. [...] The paintings of the opening scene are a quick chronological overview, with obvious shortcomings, of the most significant moments in the history and art of the entire arch [sic] of Christianity and the church' (Ivie 2017a: 2). The pope's walk through religious history 'ends with the light of a comet that becomes a meteorite striking Cattelan's pope. [...] Because, both seriously and humorously, Christianity begins with a comet that over the centuries takes on a different appearance and mysteriousness as a meteorite. And then, perhaps, for many different reasons, it turns into a rock' (Ivie 2017a: 2).[9] Sorrentino's exegesis of the title sequence as a kind of allegory of the history of Christianity, or rather of the Catholic Church, makes sense, given the series' dominant themes. Sorrentino does not call the credit sequence an 'allegory', but his enigmatic reference to the fiery comet's meta-phorical value justifies this reading; also, this 'overview' is only chronological with respect to the history addressed therein, not in terms of the order in which the paint-ings were produced, or in which they are presented, or in which they might relate to specific episodes in the series. Sorrentino's remark about Christianity beginning with a comet that transforms across the centuries, ending up as a meteorite, is particularly revealing. His final joke about the rock is as clever as it is complex: Peter was the first pope; 'Peter' derives from the Greek word for 'rock' (*pétra*); the pope is the rock on which the Church is founded, so for the pope to be crushed by a large rock is very complexly ironic – and on top of that in the sequence's reproduction of Cattelan's statue pope Jean Paul II appears not to be dead but merely to suffer stoically under the stone's weight.[10] This brings us back to the tenth and last artwork transmedi-ated in the series' credit sequence: Maurizio Cattelan's *The Ninth Hour* (1999). '[T]he title of the work refers to the Liturgy of the Hours of the Catholic Church, that is, the official set of prayers, psalms, hymns, and readings that mark the hours of, and sanctify, each day with prayer. Within this cycle, the ninth hour is the supposed hour of Christ's death on the cross, shortly after crying out "Father, father, why hast thou forsaken me?"' (Cattelan 2019: 3). Ironically, Cattelan's satirical sculpture reconnects the credit sequence, and Lenny's trajectory as protagonist, to the Gospel narrative and its protagonist.

According to Dotto:

> *The Ninth Hour* represents the end of this historical and narrative journey. Cattelan's sculpture is revealed at the end of the star-meteorite's trajectory, which, after ignit-ing the preceding paintings, flattens Pope John Paul II. The comet that initially was the shepherds' and the Church's guide, seems to acquire metaphorically more and more power, and transforms into a fiery ball. Once it exits the paintings it becomes a boulder that fells the aged pope to make room for the young and innovative Lenny Belardo, Pope Pius XIII, who will instigate a revolution.[11]
>
> (2016: 138)

Things may not be quite this neatly linear, however.

Allegory Redeemed

The Young Pope ends as it began, with the Pope addressing a huge and adoring crowd, the first episode's oneiric speech in St. Peter's Square in Rome book-ended by an actual address to the faithful outside Saint Mark's Basilica in Venice, the site of the series' opening dream sequence. From this concluding scene it would appear, as Dotto argues, that Belardo's trajectory as Pope across ten episodes has been that of the fiery meteorite seen during the credit sequence (2016: 138). Thanks to this sequence's status as macro-digital event, the meteorite streaks across the sky, or rather across the skies of a series of famous medieval, Renaissance, Baroque and nineteenth-century paintings, casting an uncanny light, leaving disruption and destruction in its wake, first guiding and illuminating and subsequently setting alight whatever it touches in its path toward its own inevitable, fiery demise atop a 3-D rendering of Cattelan's pope sculpture in the ambiguously black space of the title sequence proper. Before we too quickly align Belardo with the fiery meteorite, however, it is necessary to note how Sorrentino complicates this allegorical analogy. After all, the tenth and final episode opens not with destruction but with the pope gazing out of his windows in the Vatican over a magically nocturnal St. Peter's Square, snow falling on a giant Christmas tree. It is mid-winter, in the Catholic calendar the season of death and incipient rebirth.

Just as the image of the crucifix is juxtaposed across the series with that of the Virgin Mary, in the series' final, melodramatic moments it would seem that Belardo, or rather Sorrentino, has achieved a resolution of the 'feminine' principles of forgiveness, tolerance, unconditional love and sacrificial suffering, with the Pope's earlier identification with a 'masculine' God, compounded of vengeful wrath and an inscrutable absence. This hybrid identity resolves, or reconciles, its own paradoxical status, announced in Episode 1, the first of several scenes in which the Pope (as noted above) is asked: 'Who *are* you, Lenny?' to which he responds, 'I am a contradiction. Like God. One in three and three in one. Like Mary, virgin and mother. Like man, good and evil.' This is where his revolution begins. As the series' conclusion makes clear, however, this theological paradox conceals an epistemological one, as suggested by Belardo's dying (?) vision of a figure that may be either Christ the Redeemer or the Virgin Mary in the clouds over Venice. This vision, set over against the first episode's complementary scene of the upside-down crucifix – Christ in the ninth hour of agony on the cross – strongly suggests that we have to take not merely its allegorical but its eschatological meaning into account. (In an inversion of the dream, the shot-reverse shot sequence here shows Lenny first in a high angle close up, then the figure in the clouds, then Lenny again, but this time upside down.) The fact of its ambiguity as an image, like a visual rebus – is it a vase or two faces? – the cloudy figure only amplifies by association Belardo's ambiguous identity as pope, his gender fluidity as a man.[12] This digitally enabled cutaway reinscribes at the end the question with which we began. Put into the context of the series as a whole, narratively but also stylistically, formally, this shot stands apart as a rare moment of quasi-self-reflexivity, almost but not quite revealing the means of its own digitally enhanced production, its status as digital and allegorical event. In the end it is clear that Belardo's trajectory as pope does not follow but rather intersects with that of the fiery star in the credit sequence, in a chiasmus whose dynamic crossing point is the moment of redemption.

NOTES

1. This Episode 5 credit sequence also does not end with the meteorite smashing into John Paul II, but merely with Lenny's/Law's wink to camera and the blue neon title card.

2. The credit sequence was likely created via a combination of techniques available in a compositor such as Aftereffects, Motion or Fusion (Jeff Thompson, private communication).

3. In a 2009 interview, Sorrentino claimed to be a 'neophyte' when it came to digital technology (Bonsaver 2009a): 'Confesso di essere piuttosto reazionario, conservatore; credo nella pellicola. Sono cresciuto con un certo cinema che non è quello degli effetti speciali e quindi faccio fatica ad accettarli. Anche in questo film, li ho usati in maniera molto parsimoniosa. M'è accaduto pure che mi proponessero un film dove gli effetti speciali erano determinanti, e onestamente sono scappato. Forse un ragazzo di diciott'anni magari impazzirebbe per un film così. Mi rendo conto di essere già un po' vecchio sotto questo aspetto' (Bonsaver 2009b: 333). For the significance of digital for *The Great Beauty* and *Youth*, see Hennessey 2017.

4. The same question is asked again in Episode 6 by Cardinal Voiello.

5. It should be clear that, while in the interest of space I am invoking neither Walter Benjamin's modernist revaluation nor Paul De Man's deconstructive rethinking of allegory, my understanding of the relation between allegory in Northrop Frye's sense of a narrative-tropological-semantic structure and allegoresis as a modality of interpretation underpins all of these approaches. See, e.g., Benjamin 1985; Caygill 2010; De Man 1979, 1983; Frye 1965; Mailloux 2010.

6. In one famous example, Barthes reads an ad for 'Panzani' pasta in terms of its denotative representation of the product (spaghetti, tomato sauce, vegetables, the colours green and red, etc.) vs. its connotative level of mythical meaning: 'Italianicity' (1977: 33).

7. Frye made a similar claim for academic literary criticism in a 1965 encyclopedia entry: 'all commentary, or the relating of the events of a narrative to conceptual terminology, is in one sense allegorical interpretation' (Frye 1965: 13).

8. Rodowick notes that Aleksandr Sokurov's *Russian Ark* (2002), for instance, includes 'more than 30,000 "digital events"' (Rodowick 2007: 165), despite the fact that the film was famously shot in a single 98-minute continuous take, thanks to the new (in 2001) Sony 24-pixel HD digital camera with an extra-large hard drive that could contain that much uncompressed information (Brown 2013: 40).

9. 'I quadri sono un rapido excursus cronologico, con ovvie la cune, dei momenti tra i più significativi nella storia e nell'arte dell'intero arco del cristianesimo e della chiesa' (quoted In Perotta 2016: 3). 'Perché, tra il serio e il faceto, il cristianesimo comincia con una stella cometa che, nel corso dei secoli assume sembianze diverse e misteriose come un meteorite e poi, forse, per molti aspetti diversi si trasforma in un macigno. Giocando con la magnifica

opera di Cattelan, quel macigno abbatte un vecchio papa e lascia lo spazio a uno giovane: Pio XIII' (Perotta 2016: 2). See also Nguyen 2017.

10. 'The original installation at the Kunsthalle Basel was located directly under a shattered skylight, with shards of glass around the fallen pope' (Cattelan 1999: n.pag.).

11. Trans. Sandra Parmegiani. '*La nona ora* rappresenta la conclusione di questo percorso storico e narrativo. La scultura di Cattelan ci viene mostrato alla fine del percorso della stella-meteorite, che dopo aver infuocato i dipinti precedenti affossa Papa Giovanni Paolo II. La stella cometa che inizialmente era la guida dei pastori e della chiesa, sembra meta-foricamente diventare sempre più potente trasformandosi in una palla infuocata che una volta uscita dai dipinti diventa un macigno che abbatte il vecchio papa per lasciare spazio al giovane ed innovativo Lenny Belardo, Papa Pio XIII...il papa che vuole fare la rivoluz-ione' (2016: 138).

12. Re the ambiguous identity of the apparition in the clouds above San Marco, see Korn-haber (2017: 4): 'The very final moments of the season posed one more mystery as Lenny declared his faith to the audience and then doubled over in pain. As cardinals attended to him and his eyelids flickered, an image of the Virgin Mary appeared in the clouds'. I thank Annachiara Mariani for this insight re Belardo's final vision, and for drawing my attention to its potential implications for my reading of the series.

REFERENCES

Barthes, R. (1977), 'The rhetoric of the image', in R. Barthes, *Image/Music/Text* (trans. Stephen Heath), New York: Hill & Wang, pp. 33–37.

Benjamin, W. (1985), *The Origin of German Tragic Drama* (trans. J. Osborne), London and New York: Verso.

Bonsaver, G. (2009a), 'Dall'uomo al Divo: Un'intervista con Paolo Sorrentino', *The Italianist*, 29, pp. 325–37.

Bonsaver, G. (2009b), 'Prince of darkness', Interview, *Sight and Sound*, 19:4, April, pp. 42–44.

Brook, C. (2017), 'Post-secular identity in contemporary Italian cinema: Catholic 'cement', the suppression of history and the lost Islamic other', *Modern Italy*, 22:2, pp. 197–211.

Brown, W. (2013), *Supercinema: Film-Philosophy for the Digital Age*, New York and Oxford: Berghahn.

Cattelan, M. (1999), *La non ora* [The Ninth Hour] [wax, clothing, polyester resin with metallic powder, volcanic rock, carpet, glass, dimensions variable], Basel: Kunsthalle.

Cattelan, M. (2019), 'Maurizio Cattelan: Italian Sculptor and Conceptual Artist', *The Art Story*, https://www.theartstory.org/artist/cattelan-maurizio/. Accessed 6 June, 2019.

Caruana, J. and Cauchi, M. (2018), 'What is post-secular cinema? An introduction', in J. Caruana and M. Cauchi (eds), *Immanent Frames: Post-secular Cinema Between the Tree of Life and Melancholia*, Albany: SUNY Buffalo University Press, pp. 1–28.

Caygill, H. (2010), 'Walter Benjamin's concept of allegory', in R. Copeland and P. T. Struck (eds), *The Cambridge Companion to Allegory*, Cambridge, New York, and Melbourne: Cambridge University Press, pp. 241–53.

Deleuze, G. (1989), *Cinema 2: The Time-Image* (trans. H. Tomlinson and R. Galeta), Minneapolis: University of Minnesota Press.

De Man, P. (1979), *Allegories of Reading: Figural Language in Rousseau, Nietzsche, Rilke, and Proust*, New Haven and London: Yale University Press.

De Man, P. (1983), 'The rhetoric of temporality', in P. De Man, *Blindness and Insight: Essays in the Rhetoric of Contemporary Criticism*, 2nd. ed., Minneapolis: University of Minnesota Press, pp. 187–228.

Dotto, S. (2016), 'Paolo Sorrentino: L'arte nell'immagine cinematografica',Tesi di Laurea, Università Ca' Foscari, Venezia.

Fletcher, A. (2012), *Allegory: The Theory of a Symbolic Mode*, Princeton, NJ: Princeton University Press.

Frye, N. (1965), 'Allegory', in A. Preminger (ed.), *The Princeton Encyclopedia of Poetry and Poetics*, Princeton: Princeton University Press, pp. 12–13.

Hennessey, B. (2017), 'Reel simulations: CGI and special effects in two films by Paolo Sorrentino', *The Italianist*, 37:3, pp. 449–63.

Hunter, L. (2010), 'Allegory happens: Allegory and the arts post-1960', in R. Copeland and P. T. Struck (eds), *The Cambridge Companion to Allegory*, Cambridge, New York, and Melbourne: Cambridge University Press, pp. 266–80.

Ivie, D. (2017a), 'Paolo Sorrentino explains *The Young Pope*'s opening credits', *Vulture*, 7 February, https://www.vulture.com/2017/02/young-pope-theme-song-opening-credits-explained.html. Accessed 20 April 2019.

Ivie, D. (2017b), 'So, was that a real kangaroo on *The Young Pope*?', *Vulture*, 16 January, https://www.vulture.com/2017/01/young-pope-kangaroo-was-it-real.html. Accessed 20 April 2019.

Kermode, F. (1979), *The Genesis of Secrecy: On the Interpretation of Narrative,* Cambridge: Harvard University Press.

Kornhaber, S. (2017), 'What The Young Pope preached about love', *The Atlantic*, 14 February, https://www.theatlantic.com/entertainment/archive/2017/02/the-young-pope-season-one-finale-hbo/516600/. Accessed 15 May 2019.

Mailloux, S. (2010), 'Hermeneutics, deconstruction, allegory', in R. Copeland and P. T. Struck (eds),*The Cambridge Companion to Allegory*, Cambridge, New York, and Melbourne: Cambridge University Press, pp. 254–65.

Manovich, L. (2002), *The Language of New Media*, Cambridge, MA and London, UK: MIT Press.

'Maurizio Cattelan: Important Art' (n.d), *The Art Story*, https://www.theartstory.org/artist-cattelan-maurizio-artworks.htm. Accessed 15 May 2019.

Nguyen, H. (2017), '*The Young Pope*: Paolo Sorrentino explains that stellar opening sequence, kangaroos and more', *IndieWire*, 22 January, https://www.indiewire.com/2017/01/the-young-pope-paolo-sorrentino-title-sequence-star-meteor-kangaroo-1201771989/. Accessed 15 May 2019.

Perotta, L. (2016), 'La Sigla di *The Young Pope* spiegata di Paolo Sorrentino: "Quel Pio XII somiglia a me"', *L'Huffington Post*, 18 November.

Rodowick, D. (2007), *The Virtual Life of Film*, Cambridge, MA: Harvard University Press.

Sorrentino, P. (2008), *Il Divo*, Italy and France: Indigo Film, Lucky Red, Parco Film.

Sorrentino, P. (2016), *The Young Pope*, Italy, France, Spain, UK, USA: Wildside, Haut et Court TV, Mediapro, Sky Italia, HBO, Canal +.

Sorrentino, P. (2019), 'The New Pope' Teaser-Trailer, *La Repubblica*, 1 June, https://video.repub blica.it/spettacoli-e-cultura/the-new-pope-il-teaser-della-nuova-serie-di-paolo-sorrentino/342442/343032?ref=RHPPBT-BS-I220012994-C12-P6-S1.4-T1. Accessed 15 August 2019.

Stanska, Z. (2016), '*The Young Pope* – All 10 paintings from the opening explained', Daily Art Magazine, 5 December.

Sweedler, M. (2019), *Rumble and Crash: Crises of Capitalism in Contemporary Film*, Albany, NY: SUNY Press.

13

The 'Fabrication' of Religion in *The Young Pope*: The Double Irony of Post-Secular 'Icono*clash*'

Monica Jansen

Utrecht University

Maria Bonaria Urban

University of Amsterdam

Introduction: The Young Pope's *Post-Secular Brand of Catholicism*

'Writers and men of the cloth are the same in that way. They cannot afford to solve the mystery, because the next day they would become irrelevant'. This witty remark from Episode 8 of Paolo Sorrentino's successful TV series *The Young Pope* (2016), could be considered typical of what has been called Sorrentino's 'double irony' (Simor and Sorfa 2017): the co-presence, in the director's 'style of excess', of two antithetical models – one ironic and metafictional, one magical and transcendental. It could also be read as a statement of the 'fabrication' of religion as explained by religious studies scholar Birgit Meyer. By locating religion in the domain of aesthetics, Meyer considers it a material, sensational form rather than a doctrine, and shifts the focus to the medium that makes it possible to experience the sacred. This medium can be an art form but also the body,[1] which Meyer considers as 'practices […] through which religion becomes tangibly present' (2012: 7).

Her approach starts from Bruno Latour's assumption that the materiality of religion is derived from the fetish in its essence of being a 'factish', that is, mixing fact and fetish, and from the recognition that 'in all our activities, what we fabricate goes beyond us' (Latour cit. in Meyer 2012: 21).

At the heart of Sorrentino's sentence lies an insoluble contradiction between the mystery of a transcendental 'beyond' and the 'world-making' practices of art and religion, which is embodied by Pius XIII, who defines himself a 'contradiction', just like God is 'One and threefold', the Madonna is 'Virgin and mother', and man is 'Good and evil' (Sorrentino 2016: Episode 1). What is more, the Pontiff, who is – at the same time – orphan Lenny Belardo, confesses not to believe in God. The Pope, being at once a force of subversion and the institution of belief, thus makes it possible to establish an analogy with what philosopher Latour has coined an 'iconoclash', a neologism that combines 'clash' and 'iconoclasm'. In his interpretation, an 'iconoclash' is produced by those artworks whose act of 'breaking' a religious image proves to be inherently ambiguous (Latour 2002: 23). This is true for post-secular artworks in general, which, according to Meyer, criticize religion while taking its sacred imagery seriously (Meyer 2018: 345). In a similar manner, post-secular cinema has been identified with those films that engage with a crisis of religion rather than with religion itself (Bradatan 2014: 5). This aesthetic 'form of secular/religious hybridity' is also characteristic of contemporary post-secular fiction. John A. McClure defines the latter – with the help of Mircea Eliade, a controversial historian of religion – as corresponding to two opposed challenges: 'The first is to fashion compelling spiritually inflected alternatives to the most relentlessly secular modes of seeing and being, and the second is to ensure that these alternatives will leave room for reflection, disagreement, difference, and innovation' (McClure 2007: 9, 12).

In sum, the cinematic 'double irony' of Sorrentino's *The Young Pope* should be understood within the context of the so-called post-secular turn, which is generally dated somewhere around the 2000s. Moreover, it has been defined differently and from various disciplinary perspectives, so much so that post-secularism should be understood 'not as any kind of clear position, but as a spectrum of concerns and possibilities' (McLennan 2010: 4). Firstly, this concept can be traced back to Jürgen Habermas' influential definition of the role of religion in the 'public sphere' (2006), and the alternative proposals that have been formulated in reaction to what has been criticized as 'the privileged link between Christianity and secularism, or faith and reason' (Braidotti et.al. 2014: 1). The latter is at the basis of Habermas' conception of a 'united public sphere', which should be imagined, instead, as 'a proliferation of publics, as a contested terrain that ought to be thought of in terms of its multiplicity or diversity' (Meyer and Moors 2006: 12).

This socio-political dimension of the post-secular connects with *The Young Pope*'s representation of a reactionary, inward-looking Vatican, quite different from Pope Francis' present work of evangelization. This authoritarian image is apparently in contrast with the 'dialogue' between secular and religious institutions as envisioned by the German philosopher, on the basis of a mutually respected 'ethics of citizenship' (Habermas 2006: 6). It also contradicts the post-secular vision of a 'weakening' of religion that becomes, in the eyes of philosophers Richard Rorty and Gianni Vattimo, a 'universal ethos' promoting the 'renewal of civil life' (Zabala 2005: 7).

The series playfully reflects on the present position of the Catholic Church 'after the power' (Heimerl 2017), with its focus on Pius XIII's radical refusal to communicate through the media, thus questioning 'how religion sits in the public sphere' (Brook 2019: 144). Through the theatrical rituals and ceremonies of ecclesiastical power, which dictate the series' choreography of representation rather than of a narrative (Canova 2017: 13), Sorrentino not so much shows – according to Clodagh Brook – 'the falsity and insincerity of religion as a mere staged performance' (2019: 60), but rather reveals 'Italy's uncomfortable relationship with an unstable modernity' (62). It is precisely Sorrentino's anachronistic representation of Pius XIII's conception of a hierarchical Pope, averse to any compromise with worldly power, which raised criticism from the Italian Catholic press (Turrioni 2016).

Secondly, the post-secular also relates to the individual experience of religion in the private sphere. Religion has not disappeared in the age of secularized modernity; instead, there has been a shift from religion to spirituality. In other words, there has been a passage, on the axis of the legitimation of the sacred, from the external authority of a religious institution to the freedom of choice of the individual subject (Zonch 2017: 52–53). According to Enzo Pace, who speaks from the discipline of sociology of religions, this process has translated itself in Italy into a 'generalized symbolic code' (Pace 2007: 89) of Catholicism. Notwithstanding the growing 'tension between independence in belief and a sense of affiliation by tradition' (Pace 2007: 87), this Catholic code makes it possible for Italians to perceive 'unity in diversity' (Pace 2007: 88). This symbolic code comes close to Brook's definition of the Catholic 'cement' of contemporary Italian cinema, with its blend of 'Catholic social teaching and impegno' (Brook 2017: 207). In her book on *Screening Religions in Italy*, she reflects on 'Grace Davie's oft-cited term "believing without belonging" (1990)' (2019: 10), which for Italian filmmaking should rather be read the other way round, '"belonging without believing"', because of 'the "enveloping religious culture" of Italy's public sphere' (2019: 63). For Sorrentino, whose education – between his 14th and 18th years – in a Salesian college in Naples constitutes a 'world of memories' (Sorrentino 2017: ix), this belonging to Italy's Catholic heritage certainly represents an experience with religion that he shares with other Italian filmmakers, who 'define themselves as atheists, agnostics, or anticlerical, but are nonetheless unable to detach themselves from the rituals and icons of Catholicism' (Brook 2019: 62).

Finally, philosopher Charles Taylor defines – in *A Secular Age* – the post-secular as the 'new conditions of belief' (2007: 20) created by secularism. In his view, secularity is the 'context of understanding in which our moral, spiritual or religious experience and search takes place' (2007: 3). According to Taylor, the crucial transforming move in the process of secularization is 'the coming of exclusive humanism' (or of 'self-sufficing humanism'), which makes that 'a secular age is one in which the eclipse of all goals beyond human flourishing becomes conceivable; or better, it falls within the range of an imaginable life for masses of people' (2007: 19–20). This means that, in modernity, the debate between religion and unbelief is shaped by 'the two extremes, transcendent religion, on one hand, and its frontal denial, on the other' (Taylor 2007: 20). The main feature of this new context of belief is 'that it puts an end to the naïve acknowledgment of the transcendent, or of goals or claims which go beyond human flourishing. [...] Naïveté is now unavailable to anyone, believer or unbeliever alike' (Taylor 2007: 21).

This argument brings us back to the unresolvable contradiction between exclusive humanism and a longing for transcendental truth, which emerges from Sorrentino's comment on the kinship between writers and priests that we quoted at the beginning of this chapter. Our aim is to investigate how this new 'context of understanding' is translated into the 'double irony' of *The Young Pope*, and how this narrative strategy might be indicative of Sorrentino's interpretation of the post-secular. Therefore, the medium of this TV series is treated, first and foremost, as a 'sensational form' of religion (Meyer), which at the same time configures an 'icono*clash*' (Latour).

The 'fabrication' of religion through the 'icono*clash*' will be illustrated, first of all, through the example of Maurizio Cattelan's famous sculpture of John Paul II being hit by a meteorite, which Latour mentions in his 2002 essay and which is set in motion in the opening credits of the individual episodes. Why have Catholic believers considered this work of art sacrilegious, whereas *The Young Pope* has been received as a provocation within the limits of the acceptable? What form of 'irony' is considered appropriate for what has been termed 'Catholic modernity' (Collins 2017)? Secondly, one of the key notions in *The Young Pope* is that of the Catholic Church being a 'hyperbole' turned upside down. What this means is shown by the 'icono*clash*' of the reversed image of Christ on the cross – a strongly codified image in Catholic iconography[2] – and its replication in the icon of the Pope. The third case study is also linked to a recurrent expression used in the series, namely that the Church ought to be thought of as 'female' (Sorrentino 2016: Episode 2). 'Icono*clash*', in this case, should be understood in the plural: different conflicting female typologies that, together, comment on this assumption and force a spiritual opening up of the restrictions on female liberty advocated by Pope Pius XIII.

What these three examples show is that the 'icono*clash*' helps explain how 'double irony' in *The Young Pope* works as a post-secular 'context of under-standing', in which the 'weight of God' – the book that Sorrentino based on the series is entitled *Il peso di Dio. Il vangelo di Lenny Belardo* ('The weight of God. The gospel of Lenny Belardo') (2017) – is part of a post-metaphysical conscience as well as materially present in aesthetic and religious practices. Its double bind comes close to the paradox represented by what Eliade has called a 'hierophany', that is, 'the act of manifestation of the sacred [...] in objects that are an integral part of our material "profane" world' (1957: 11).

*Representations of 'Icono*clash*' and 'Double Irony' in* The Young Pope

If we accept Meyer's suggestion to study the sensational form as a 'format to be followed and a performance to effect a particular reality' (2012: 29), the study of artworks can offer insight into the 'cleavages between sensational forms, and hence between religious aesthetics and broader modes of world-making' (2012: 29). Meyer's reference to Latour's positive concept of 'factish' can be coupled with Latour's neologism of 'icono*clash*'. This concept 'acknowledges the multi-direc-tional transgressions taking place in contemporary accusations of blasphemy and sacrilege, and it considers them as manifestations and collisions of different but not necessarily opposing or exclusive world views' (Korte 2014: 237). Latour, in an essay written for the catalogue of the exhibition *Iconoclash. Beyond the Image Wars in Science, Religion and Art*, mentions that he has 'chosen only those sites, objects, and situations where there is an ambiguity, a hesitation, an icono*clash* on how to interpret image-making and image-breaking' (Latour 2002: 23). Through-out the text, the author consistently uses italics in 'icono*clash*'.

In this view, 'world-making' and 'world-breaking' are two possible outcomes that are both contemplated by Latour's notion of 'icono*clash*', which allows for the sensational form of religion that is represented by a post-secular work of art to be intrinsically ambivalent in its reference to the role of religion in the public sphere. 'Icono*clash*', because of its open-ended ambivalence, might therefore disclose the contradiction, in the 'context of understanding', between exclusive humanism and transcendence (Taylor 2007) as well as the 'double irony' employed by Paolo Sorrentino in his TV series.

In order to measure the 'icono*clash*' that is provoked in the viewer of *The Young Pope*, this chapter refers to the transnational reception of the TV series in Catholic media in the United States, where HBO launched the first episode on 15 January

2017, and its ratings made up for an 'unexpected victory'.[3] The sensational form of Sorrentino's 'icono*clash*' is approached through the concept of 'double irony' as this is expressed in the director's 'excessive cinematic style'. According to Eszter Simor and David Sorfa, the Neapolitan director's 'aesthetically pleasing images' (2017: 5) are never an end in themselves, since it is the very 'excessive cinematic style that creates room for ambiguity and thus makes an ironic interpretation possible' (2017: 2). They explain how 'Sorrentino creates a radically ironic space here, a sort of double irony, the irony of irony. This extreme ironic position seems to be in stark contrast with the spiritual yearning of magical characters. However, in Sorrentino's work even ironic characters can yearn for spirituality. The Pope is arrogant and cynical but he is magical, he is able to perform miracles' (2017: 12). Moreover, as Lydia Tuan has pointed out, the 'excess as a style' in Sorrentino's productions, together with 'its intense aestheticism', has an impact on 'how viewers understand the inner turmoil of Sorrentino's protagonists' (Tuan 2019: 429).

Cattelan's 'Irony Against All Mediators'

It is striking how, in *The Young Pope*, religious symbols and icons are displayed in a way that both enhances and desacralizes the sacred. We may therefore assume that Sorrentino's style of cinematic excess, which emphasises the 'lure' of Catholicism (Brook 2019: 21), also accentuates the 'sensational forms' (Meyer 2012) of religious symbols and icons, to such an extent that they can be described as an 'icono*clash*' (Latour 2002): their ambivalence causes the subjects and objects of representation to simultaneously manifest something sacred and profane.

This double tension within sacred images is remediated in *The Young Pope* by artist Maurizio Cattelan's *La nona ora* (*The Ninth Hour*), a sculpture showing Pope John Paul II lying on the ground after being struck down by a meteorite. This sculpture is included, with some variations (Canova 2017: 29), in the opening credits of the individual episodes of Sorrentino's series.

It is worth focusing on the post-secular irony of this work by Cattelan, which Latour considers an example of an 'icono*clash*' before which 'one does not know, one hesitates, one is troubled by an action for which there is no way to know, without further enquiry, whether it is destructive or constructive' (2002: 16). How can we indeed assess this 1999 artwork, asks Latour? Does it 'demonstrate a healthy irreverence for authority', or is it 'a deeply respectful image showing that, in Catholicism, the Pope is requested to suffer the same breaking, the same ultimate destruction as Christ himself' (Latour 2002: 30)? The mimetic effigy of the Pontiff provoked violent reactions from the Polish public; when the sculpture was exposed in the Zacheta National Gallery of Art in Warsaw, in 2000, three men tried to 'rescue' the Pope by removing the meteorite. What had been recognized as an act of iconoclasm on the Polish Pope, in turn provoked an act of iconoclasm concerning the image of the Pope as created by the artist (Gennari-Santori 2015: 84). Flaminia Gennari-Santori deduces from the nature of this incident that iconoclasts 'make war on images, not on reality' (2015: 86), and that they act collectively in the name of a political idea about what may be displayed in public and what, on the contrary, transgresses the rules of the religious community they represent (2015: 86–87).

By quoting the 'icono*clash*' of Cattelan's *La nona ora*, and by inserting the sculpture at the end of a gallery of paintings belonging to Christian iconology, Sorrentino performs, in turn, an 'icono*clash*' that is expressed, however, with double irony. The contrastive moods of Pope Pius XIII walking straight ahead and winking at the public until a meteorite – materialized from one of the paintings – hits the image of Pope John Paul II, could be analysed as an example of 'double irony'. Lenny Belardo's winking has been interpreted differently, as an act of iconoclasm by Pius XIII against his predecessor (Rodríguez Serrano 2017: 88), and as a suggestion that his refusal to show his face to the community of believers within the story does not diminish the Pope's popularity among the public in terms of a commodity (Brook 2019: 137) being shared on social media (Manzato and Mascio 2019), and recreated through the production of GIFs (Prosperi 2016) and Internet memes (Adalian 2017). In this case, the ambivalence of the 'icono*clash*' triggers the complicity of the viewer.

The question that arises here is why Cattelan's image of the Pope, fulminated in the hour of Christ's death, has been experienced as offensive by believers, while Sorrentino's Pope – positioning himself ironically in the long tradition of religion and art – has not, apart from the Catholic press commenting on irony and its use in a proper Christian way (Blanski 2017). Indeed, it is striking to see how *The Young Pope*, except for the already mentioned criticism of its anachronistic representation of the Catholic Church by *Famiglia cristiana*, in the United States has generally been received as a cultural product that corresponds with the definition of post-secular fiction as a hybrid form of secular and religious contents (McClure 2007: 9). In the *Religious Studies Review*, the TV series is hailed as a useful resource for religion and film courses, in that it supposedly allows students to gain familiarity with 'Catholic modernity' (Collins 2017). This modernity consists of contradictions and opposites, which question not so much the Christian religion, but rather secularism's preconceptions of it (Malone 2017). Therefore, in Sorrentino's series, as Tyler Blanski writes in *Crisis Magazine*, 'the mash-up of seeming opposites ("sexy" and "priest") might actually be salutary', and

[t]he juxtaposition of opposites – the unexpected love for those in Catholic power combined with outrage when they commit grievous sins, the surprising delight in

liturgical beauty mixed with horror at the extravagance, the way you can't pin a single person down as either a sinner or a saint – combine in such a way that leaves us wondering, What is the Catholic Church, really?

(Blanski 2017)

This means that the ambivalence of an artwork that contains an 'intrinsic icon-oclash' (Meyer 2018: 350) can act in different ways, depending on the material-ity of the sensational form. The clash caused by Cattelan's work can be related to the avant-garde tradition in which 'artworks were expected to break the yoke of religion and tradition' (Meyer 2018: 345). Latour, in his exhibition, classified Cattelan's sculpture as an example of iconoclastic gesture 'E', that of a 'devastating irony against all mediators' (2002: 30). This cynical and ironic, anti-religious stance is considered typical of the modern art world before 9/11 and, according to Meyer, has been replaced by a post-secular perspective typical of works of art that look for new kinds of provocations, at the same time taking seriously Catholic imagery and its role as a factor in a contemporary, pluralist society (Meyer 2018: 345).

This new kind of post-secular 'icono*clash*', in Sorrentino, is to be found in the recognition that a work of art exemplifies the 'fabrication' of religion, both as a human construction and as a medium that offers access to the 'beyond' of the sacred. In this sense, there is a similarity with how S. Brent Plate, in his introduc-tion to *Religion and Film*, formulates the analogy between religion and aesthetics: '[R]eligion and film are akin. They both function by recreating the known world and then presenting that alternative version of the world to their viewers/worship-pers' (Plate 2008: 2). Sorrentino's *The Young Pope* offers a perfect illustration of Meyer's idea of 'religion as not limited to doctrines and meanings, but as material and embodied' (2018: 359). By including Cattelan's artistic heresy in the creative space occupied by Pius XIII, room is created for ambiguity that makes an ironic interpretation of 'icono*clash*' possible (Simor and Sorfa 2017: 2), without the latter being experienced as offending the Catholic faith.

Upside-Down Imageries of Christ and the Pope

Pius XIII's playfulness thus de-dramatizes the Pope's destitution as a spiritual father, and retrieves his role as a medium to reach the 'beyond', albeit a contra-dictory one. His theology of 'mystery' is coupled with the Pope's refusal to show his face to the community of believers, thus preserving his holy 'aura'. His deci-sion, to follow the example of famous artists who neither appear in public nor allow themselves to be photographed, is explained to his rival, Cardinal Voiello, as follows: 'The Vatican survives thanks to hyperboles. So, we...we will generate the hyperbole, but this time in reverse' (Sorrentino 2016: Episode 2).

The so-called 'upside-down' imaginary is one of the many visual strategies the Neapolitan director adopts so as to generate contradictory images, and is a recurrent one in all his works. In the opening scene of *The Great Beauty* (2013), for instance, when Jep Gambardella celebrates his 65th birthday, we first see the main character 'kissing and flirting' with the female guests of his party; then, suddenly 'the image turns upside down and this striking visual element [...] calls the viewer's attention to the importance of narration over narrative' (Simor and Sorfa 2017: 4).

A similar situation is displayed at the beginning of the first episode of *The Young Pope*. The 'contradiction' of the orphan Lenny Belardo, being a Pontiff who does not believe in God, is expressed with the help of 'overturned' spiritual symbols, starting with the reversed image of Christ with which the audience is confronted at the beginning of the first episode. In fact, we see the cross hanging on the wall by the headboard of the bed, but from the perspective of the newly elected Pope, who is supine on the bed like a corpse, and so the crucifix appears overturned (Sorrentino 2016: Episode 1). The Pope's ambiguous identification with the image of Christ as a symbol of sacrifice and redemption, mediated by the iconography of a shared Catholic 'symbolic code' (Pace 2007: 89), could be seen as an 'icono*clash*' on an allegorical level.

This 'upside-down' imaginary is further developed throughout the series, as demonstrated by the scene in which Pius XIII visits the storehouse where the gifts for the Pontiff are collected (Episode 2). Among these he finds a letter written by a child, who asks the following question: 'Dear Pope, What do I have to do to believe in God?'. The drawing that accompanies the question – not just *a* question, but *the* question around which the whole narrative is built – shows us, in a typically childlike style, some houses with red roofs and trees, and the figure of the Pope at the top, dressed in white and wearing red shoes, but upside down. Such a powerful image seems to recall that of the inverted crucifix; despite being ambiguous, it will reveal its meaning when the child's drawing reappears on Pius XIII's lectern during his first shocking homily (Episode 2), in which the Pope ideally turns the post-conciliar pastoral teaching upside down. It is therefore through this visual clue, which mediates religious images and icons in an uncertain way, that the series urges its audience to reflect on the religious message and to make sense of the story.

In this reversed order of seeing, the profane and the sacred form the paradox represented by the 'icono*clash*'. The upside-down symmetry between Christ on the cross and the child's drawing of the Pope establishes a visual correspondence of immediacy between the two dimensions, and at the same time confirms the series' logic of belief through disbelief. It can be said that, in this reversed order, the image of the Pope represents a 'hierophany', in that he becomes 'something else' (Eliade 1957: 12) and represents 'a break in the homogeneity of space' (1957: 21). Its 'revelation of an absolute reality' (1957: 21), however, is questioned by this infantile point of view on faith. His doubt is inherent in the ambivalence between a religion of love – which will return later in the series, with the example of the Blessed Juana – and a religion of fear, two opposite – but not mutually exclusive – dimensions of belief that are continuously discussed during the series.

The contradiction between these two affects does not seem to find a unique solution in redemption, because the Pope's judgement does not always seem to be guided by Christian piety.[4] This ontological undecidedness results in an 'intrinsic iconoclash', and could be interpreted as Sorrentino's ambivalent and provocative response to Brook's exhortation that Italy's cinema must 'look more closely at the "inner bastard" if it is to heal the cracks in the fragile cement of its emerging post-secular identity' (2017: 208).

Female 'Iconoclash' as the 'Opening Line' of Religion

Throughout the series, Sorrentino seems to depict female subjectivity against, but also in line with, the formats of religion consecrated by the Catholic Church. While the director's 'male gaze' on female subjects has been judged as prevalently sexist, notwithstanding his apparent critique of 'specific gender-based [...] stereotypes of femininity' (Kilbourn 2019: 381), in *The Young Pope* it is possible to distinguish a multiplicity of images of the female, which – in their hybrid secular/religious composition – form an 'iconoclash' constellation.

Within the Catholic practice of seeing, Cardinal Voiello associates the Palaeolithic statue of the Venus of Willendorf (which is preserved in the Pope's library) with sin, as it evokes 'impure thoughts' in him (Sorrentino 2016: Episode 1). At the same time, Voiello is shown praying on his kneeler in front of a wall covered with crucifixes (Episode 4), a scene where Sorrentino experiments with a multiplying effect that strengthens the visual impact of a religious object or icon. Voiello, in his confession, admits to suffering from an internal dualism between being an 'idol breaker' and an 'icon worshipper', two roles discussed by Latour in his essay on 'iconoclash' (2002: 30). What is more, Voiello, who incarnates the Vatican's political cynicism, is also the writer of a homely in which religion is professed as love.

This unresolved dualism of the sacred and the profane is parallelled in the orphan Pope's search of mother figures, which makes of him simultaneously a worshipper of Mary, the iconic woman of Catholicism, and a 'breaker' of female freedom as he expresses himself against the right to abortion, in defence of the Christian dogmas of faith. His doctrinarian act unleashes the anger of the Femen, who – in the series – protest naked with the word 'Bastard' written on their bodies in front of Pius XIII, in the Vatican gardens (Episode 8). This episode can be read as a reference to the feminist blasphemous art of 'Pussy Riot' (Korte 2014).

These female subjectivities, which are considered incongruent with the Catholic faith as a doctrine,[5] also point to the centrality of the fetish in the 'fabrication of religion' (Meyer 2012) and to the 'icono*clash*' as a subversive meaning that opens alternative ways of provocation. In its ultimate analysis, it seems that the ambivalence of the 'icono*clash*' opens itself to the alternative of revelation, with the introduction to the story of Blessed Juana, a little girl who was worshipped in Guatemala and Central America. When she died of leukemia at the age of 18, she uttered the following words: 'All the world will be infatuated with me because all my life I have been infatuated with the world' (Sorrentino 2016: Episode 8). The French Cardinal Michel Marivaux, trying to convince the Pope to canonize her, adds to the story by saying that she told invented fables about the Madonna to make ill children laugh (Episode 8). The message is brought across in the final homely the Pope pronounces in Venice, on St Mark's Square, where he recounts – this time speaking frontally to the people present there – Juana's parable: 'When they asked her: "Who is God?" "God is a line that opens," replied the Blessed Juana. She was just fourteen years old, and no one understood what it was what she was trying to say' (Episode 10).

Conclusion

The examples of 'icono*clash*' in *The Young Pope* that we analysed here, in its broad definition of subjects and objects that are ambivalent between the destruction and the construction of a material form of religion (Meyer 2012), all foreground the 'remediation of religious iconography' (Brook 2019: 56) within a secular 'context of understanding' (Taylor 2007: 3). Sorrentino's 'double irony' (Simor and Sorfa 2017) is functional to the double bind of the 'icono*clash*' as this has been theorized by Latour (2002), in the sense that the series, with its prevalence of narration over narrative, playfully mocks stereotypical images of the power of the Church while at the same time creating room for transcendence. However, this happens without a unique and absolute truth being reached. Pius XIII's vertical aspiration to an immediate access to the 'beyond' – an aspiration that is reflected in Eliade's image of 'hierophany' – is remediated by the reversed image of Christ and that of the child's drawing, in which the Pope is turned upside down. This reversed symmetry thus established can be considered an 'icono*clash*', in that it offers no guarantee for a post-secular 'ethics' of religion.

The ethical dimension of subverting religion, while taking its potential for the creation of an alternative vision seriously, is introduced by the examples of incongruent female figures; the fable of the Blessed Juana comes closest to that of Meyer's vision of material religion as a set of visual and bodily practices, rather than as a mental construction. By advocating a religion of love, one could suggest that Sorrentino, in the end, reaches an affirmative form of 'icono*clash*'. This interpretation also seems to be in tune with Latour, when he says that he prefers a constructive interpretation of the 'icono*clash*' to a destructive one; this is, according to the French philosopher, the difference between 'iconoclast distortion, which always relies on the power of what is destroyed, and a productive cascade of re-representation' (2002: 36).

NOTES

1. In her publications, Meyer stresses the important role of the body in creating access to the religious experience of the supernatural. In her 2012 inaugural speech, she formulates it as follows: 'Importantly, focusing on sensational forms draws our attention to the triple role of the body as a producer, transmitter and receiver of the transcendent. [...] Therefore, the (physio-cultural) body is the key to understanding how fabrications that reach out to what is posited as "beyond" eventually conjure a being (or beings) that command belief: how, in short, the genesis of extraordinary presence occurs' (Meyer 2012: 28).

2. Anne-Marie Korte, when discussing female crucifixion in feminist works of art, observes that in these cases 'the judgement of blasphemy is founded upon the idea that the (religious) symbol of crucifixion is confined and closed in its actual form, content, and meaning (because of its transcendent or God-given nature). The offence of blasphemy here involved concerns the violation of established, authorized, and familiar representations of the crucified Christ' (Korte 2014: 236).

3. According to *Vulture*, 'The network estimates each episode has been seen by an average of 4.7 million viewers across the network's various linear and digital platforms' (Adalian 2017).

4. An example of an unethical form of transcendence in post-secular terms is the heavenly vengeance enacted by the Pope in Episode 8 upon a corrupt nun, Sister Antonia.

5. We could add to these Jusepe de Ribera's 'Donna barbuta', discussed by Canova, a painting that appears repeatedly in the series (in particular Episode 7), and thus exemplifies the oxymoric dimension of the Pope's dual personality (2017: 24–25).

REFERENCES

Adalian, J. (2017), 'Why The Young Pope was an unexpected victory for HBO', *Vulture*, 14 February, https://www.vulture.com/2017/02/hbo-young-pope-unexpected-victory-for-the-network.html. Accessed 6 November 2019.

Blanski, T. (2017), 'What we talk about when we talk about *The Young Pope*', *Crisis Magazine: A Voice for the Faithful Catholic Laity*, 22 February, https://www.crisismagazine.com/2017/talk-talk-young-pope. Accessed 6 November 2019.

Bradatan, C. and Ungureanu, C. (eds) (2014), *Religion in Contemporary European Cinema: The Postsecular Constellation*, New York: Routledge.

Braidotti, R., Blaagaard, B., De Graauw, T. and Midden, E. (2014), 'Introductory notes', in R. Braidotti, B. Blaagaard, T. De Graauw and E. Midden (eds), *Transformations of Religion and the Public Sphere: Postsecular Publics*, Houndmills, Basingstoke, Hampshire: Palgrave Macmillan, pp. 1–13.

Brook, C. (2017), 'Post-secular identity in contemporary Italian cinema: Catholic "cement", the suppression of history and the lost Islamic other', *Modern Italy*, 22:2, pp. 197–211.

Brook, C. (2019), *Screening Religions in Italy: Contemporary Italian Cinema and Television in the Post-secular Public Sphere*, Toronto: Toronto University Press.

Canova, G. (2017), *Divi, duci, guitti, papi, caimani: L'immaginario del potere nel cinema italiano, da Rossellini a The Young Pope*, Milano: Edizioni Bietti.

Collins, B. (2017), '*The Young Pope*', *Religious Studies Review*, 43:2, pp. 157–58.

Eliade, M. (1957), *The Sacred and the Profane: The Nature of Religion*, New York: Harper & Row.

Gennari-Santori, F. (2015), 'Images in the Piazza: The destruction of a work by Maurizio Cattelan (Milan, May 2004)', *Change Over Time*, 5:1, pp. 78–94.

Habermas, J. (2006), 'Religion in the public sphere', *European Journal of Philosophy*, 1, pp. 1–25.

Heimerl, T. (2017), 'Nach der Macht ist vor der Macht. *The Young Pope* als spielerischkritische Reflexion zu kirchlicher Macht heute', *Disputatio Philosophica: International Journal on Philosophy and Religion*, 1, pp. 103–14.

Kilbourn, R. (2019), 'The "primal scene": Memory, redemption and "woman" in the films of Paolo Sorrentino', *Journal of Italian Cinema & Media Studies*, 7:3, pp. 377–94.

Korte, A. (2014), 'Blasphemous feminist art: Incarnate politics of identity in postsecular perspective', in R. Braidotti, B. Blaagaard, T. De Graauw and E. Midden (eds), *Transformations of Religion and the Public Sphere: Postsecular Publics*, Houndmills, Basingstoke, Hampshire: Palgrave Macmillan, pp. 228–48.

Latour, B. (2002), 'What is iconoclash? Or is there a world beyond the image wars?', in P. Weibel and B. Latour (eds.), *Iconoclash, Beyond the Image-Wars in Science, Religion and Art*, Cambridge: ZKM and MIT Press, pp. 14–37.

Malone, P. (2017), '*The Young Pope*: Popes are people, too', *Catholic Stand*, 26 August, https://www.catholicstand.com/young-pope-popes-people/. Accessed 6 November 2019.

Manzato, A. and Mascio, A. (2019), '*The Young Pope*: An Italian "celevision" case study', *Journal of Italian Cinema & Media Studies*, 7:3, pp. 411–24.

McLennan, G. (2010), 'The postsecular turn', *Theory Culture Society*, 27:4, pp. 3–20.

Meyer, B. (2012), *Mediation and the Genesis of Presence: Towards a Material Approach to Religion*, Utrecht: Faculteit Geesteswetenschappen, Universiteit Utrecht.

Meyer, B. (2018), 'The dynamics of taking offense: Concluding thoughts and outlook', in C. Kruse, B. Meyer and A. Korte (eds), *Taking Offense: Religion, Art, and Visual Culture in Plural Configurations*, Paderborn: Wilhelm Fink, pp. 340–72.

Meyer, B. and Moors, A. (2006), *Religion, Media and the Public Sphere*, Bloomington: Indiana UP.

McClure, J. (2007), *Partial Faiths: Postsecular Fiction in the Age of Pynchon and Morrison*, Athens: University of Georgia Press.

Pace, E. (2007), 'A peculiar pluralism', *Journal of Modern Italian Studies*, 12:1, pp. 86–100.

Plate, S. B. (2008), *Religion and Film: Cinema and the Re-creation of the World*, London and New York: Wallflower.

Prosperi, G. (2016), 'Tra TV e *GIF quality: The Young Pope* come esempio di complessità televisiva', *Annali Online UniFE*, 11:2, http://annali.unife.it/lettere/article/viewFile/1404/1192. Accessed 6 November 2019.

Rodríguez Serrano, A. (2017), 'El hombre, el otro y Dios: Reflexiones sobre la mirada y la serialidad en *The Young Pope*', *L'Atalante: Revista de estudios cinematográficos*, 24, pp. 85–97.

Rorty, R. and Vattimo, G. (2005), *The Future of Religion* (ed. S. Zabala), New York: Columbia University Press.

Simor, E. and Sorfa, D. (2017), 'Irony, sexism and magic in Paolo Sorrentino's films', *Studies in European Cinema*, 14:3, pp. 200–15.

Sorrentino, P. (2013), *La grande bellezza (The Great Beauty)*, Italy and France: Indigo Film and Medusa Film.

Sorrentino, P. (2016), *The Young Pope*, HBO, Canal+, Sky Atlantic.

Sorrentino, P. (2017), *Il peso di Dio. Il vangelo di Lenny Belardo*, Turin: Einaudi.

Taylor, C. (2007), *A Secular Age*, Harvard: Harvard UP.

Tuan, L. (2019), 'Paolo Sorrentino's cinematic excess', *Journal of Italian Cinema & Media Studies*, 7:3, pp. 425–42.

Turrioni, M. (2016), 'Che grande bluff il giovane Papa di Sorrentino', *Famiglia cristiana*, 5 September, https://m.famigliacristiana.it/articolo/the-young-pope-sorrentino8451.htm. Accessed 6 November 2019.

Zonch, M. (2017), 'Il testimone di fede: Verità e spiritualità nella narrativa di Saviano', *Incontri. Rivista europea di studi italiani*, 32:1, pp. 50–64.

14

The Young Pope:
Between Television and Celebrity Studies

Anna Manzato

IULM University

Antonella Mascio

University of Bologna

Introduction: Looking at Celebrity Studies[1]

In the panoply of Italian television series that have been produced in recent years, productions such as *Romanzo Criminale* (2008–10), *Gomorrah* (2014–present) and *1992–1993* (2016–17) stand out. These series are well known by a large and global audience, and their popularity is linked to the celebrities in them. Through their participation, these famous actors and directors seem to contribute to adding a value-laden aura that is increasingly sought after in the stories represented on television. Undoubtedly, celebrities become an important component in medial texts. They work as connecting nodes with the other texts they have previously participated in by engendering recognition and intermediality processes; they shift the attention of fan groups towards new productions in which they appear; and they influence the audience's tastes and habits. As stated by Nick Couldry, 'celebrity is part of the related "myth of the media center"' (2016: 98). The theoretical backdrop that has guided the present study, which is specifically focused on the television series *The Young Pope* (2016), has drawn inspiration from celebrity studies – a widely recognized field of studies (especially in the United States and the United Kingdom) that is closely linked to both media and cultural studies. In fact, *The Young Pope* has seen the participation of actors such as Jude Law and Diane

Keaton as its protagonists. Its director is Paolo Sorrentino, another world-famous celebrity. However, before turning to a specific analysis of the chosen text, we would like to briefly explore celebrity culture, a field of study that does not only refer to people wearing the mantle of notoriety, but also and primarily deals with the very concept of 'celebrity': the processes that are moved by it, the meanings that it refers to and its ability to generate 'real-life consequences' (Turner 2010: 14) and produce a 'cross-field effect' (Couldry 2016: 101).

As David Marshall (2006) has highlighted, for several decades now medial systems have been attributed to having the most relevant role in the cultural construction of celebrities. People who become celebrities owe much of their noto-riety to the opportunity they have to appear on television and cinema screens, in newspapers and magazines, on websites and on social media. Celebrities are stud-ied for the developments taking place in these settings, and for the productions that are generated there and the consumption that is fostered. With new technol-ogies and social media, the latest trend for celebrities is that of becoming media (Boccia Artieri 2012): the communication of their images increasingly involves not only the public sphere but also the private or semi-private sphere, thus staging traits of their own (ordinary) everyday lives in a regime of constant connection to the user audience. We can therefore say that 'celebrity' is not only a category of medial texts, but rather a medial representation genre, a *'feature of the discourse'* (Turner 2004, emphasis added), and therefore a construction that is made by the media together with audiences. Its perimeter of incidence and meaning would be changing, so that it takes on new orders of magnitude: from the 'micro' celeb-rity (Marwick and Boyd 2011) to the 'meso' celebrity (Pedroni 2016),[2] which are useful for exploring new logics of social affirmation that are typical of the web. The many definitions that can describe the celebrity 'as representation, as discourse, as an industry and as a cultural formation' (Turner 2010: 13) contribute towards the possibility of considering it as a good interpretation key for medial phenomena: 'the way the social world organizes and commodifies its representa-tions, discourses and ideologies, sensations, impressions and fantasies' (Holmes and Redmond 2010: 1).

Marshall (1997) uses the expression 'the celebrity-commodity' to describe the way in which celebrities are manufactured, marketed and traded. Chris Rojek describes the celebrity as the attribution 'of glamorous or notorious status to an individual within the public sphere' (2001: 10) by using a range of possible spec-ifications to this end: ascribed, achieved (i.e., gained through talent or skills) or attributed (by cultural intermediaries), and celetoids (evanescent, media generated, sometimes accidental) or celeactors (linked to fictional characters).

For current research, the status of the celebrity – and their presumed vulner-ability – has resulted in an important feature in the shift from a noble medium (cinema) to a more popular one (television). By observing the cast of *The Young Pope*, in particular its director and leading actors, we have questioned how the shift from one screen to another could have an impact on the way the celebrity levels are measured. Could we say that the creative process takes into account the presence of specific celebrities who are used to working according to a filmic grammar? In which way do fans participate in the support, implementation or creation of the celebrity aura in Social Network Sites (SNS)? In these settings, how does the relationship between fans and celebrities change? Again: how much impact can mobility, which is typical of 'celevision' (Kavka 2016), have in building a transnational status of celebrities? Could the role of celebrities be considered 'promotional' for the medial products? These are some of the questions that have driven our analysis based on the study of the *The Young Pope* series in its Italian broadcast, by considering a series of texts as a corpus linked to the medial and para-textual discourses that have accompanied it, together with some Facebook pages that have been organized and inhabited by fans.

The Young Pope: *The Celebrity* in *The Text*

Before moving to an analysis of the text, we should provide a better definition of 'celevision', which *The Young Pope* seems to represent as a relevant case. Misha Kavka describes it as a process involving 'the everyday circulation of celebrity through the extensions of television culture as supported by the spread of screen technologies' (2016: 297). If, in fact, up to a few years ago outlining a hierarchy between celebrities coming from the cinema world and celebrities belonging to television seemed to be feasible, today – due to medial convergence and the dissemination of contents on different screens – supporting this separation would be untenable. Mobility, based on new technologies, production modes and social habits, makes the fruition of medial texts possible on any device, thus involving men and women from show business, sports and politics as well. In focusing on the television series, for example, we found, increasingly, cases of actors shifting to and from television and cinema. Kevin Spacey and Robin Wright in *House of Cards* (2013–18), Nicole Kidman in *Big Little Lies* (2017), Bryan Cranston in *Breaking Bad* (2008–13) or Susan Sarandon and Jessica Lange in *Feud* (2017): 'celebrity culture seems to be proliferating along with television's proliferating screens' (Kavka 2016: 296). In taking this reference framework into account, it seems feasible to say that *The Young Pope* displays several examples of 'celevision'; some of these examples belong to the text narrative, while others are linked to its production and implementation. The same product, in being a television series, follows a double track in getting closer to audiences: the viewing setup is typical of television, while the presentation mode seems specifically filmic.

The Young Pope was aired in Italy from 21 October to 18 November 2016 by Sky Atlantic, following the usual programming rules: the episodes were screened every week following the network schedule. It was aired for the first time during the 73rd edition of the Venice Film Festival in 2016, where the screening of the first two episodes was acclaimed by the audience. The authorship mark of director Paolo Sorrentino – world-level celebrity as a recent Academy-Award winner – seems to convey quality and originality to a text that also appears in a non-television context. His direction contributes to ascribing some typical values of the filmic text to the television series: narrative, acting, directing, set design quality and so on. In his first television experience, Sorrentino seems to focus on some specific elements: the use of a specific grammar that makes his style recognizable (many close-ups; a timing that is, at times, overtly slow, and so on) and the presence of well-known actors. *The Young Pope* appears to be a product that is marked by celebrity, which puts whoever is invested in it 'in between' several screens.

The plot tells the story of the papacy of Pius XIII (Jude Law), a fictional character moving within a contemporary setting. The first Pope from the United States – young and extraordinarily handsome – stands out from his predecessors due to his controversial personality; he is a seemingly resolute character, at times capricious and at other times very fragile. The events that are narrated focus on his past and his present, and on the characters that are beside him during his progression, from Cardinal Angelo Voiello, the Vatican's Secretary of State (Silvio Orlando), to Sister Mary (Diane Keaton), to Cardinal Michael Spencer (James Cromwell).

In considering the celebrity culture as our vantage point – and celevision as the category of reference – we can say that the text of *The Young Pope* is rich in relevant elements that enable us to look at the phenomenon from an across-the-board viewpoint. The above-mentioned names, together with those of Javier Cámara, Cécile de France, Ludivine Sagnier and Stefano Accorsi, are part of a group of famous actors who are more closely related to the world of cinema than that of television. This is an international cast and a co-production (HBO, Canal+) that is capable of attracting the attention of Italian and foreign media, and that focuses the discourse on celebrities before discussing the actual product.

Celebrity thus inhabits the text and enhances it through its presence, engendering high expectations in audiences even before the series is broadcast. This is a kind of celebrity that we might be called extra-diegetic: it belongs to the director and actors more than to the text and its characters, and provides the series with an aura and atmosphere that are capable of preparing the audience for its viewing. Another narrative course linked to celebrity develops at the intra-diegetic level. The stages marking the evolution of Pius XIII's character correspond to an increase in popularity among the audience inhabiting the text (the clergy and the faithful) and the television audience. The Pope progressively acquires a biography, a private sphere that makes him interesting: in several instances he shows himself as Lenny Belardo (his birth name), thus laying bare his personal life and frailties.

However, two levels seem to be worthy of further analysis of the Pope's character for us: the first refers to his role as the Catholic religion's highest authority; the second refers to his growth as a charismatic narrative character. Within the framework of the text, Pius XIII becomes famous per se at the moment of his election: this is a great religious event that is followed by worshippers and journalists from all over the world. The depiction of this moment is displayed accurately, on-screen: St. Peter's Square, a symbolic location for Catholic culture, is placed at the centre of the narrative moment, giving Lenny sovereignty, and therefore celebrity, in the religious world that is being portrayed. However, the promotion of his figure, primarily through relations with the merchandising and consumer industry, places Pius XIII in an enigmatic and somewhat unexpected position in terms of celebrity management: the Pope seems to reject it, to be coherent with the Christian teachings that he constantly and learnedly quotes. Indeed, this way of ruling by subtracting his figure produces celebrity as a result: 'Presence is absence' (third episode); 'I'm creating expectation' (fourth episode); '[w]e must revert back to being forbidding, inaccessible and mysterious' (fifth episode). By using the ploy of absence, Lenny fosters a strategic sort of frenzy in the worshippers' audience, as he openly states in his first meeting with the Vatican's head of marketing: 'What is the *fil rouge* linking the most important figures in their respective fields?' – he says, referring to some of the most famous figures of the contemporary world, such as Bansky, Daft Punks and Mina – 'None of them show themselves. None of them want to be photographed'. Celebrities place themselves at the centre of the narrative layout: Lenny portrays a controversial figure that is full of contradictions, especially in how he relates to both his audiences – the clergy and the faithful. Thus, the denial of his image gives him lots of freedom: he can walk around Rome wearing a simple track suit, he can enter a café and be taken for an ordinary man and so on. He seems then to be extremely familiar with the mechanisms comprising the device of celebrity, and uses them with great mastery.

Around the Text: The Paratexts of The Young Pope

The second level of analysis regards the elements that surround the text, that is, what Gérard Genette (1987) calls 'paratext': the paratext is defined as the set of practices that go along with text production and reception, such as physical format or launching. More precisely, the forms that lie outside the text and provide it with a track for comments (advertisement, interviews with the author, reviews) are defined as 'epitext', and contribute to the text's overall meaning.[3] We systematically examined two Italian newspapers, *La Repubblica* and *La Stampa*, from 1 September to 24 December 2016, along with an occasional look at other daily papers – including those online – if their content was relevant. Although the first episode was aired on 21 October, we thought that it was important to begin the analysis in September because of the presentation of the series as a special event at the Venice Film Festival, with Sorrentino, Jude Law and other leading actors from the series in attendance. *The Young Pope* is defined as 'the television project of Paolo Sorrentino, an original production by SKY, HBO, Canal+, sold in 110 countries [...] After the projection for the public seven minutes of ovation are recorded' (Ugolini 2016). An enthusiastic reception also appears outside our sample: the *Wall Street Journal* is reported to have commented on *The Young Pope* as '[t]he Renaissance of Italian television' (Anon. 2016). Following the period under consideration, we continued a less systematic analysis of the press: *The Young Pope*, in fact, continues to appear as a newsworthy element even after the series ended, thus confirming a kind of long wave of interest for the subject. We also considered the website and specials on Sky Atlantic, the channel where the series was aired alongside Sky Cinema Uno: this is, in fact, the institutional place where the readings of the series were constructed for the audience, thus representing a typical case of epitext.

The Press: Making The Young Pope a Celebrity Event

During the period under consideration for our study, the press focuses primarily on Paolo Sorrentino, Jude Law and Silvio Orlando, while less attention is paid to the female character portrayed by Diane Keaton. This simple datum confirms the weight of celebrities in this series: the connotation of the product passes through an international award-winning director and famous international actors. Recurrent words are 'Church', 'Pope', 'religion', 'God', 'spirituality' and 'beauty': the series' subject matter appears to be handled extensively, with detailed comments on the characters and storylines.

As noted before, the press' attention begins during the presentation at the 73rd edition of Venice Film Festival, in September 2016: the series is placed side by side with other successful television products ('a monumental series' [Ugolini 2016a]), but an immediate superposition between cinema and television is thematized. These newspapers report, with great emphasis, a statement from Sorrentino: 'I made a film that is ten hours long, and gave it a harder narrative structure than my previous works'. Moreover, Sorrentino says, 'television has a wider breath, like the great nineteenth-century novel' (Anon. 2017c). Furthermore, *The Young Pope* is defined as 'the latest great film of Sorrentino' (Recalcati 2016). This adoption of a filmic definition also recurs in the television special *The Young Pope: Behind the Scenes* (2016) and represents the key concept for our analysis, centred on celevision. This concept is made possible by the collapsing boundaries between cinema and television; it is an area where characters – but also formal elements – can trespass the threshold between the two media. It is also an area where celebrities can gain visibility and power, thus doubling their presence in both media. The series is even defined as a 'non series' (Ruozzi 2017,), or 'an anti-series, an anti-narration' (Grasso 2016). Attention is also focused on the 10 October 2016 premiere, with Italian Minister Boschi attending: the event is definitely on the press' agenda, and an expectation for the first episode is established.

We then witness both the cultural legitimation of a television product in the cinema area (Menarini 2017) and the difficulty of defining a product that a cinema celebrity comprises in another medium: celevision, once again. There are many interviews with the director and actors, which almost all precede the first episode (see Anon. 2016b, 2016c, 2016d, 2016e, 2016f, 2016g, 2016h, 2017c), in which they talk about the product's peculiarity and, even more, about the leading character Pius XIII: 'Lenny is an open possibility in the face of Catholicism' (Finos 2016).

Irrespective of the thematic level, from our standpoint the interesting data are the short-circuits between movie stars and television personalities (Langer 1981), and the overall construction of a hybrid area where celevision appears to be the key element once again: migrating across screens, directors and actors develop an everyday circulation of celebrities and their enhanced visibility across a socially convergent terrain (Kavka 2016). Considerable attention is paid to the first episode's success: both newspapers comment about the record in terms of audience ('three times superior to *Games of Thrones*' [Ugolini 2016b]) and the number of interactions on Facebook and Twitter ('the Facebook accounts of SkyAtlantic and SkyCinema have generated a social audience of 730.000' [Ugolini 2016b]). At a more general level, many comments in the press use Sorrentino's figure to characterize the series: 'it's a Copernican revolution: you must see the series whether you are Sorrentinians or not [...] there is all the Sorrentinism in this fresco' (Naso 2016); the director is also indicated in the same article as both a pro and a con of *The Young Pope*, which is defined as a series that inspires 'uncompromising hate or blind enthusiasm'. Moreover, the 'magic realism' of Sorrentino produces a personal narrative universe, comprising grotesque and exaggerated portraits, slow rhythms and implausible events that represent both a strong point and a weakness (Pierri 2016). Nevertheless, on the whole, the comments are enthusiastic: 'it's the overturn of every narration made in the last 60 years' (Infelise 2016); Sorrentino is an 'extraordinary talent', who stages 'a saint, a sinner, a Pope, a man' with a high-level direction (Caprara 2016).

After the end of the series, other events related to *The Young Pope*, and particularly to Sorrentino, attract the press' attention: the release of the book *Il peso di Dio* (Sorrentino 2017), which is a collection of Pius XIII phrases, the series' presence at the Roma Fiction Festival in December, an exhibition in Naples of photographs from the set (5 April 2017) and the announcement of the new season, *The New Pope* (19 March 2017). However, the main event covered by the press is the HBO airing in January 2017: 'Record of audience in the United States' (Anon. 2017a), 'America discovers Sorrentino's Pope' (Caprara 2017). The American press and its divergent judgements are also reported by another article in *La Stampa* the same day (Caprara 2017): '"a narrative structure never seen before" (*Variety*), "visually sublime, textually ridiculous" (*New York Times*), "a perfect actor for the role" (*Boston Globe*)'. In an attempt to sum up press behaviour towards *The Young Pope*, we can say that attention has been paid to the whole production cycle, from the preview, to the launching in the United States in January 2017, to the announcement of a second season in spring 2017. We could define the overall coverage as the construction of a celebrity event, starting from the centrality of directors and actors in the press narration. We can now add that the entire series assumes the connotation of a special event due to its characters and peculiar theme; celebrity, in this sense, can be attributed not only to individuals who take part in the series, but also more generally to the product itself, which takes on a peculiar resonance thanks to the superposition of cinema and television. It is Sorrentino's prominence and Jude Law's figure, their notoriety and shifting across different screens, that develop a celevision success. Moreover, the collateral events reported after the series ending correspond to a general construction of an aura that depicts *The Young Pope* as an 'anomalous' and yet intriguing product.

The Institutional Point of View

From the production side, we considered two kinds of data that drive the audience to a specific reading of the series, and thus construct the connotation of *The Young Pope* that is preferred from an institutional point of view: the television specials aired by Sky, and the Facebook accounts of Sky Atlantic and Sky Cinema. The television specials were aired the day before the first episodes (*The Young Pope: Behind the Scenes*), immediately before the first episodes (*The Young Pope Speciale* [2016]) and before the last episode (*The Young Pope: A Tale of Filmmaking* [2016]). All the products have a documentary format that focuses on Sorrentino, with images of the shootings, often without comments.

The most interesting among the three cases is *The Young Pope Speciale*, an alternation of close-ups of the director and actors and sequences from the series. Each actor explains his character, and once again Sorrentino has the opportunity to make a key feature of his work explicit: according to the director, Lenny Belardo is 'a complex character' and the series is 'a very long film about solitude'. Furthermore, the director talks about the genesis of his work, the choice of actors, his opinion about the relationship between cinema and literature, while Jude Law says he performed as 'an orphan, not a Pope', pointing to the complex mixture of faith and doubt in Pius XIII. So the audience gains an overview of the series' themes and tones not only before viewing it but also at its ending, thus closing the circle of interpretation with an intended point of view. Overall, the three documentaries demonstrate Sky's great investments in this product: an international co-production, aired on the channel that hosts quality drama, and simultaneously on the cinema channel (celevision, again), which requires enormous support due to its quality. This has been the case for other serial products by Sky,[4] such as *Gomorrah*.

The same aim of directing the audience's interpretation can be found on the Sky Atlantic and Sky Cinema websites. In the first instance, they show a lot of photographs of Lenny and the other characters, along with videos from the episodes and the shootings, episodes' reviews and news: from the marathon on Christmas Day, to Jude Law's birthday, to the release of the book *Il peso di Dio*. There is also a part dedicated to fan art, thus stressing the audience's participation in the programme. Overall, the institutional point of view aims at creating an aura around the programme: 'an event series', 'the new masterpiece series', *The Young Pope* is depicted as an exceptional TV event that no one can miss. The advertisements that appeared in the press also follow this trend. A full page picture shows Pius XIII walking in a pool, surrounded by the captions taken from Italian and foreign press: 'A Pope like Lenny Belardo was never seen before' (*Vanity Fair*), 'Law offers us his best interpretation ever in the character of the enigmatic Pope' (*The Times*), 'Sorrentino's contradictory and smoker Pope conquers Venice' (*Il Messaggero*). The names that appear are those of the best known: Jude Law, Diane Keaton and of course Paolo Sorrentino. Celebrities are at the centre of the communicative strategy: high-profile actors, high-profile director and enthusiastic reception all over the world: the celebrity event is ready to be celebrated.

The Reception of Celebrity

If in the previous paragraph we dealt with celebrity construction in celevision, our third level of analysis regards the appropriation of celebrity by the audience: what kind of engagement emerges on the side of spectatorship? How has *The Young Pope* been commented, appropriated and elaborated? How is the celebrity-series valorized? To answer these questions, we have analysed two Facebook pages dedicated to the series: 'The Young Pope Italia' and 'The Young Pope ITA', considering both the posts and the comments. Also in this case, as we did regarding the press, we extended our analysis from the strict period of the airing to more recent posts, which confirm what we previously said about newspapers: attention for the Facebook profile does not stop with the end of the episodes, instead extending to the announcement of the new season in May 2017, and giving notice that Sorrentino was awarded the Nastro d'argento (Silver Ribbon) in June 2017.[5] In the first place, our results demonstrate contents that reverberate the series timing: promos and reviews follow the line of the episodes, thus defining a kind of engagement that is more televisual than social. The weekly reports look more like the old television reception mode that is tied to precise schedule appointments than the 'anywhere, anytime' mode linked to the spread of new reception types made possible by the evolution of technologies and devices.

As for the visual aspect, the images are mostly of Lenny, even if other characters are present, like Cardinal Voiello first and foremost, who is performed by Silvio Orlando. Many posts deal with linguistic elements such as the music or the opening titles: reflections on the use of artistic masterpieces or the sudden popularity of an old song by Italian pop singer Nada used in one episode can be found. Moreover, many posts repeat phrases by Lenny and the characters, which become specific attributes of their personalities ('first-rate' Silvio Orlando). Comments by followers (The Young Pope ITA n.d.; The Young Pope Italia n.d.) show a definite polarization around Sorrentino ('genial genius', 'a legend and a genius') and Jude Law ('very much intriguing', 'the perfect Pope', 'excellent', 'magnetic'), who appears as the leading subject starting with Episode 4. Topics include his physical beauty and his character's personality.[6] Secondary characters and especially female characters appear in the background. The emotional tone rises up following the series' ending, with frequent complaints and a general appreciation for the announcement of a second season, even if it is not still clear whether Lenny will be the main character again, since the final scene is open to different interpretations (and the comments are quite numerous on this point as well).

What kind of use of *The Young Pope* can be found, then, on social media? One clear occurrence regards an (almost) total love for the series in a relationship of (almost only) enthusiastic approval of the product. Even if some negative comments can be found ('boring', 'eccentric'), starting with the earliest comments, the greatest proportion of Facebook users insist on positive judgements: 'everything absolutely perfect', 'best series ever', 'the true cinema in TV', 'a real masterpiece', 'out of schemes', 'measure and madness', 'extraordinary' (The Young Pope ITA n.d.; The Young Pope Italia n.d.). In other words, excess seems to be the key element in the appropriation of *The Young Pope*, both in positive and in negative terms.

Another interesting piece of data regards what seems to be a complete appropriation of the celebrity features: users comment on the series, but mostly on the two stars of *The Young Pope*: Sorrentino and especially Jude Law. This focalization on a movie star confirms, in our opinion, what Chris Rojek (2001) says about the increasing importance of the public face in everyday life: celebrity culture relies on favourable public recognition and, in the case of celevision, this public recognition doubles the original filmic area into the televisual one, expanding its audience and enlarging its borders. If we talk about *Complex TV* (Mittell 2015) to describe transmedia storytelling, orienting paratexts and new authorialities, then the concept of celebrity may not be inconsistent with this scenario: the construction and reception of celebrity, by the paratextual level and the social network level, seems to enter into this new televisual scape, and television can also be an important element in its analysis.

Conclusions

As we have discussed above, *The Young Pope* is a typical text of complex television (Mittell 2015), where features linked to the celebrity culture clearly emerge at different stages. The double – and blurred – cinema-television level and the participation of a famous cast and director become essential elements in the product's construction. The medial story, or the way in which the media have talked about *The Young Pope*, is based precisely on these elements as we have stressed in our analysis, by first presenting the audience with a sort of quality certification that is based primarily on a group of participating celebrities.

While the episodes are being broadcast, the audiences liven up and speak out, together with the media. Our analysis of Facebook pages has shown how much interest viewers had for the series, and it generated a related traffic consisting of textual, visual and audio-visual messages. The effectiveness of online participatory culture is mirrored in the making of celevision: in social settings we find a participation-based and multi-screen narrative of celebrities, in particular focused on Jude Law – Lenny Belardo. Celevision thus appears to be a phenomenon that, besides taking into account medial resonance, also becomes possible thanks to audience appropriation.

To conclude this analysis we would like to highlight in *The Young Pope* two levels of 'celebrity' presence. The first, which has been highlighted several times during our analysis, refers to the celebrity status that participating actors and the director already had, and that also has an impact on the texts. The second level coincides instead with the textual perimeter: here it is the Lenny Belardo character managing his celebrity strategically. In this progression, the young Pope acts as a guide for the audience, interpreting a pedagogical function, thus showing the opportunities that the 'celebrity' device provides. It should also be emphasized that two important orders of 'celebrity' are found, superimposed, in the text: one belongs to the religious realm and the other to show business. Pius XIII's character – precisely because it is played by Jude Law – takes the two roles upon himself and strengthens them, thus turning into the summa of the religious cult and the celebrity cult (Rojek 2001). The portrayal of a symbolic power, embodied by the Pope, also determines the power 'of constructing reality' (Bourdieu 1991: 166), therefore both inside and outside the text. In fact, this overlapping is so well highlighted in the media discourse that during the broadcasting of the series, ongoing comparisons between Pope Bergoglio and Pope Belardo were presented, thus creating imaginary exchanges between the two (Anon. 2016a). Thus, a celebrity capital put to test can be observed, 'which works in particular fields related to the other types of media-related capital' (Couldry 2016: 104).

The construction of celebrity in the text is then organized by taking into consideration several reference areas: show business, which the well-known names already belong to, and religion, which helps to define in the story-telling a series of features typical of celebrity, such as the relationship with audiences, managing famous people, rituals and large Church events (one of each is put into every episode: the Pope's election, the Pope's first speech, the travels abroad…) – and so on. Obviously there is the construction of the series' main character, Pope Pius XIII, who chooses to become famous through denial, and at the same time reveals himself only in the privacy of relationships with the characters who are closest to him. These levels of celebrity follow one another and contribute to the success of the text by exploiting the ongoing shifting of the screens, as highlighted in the analysis of para-textual materials: the discourse about Lenny Belardo is often paired with a remark about the actor Jude Law's artistry and beauty, and a reference to Pope Francis' speeches and policies.

In these practices we can find the expression of what Couldry defines as media 'metacapital', 'through which *media* exercise power over other forms of power' (2016: 102, original emphasis): many features of celebrity culture are an expression of this (Driessens 2013). Besides being attractors of audiences, celebrities then appear to be part of a complex medial process comprising cultural phenomena and impacting the social realm through the deployment of symbolic power, as the case of *The Young Pope* has shown.

NOTES

1. The article is a work of both the authors. Specifically Anna Manzato wrote the parts 'Around the text: the paratexts of *The Young Pope*', 'The press: making *The Young Pope* a celebrity event', 'The institutional point of view' and 'The reception of celebrity'; Antonella Mascio wrote: 'Introduction. Looking at Celebrity Studies', '*The Young Pope*: the celebrity in the text' and 'Conclusions'.

2. Marco Pedroni uses the 'meso-celebrity' concept to describe some particular cases of fashion bloggers: 'The meso-celebrities are described as occupying a position far from both the few celebrities in the field and the thousands of micro-celebrities who live in the shadows of the web' (2016: 103).

3. Genette talks about the various productions that surround and extend the text: 'This accompainment, of variable scope and modes, is what I call the paratext' (1987: 3). The epitext is defined as 'any paratextual element which is not annexed to the text, but that somehow circulates freely, in a virtually unlimited physical and social space' (1987: 337).

4. On the specific features of pay television series production, and especially the case of Sky Italia, see Barra and Scaglioni (2013).

5. On this occasion, a post in *The Young Pope ITA* reports, stresses again the closeness between cinema and television: 'series can become new authorial films' (Anon. 2017b).

6. The fictional dimension of celebrity, that is comments about characters, in this case replaces what Redmond (2014: 13) calls 'celebaesthetic', that is, the sensorial and emotional dimension tied to the celebrity body.

REFERENCES

1992–1993 (2015–17, Italy: Sky Atlantic and Sky).

Anon (2016a), 'Aborto, il dialogo immaginario tra papa Francesco e Jude Law', *Corriere della* Sera, 21 November, http://corriere.it/spettacoli/16_novembre_21/aborto-dialogo-immaginario-papa-francesco-jude-law-sorrentino-young-pope-ab8171ea-b006-11e6-a471-71884d41097a.shtml. Accessed 7 November 2017.

Anon (2016b), 'Interview with Paolo Sorrentino', *La Repubblica*, 26 September, https://repubblica.it/venerdi/interviste/2016/09/26/news/papalepapaleintervistaapaolosorrentino-sutheyoungpope-148575057/. Accessed 7 November 2017.

Anon (2016c), 'Interview with Jude Law', *La Repubblica*, 20 October, https://www.repubblica.it/spettacoli/tv-radio/2016/10/20/news/the_young_pope_sorrentino_jude_law-150149369/. Accessed 7 November 2017.

Anon (2016d), 'Interview with Silvio Orlando', *La Repubblica*, 1 October, https://repubblica.it/spettacoli/tv-radio/2016/10/01/news/youngpopesilvioorlando-148867567/. Accessed 7 November 2017.

Anon (2016e), 'Interview with Diane Keaton', *La Repubblica*, 17 November, https://repubblica.it/spettacoli/cinema/2015/11/17/news/diane-127528929/?ref=search. Accessed 7 November 2017.

Anon (2016f), 'Interview with Jude Law', *La Stampa*, 20 October, https://lastampa.it/2016/10/20/spettacoli/jude-law-adesso-so-il-latino-e-mi-faccio-domande-sulla-vita-e-sudio-xbqziclNMv8RN1qfGl80EM/pagina.html. Accessed 7 November 2017.

Anon (2016g), 'Interview with Silvio Orlando', *La Stampa*, 5 November, https://lastampa.it/2016/11/05/alessandria/il-cardinale-voiello-di-the-young-pope-sar-al-teatro-civico-con-uno-spettacolo-sul-disamore-q6sPSj8sZVwkJE0NJwoqSJ/pagina.html. Accessed 7 November 2017.

Anon (2016h), 'Interview with Paolo Sorrentino', *La Stampa*, 25 November, https://lastampa.it/2016/11/25/spettacoli/paolo-sorrentino-me-ne-sono-andato-da-napoli-per-stanchezza-gvnKqYE9VpmCfDkcVRgjpL/pagina.html. Accessed 7 November 2017.

Anon (2016i), '*The Young Pope a Venezia*', *Corriere della Sera*, 16 September, https://www.corriere.it/spettacoli/16_settembre_03/mostra-cinema-venezia-2016-papa-provocatorio-sorrentino-012eb5c4-71bb-11e6-a5ab-6335286216cb.shtml. Accessed 7 November 2017.

Anon (2017a), 'Record di ascolti USA per *The Young Pope*', *La Repubblica*, 18 January, https://www.repubblica.it/spettacoli/tv-radio/2017/01/18/news/record_di_ascolti_in_usa_per_the_young_pope_-156335797/. Accessed 7 November 2017.

Anon (2017b), 'The Young Pope ITA', Facebook, 24 February, https://facebook.com/theyoungpopita/. Accessed 2 November 2017.

Anon (2017c), 'Interview with Paolo Sorrentino', *La Repubblica*, 8 April, https://www.repubblica.it/spettacoli/cinema/2017/04/08/news/paolo_sorrentino_berlusconi_the_young_pope-162457314/?ref=search. Accessed 7 November 2017.

Barra, L. and Scaglioni, M. (eds) (2013), *Tutta un'altra fiction: La serialità pay in Italia e nel mondo: Il modello Sky*, Rome: Carocci.

Boccia Artieri, G. (2012), *Stati di connessione*, Milan: Franco Angeli.

Bourdieu, J. (1991), *Language and Symbolic Power*, Cambridge: Polity.

Caprara, F. (2016), '*The Young Pope* di Sorrentino da record: Ecco perché ci è piaciuto il primo episodio', *La Stampa*, 22 October, https://lastampa.it/2016/10/22/spettacoli/young-pope-di-sorrentino-incanta-ecco-perch-ci-piaciuto-il-episodio-Hpgae1gg9hTG5h4fEy1FIM/pagina.html. Accessed 7 November 2017.

Caprara, F. (2017), '*The Young Pope*, buona la prima: Al debutto USA batte Homeland', La Stampa, 19 January, https://lastampa.it/2017/01/19/spettacoli/the-young-pope-buona-la-prima-al-debutto-usa-batte-homeland-LRAzkyX1OjTW1kXqueaxTK/pagina.html. Accessed 7 November 2017.

Couldry, N. (2016), 'Celebrity, convergence and the fate of media institutions', in P. D. Marshall and S. Redmond (eds), *A Companion to Celebrity*, London: Wiley, pp. 98–113.

Driessens, O. (2013), 'Celebrity capital: Redefining celebrity using field theory', *Theory and Society*, 42:5, pp. 543–560.

Elkann, A. (2017), 'Paolo Sorrentino: "Siamo tutti soli. Il cinema è fatto per consolarci"', La Stampa, 5 March, https://lastampa.it/2017/03/05/societa/siamo-tutti-soli-il-cinema-fatto-per-consolarci-kArSLMHrts2oFD2jBrC2bJ/pagina.html. Accessed 7 November 2017.

Finos, A. (2016), 'Il Young Pope di Sorrentino: Ai cattolici piacerà se lo guarderanno come si fa con un quadro', La Repubblica, 10 October, https://repubblica.it/spettacoli/tv-radio/2016/10/10/news/sorrentino-149415120/. Accessed 7 November 2017.

Genette, G. (1987), *Seuils*, Paris: Seuil.

Grasso, A. (2016), 'Il Papa di Sorrentino: Un antiracconto troppo compiaciuto', Corriere della Sera, 21 November, https://www.corriere.it/spettacoli/16_novembre_21/papa-sorrentino-antiracconto-troppo-compiaciuto-175cae78-af3c-11e6-8815-37f3520714e8.shtml. Accessed 7 November 2017.

Holmes, S. and Redmond, S. (2010), 'A journal in celebrity studies', *Celebrity Studies*, 1:1, pp. 1–10, http://tandfonline.com/doi/abs/10.1080/19392390903519016. Accessed 7 November 2017.

Infelise, A. (2016), 'Con il papa cattivo Sorrentino fa ascolti da record', La Stampa, 23 October, https://lastampa.it/2016/10/23/cultura/con-il-papa-cattivo-sorrentino-fa-ascolti-da-record-1eLm3Ey81Z7Qh5OyDPjBdK/pagina.html. Accessed 7 November 2017.

Kavka, M. (2016), 'Celevision: Mobilizations of the television screen', in P. D. Marshall and S. Redmond (eds), *A Companion to Celebrity*, London: Wiley, pp. 295–314.

Langer, J. (1981), 'Television's personality system', *Media, Culture & Society*, 3:4, pp. 351–365.

Marshall, P. D. (1997), *Celebrity and Power: Fame in Contemporary Culture*, Minneapolis: University of Minnesota Press.

Marshall, P. D. (2006) (ed.), *The Celebrity Culture Reader*, London: Routledge.

Marwick, A. and Boyd, D. (2011), 'To see and be seen: Celebrity practice on Twitter', *Convergence*, 17:2, pp. 139–58, http://journals.sagepub.com/doi/pdf/10.1177/1354856510394539. Accessed 7 November 2017.

Menarini, R. (2017), 'It aliano/internazionale: Paolo Sorrentino e il caso *The Young Pope*, ricezioni critiche a confronto', International Congress Innovations and Tensions. Italian Cinema and Media in a Global World, Rome, 9–10 June.

Mittel, J. (2015), *Complex TV: The Poetics of Contemporary Television Storytelling*, New York: New York University Press.

Naso, D. (2016), '*The Young Pope*, che siate sorrentiniani o no guardate la serie: È una rivoluzione copernicana', Il fatto quotidiano, 22 October, https://ilfattoquotidiano.it/2016/10/22/the-young-pope-che-siate-sorrentiniani-o-no-guardate-la-serie-e-una-rivoluzione-copernicana/3114847/. Accessed 7 November 2017.

Pedroni, M. (2016), 'Meso-celebrities, fashion and the media: How digital influencers struggle for visibility', *Film, Fashion & Consumption*, 5:1, pp. 103–121, http://ingentaconnect.com/content/intellect/ffc/2016/00000005/00000001/art00008. Accessed 7 November 2017.

Pierri, M. (2016), '*The Young Pope*, pro e contro della serie tv di Paolo Sorrentino', Wired, 8 November, https://wired.it/play/televisione/2016/11/08/young-pope-serie-tv-sorrentino/. Accessed 7 November 2017.

Recalcati, M. (2016), 'La ferita del giovane Papa potrà diventare poesia', La Repubblica, 18 November, https://www.repubblica.it/spettacoli/tv-radio/2016/11/18/news/young_pope_ferita_giovane_papa_diventa_poesia-152274959/. Accessed 7 November 2017.

Redmond, S. (2014), *Celebrity and the Media*, Basingstoke: Palgrave Macmillan.

Rojek, C. (2001), *Celebrity*, London: Reaktion Books.

Romanzo Criminale (2008–10, Italy: Sky Cinema and Sky).

Ruozzi, F. (2017), '*The Young Pope*: L'anno dei tre papi', Micromega, 4 January, http://temi.repubblica.it/micromega-online/the-young-pope-l%E2%80%99anno-dei-tre-papi/. Accessed 7 November 2017.

Siri, S. (2017), 'L'America scopre il Papa di Sorrentino: È come Trump', La Stampa, 19 January, https://lastampa.it/2017/01/17/spettacoli/lamerica-scopre-il-papa-di-sorrentino-come-trump-roob0Xb79E6wAWZEZwOFgL/pagina.html. Accessed 7 November 2017.

Sorrentino, P. (2017), Il peso di Dio. Il vangelo di Lenny Berardo, Turin: Einaudi.

The Young Pope: A Tale of Filmmaking (2016, Italy: Sky Atlantic).

The Young Pope: Behind the Scenes (2016, Italy: Sky Uno).

The Young Pope ITA (n.d.), Facebook, https://facebook.com/theyoungpopita/. Accessed 4 June 2019.

The Young Pope Italia (n.d.), Facebook, https://www.facebook.com/santissimolenny/?__tn__=%2Cd%2CP-R&eid=ARA71ViXj6krzXPoNSTxbcuf4373dq5fFBDiDChvGDWoZTMYYJwOmsE8Yoz5ce28NVznMPu6fdMuvnAm. Accessed 4 June 2019.

The Young Pope Speciale (2016, Italy: Sky Atlantic).

Turner, G. (2004), *Understanding Celebrity*, London: Sage.

Turner, G. (2010), 'Approaching celebrity studies', *Celebrity Studies*, 1:1, pp. 11–20, http://tandfonline.com/doi/abs/10.1080/19392390903519024). Accessed 7 November 2017.

Ugolini, C. (2016a), '*The Young Pope*: House of Cards in Vaticano', La Repubblica, 3 September, http://repubblica.it/speciali/cinema/venezia/edizione2016/2016/09/03/news/houseofcardsin-vaticanosorrentinoilmiopapanoneunaprovocazione–147118370. Accessed 7 November 2017.

Ugolini, C. (2016b), '*The Young Pope* da record, + 45% di Gomorra nella prima puntata', La Repubblica, 22 October, https://www.repubblica.it/spettacoli/tv-radio/2016/10/22/news/_the_young_pope_da_record_quasi_il_doppio_del_debutto_di_gomorra_-150331547/. Accessed 7 November 2017.

15

Interview with Carlo Poggioli

Author: Annachiara Mariani
Date and location: 1 August 2019 at Cinecittà (Rome, Italy)

Biography

Carlo Poggioli was born in Torre Annunziata, a suburb of Naples. After graduating from the Academy of Fine Arts in Naples, he moved to Rome and started his professional training at the costumier's Tirelli Costumi. There, he began work as an assistant for several renowned costume designers: Gabriella Pescucci (*The Name of the Rose, The Adventures of Baron Munchausen, The Age of Innocence*, etc.), Piero Tosi (*History of a Blackcap*), Maurizio Millenotti (*The Voice of The Moon*). Moreover, Poggioli worked with Ann Roth on *The English Patient* and *The Talented Mr. Ripley*, with Federico Fellini on *The Voice of The Moon*, with Martin Scorsese on *The Age of Innocence*, and Franco Zeffirelli on *History of a Blackcap*. He made his debut in theatre with Luca Ronconi. For several years now he has been collaborating with Ruggero Cappuccio, with whom he has worked on many plays and operas including *Falstaff, Nina pazza per amore* produced by the Teatro alla Scala, and *Don Calandrino* at the Salzburger Festspiele, all directed by Riccardo Muti. He has worked on about 40 films, including international television productions such as *Cold Mountain* by Anthony Minghella, *The Brothers Grimm* and *Zero Theorem* by Terry Gilliam, and *Divergent* by Neil Burger. He teamed up with Paolo Sorrentino on *Youth, Loro, The Young Pope* and *The New Pope*. The film *Loro* earned him a nomination for best costume design at the 2019 David di Donatello film awards. Finally, Poggioli is President of the A.S.C. (Italian Association of Costume Designers and Interior Decorators).

Awards

2008 Genie Award for Best Achievement in Costume Design – *Silk* – Won (with Kazuko Kurosawa)

2005 Saturn Award for Best Costumes – *Van Helsing* – Nominated (with Gabriella Pescucci)

2005 Silver Ribbon for Best Costume Design – *Van Helsing* – Nominated (with Gabriella Pescucci)

2004 BAFTA Award for Best Costume Design – *Cold Mountain* – Nominated (with Ann Roth)

2002 Emmy Award for Outstanding Costumes for a Miniseries, Movie or a Special – *The Mists of Avalon* – Nominated (with Giovanni Casalnuovo and Lindsay Pugh)

Interview

Mariani: Can you describe your career path so far?

Poggioli: I was born with a passion for theatre and for cinema. Even though no one in my family has ever been involved in the theatre or film business, I have always been fascinated by these art forms. As a child, I was lucky that my family regularly took me to the opera at the San Carlo Theatre in Naples. My parents loved the theatre and opera, and they went regularly. To begin with, I got bored because I was only four or five years old. Little by little, my passion grew, and I learned to love the performances. My mother was fond of Eduardo de Filippo, so we went to all of his plays at the San Ferdinando Theatre in Naples, with Pupilla Maggio as the lead actress. I know a lot of de Filippo's plays by heart, thanks to the passion my parents instilled in me. Later on, I attended the Art Institute in Torre Annunziata, and finally the Academy of Fine Arts in Naples. As soon as I got my diploma from the Academy, I decided to move to Rome to look for a job because it clearly offered far more opportunities in the film industry than Naples. Some friends of mine had an apartment in Rome that I was able to rent, so I moved there with Sasà, a dear friend of mine who is still working with me after all these years. After we moved, our adventure began. We had no contacts in Rome who could help us. It was very hard initially because we arrived in Rome at the beginning of the 1980s and the film industry was undergoing a 'critical period'. Luckily, a few costume design firms contacted us and I went to work for Tirelli, one of the world's greatest names. At Tirelli, I worked as an assistant designer for some of the most important Italian costume designers, such as Gabriella Pescucci, Piero Tosi and Maurizio Millenotti. I worked on several films: J. J. Annaud's *The Name of the Rose* (1986), Terry Gilliam's *The Adventures of Baron Munchausen* (1988), Martin Scorsese's *The Age of Innocence* (1993), Franco Zeffirelli's *Sparrow* (1993) and Federico Fellini's *The Voice of the Moon* (1990). Working with Fellini for over a year marked me deeply; we were also neighbours in Rome, and we became good friends. He asked me to help him with other projects and I was always happy to help him out. After Fellini's death in 1993, I continued working with Gabriella Pescucci for many years. I also worked alongside Ann Roth as assistant on *The English Patient* (1996), and as associate designer for *The Talented Mr. Ripley* (1999) and *Cold Mountain* (2003), directed by Anthony Minghella. Unfortunately, although we had planned to collaborate on more films, Minghella died suddenly in 2008. As a costume designer for film and television, I have designed costumes for *Marquise* (1997) directed by Vera Belmont, *Jason and the Argonauts* (2004) and *The Mists of Avalon* (2001) directed by Uli Edel, *Van Helsing* (2004) directed by Steven Sommers, *Doom* (2005) directed by Andrzej Bartkowiak, *The Fine Art Of Love: Mine-Haha* (2005) directed by John Irvin, *The Inquiry* (2006) directed by Giulio Base and *The Brothers Grimm* (2005) directed by Terry Gilliam. My most recent films are: *Romeo and Juliet* (2013) directed by Carlo Carlei, *The Zero Theorem* (2013) directed by Terry Gilliam, *The Raven* (2012) by James McTeigue, *The Rite* (2011) by Mikael Håfström, *Season of the Witch* (2011) by Dominic Sena, *Miracle at St. Anna* (2008) by Spike Lee and *Divergent* (2014) directed by Neil Burger. Five years ago, I met Paolo Sorrentino and we worked on his film *Youth* (2015), then on the TV series *The Young Pope* (2016), the film *Loro* (2018) and we've just finished *The New Pope* (2019). Last summer, I worked on a very interesting film by Siro Guerra, called *Waiting for the Barbarians* (2019), filmed in Morocco and starring Johnny Depp, Mark Rylance and Robert Pattinson. This film had its world premiere at the Venice Film Festival on 6 September 2019.

Mariani: In an interview with Valentina De Giorgi for the docuseries *Meet the Hollywood costume designers*,[1] you said that 'the costume designer's task is to help the actor become the character he/she has to play'. Can you give us a specific example of this concept in relation to Sorrentino's films?

Poggioli: Sorrentino's films are different from those by the other directors I've worked with. Paolo is not just the director, he is also the screenwriter of his films. Therefore, when he writes the script, he has a very clear idea of how he wants his characters to be, of their personalities and their clothing. As he is a very intelligent artist, he is always open to my suggestions and ideas on the actors' attire. Analysing my designs, we discuss the way I visualize the characters. We work extremely well together because when we exchange our ideas we build and transform the characters together. Paolo usually accepts my input on the characters. However, the most crucial moment is when we try the costumes on the actors. Sometimes, it happens that the actors do not like what we have visualized for them. At times, they say that the outfits do not help them 'become' the character. However, this decisive phase always goes very smoothly in Paolo's films because he works very closely with the actors he casts. So, when the actors arrive on set, they are already familiar with their costumes. I show them my designs, the fabrics and prepare them for their cinematic transformation. Sometimes we have to alter an actor's body shape, with prosthetic bellies, humps and so on. Sometimes, we need to give an actor with a lot of hair a bald head. The most important part of my job is to create the best costume for the actors and help them 'morph' into their fictional roles.

Mariani: Was it challenging to help Jude Law 'assume' the Pope's role?

Poggioli: Jude Law was very curious and involved in his role as Pope. He knew very well that it would not be easy to 'become' such a big character. I'll tell you about one peculiar anecdote that surprised me a little. Here in Cinecittà, he was filming the famous scene of his entrance into the Sistine Chapel before his address to the Cardinals. As you may recall, he was wearing a papal tiara encrusted with jewels, an ornately decorated three-tiered conical crown and a very heavy cloak. The papal tiara he was wearing was modelled on the one Pope Paul VI donated to Washington in 1964, abandoning the tradition of wearing that very heavy crown that caused headaches and made it difficult to move. Even though I had used the lightest fabric and materials possible to recreate the tiara and the cloak, his costume was still extremely heavy. I remember that the filming for that scene took place during the month of August, and I apologized to Jude for how very hot he must have felt underneath his costume. I was very impressed when he told me not to worry. In fact, he was happy to be wearing such heavy clothing because it helped him to realize the weight the popes had to bear with the immense responsibility of leading the Catholic Church. Jude's answer struck me deeply because I had never received such an insightful remark during my work before, and I will always remember it.

Mariani: Let's talk about the film *Loro*. How did you help Toni Sevillo 'inhabit' the character of Silvio Berlusconi?

Poggioli: For this particular film, I had to work on the physicality of the character. When the actor has to portray and resemble an historical character, it's the job of the costume designer to recreate his external appearance, including any physical defects. Since Toni Servillo is slimmer than Silvio Berlusconi, I had to create a prosthetic belly for him. Even using the lightest material possible, the belly was still cumbersome and slightly uncomfortable to wear since the film was shot in the summer. Moreover, Toni had to sit for makeup for several hours every morning to make him look like Berlusconi. So, although it can't have been easy for him to film using prosthetics and makeup, he was always appreciative, cordial and professional as real artists are.

Mariani: What is the most pleasing aspect of your job as costume designer?

Poggioli: The most enjoyable aspect is when I finally see my planning and designs realized on screen. The elaborate process of devising a character takes a very long time, and people do not realize that. This involves several stages, including: talking to the directors, drawing the costumes with hairstyles and makeup, choosing the fabrics, having the tailors create them, trying the costumes on the actors, adjusting them if needed and finally checking how they look on screen. I usually see some little things I'd like to improve in my creations, but that's normal. I always wish I could start over, but it is still very rewarding to see the actors on screen looking the way I'd visualized them.

Mariani: You work in cinema, theatre, opera and television. Can you explain how creating costumes for these art forms differs?

Poggioli: Clearly, working in cinema requires a closer attention to detail because close-ups and medium shots demand precision and meticulous attention to even the smallest stitch or decoration. On the other hand, in the theatre or opera, since there is a certain distance between the audience and the stage, the spectators cannot see every detail of the performers' costumes. However, there is not much difference for me because I work with obsessive precision in every art form. Perhaps I pay closer attention to form and colour in my work for the theatre because the audience has a wider point of view of the whole scene and it is important to create visual balance. The viewers 'consume' films more quickly, so it is less important to find balance as a whole, but it is paramount to attain precision in every detail.

Mariani: Do you prefer to create historical costumes or contemporary ones?

Poggioli: It depends. Obviously, creating costumes for both types of characters requires a lot of research and study, so the process is similar. Perhaps I prefer creating costumes for period films because it allows me to play with them, allowing me free reign for my creativity and the ability to make my own decisions. Instead, when I work on a film with contemporary characters, a lot of people have an opinion about my choices, and it's harder to please everyone. However, sometimes directors have their own ideas of how an historical character should look. If they have a particular painting or picture in mind, they may wonder how and why we chose to dress a character a particular way. Of course, this situation is rare.

Mariani: Finally, can you comment on your work with Paolo Sorrentino?

Poggioli: There is great chemistry between Paolo and I. First of all, we are both from Naples and that alone means a lot because I think that people from Naples have a different outlook on life. Moreover, since Paolo is a director and screenwriter, he has very clear ideas on how everything has to be handled. I really like working with him because we are always confident about what we want, and we immediately understand each other. We have been working together for several years and we know each other so well that when we start working on a new film or TV series, we know exactly what we want and how to achieve it without too much discussion. This is extremely important because we don't often have a lot of time to prepare for a film, so our mutual understanding allows us to work efficiently and at our best. I think highly of Paolo Sorrentino as a director, and I enjoyed his films even before I met him, so I understood his poetics and his approach to films quickly. Therefore, I knew exactly what was expected of me and how to meet Paolo's expectations.

NOTE

1. Here is the link for De Giorgi's interview: https://www.aesseci.org/component/k2/item/39-carlo-poggioli-a-life-between-hollywood-and-cinecitta-and-a-sexy-pope.

Notes on Contributors

Michela Barisonzi has a Ph.D. in Italian studies from Monash University (Melbourne, Australia), a BA in translation and interpretation, and three MAs respectively in foreign literatures and cultures, international relations, and teaching. Her current research is centred on nineteenth-century Italian literature and gender discourse with a focus on rape and violence against women. Other areas of research include Italian cinema, the juridical language of skilled migration in the European Union and Australian governmental frameworks, and the language of political discourse in South America. In 2019 she published a book on sexuality, hysteria, and adultery in the novels of Gabriele D'Annunzio, and she has published various articles and presented papers based on nineteenth-century Italian literature and contemporary Italian cinema at several national and international conferences.

Mimmo Cangiano received his Ph.D. from Duke University. He has been 'Lauro De Bosis' postdoctoral fellow at Harvard University and he taught as an assistant professor at The Hebrew University of Jerusalem. He currently teaches at Colgate University. His publications include the books *L'Uno e il molteplice nel giovane Palazzeschi (1905–1915)*, *La nascita del modernismo italiano. Filosofie della crisi, storia e letteratura (1903–1922)*, and *The Wreckage of Philosophy: Carlo Michelstaedter and the Limits of Bourgeois Thought*. A specialist of nineteenth- and twentieth-century Italian culture, he has published essays dedicated to authors such as Pirandello, Michelstaedter, Boine, Soffici, Gozzano, Prezzolini, Sanguineti, Rosi, Wu Ming, as well as articles dedicated to the relationships between Italian and Austrian culture, and to prominent Marxist theoreticians such as György Lukács and Antonio Gramsci.

Monica Facchini is an associate professor of Italian and film and media studies at Colgate University. Her main research interests include Italian cinema and literature, and her approach is interdisciplinary, spanning from film studies to visual arts, cultural anthropology and postcolonialism. Her publications include essays on Pier Paolo Pasolini and Francesco Rosi's cinema, and her analyses on the role of sound and soundtrack in Italian cinema and postcolonialism in Gillo Pontecorvo's films are forthcoming. She is currently working on a book manuscript on the relationship between death, mourning rituals and politics in Italian cinema from Pier Paolo Pasolini to Paolo Sorrentino.

Alex Gammon is an independent scholar and an alumnus of Florida State University where he earned his B.A. in English, with an honours in the major creative project of short stories, and international affairs with a concentration in anthropology. His pursuit of anthropological studies has taken him to the Cosa Excavations site in southwest Tuscany for the 2016 season to excavate the colony's bath complex and catalogue findings. His research interests include the anthropology of children and their cognitive and ethical development as well as the anthropology of sleep and the ramifications of the siesta and truncated monophasic sleeping on the labour force. A strong interest in Italian cinema drives a portion of his academic work, specifically an interest in Paolo Sorrentino's use of environment as an existential confrontation for his films' protagonists.

Matteo Gilebbi holds a Ph.D. in Italian from the University of Wisconsin-Madison and is currently a lecturer in the Department of French and Italian at Dartmouth College. He is also the co-founder of the 'Anthropocene Working Group' and a member of the 'Environmental Humanities Initiative' at Dartmouth. His research focuses on the connections between literature, cinema, and philosophy, using theories from ecocriticism, posthumanism, new-materialism, and animal studies. His most recent work has been published in the edited volumes *Towards the River's Mouth* (Lexington Books, 2018); *Landscapes, Natures, Ecologies: Italy and the Environmental Humanities* (University of Virginia Press, 2018); *The Carol J. Adams Reader: Writings and Conversations 1995-2015* (Bloomsbury, 2016); and *Animals and the Posthuman in Italian Literature and Film* (Palgrave Macmillan, 2014). He recently translated two books of poetry by Ivano Ferrari, published in the single volume *Slaughterhouse* (Legas, 2019).

Monica Jansen is an assistant professor of Italian at the Department of Languages, Literature and Communication (TLC) at Utrecht University. Her research interests include modernism and postmodernism studies, and more specifically new forms of Italian cultural engagement. She investigates cultural representations of socially relevant topics such as religion, precarity, youth and migration, from an interdisciplinary, transmedial and transnational perspective. She published *Il dibattito sul postmoderno in Italia: in bilico tra dialettica e ambiguità* (Franco Cesati, 2002) and co-edited the following volumes and themed issues: 'Spanish Exile and Italian Migration in Argentina' (*Romance Studies*, 2019); 'Raccontare la giustizia' (*Forum*

Italicum, 2017); *Televisionismo. Narrazioni televisive della storia italiana durante la Seconda Repubblica* (Edizioni Ca' Foscari, 2015); *The History of Futurism: The Precursors, Protagonists, and Legacies* (Lexington Books, 2012). She is an editor of the book series 'Moving Texts' (Peter Lang), member of the editorial board of *Journal of Italian Cinema & Media Studies* and book review coordinator of the 'Italian Bookshelf' of *Annali d'Italianistica*.

Russell J. A. Kilbourn is a professor in English and film studies at Wilfrid Laurier University, specializing in film theory, memory studies, comparative literature and adaptation. He has published many book chapters and journal articles; his books include: *Cinema, Memory, Modernity: The Representation of Memory from the Art Film to Transnational Cinema* (Routledge, 2010); *The Memory Effect: The Remediation of Memory in Literature and Film* (WLU Press, 2013), co-edited with Eleanor Ty; *W.G. Sebald's Postsecular Redemption: Catastrophe with Spectator* (Northwestern University Press, 2018); and *The Cinema of Paolo Sorrentino: Commitment to Style* (Columbia University Press, 2020). Kilbourn is also one of the founders of the Posthumanism Research Network (based at Brock University and Wilfrid Laurier University), and his current research interests include posthumanism and postsecular cinema.

Anna Manzato is an assistant professor of sociology of communication at IULM University, Milan. She has taken part in research about media for Rai-VQPT, OssCom-Catholic University, Istituto Gemelli-Musatti, Milan, Associazione Interessi Metropolitani, Milan. In several essays she has dealt, among other themes, with media and everyday life, in the perspective both of the incorporation of technologies and of the transformation of contents, especially television's. Among her recent publications are 'Oltre la fiction. La serialità tra realtà e scrittura' (2015) in D. Cardini (ed.), *Le serie sono serie: Seconda stagione*, Milano: Arcipelago Edizioni, pp. 115–27; 'Il consumo televisivo' (2016) in OSI, *La società italiana: Cambiamento sociale, consumi e media*, Milano: GueriniNext, pp. 163–73.

Antonella Mascio (Ph.D. New Media Studies) is an associate professor in sociology of cultural and communication processes at University of Bologna. In recent years she focused her researches on online social relations and on relationships between the Internet, TV Drama, and Fashion. She has recently published *Fashion Convergence* (with Junji Tsuchiya, ZMJ, 2015), *Virtuali Comunità* (Guerini e Associati, 2008), *Visioni di moda* (Franco Angeli, 2008), *Fashion Games* (Franco Angeli, 2012).

Nicoletta Marini-Maio is a professor of Italian and film studies at Dickinson College. She authored the monograph *A Very Seductive Body Politics: Silvio Berlusconi in the Cinema* (Milan: Mimesis International, Italy, 2015) and a number of articles and book chapters on the representation of the so-called *years of lead* (1970s) in Italian film and theatre, coming of age in Italian film, and Paolo Sorrentino's cinema. She co-edited with Ellen Nerenberg and Thomas Simpson a critical translation of *Corpo di stato*, by the Italian playwright Marco Baliani (2011, Fairleigh Dickinson UP), and with Colleen Ryan the volumes *Set the Stage! Teaching Italian through Theater. Theories, Methods, and Practices* (Yale University Press, 2009) and *Dramatic Interactions* (Cambridge Scholars Publishing, 2011). With Ellen Nerenberg, she is co-author and co-principal investigator of *La nazione Winx: Educare la futura consumista* (Winx Nation: Grooming the Future Female Consumer), forthcoming from Rubbettino, Italy, in 2021. Marini-Maio is the founder and editor of *gender/sexuality/italy* (g/s/i), an academic journal on constructions of femininity and masculinity in Italian culture.

Carla Molinari is currently a senior lecturer in architecture at the Leeds Beckett University and Honorary Associate of the University of Liverpool, conducting research on innovative interpretation of sequences and montage in architecture. She has a Ph.D. in theory and critic of architecture (University Sapienza of Rome) and she has published on cinema and architecture, on the conception of architectural space and on cultural regeneration. In 2016, she was awarded the prestigious British Academy Fellowship by the Accademia Nazionale dei Lincei and in 2014 she was the recipient of the Best Young Critic of Architecture Prize (presS/Tletter, Venice).

Ellen Nerenberg is Hollis Professor at Wesleyan University. She is author of *Prison Terms: Representing Confinement During and After Italian Fascism* (2001) awarded the Marraro 38 Prize from the MLA, and *Murder Made in Italy: Homicide, Media, and Contemporary Italian Culture* (2012). She is the co-editor of *Writing Beyond Fascism* (2000) and *Body of State* (2012). She is a founding editor of *g/s/i-gender/sexuality/Italy* and reviews editor of the *Journal of Italian Cinema and Media Studies*. Publications include essays on serial television in Italy and North America. She is currently working on *Winx Nation: educare la futura consumista* with Nicoletta Marini-Maio.

Lydia Tuan is a first-year Ph.D. student in the Departments of Italian and Film & Media Studies at Yale University. Her research explores moving images and interactive forms of visual representation in Italian contexts, focusing particularly on

Italian cinema, contemporary art practices, and moving image installations. Her essays and reviews have appeared in or are forthcoming in the *Journal of Italian Cinema and Media Studies, Annali d'Italianistica*, and *Cinéma & Cie*.

Maria Bonaria Urban is an assistant professor in Italian language and culture at the Department of Italian Studies of the University of Amsterdam. Her fields of research are: memories studies, film and television studies, public history, Italian migration and new mobilities, imagology and women's writing, with a strong focus on the intersection between history, media and nationalism. She published the monograph *Sardinia on Screen: The Construction of the Sardinian Character in Italian Cinema* (Rodopi, 2013) and co-edited the following volumes and themed issues: 'Spanish exile and Italian migration in Argentina' (*Romance Studies*, 2019); 'Raccontare la giustizia' (*Forum Italicum*, 2017); *Televisionismo. Narrazioni televisive della storia italiana durante la Seconda Repubblica* (Edizioni Ca' Foscari, 2015); *Le frontiere del Sud. Culture e lingue a contatto* (CUEC, 2011). She coordinates the research group *Mediating Memories of Fascism, Dictatorship and War* and is member of the editorial board of *Journal of Italian Cinema & Media Studies*.

Sandra Waters received her Ph.D. in Italian from Rutgers University, and is the managing editor of *Italian Quarterly*. Her fields of research include the historical novel, gender theory, 20-21st-century Italian literature, Italian film, contemporary horror film, surveillance, the collective author, and trauma theory. Her recent publications include work on American horror films, Paolo Sorrentino's films and tv series, Dario Argento, Luther Blissett and Wu Ming, and Maria Rosa Cutrufelli. Her most recent publication is *Spaces and Places of Horror* (Vernon Press, 2020), which she co-edited with Francesco Pascuzzi.

Bibliography

Antonello, P. and Mussgnug, F. (eds.) (2009), *'Postmodern Impegno': Ethics and Commitment in Contemporary Italian Culture*, Bern: Peter Lang.

Antonello, P. and Mussgnug, F. (2010), 'The Ambiguity of Realism and Its Posts: A Response to Millicent Marcus', *The Italianist,* 30, pp. 258–62.

Antonello, P. and Mussgnug, F. (2012), 'Di crisi in meglio: Realismo, impegno postmoderno e cinema politico nell'Italia degli anni zero: da Nanni Moretti a Paolo Sorrentino', *Italian Studies*, 67: 2.

Antonello, P. and Mussgnug, F. (2016), 'Il Divo: Paolo Sorrentino's Spectacle of Politics'. in G.Lombardi and C.Uva (eds.), *Public Life, Imaginary, and Identity in Contemporary Italian Film*, Oxford: Peter Lang, pp. 291–306.

Bagnall, R., Brodersen, K., Champion, C., Erskine, A. and Huebner, S. (eds.) (2012), *Encyclopaedia of Ancient History*, Malden, MA: Wiley-Blackwell.

Bisoni, C. (2016), 'Paolo Sorrentino: Between Engagement and *savoir faire*', in G. Lombardi and C.Uva, *Public Life, Imaginary, and Identity in Contemporary Italian Film*, Oxford: Peter Lang, pp. 250–62.

Bonsaver, G. (2009), 'Dall'uomo al Divo: Un'intervista con Paolo Sorrentino', *The Italianist*, 29, pp. 325–37.

Cangiano M., Gammon A., Gilebbi M., Kilbourn R., Mariani A, Manzato A., Mascio A., Tuan L. and Waters S, (2019), *Journal of Italian Cinema and Media Studies, Special Issue on Paolo Sorrentino's Cinema*, 7: 3, Bristol UK: Intellect Publishers.

Canova, G. (2017), *Divi duci guitti papi caimani: L'immaginario del potere nel cinema italiano, da Rossellini a The Young Pope*, Milan: Bietti Heterotopia.

Canova, G. (2009), 'Exposing the Dark Secrets of Italian Political History: An Interview with Paolo Sorrentino', *Cineaste*, 34: 3, pp. 32–37.

Crowdus, G. (2014), 'In Search of *The Great Beauty*: An Interview with Paolo Sorrentino', *Cineaste,* 39: 2, pp. 8–13.

De Santis, P., Monetti, D. and Pallanch, L. (2010), *Divi e Antidivi: Il Cinema di Paolo Sorrentino*. Roma: Laboratorio Gutenberg.

Fiorito, G. (2013), *Paolo Sorrentino, 'La grande bellezza': Diario del film*, Milano: Feltrinelli.

Fonzi- Kliemann, C. (2014), 'Cultural and Political Exhaustion in Paolo Sorrentino's *The Great Beauty*', *Senses of Cinema*, 70.

Hennessey, B. (2017), 'Reel Simulations: CGI and Special Effects in Two Films by Paolo Sorrentino', *The Italianist*, 37: 3, pp. 449–63.

Hipkins, D. (2008), 'Why Italian Film Studies Needs A Second Take on Gender', *Italian Studies*, 63: 2, pp. 213–34.

Iannotta, A. (2016), 'Le immagini del potere: Note sull'identità italiana nel cinema di Paolo Sorrentino,'*California Italian Studies*, 6: 2, pp. 1–17.

Johnston, T. (2012), 'This Must Be the Place', *Sight and Sound*, 22: 4, pp. 78–79.

Kilbourn, R. (2020), *The Cinema of Paolo Sorrentino: Commitment to Style*, Columbia University Press.

Marcus, M. (2010), 'The Ironist and the Auteur: Post-realism in Paolo Sorrentino's *Il Divo*', *The Italianist,* 30, pp. 245–57.

Mariani, A. (2017), 'The Empty Heterotopic (Non-)Space of Sorrentino's Female Characters in *The Great Beauty* and *The Consequences of Love*', in S.Byer and F.Cecchini (eds.), *Female Identity and Its Representations in the Arts and Humanities*, Newcastle upon Tyne: Cambridge Scholars Publishing, pp. 168–84.

Mariani, A. (2018), 'The Antithetical Coherence in Sorrentino's Youth: Visual (Ab)use and Male Dominance', *South Central Review*, 35: 2, pp. 117–32.

Mariani, A. (2019), 'Experiencing *Panismo* in Sorrentino's *The Great Beauty*, *Youth,* and *Loro*', *Italica*, 96: 3, pp. 486–510.

Mariani, A. (2020), 'Viral (Per)Versions of Power in Paolo Sorrentino's Diptych *Loro*', Cambridge University Press, 25: 3, pp. 299–315.

Marlow-Mann, A. (2010a), 'Beyond Post-Realism: A Response to Millicent Marcus', *The Italianist*, 30, pp. 263–71.

Marlow-Mann, A. (2010b), 'Characters Engagement and Alienation in the Cinema of Paolo Sorrentino', in W. Pope (ed.), *Italian Films Directors in The New Millennium*, Newcastle upon Tyne: Cambridge Scholars Publishing, pp. 161–73.

Mecchia, G. (2018), 'Birds in the Roman sky: Shooting for the Sublime in *La Grande Bellezza*', *Forum Italicum* 50: 1, pp. 183–93.

Mori, G. (2018), *Del desiderio e del godimento: Viaggio al termine dell'ideologia ne 'La grande bellezza' di Paolo Sorrentino*, Milano: Mimesis.

O'Leary, A. (2017), 'What is Italian Cinema?', *California Italian Studies*, 7:1.

O'Rawe, C. (2018), 'Editorial: Contemporary Italian Film Culture in the Light of #MeToo', *The Italianist*, 38: 2, pp. 151–52.

Renga, D. (2013), 'The Mafia Noir: Paolo Sorrentino's Le conseguenze dell'amore', In *Unfinished Business: Screening Screening the Italian Mafia in the New Millenium*, Toronto: University of Toronto Press, pp. 65–79.

Salvestroni, S. (2017), *'La grande bellezza' e il cinema di Paolo Sorrentino*, Bologna: Archetipolibri.

Simor, E. and Sorfa, D. (2017), 'Irony, Sexism and Magic in Paolo Sorrentino's Films', *Studies in European Cinema*, 14: 3, pp. 1–16.

Spoladori, S. (2014), *Paolo Sorrentino: Le conseguenze di un autore*, N.p.: Le Mani Microart S.

Toumarkine, D. (2013), 'La Dolce Bellezza', *Film Journal International*, 116: 12, pp. 28–30.

Viano, M. (2010), 'Between Modernity and Eternity: *Il divo* in Cinematic Rome', *Annali D'Italianistica*, 28, pp. 341–62.

Vigni, F. (2012), *La maschera, il potere, la solitudine: Il cinema di Paolo Sorrentino*, Firenze: Aska.

Zaccagnini, E. and Spagnoletti, G. (2007), 'Intervista a Paolo Sorrentino', *Close-up*, 23, pp. 109–16.

Zagarrio, V. (2016), 'The 'Great Beauty,' or Form Is Politics', in G.Lombardi and C.Uva (eds.), *Public Life, Imaginary, and Identity in Contemporary Italian Film*, Oxford: Peter Lang, pp. 119–32.

FILMOGRAPHY

Sorrentino, P. (1998), *L'amore non ha confine (Love Has No Boundaries)*, Italy: Indigo Film.

Sorrentino, P. (2001a), *La notte lunga (The Long Night)*, Italy: Indigo Film.

Sorrentino, P. (2001b), *L'uomo in più (One Man Up)*, Italy: Indigo Film and Key Films.

Sorrentino, P. (2002), *La primavera del 2002: L'Italia protesta, l'Italia si ferma* (video documentary).

Sorrentino, P. (2004a), *Giovani talenti italiani* (video; segment: 'Quando le cose vanno male').

Sorrentino, P. (2004b), *Le conseguenze dell'amore (The Consequences of Love)*, Italy: Fandango, Indigo Film, Medusa Film.

Sorrentino, P. (2004c), *Sabato, domenica e lunedì* (TV movie).

Sorrentino, P. (2006), *L'amico di famiglia (A Family Friend)*, Italy: Indigo Film.

Sorrentino, P. (2008), *Il Divo*, Italy and France: Indigo Film, Lucky Red, Parco Film.

Sorrentino, P. (2009a), *La partita lenta* (short).

Sorrentino, P. (2009b), *L'aquila 2009: Cinque registi tra le macerie* (video documentary short; segment: 'L'assegnazione delle tende').

Sorrentino, P. (2010), *Napoli 24* (short).

Sorrentino, P. (2011a), *In the Mirror* (short).

Sorrentino, P. (2011b), *This Must Be the Place*, Italy, France and Ireland: Indigo Film and Medusa Film.

Sorrentino, P. (2012), *Tony Pagoda e i suoi amici (Tony Pagoda and his Friends)*, Milan: Feltrinelli.

Sorrentino, P. (2013a), *Hanno tutti ragione (Everybody's Right)*, Milan: Feltrinelli.

Sorrentino, P. (2013b), *La grande bellezza (The Great Beauty)*, Italy and France: Indigo Film and Medusa Film.

Sorrentino, P. (2014a), *Le voci di dentro* (TV movie).

Sorrentino, P. (2014b), *Rio, I Love You (segment: 'La Fortuna')*, Brazil, United States, and France: Conspiração Filmes.

Sorrentino, P. (2014c), *Sabbia* (short).

Sorrentino, P. (2014c), *The Dream* (short).

Sorrentino, P. (2015), *Youth*, Italy, France, United Kingdom, and Switzerland: Barbary Films, Pathé, Indigo Film.

Sorrentino, P. (2016), *Gli aspetti irrilevanti (The Irrelevant Aspects)*, Milan: Mondadori.

Sorrentino, P. (2016) *The Young Pope*, Italy, France, Spain, United Kingdom, and United States: Wildside, Haut et Court TV, Mediapro, Sky Italia, HBO, Canal+, (10 episodes).

Sorrentino, P. (2017a), Il peso di Dio. Il Vangelo di Lanny Belardo// God's Weight, Lenny Belardo's Gospel, Torino: Einaudi.

Sorrentino, P. (2017b), *Killer in Red* (short).

Sorrentino, P. (2018a), *Loro 1*, Italy, France: Indigo Film, Pathé Production, France 2 Cinéma.

Sorrentino, P. (2018b), *Loro 2*, Italy, France: Indigo Film, Pathé Production, France 2 Cinéma.

Sorrentino, P. (2019), *The New Pope*, Italy, France, Spain, United Kingdom, and United States: Wildside, Haut et Court TV, Mediapro, Sky Italia, HBO, Canal+.